A Taste of America

A Taste of America

Jane and Michael Stern

Andrews and McMeel

A Universal Press Syndicate Company

Kansas City / New York

Library of Congress Cataloging-in-Publication Data
Stern, Jane.
    A taste of America.
    Includes index.
    1. Cookery, American. I. Stern, Michael, 1946–
II. Title.
TX715.S8394   1988   641.5973   88-22158
ISBN 0-8362-2125-7
ISBN 0-8362-2126-5 (pbk.)

These photos and memorabilia are from the scrapbooks of Jane and Michael Stern.

A Taste of America book design by Cameron Poulter.

Contents

Acknowledgments

We travel alone, but have many good companions. Readers volunteer restaurant tips and updates. Chefs give us their secret recipes. Home cooks send suggestions for favorite dishes they want us to track down. To all, we are grateful for guiding us along the way. Without such help, we could never have found the treasures this book contains.

Once we get a recipe home, we test it. But we don't do that by ourselves either. To make certain every dish turns out the way it is supposed to, we rely on Brooke Dojny and Melanie Barnard. They verify almost every recipe after we have proofed it to our satisfaction. Their ability to spot potential pitfalls lets us—and our readers—rest assured that each recipe works right and tastes good.

We owe our fondest thanks to friends at Universal Press Syndicate. It is inspiring to have the A-team of John McMeel, Kathleen Andrews, Lee Salem, and Donna Martin on our side. We especially thank Donna Martin, who encouraged us to start writing a weekly column, then to shape the best of it into this book. Thanks also to Bob Duffy and his band of resolute salespeople, who have taken our column to newspapers in fifty states. And to Alan McDermott, who fine-tooth-combs everything we write. It is a privilege to be published by this extraordinary group of people in Kansas City, and not just because they take us out to eat fried chicken every time we visit them.

Introduction

For fifteen years we have had the world's greatest job. We drive around America eating the best food we can find, then we tell people about it in our books and in a weekly newspaper column called "A Taste of America." The column always includes a recipe that gives the flavor of the restaurant.

This book is what we consider the cream of the crop—our way of applauding those recipes and restaurants that have kept us happy travelers for such a long time.

When we first lit out in search of good food, our goal was simple: to locate restaurants where a person could eat cheaply and well. We explored the byways and back roads of America and drove the tires off nineteen cars. We stayed in towns so small they weren't on any road map. We debated the merits of North Carolina–style barbecued pork versus Memphis wet ribs and dry ribs; we compared and contrasted skillet-fried chicken across the country; we feasted in small-town cafés, roadside diners, fish shanties, rustic inns, city bistros, cattle barns, and cafeterias.

As we ate our way around the country, our aim sharpened. We began looking for meals with personality, and for restaurants that embodied the spirit of their region or neighborhood. As we see it, there is no better place to get to know the heart and soul of this country than at the tables where everyday people eat.

Each recipe in this book expresses the character of a restaurant that is very special to us: dishes such as Quahog Hash from the menu of a friendly hash house along the shore in southern Connecticut, Whole Wheat Hazelnut Waffles from a swank Seattle café, Tipsy Sweet Potato Pudding from the dining room of a one hundred-year-old boardinghouse in Lynchburg, Tennessee. These are the kinds of treasures that make writing "A Taste of America" such delectable work. We think they represent the best of our country's diverse and far-flung cuisine.

It would be wrong to give such recipes without telling you the stories behind them and describing the exceptional places they come from. You would miss the fun if you made Throwed Rolls like those at Lambert's Cafe in Sikeston, Missouri (page 47), but didn't know that they get their name because tradition demands they be thrown from the stove to the table as soon as they are cool enough to handle! Recipes that diagram only how to make the food tell only half the story. That is why each recipe in this book gets a proper introduction, explaining why it's something special.

People ask how we find the places we write about. When it comes to prospecting for good restaurants, we have it easier than most travelers. Since we began writing about food, readers have endowed us with tips galore suggesting where we ought to go next. Now whenever we hit the road we leave home with a shoebox full of suggestions.

Still, it can be tough finding the best food in a strange place. Our million miles on the American highways have helped us develop culinary radar that works pretty well. It is a combination of experience, logic, intuition, and willingness to get lost. Here are a few tips we can share:

Excellent restaurants rarely put up billboards or advertise. Many don't *look* like anything special. To find the really choice ones, you have to get away from the big roads, off the beaten path. Good eats are found on wharfs, in gas station cafés, in ungentrified neighborhoods, sometimes on the wrong side of the tracks. Eating America's finest food can be an adventure as well as a satisfying meal.

In a small town where we don't have a clue, we eat breakfast at any café where the sheriff's car is parked. The local police force is usually able to track down the tastiest biscuits for miles around.

On the subject of breakfast: You have almost certainly found the town's best if it is being served at a restaurant that sports a large round table at which locals gather to exchange news and gossip each morning. That's the way it happens every day at the Courtesy Coffee Shop in Winchester, Indiana (page 1), where tidings are traded over buckwheat cakes and freshly squeezed orange juice.

Look in the Yellow Pages and eliminate all places with splashy ads bragging about the size of their banquet rooms and vast parking lots for tour buses. Forget restaurants that bill themselves as "emporiums," "circuses," or "eating establishments"; also, drive fast past any place that serves "potables and victuals" instead of food.

Beware of restaurants with brightly colored roof tiles or mansard roofs. Don't ask us to explain; we don't know why, but these places are almost always bad. Equally unexplainable but true is the fact that restaurants with plaster cows on the roof or neon pigs as window signs are usually excellent.

We generally look for restaurants that have been around forever. "Since 1916" is guaranteed to catch our eye. El Charro in Tucson, Arizona (page 92), has walls plastered with souvenir calendars going back to 1946. At Shapiro's Delicatessen in Indianapolis (page 100), we met a customer who told us that her grandmother used to take her there during the 1930s, every Thursday night, for chicken soup with matzoh balls. Now she takes her grandchildren to Shapiro's every Thursday night for the same trustworthy meal.

When in doubt, check out the pie case. Cafés proud of their pies display them so customers can admire their beauty during lunch. At Henry's Sohio in West Jefferson, Ohio (page 189), Madge Knox exhibits the daily pie selection behind a display of all the ribbons she has won at local and state fairs.

Our kind of restaurant is often unconventional. At Gladys Breeden's in the hills of eastern Tennessee (page 147), we walked in and Gladys told us to go to the stove and "dip a plate." At this homiest of home cooking establishments, you take your own plate out of her kitchen cupboard, then proceed to help yourself to pork chops and candied apples at Gladys's stove, just as you might do at your mother's house. At Zaharako's Soda Fountain in Columbus, Indiana (page 240), you will likely be serenaded by an eighty-five-piece player pipe organ while eating "Cheese-Br-Grs" and sipping Green River sodas. At the Branch Ranch in Plant City, Florida (page 150), dinner comes to the table in a stack of six serving pans, to which customers are expected to help themselves. Eccentricity is no guarantee of superior eating, but it is a hint of real character in the kitchen.

We have sampled each place in this book and include it because we think it is worth visiting. As for the recipes, although they come from restaurants all over the country, we take responsibility for them as they are printed here. We have adjusted and tested each one so it works right in a home kitchen. Don't worry, though—we would never pretty-up a dish to make it fancier than it is, nor would we take the kick out of a spicy one to make it more polite. In every case, our goal has been for the recipe to honestly convey what the restaurant and its region are like.

Unlike most cookbook writers, we seldom invent recipes. We collect them. That is why we think of this book as something more than an assortment of things that the two of us happen to like to eat. We do indeed like this food, but it isn't merely the taste of the food we love. It's the taste of America.

JANE AND MICHAEL STERN
West Redding, Connecticut

1
Breakfast

1

Courtesy Buckwheat Cakes

WINCHESTER, Ind.—When you travel the two-lane highways of the American Midwest, through central Illinois and Indiana in particular, there is a gentle pastoral rhythm to the journey. Long, straight roads lead along fields of corn, past pigpens and cow barns and distant swirls of dust where tractors work the earth. Phone poles tick by, and the vast openness is punctuated by an occasional Gothic farmhouse, then a crossroads café or a one-pump garage. Every twenty to fifty miles, you slow to a crawl as the road feeds you straight into a town.

Many of these towns are built around a courthouse on a square in such a way that anyone passing through must navigate at least halfway around the town square to continue in the same direction. For us, that's the exciting part of the trip. We circle all the way around at least once, looking for an appealing café, or an irresistible old-time hardware store or soda fountain pharmacy or grocery or antiques-and-junk shop.

When we got to Winchester, Indiana, we weren't quite so aimless in our search. "Taste of America" reader Jean Jacobs of Peru, Indiana, had written us a letter recommending a restaurant just off the town square. She said it was a small café with cooks who were all farmers' wives. "Believe me," Jean wrote, "they are good! Pies, biscuits, chicken and dumplings: If they make it, you are sure to enjoy it."

We sensed Jean had steered us right even before we walked in the door. It was 7 A.M., and the quiet street outside the Beachler Apartment Building was parked with pickup trucks and cars with local license plates. An appealing old neon sign hung outside the brick building announcing "Courtesy Coffee Shop." The entrance was through the lobby of the apartments.

We walked in and gazed upon a heartwarming vista of Midwestern morning life: the small-town café. Customers were seated on pink stools at a short counter, and on pale green kitchenette chairs at tables covered with boomerang-pattern Formica. In a big open kitchen at the back, we saw the ladies hard at work: mixing salads, popping breads in the oven, squeezing glasses of orange juice one by one. A rack held pie crusts so hot from the oven they were still steamy in the cool morning air.

We were the only strangers in the place. "Elsie, Tom, you want more coffee?" asked the waitress of a table near the door. "Al, your French toast will be right up. You folks"—she was addressing us as we gaped with pleasure at the friendly scene—"you have a seat right here. Can I bring you some juice?"

COURTESY BUCKWHEAT CAKES

I egg
I to I¼ cups buttermilk or sour milk
½ cup buckwheat flour
½ cup white all-purpose flour
½ teaspoon baking soda
2 tablespoons sugar
½ teaspoon salt
2 tablespoons melted butter, plus butter for frying

Beat egg with I cup buttermilk.
Mix flours, baking soda, sugar, and salt.
Combine both mixtures, stirring only enough to blend, stirring in butter last, and adding up to ¼ cup of buttermilk if needed to thin batter. (It should be barely thicker than heavy cream.)
Lightly butter a griddle or frying pan over medium heat. Pour out pancakes 6 inches in diameter. When crisp and light brown, flip and cook other side. They are best served immediately from the griddle; but if necessary, pancakes may be kept warm on an ovenproof plate in a very low (175–200 degrees) oven.
Makes six 6-inch pancakes.

Courtesy Coffee Shop: 202 S. Meridian, Winchester, Ind.; (317) 584-1851.

So began a memorable breakfast, inscribed in our little black book of culinary treasures as much for the country feeling of the place as for the food. Oh, the food was good—make no mistake about that. We each had a buckwheat cake, nearly as large as its plate, accompanied by sausage patties, fresh OJ, and good coffee. And we look forward to coming back someday for lunch (which they call dinner) or dinner (known hereabouts as supper), when the service is cafeteria-style, and the menu lists meals of pan-fried steaks, ham loaf, and the chicken and dumplings about which Jean Jacobs had raved.

For now, though, until we eat again at the Courtesy Coffee Shop, whenever we want to remember that fine Indiana morning, we do it with a breakfast of buckwheat cakes made the way the farm ladies make them in Winchester: broad, delicate-textured, but with that distinctive earthy buckwheat flavor, steaming hot off the griddle. (Buckwheat flour is available in health food stores.)

Migas

AUSTIN, Texas—Tourist, beware of the salsa on the tables at Joe's. It looks innocent enough, sitting in a small jar of the type that might hold pickle relish or some such wan condiment in an ordinary café. It is pale green, chunky, loose enough to seep and slither into the wrinkles of your enchiladas as soon as a spoonful is ladled on. Wow, is it ever hot! Hot enough to clear your ears, nose, and throat, open your eyes wide, and send a shiver down your spine. Hot enough to set your tongue buzzing for hours after you have finished eating.

Shocking as it is, the salsa is part of what makes Joe's Bakery and Coffee Shop feel so *real*. Located on East 7th Street, a mostly Spanish-speaking neighborhood in Austin, Joe's is one of the capital city's great authentic Tex-Mex restaurants, patronized equally by local Chicanos and Anglos, blue-collar folk and students from the University of Texas.

The first thing you see when you enter the hunkering cinderblock building are shelves of cookies, cakes, and doughnuts—fanciful pastries the likes of which one finds only in Mexican bakeries. Here are wide-bodied gingerbread pigs, sheet cakes with bright pink icing, cinnamon-sheathed fried dough, and sweet rolls in a dozen different configurations. Many customers come to Joe's for bags of pastries to go.

Beyond the bakery cases is a wide dining room with seating at booths and tables where menus are semipermanently encased

MIGAS

3 eggs
2 tablespoons milk
1 tablespoon butter or margarine
²/₃ cup crisp corn tortilla chips, broken into
*   bite-size pieces*

OPTIONAL: *one or two of the following:*
½ cup cooked, crumbled spicy sausage
*   (preferably chorizo)*
½ cup grated sharp cheese
¼ cup sautéed onions
½ cup diced fried potatoes

Thoroughly beat eggs with milk.
Melt butter or margarine in omelette pan over medium heat. Pour in eggs. Stir almost constantly. As eggs begin to set (within just a few seconds), stir in tortillas and any of the other optional ingredients. Continue stirring as eggs set. Salt to taste.
Serve with warm flour tortillas and refried beans. Makes 1 serving. (Double or quadruple amounts to serve 2 or 4 people.)

Joe's Bakery & Coffee Shop, 2305 E. 7th St., Austin, Texas; (512) 472-0017.

underneath plastic tablecloths. Fans spin overhead. Decor is south-of-the border eclectic, including a velvet painting of a bull-fighter, scenic vistas of Mexico, high-tone art prints, and a souvenir banner from Niagara Falls.

We were strangers when we entered, and a bit timid, but the man at the cash register made us feel welcome. He guided us to a table and explained that Joe's is famous for having the best menudo (tripe stew) in town. Menudo and chili, he advised, were available by the pint or quart, to go, if we needed to get dinner to take home. Joe's is open only for breakfast and lunch, until 5:30 P.M. weekdays (except Monday), and 3:30 on Sunday.

We had come early, for breakfast, so we got plates of huevos rancheros and migas with beans. The former is the classic Tex-Mex morning meal: eggs over easy, embellished with chunky red salsa, served alongside fried potato disks, bacon, and refried beans. Instead of toast, we received a covered plastic bowl holding warm flour tortillas.

The surprise treat of the day were the migas, a mess of scrambled eggs, broken-up corn tortillas, and chorizo sausage. They looked like a haywire omelette, made with an exuberant hand that threw everything together with no worry about how it looked. Our waitress explained that many customers like to customize their migas. They order cheese, sautéed onions, extra sausage or potatoes to mix in with the eggs. And, of course, those who are serious about getting the true Tex-Mex experience dollop their migas with four-alarm hot sauce.

The recipe for migas is an easy one, and as flexible as you want it to be. The minimum ingredients are eggs and corn tortillas. Although any common tortilla chips will work, handmade ones are infinitely more delicious than the kind you buy in bags.

Jo-Ann's New Joe

SOUTH SAN FRANCISCO, Calif.—Tucked into our file cabinet of tips, in the California section, is a napkin on which we long ago wrote these words: BUTTERMILK SHAKE AT JO-ANN'S—HARVEY STEIMAN SAYS THE BEST. Nobody knows more about San Francisco restaurants than Harvey Steiman, who hosts the "KCBS Kitchen" radio show, so this was a suggestion we took seriously. Not only did he extol the milk shakes; he sang praises about the unaffected atmosphere and home cooking; he rhapsodized about feather-weight omelettes; he implored us to eat a plate of pancakes. "Jo-Ann's is your kind of place," he assured. After a few breakfasts

JO-ANN'S NEW JOE

1 tablespoon olive oil

1 clove garlic, crushed

1/3 pound ground beef

1 tablespoon butter

3 eggs

1/4 cup grated sharp cheddar cheese

1/3 cup chopped tomato

1–2 tablespoons chopped olives, to taste

Heat olive oil in an omelette pan over medium-high heat. Sauté garlic in oil until it softens. Remove with slotted spoon. Cook beef in oil, stirring constantly to keep it loose. Remove from pan, drain off fat. Quickly wipe pan clean and melt butter in it. (Reduce heat: Don't let the butter burn.)

Beat eggs well with 2 tablespoons water. Pour into pan when butter is sizzling. As eggs set, sprinkle in cheddar cheese, then beef, then tomatoes and olives. When bottom of omelette is firm, fold it over. Slide onto plate and serve.

Makes 1 serving.

Jo-Ann's Cafe, 1131 El Camino Real, South San Francisco, Calif.; (415) 872-2810.

there, we are happy to report that he was right.

We never did try the milk shakes. Each time we have eaten at Jo-Ann's, our attention has been riveted by breakfast. You will see what we mean if you arrive about seven or eight in the morning, when the muffins are out in their trays near the cash register. Who can resist these big-topped beauties? Blueberry, apple, banana—the selection varies. Our favorite is raisin-nut, a tawny giant that looks just grand when you pull it apart and set some butter on it to melt.

Another fresh-baked breakfast attraction is orange bread, which is sliced thick and made into French toast. There are marvelous pancakes, too—the batter spiked with mashed bananas or pumpkin; or you can get a stack of exemplary buckwheat cakes. Jo-Ann's granola is a lavish composition of nuts, raisins, honey-flavored grains, brown sugar, and fruit. And there is a delightfully direct item on the menu known as "Jose Pappas." It is a mound of home-fried potatoes topped with cheddar cheese, hot salsa, and sour cream.

The single greatest thing to eat at Jo-Ann's is an omelette. Name your filling: Italian sausage, Cajun sausage, bacon, turkey, cheddar cheese, Monterey Jack cheese, Swiss cheese, cream cheese, blue cheese, Parmesan cheese, jalapeño peppers, chili peppers, bell peppers, mushrooms, green onions, caviar, sour cream, or black olives. A three-egg omelette comes with your choice of any two ingredients. If you want more than two, you pay ninety-five cents per addition.

The first time we visited Jo-Ann's, the blackboard above the counter listed a special omelette of the day: spinach, ground beef, cheddar cheese, tomatoes, and olives. It had no name, but anyone with an interest in arcane Bay Area cuisine could spot it as an omelettized version of the weird local dish known as a "New Joe Special." Since the 1930s, a variety of Italian restaurants named Joe's, New Joe's, Baby Joe's, and the Original Joe's have been serving variations of the same thing: a jumble of ground beef, spinach, and eggs. Customarily, all the ingredients are stirred together in a frying pan along with spices, maybe mushrooms, and whatever else the kitchen has on hand. Here at Jo-Ann's (no relation to any other Joe's), the eggs are a pocket for all the ingredients. It is a super idea—an informal hearty meal suitable for brunch or supper.

Tahitian Toast

SEATTLE—On any list of American places where breakfast is big, put Seattle at the top. Seattleites are fanatical about breakfast—about strong coffee, elephantine muffins, swirling cinnamon rolls, maple bars, hotcakes, honey buns, and hash browns.

No doubt some of the city's lust for breakfast derives from its coffee mania. Throughout Seattle, vendors hawk freshly brewed espresso from sidewalk carts. Locals consume this potent brew with the kind of nonchalance most of us have toward a glass of water or soda pop. For those who prefer coffeeing up sitting down, there are dozens of comfortable coffeehouses suitable for sipping.

Grazers can pick and choose their breakfast down at the Pike Place Market, where greengrocers and fishmongers set up their stalls in the cool morning air, which is perfumed by the aromas of warm crumpets (at The Crumpet Shop), croissants (at Au Gavroche), sourdough rolls (at Three Girls Bakery), hazelnut waffles (at Cafe Sport), and whole-grain griddlecakes (at Sound View Cafe).

Up in the Green Lake part of town, by the time it is 8 or 8:30, there will likely be a line of hungry customers waiting for a table at Julia's 14 Carrot Cafe on Eastlake—our pick as the best place for a serious, Seattle-size breakfast.

Julia's is a laid-back eatery, casual and comfortably disheveled, where the customers are a helter-skelter assortment of shaggy university types, newspaper addicts, and a few pinstriped business people. When you walk in the door, you smell the powerhouse Stewart Brothers coffee that is served in thick mugs and hottened up as often as required. And you see vistas of glorious good food, piled high on plates, overcrowding the small unclothed tables.

What to eat? It's a tough decision. Even putting aside lunch and dinner, breakfast presents a befuddling set of choices. For omelettes, there are nineteen different fillings, including five kinds of cheese; on the side come hash browns and your choice of toast, English muffin, or streusel-yogurt coffee cake. The coffee cake is a big, moist, crumb-topped block, served with a crowning sphere of butter as big as a pingpong ball. For fifty cents extra, you can get Julia's cinnamon roll instead of the regular breadstuffs. "Large and gooey" is how the waiter describes the roll—a vast spiral of pastry with clods of raisins and veins of dark sugar gunk packed into its warm furrows. It, too, comes blobbed with a ball of melting butter.

If eggs aren't your dish, there are hotcakes, all kinds of hotcakes: sourdough or regular, with sliced bananas, apple slivers or blueberries, with bacon on the side or cooked into the 'cakes. You

TAHITIAN TOAST

8 broad slices of sourdough or other sturdy bread

⅓ cup tahini dip (sesame butter), stirred so oil is blended into butter

4 eggs, well beaten

4 tablespoons butter

Make 4 sandwiches by spreading bread with a thin layer of tahini dip. Soak sandwiches in beaten egg, turning so both sides are well-sopped with egg.

Melt butter in large skillet over medium heat. Grill sandwiches in butter until golden brown. Flip and grill other side. Serve immediately, with or without syrup.

Makes 4 servings.

Julia's 14 Carrot Cafe: 2305 Eastlake E., Seattle, Wash.; (206) 324-1442.

can order hot oats with dates and cashews, homemade granola or sourdough French toast.

The 14 Carrot breakfast we like best is a dish dubbed Tahitian Toast by Julia's menu-writer. It is an inspired combination: a French toast sandwich glamorized by a thin vein of tahini dip (sesame butter). The hard part, for people who don't live on the West Coast, is getting the kind of tasty sourdough bread used at Julia's. If you cannot find a large loaf of sourdough, though, don't despair. We have tried this recipe with big slices of good quality non-sourdough bread, and it's swell. Serve Tahitian Toast for breakfast or brunch, with fresh fruit and yogurt on the side.

Quahog Hash

OLD SAYBROOK, Conn.—Lobster may be king of seafood on Yankee shores, but it is clams that are the people's choice. New Englanders adore clams and have devised a thousand ways to eat them. Clam chowder, fried clams, clams casino, stuffed clams, deep-fried clam fritters, baked clam casseroles: From raw in the shell to the top of thin-crusted pizzas, the almighty bivalve is as common hereabouts as turnip greens in Dixie or burritos in L.A.

One of the most delicious ways with clams happened as an accident about ten years ago. Pat Brink, who used to run a small coffee shop in Old Saybrook, had recruited her children to help her make the clam chowder. The young ones shucked a mountain of clams, but instead of carefully saving the briny broth inside the shells, they kept only the meat. Chowder cooks know that you cannot make clam chowder without clam liquor. "What to do with two bushels of clams and no broth?" Pat wondered.

The answer to her question was clam hash, a spur-of-the-moment invention that has since become the signature dish at Pat's Kountry Kitchen—a family-size restaurant that grew out of her popular town café.

Like chowder, the hash is made from the big clams known as quahogs (say co-hog), too chewy to eat whole. They are chopped up, mixed with potatoes and onions, then griddle-fried until crusty brown outside, with a moist, ocean-scented center.

Pat told us that many new customers, especially those from clam-deprived regions of the country, don't cotton to the idea of clam hash right away—especially for breakfast. That's why she often offers strangers a sample. "I bet I've given out ten thousand tastes of clam hash since we started making it," Pat grinned, telling us about hungry travelers from all over the country, as far as Cal-

QUAHOG HASH

3 medium potatoes (about 1 pound)

1 dozen large chowder clams (or two 6½-
    ounce cans chopped clams, drained of
    most juice)

1 rib celery, diced (about ⅓ cup)

½ bay leaf, thoroughly crushed

2 bunches scallions, chopped, including
    some of the greens (½ to ⅔ cup total)

2 to 4 tablespoons cream

½ to 1 teaspoon salt, to taste

½ teaspoon black pepper

¼ teaspoon thyme

2 to 3 ounces salt pork, cut into small
    pieces

Peel and boil potatoes until they can be pierced with a fork. Cool and dice.

Scrub clam shells thoroughly clean. Place in kettle with about one inch of water with celery and bay leaf. Cover and steam over medium heat about 15 minutes, or until the shells are open wide. Remove clams from broth, and when cool enough to handle, cut out meat. Chop clam meat into nuggets no bigger than peas. (If you're using canned clams, omit celery and bay leaf.)

Combine chopped clams, potatoes, and scallions with enough cream so mixture holds together, but isn't wet. Stir in seasonings.

In a 12-inch Teflon skillet, fry salt pork over medium-high heat until fat is rendered. Remove most of "cracklings." Flatten hash into a patty in the hot fat. Fry 10–15 minutes, until crusty. Flip and fry other side 10–15 minutes, until crusty. Garnish with cracklings if desired.

Makes 4 servings.

Pat's Kountry Kitchen: Junction of Route 154 & Mill Rock Road, Old Saybrook, Conn.; (203) 388-4784.

ifornia, who come back for hash every summer.

The Kountry Kitchen is a genuine hash house—the only place we know that regularly makes not only clam, but corned beef hash, too. And every weekend, the menu lists an old down-east favorite called red flannel hash—chopped up corned beef, potatoes, onions, etc., turned vivid red by the addition of beets. Pat's version is further pepped up with pastrami.

At breakfast, Pat's is packed with hash hounds who accompany their crusty hot-off-the-griddle slabs with eggs and home fries and crumbly blueberry muffins. Coffee comes from the school of the bottomless cup, replenished throughout the meal.

The first time we sat down, it was a hectic weekend morning, but Pat recognized us as newcomers and zeroed in as we read the menu, advising us to be sure to order our hash well-done. Then she table-hopped among her regulars (some of whom told us they come here for three meals every day), offering them tastes of her freshly baked Pilgrim pie (apples, raisins, cranberries) or vanilla chip pie or Grape-Nut tapioca pudding.

Pat's is a happy place, imprinted with the personality of its owner, who watches over the boisterous dining room with all the sass of a diner moll. The decor is a hodgepodge of Pat's favorite bric-a-brac, including a teddy bear collection, antique implements and china, and a sign in the lobby asking, "Next to the flag, whom do you love?"

FRIED MATZOH

6 to 8 matzohs
2 eggs
½ cup sour cream
6 to 8 tablespoons butter
salt to taste

Break matzohs into large pieces in a large bowl. Fill bowl with water and immediately drain all water out. Matzohs should be barely dampened.

Beat eggs and sour cream together. Stir gently into matzohs, coating all the broken crackers but trying not to break them into smithereens.

Melt 4 to 5 tablespoons of butter in wide skillet over medium heat.

Empty moistened matzohs into pan and spread out evenly. Dot tops of matzohs with remaining butter. When bottom of the pile of matzohs begins to brown, begin flipping them over. They will break into ragged pieces as you flip them. Continue cooking, stirring and flipping until all shreds and pieces of matzoh are cooked through, but not burned. Remove from heat and serve. Makes 3 to 4 servings.

Cafe Beaujolais: 961 E. Ukiah St., Mendocino, Calif.; (707) 937-5614. (Note: Cafe Beaujolais closes for a couple of months in the winter, usually starting December or January.)

Fried Matzoh

MENDOCINO, Calif.—If scenery whets your appetite, take the coast highway north out of San Francisco. Stop for biscuits and homemade strawberry preserves at Jerry's Farmhouse in Olema, for barbecued oysters at Tony's Seafood in Marshall. Cruise up the rocky shore and spend the night in Mendocino. Get up early the next day, drive out to the water's edge, sniff the salty air, perhaps even spot a spouting whale, then prepare to enjoy one of the best breakfasts of your life, at Cafe Beaujolais.

Among breakfast aficionados, this restaurant in a 1910-vintage Victorian house on Ukiah Street has become a legend. "When I die and go to heaven," one anonymous fan wrote to chef/owner Margaret Fox, "there had better be a Cafe Beaujolais there, or I'm not going."

Even the ordinary items on Margaret Fox's morning menu are extraordinary. Fluff-textured omelettes are filled with mushrooms and sour cream, or herbed cream cheese, or linguica sausage. Granola, served with fresh fruit, is studded with sunflower seeds and chunky with cashews. Waffles—Margaret's best-known breakfast specialty—are made with batters of buttermilk and oatmeal or sour cream and wild rice. And of course there is a full array of freshly made muffins, rolls, and coffee cakes.

One of our favorite breakfast items in Margaret Fox's repertoire is fried matzoh, also known as "matzoh brie." Matzoh, in case you aren't familiar with Old Testament cuisine, is the unleavened bread made by Jews when they beat a fast retreat from Egypt and had no time to wait for yeast to work. Now, by Biblical commandment (Exodus 12:15), it is the traditional bread of Passover season—wafer-thin, brittle, baked in perforated sheets so it can be broken into bite-size pieces.

Year around, matzohs make a good substitute for crackers. You can buy them plain or enriched with eggs and onions. You can crumble them into powder and make matzoh balls (dumplings especially well-suited for chicken soup), or you can eat them on a diet in lieu of more fattening kinds of leavened bread. And at breakfast, matzohs are transformed into a wonderful dish that might be described as a cross between an omelette and French toast.

Margaret's fried matzoh is made from a single cracker broken into raw scrambled eggs, then cooked in a skillet. It's simple and delicious. Our own version is more wieldy than her eggy version—dry enough to eat pieces of it with your fingers, and more substantial than scrambled eggs. It is moist but not wet; and if you fry it just long enough, it will be crisp around its edges but not dried out anywhere.

Serve fried matzoh plain or garnished with sour cream. Or you can even serve it accompanied by maple syrup, like French toast.

Cheddar Corn Pancakes

WEST REDDING, Conn.—If there was ever a restaurant where we run the risk of turning into health food nuts, Gail's Station House is it. Located a mere two miles from our home, the Station House is the place we go if we are too lazy to cook breakfast or lunch; if we want to take out-of-town visitors to a picturesque little Connecticut country café; or whenever we get a craving for Gail's cheddar corn pancakes.

Gail Gilbert is a vegetarian. Her menu is filled with healthy things, from freshly squeezed carrot juice (you can hear the juicer whir in the kitchen when you order it) to vegetable and brown rice casseroles, fruit salads, and even a "veggie burger." Gail bakes her bread using unsprouted wheat; her peanut butter (for PB&J or peanut butter and banana sandwiches) is the natural kind; soups, of course, are made from scratch. Believe us, it's a pleasure to eat healthy in this restaurant.

Health food isn't the only thing on the menu, though. In addition to good-for-you things, the Station House also specializes in giant bad-for-you (but irresistibly tasty) hamburgers made of beef—oozy half-pounders draped with cheddar cheese or cheddar

CHEDDAR CORN PANCAKES

1¼ cups flour

1 tablespoon sugar

4 teaspoons baking powder

1 teaspoon salt

2 eggs

1 to 1¼ cups milk

4 tablespoons butter, melted and cooled

1 7-ounce can corn niblets, thoroughly
   drained

butter for frying pancakes

2 cups grated cheddar cheese

Mix together flour, sugar, baking powder, and salt.

Beat eggs and 1 cup milk together. Stir in melted butter.

Combine both mixtures, then add corn niblets, stirring only enough to blend. If mixture seems too thick to pour, stir in up to ¼ cup milk.

Over medium-high heat, melt butter on a griddle or skillet. When butter begins to sizzle, pour out pancakes about 4 or 5 inches in diameter. Sprinkle each with about ⅛ cup cheddar cheese. When bubbles begin to pop on the surface of the pancake, flip and cook until cheese is crusty and gold.

Makes about 16 5-inch pancakes.

The Station House, 3 Sidecut Road, West Redding, Conn.; (203) 938-8933.

and bacon, served on homemade buns. If you really want to be a pig about it, you can get a mess of grilled onions and mushrooms on the side; and complete the naughty platter with a serving of fried potatoes drizzled with melted cheese. Now, that's good eating!

Breakfast, served until 3 P.M. closing, is the great meal at Gail's: fresh-squeezed juice, toast from the unsprouted wheat bread, different kinds of muffins every day, even homemade granola—honey-sweet and jam-packed with raisins.

The menu lists all the usual omelettes, plus a trio of "Station House Skillet Specials" brought to the table in their own cast-iron frying pans. Our favorite skillet is "Texas Pink"—a combination of red-skinned hash browns, jalapeño peppers, scrambled eggs, salsa, and sour cream, garnished with a wedge of grapefruit. "Barney's Breakfast" is a layering of hash browns, Canadian bacon, melted cheese, and scrambled eggs, accompanied by an English muffin. "Leo's Skillet" is eggs scrambled with nuggets of Nova Scotia lox and green onions, served with a bagel and cream cheese.

We've saved the best for last: pancakes and French toast. The French toast is made with Gail's bread. The pancakes are made with buckwheat flour or plain, or with all sorts of goodies added to them: blueberries, bananas, even chocolate chips, or—our favorite—cheddar cheese and corn, with their cheese side crusty from the grill.

Gail told us how to make cheddar corn cakes at home, explaining that the only problem is readying quantities for several people. You need a broad griddle to do it right, so that all the pancakes, for everyone, are ready at the same time. (It is possible, although not as good, to keep pancakes warm in a low oven on a heat-proof plate.)

BAKED PANCAKE

1 egg
1/3 cup flour
pinch of cinnamon
pinch of nutmeg
2 teaspoons sugar
2 drops vanilla extract
1/2 cup milk
2 tablespoons butter

Preheat oven to 375 degrees.

Combine egg, flour, cinnamon, nutmeg, sugar, vanilla, and milk. Mix well.

Melt butter in 7- to 8-inch ovenproof skillet until bubbly (but not brown). Quickly pour all of batter into pan and scoot it into the preheated oven. Bake 8–10 minutes or until golden brown and firm.

Sides will be high and dry; center will be shallow and soft. Slip the pancake onto a plate and fill center with fruit and/or sour cream, jam, etc.; or sprinkle with powdered sugar and a squeeze of lemon.

Serve immediately. Makes 1 serving.

Big 3 Fountain: Route 12, Sonoma, Calif.; (707) 996-8132.

Baked Pancake

SONOMA, Calif.—Awhile ago at dinner, we were discussing breakfast—pancakes in particular. It was an impassioned argument about who made the best. We were staunch partisans of Polly's Pancake Parlor in Sugar Hill, New Hampshire, or maybe Walker Brothers in Wilmette, Illinois; but then our dinnermates threw the discussion into chaos by suggesting that the best in all the land were the baked pancakes served at the Big 3 Fountain in California's Sonoma Valley.

We could not deny that Big 3 baked pancakes are one of the swellest meals anywhere, but we argued that they are so distant from the Platonic ideal of pancakehood that they are pancakes only in name. Pancakes, it seemed to us, are by definition fried and flipped on a griddle, as suggested by synonyms such as flapjack and griddlecake. Baked pancakes are poured into a pan and, as the name says, baked in an oven. Then, rather than getting sloshed with maple syrup, they are customarily filled with fresh fruit and sour cream, or a heap of caramelized apples or bananas. They wind up looking more like an open-face omelette than a stack of hotcakes.

The discussion then drifted into types of syrups—pure maple, Mrs. Butterworth's, sorghum, (each had its champions)—and we never did resolve the issue of the ultimate pancake. But that dinner" left us with a major hankering for a baked pancake.

So the next time we headed west, the Big 3 Fountain topped our agenda. Even aside from the pancakes, it is a great place to visit. Attached to the Sonoma Mission Inn, it opened as a combination soda fountain, bus depot, dry cleaners, drugstore, and post office in the 1920s. In 1959, it was named the Big 3 after three men who bought it: a butcher, a grocer, and a fountainmaster.

Our first visit was in the early 1980s, after the Sonoma Mission Inn had been turned into a swanky spa, and the Big 3 had been spiffed up to high 1950s style again, including a gleaming pop-up toaster on every table (for regular customers who insisted on toasting their own). It now sports many of the hallmarks of the California culinary style: a stylish open kitchen, a wood-burning oven, and a retro-chic menu of down-home diner cuisine. You can purchase (or merely sample) wine from local boutique vineyards, and you can have the gourmet delicatessen make up a picnic basket for afternoon jaunts into wine country.

But of course our recommendation, before you avail yourself of anything else the Big 3 has to offer, is to sit down for breakfast. Have a baked pancake, served plain (to be dusted with powdered sugar and sprinkled with a squeeze of lemon) or filled with fruit (fresh berries or baked sliced apples). The other noteworthy breakfast item is sourdough French toast, soaked in orange liqueur marinade, then topped with baked apple slices.

If you won't be in northern California soon, the good news is that baked pancakes are ridiculously easy to make at home. All you need is an ovenproof sauté or omelette pan, about eight inches across. Be sure to have your filling (if any) prepared in advance, ready to get plopped into the center of the pancake when it emerges from the oven. These 'cakes should be served immediately. (Therefore the only practical way to serve several people is to have several pans—and multiply this recipe accordingly.)

Whole Wheat Hazelnut Waffles

SEATTLE, Wash.—"Creative" is the word that describes what is on the menu at Cafe Sport. The kitchen blithely mixes traditions: Chinese, Pacific Northwestern, and square American; and it seeks out rare and exotic ingredients. Such restlessness can be risky if the chef isn't good. Fortunately, this kitchen is overseen by a wizard named Tom Douglas, who knows what he is doing; during our last visit to Seattle, we had breakfast, lunch, and dinner at Cafe Sport and enjoyed every meal.

It is located on a snug site at the north end of the Pike Place Market, sufficiently far from the commotion to provide some peace, but close enough so that when you step outside after lunch, you are only a short stroll away from the thick of the shopping and street bustle that make the market fun.

Interior lighting is provided by a mixture of table candles and neon. The café is romantically dark at night; during the day, sun streams in through picture windows. Walls are beige, turquoise, and bright red, spangled with multicolored sequins. Booths are plush leather; tables are covered with thick white cloths. We would summarize the ambience as fashionable, but not repulsively so.

What is nice about lunch and dinner is that they offer a real choice among plain and fancy foods. You can get a hamburger and French fries or baked Pacific ling cod with a *coulis* of fresh thyme and tomato. The hamburger, it must be said, isn't really *plain*; the day we had lunch at Cafe Sport, it was a chiliburger with Gouda cheese. It was swell. And the French fries were good too: crisp curly shoestrings with honest potato-and-clean-oil flavor. The ling cod was inspired: a big meaty filet that fell into moist flakes when probed with a fork, the heft of the fish impeccably complemented by its boggy tomato blanket.

WHOLE WHEAT HAZELNUT WAFFLES

1 cup white flour
1 cup whole wheat flour
¾ cup ground roasted hazelnuts
3 tablespoons brown sugar
grated rind of one orange
1½ teaspoons baking powder
1 teaspoon baking soda
½ teaspoon salt
4 eggs, separated
1 cup yogurt
1 cup milk
2 tablespoons butter, melted

Preheat waffle iron.
Combine all dry ingredients in large mixing bowl.
In a smaller bowl, combine yogurt, milk, and melted butter.
Beat egg yolks until foamy. Add yogurt, milk, and melted butter. Mix gently into dry ingredients.
Beat egg whites until soft peaks form and fold carefully into batter.
Spoon just enough batter into preheated waffle iron to cover the bottom griddle. Cook until waffle is golden brown (time will vary depending on waffle iron).
Serves 4–6 (makes six 8-inch waffles).

Cafe Sport, 2020 Western Ave., Seattle, Wash.; (206) 443-6000.

The menu always changes, but one exceptional dish nearly always available at lunch and dinner is grilled chicken with spicy noodles, a vaguely oriental-flavored composition of strips of grilled and glazed white meat resting atop a slippery bundle of noodles bathed in peanut sauce.

Salads are uncommon; there is one made with wild greens, baked goat cheese, and pecans, another weighted with hunks of sharp Oregon blue cheese. A favorite appetizer among many Cafe Sport regulars is black bean and chili pepper soup garnished with salsa and sour cream. For finishing a meal, there are ravishing desserts: apple, pear, and hazelnut tart; persimmon pudding topped with cognac-flavored whipped cream; or classic pecan pie.

We wish we had been able to eat more breakfasts at Cafe Sport. The menu lists enticing things such as corned beef hash with Mexican chilies, cinnamon French toast, and eggs scrambled with chorizo sausage, cheddar cheese, and tomato salsa on a tortilla. We were able to sample scones, apple-flecked sausages, and a superb whole wheat hazelnut waffle, the recipe for which Tom Douglas was good enough to give us. Hazelnuts, he explained, are an Oregon crop, so he works them into his menu in many ways. He serves the waffles with fresh fruit and orange butter (made by whipping unsalted butter with a bit of marmalade, sugar, and orange rind). Maple syrup is fine, too.

Ham and Red-Eye Gravy

ROANOKE Va.—Most people will tell you (correctly) that breakfast is the specialty of the house, but we would never kick lunch off the table at the Roanoker Restaurant.

The last midday meal into which we plunged at this "Home of Good Food Since 1941" was a staggering vista of victuals, the kind of bounteous plate lunch that signals good café cooking in the South. There were a mere two of us in the booth, and we ordered only two meals, but by the time the food was served, there were ten different plates on the table: one for the turkey divan, one for the pan-fried flounder filets, two plates holding crunch-crusted corn sticks and one jumbo hot biscuit each, four separate little bowls of side dishes (shellie beans, potatoes au gratin, candied yams, and spiced applesauce), and two plates of sugar-crusted apple pie.

What a feast! Our only regret was that we couldn't stick around another day until breakfast and return for the Roanoker's country ham and red-eye gravy.

Oh, sure, there would be more ham and red-eye gravy along the road, but few restaurants serve this country classic with Roanoker panache. First, there are the biscuits: big ones, cat-head size, but smooth-topped and not so knobby, with a faint sour milk tingle. And of course there's honey and jelly and grits and eggs. But the great thing about the meal is the look of that ham on its giant platter.

Paper-thin slices, nearly as deep red as mahogany, are fanned out partially submerged in a pool of the wondrous amber gravy known as red-eye. There is nothing to this hammy stuff, really; it's merely drippings cooked down with a little water or black coffee until the viscous liquid darkens to its proper shade of pink or brown.

Therein, however, lies serious controversy: pink or brown? Water or coffee? Some red-eye aficionados say the gravy comes by its name from a bleary morning-after appearance, which is best created by adding nothing other than water to the rendered fat. Flecks and bits and pieces of country ham (which gets fried in the fat before the gravy is made) give it the bloodshot look.

Others contend that the point is to make the gravy boat or bowl actually resemble an eye. Based on the principle that water and oil do not mix, their recipe calls for the rendered fat and all the ham scrapings to be poured in the bowl first. Then coffee is added, slowly and without undue turbulence. If it is poured in just right, it will submerge as a single mass of darker liquid, then bob to the surface of the pink-eye drippings, just like an eyeball, causing the bowl to look exactly like a reluctantly opening eye.

As many times as we have tried the latter method, our eye always turns out as segmented as a fly's. At the Roanoker, they are purists, using nothing but water to thin out the ham drippings, creating a gravy that is thin but overwhelmingly porcine. If you use coffee instead of water, the roasted flavor of the bean tends to diminish the salty zest of the rendered ham.

The only thing that cannot be monkeyed with when making red-eye gravy is the ham itself. It is absolutely essential that cured country ham be used. City ham doesn't have what it takes.

The problem is that a whole country ham is a major investment. If you don't have a store near you that sells it by the piece, you might want to try our favorite mail-order source for country hams—whole or by the one-pound slab: The Loveless Café, Route 5, Highway 100, Nashville, Tenn. 37221; (615) 646-9700.

HAM AND RED-EYE GRAVY

½ pound country ham, untrimmed, sliced
   very thin
salt pork (if necessary)
½ to ⅔ cup water or black coffee

Trim some of the excess fat from the edges of the ham and fry the fat over medium heat in a heavy skillet until rendered.

Fry ham slices in rendered fat, turning frequently, until they begin to brown. Do not overfry. Remove ham to serving platter. (If the ham is fairly lean, you may need to render more fat in the pan—either from another hunk of ham, or, if necessary, by using salt pork. Yield should be about ¼ cup of drippings.)

Gradually drizzle water or black coffee into ham drippings, continuing to cook, stirring constantly, scraping any bits and pieces of ham off the skillet into gravy.

Spoon gravy over ham or grits, or serve in bowl suitable for biscuit-dunking.

Makes 4 servings.

Roanoker: 2522 Colonial Ave., Roanoke, Va.; (703) 344-7746.

Sawmill Gravy

PADUCAH, Ky.—We are a couple of fuddy-duddies. We don't much like progress, and we are suspicious of anything new. Especially new restaurants. We like places that have been in business a long time, that cook good old-fashioned American food and serve it just as they always have.

Our job is to encourage the good places to keep the faith. By sharing our discoveries with readers, we hope to do our part to keep the good guys thriving.

Nothing makes us happier than returning to a place we once loved and finding it just as beautiful as ever, or even better. On a recent trip through the mid-South, we relished the familiar (and expected) excellence of biscuits at the Loveless Café in Nashville, fried chicken at Rowe's Family Restaurant in Staunton, Virginia, and coconut pie at Buntyn in Memphis.

Then we headed north, through Paducah, a town we hadn't visited in a dozen years. There used to be a restaurant we liked a lot in Paducah. It was a ragtag hut named Skin Head's. Long ago, when we first hit the road, it was at Skin Head's that we had our first real taste of Southern-style breakfast: biscuits, gravy, country ham, hash browns, and eggs. Given the economic ups and downs of the last decade, as well as Skin Head's helter-skelter appearance, we held out little hope it would still be baking biscuits.

But there it was! Looking every bit as declassé as we remembered: a squat cinderblock building with a metal awning that looks as if it had been used for carhop service years ago, and a sign outside announcing it as "The Breakfast House of the South." The inside is still a spill of rattle-legged booths and tables, wood-paneled walls, overhead fluorescents. "Remember now," the menu says, "short, fat, thin or tall, 'Ole Skin Head' will try to feed y'all."

We arrived at noon, and the midday meal was in full swing, as every sort of Paducahan from truck drivers to prom queens and businessmen streamed in to feast on handsome plates of skillet-fried catfish, crisp tenderloin sandwiches, or that cheap and wonderful mid-American ploughman's lunch of white beans, corn sticks, hot sauce, and a slab of onion (costing a grand total of $1.25).

What a fine time we had wallowing in the high spirits of Skin Head's and devouring its blue-plate food! If you are passing through Paducah and want a sassy taste of real American café life, it's an experience you won't soon forget.

A great stop for lunch; but it is the morning meal that still maintains Skin Head's in the first line of homecooking restaurants. "At Skin Head's," the menu boasts, "breakfast is a full-time job—not a

SAWMILL GRAVY

¼ cup cold bacon grease
⅔ cup flour
2½ cups milk, heated
2 teaspoons black pepper
2 teaspoons salt

Melt grease in heavy saucepan over medium heat. Sprinkle in flour, whisking constantly. Cook about 1 minute, then whisk in hot milk, pepper, and salt. Cook and stir 5 minutes. (It will keep several days in the refrigerator, but you may need to add a bit of milk to thin it out when reheating.)
Yield: about 2 ¾ cups.

Skin Head's: 1021 S. 21st St., Paducah, Ky.; (502) 442-6471.

sideline . . . seldom equaled, never excelled, imitated but never duplicated."

The roster of items is traditional, each made to perfection. Eggs and potatoes, of course. Slabs of griddle-fried country ham, their scarlet centers edged with halos of translucent amber fat, are accompanied by red-eye gravy. Buttermilk biscuits, the menu brags, "are made from Sunflower Self-Rising Flour, not that stuff they are calling scratch." However they are made, they are hot and good, perfect for dunking—either in the red-eye, made from ham drippings, or into bowls of "sawmill gravy."

We'll admit that the first time we tasted it, we were a little bit horrified by this thick white gunk, supercharged with pepper. And even today, as much as we enjoy sawmill gravy, we must warn you that it is one of the most rib-sticking foods on earth, not for dieters. Serve it along with jam and honey and other good biscuit toppers, and use it for an occasional dunk. No true Southern breakfast table should be without it.

2 Eggs with a choice of 4 strips bacon or 2 sausage patties or 3 links, hash brown potatoes, biscuits or toast, choice of grits or sawmill gravy, coffee $2.45
Or With Ham $2.70

2
Appetizers

Roasted Garlic

YOUNTVILLE, Calif.—The bar at Mustard's Grill is packed . . . but nobody is drinking liquor. Mustard's beverage list is wine and beer only; this is a wine crowd, for sure.

Listen to their conversations as they wait for a precious table in the dining room: There is little palaver about sports or politics or the usual tavern topics. Instead, one hears about varietals and private-reserve cabernets, about noble rot and fermentation.

There is nothing affected about these oenophilic discussions. Wine happens to be the local business hereabouts, and just as you'll hear automobile gossip in a Detroit bar or grain price futures in Des Moines, so the conversation at Mustard's is shoptalk about the lifeblood of the Napa Valley.

Here is a restaurant of the 1980s. As the wine business prospered, so did wine country cuisine; and now the land north of San Francisco is a gold mine of young-hearted places to eat. When Mustard's opened a few years ago, grape growers, vintners, and oenophiles fell in love with it; now the handsome grill is theirs.

Casual lifestyle is an art among these open-shirted customers, who are served by an attractive staff in long white uniforms reminiscent of San Francisco's grills. The restaurant is hip in a uniquely northern California way—laid-back, yet earnest about its food and drink. For a taste of what has become classic wine country cooking—sunny fare that the rest of us consider "California cuisine"—this is the best place we know.

From the wood-burning oven come beautiful herbed chickens, charred nearly sooty with a tangy mustard sauce. Grilled duck leg is served with a moist, heavy square of polenta. Calves' liver, rabbit, steaks, and fresh fish are cooked on a mesquite grill. Hamburgers are only-in-California excellent, available with lacy heaps of fried onion rings. Homemade banana rum ice cream is one of the most wonderful desserts we have ever lapped up.

We returned to Mustard's five times during a weeklong eating expedition north of San Francisco, and although our goal was to try as many things as possible, we could not resist beginning every meal with chef Cindy Pawlyson's goat cheese salad. It is a round of white-as-alabaster chevre rolled in pulverized almonds and heated, but not quite to the melting point. Moistened with an herb vinaigrette and decorated with sun-dried tomatoes in virgin olive oil, it is as smooth as velvet, with just the faintest goaty tang that does exactly what an appetizer is supposed to do . . . whet your whistle for all the good things to come.

Among those things is an item listed on the menu

19

ROASTED GARLIC

4 heads garlic (large-budded heads preferred)
4 tablespoons butter, melted
salt and pepper
4 tablespoons olive oil

Preheat oven to 275 degrees.
Carefully remove the outer parchmentlike skin of the garlic heads. Using a sharp knife, evenly cut the base (without cutting into the head) so the garlic will sit with the pointed parts of the cloves upward.

Place heads of garlic in a small baking dish and drizzle butter over them. Sprinkle with salt and pepper. Place in oven and bake 30 minutes. Pour one tablespoon of olive oil onto each head. Bake one more hour, basting frequently to keep heads moist.

When done, buds should pull easily away from the heads. Let cool to tepid. Each bud should be squeezed from its skin directly onto bread, then spread with a knife. Accompany garlic with French bread and mellow, spreadable cheese.

Mustard's Grill: Route 128 north of Yountville, Calif.; (707) 944-2424.

KNISH

PASTRY
4 cups sifted flour
4 teaspoons baking powder
1 tablespoon salt
4 tablespoons butter
4 tablespoons rendered and chilled chicken fat or solid vegetable shortening
1 cup milk
2 eggs, beaten

inconspicuously among "sides and condiments" as "roasted garlic." It is an entire head of garlic, slow-cooked until tender, served with toast. What do you do with it? Simple. Pull off the buds, one by one, and squeeze them out of their parchmentlike natural wrapping onto the toast. Tempered by heat, each pod of garlic is soft and nearly butter-textured, so it oozes easily and spreads with a knife.

We learned to order the garlic along with the warm goat cheese, and combine the two. First, spread some cheese on the toast, then top that with garlic, then an oily sliver of tomato for its zest. Sheer heaven!

Whole buds of garlic? Yes, indeed: Down the hatch! You see, consuming a head of roasted garlic, bud by bud, is not nearly as daunting as chewing even one tiny bud in the raw. When cloves of garlic cook, they not only soften, they yield their sting. In fact, James Beard used to tell us that one of his proudest creations was a dish he called "Chicken with Forty Cloves of Garlic." Jim especially liked it because he loved to shock people—as a recipe calling for forty cloves of garlic was bound to do. But amazingly, there is nothing offensive or smelly about the finished dish. As the garlic cooks, sealed in foil with the chicken, it mellows, flavoring the meat but not overwhelming it.

The same principle is what makes roasted garlic such a delicious conversation-piece hors d'oeuvre. Allow one entire head of garlic for each person. And if your guests have not eaten roasted garlic before, assure them that this is definitely finger food. Provide plenty of napkins!

Knish

FOREST HILLS, N.Y.—Queens Boulevard, from Rego Park through Forest Hills out to Kew Gardens, is a New York food bazaar.

Argentine bakeries, Italian pasta parlors, Greek diners, Kosher delis, Chinese dumpling houses, Hungarian strudel shops, falafel merchants from the Middle East: Name the nationality, and chances are good you can find its food on the boulevard. In Forest Hills, a storefront shop named Knish Nosh has concentrated exclusively on knishes for more than thirty years.

A knish—in case you never ran into one—is a building block of Jewish gastronomy. And we do mean block. A good knish is one of mankind's most substantial foodstuffs. The size of a hardball, it is a pastry dough wrapped around a compressed lode of filling—kasha

FILLING

2 tablespoons butter

1 medium onion, chopped (about ¹/₂ cup)

*1¹/₂ to 2 pounds potatoes, boiled and
mashed with ¹/₄ cup sour cream and 2
tablespoons butter (2¹/₂ to 3 cups)*

1 egg

¹/₂ cup sifted flour

¹/₂ teaspoon salt

¹/₈ teaspoon white pepper

1 tablespoon grated onion

*To make pastry: Sift together flour,
baking powder, and salt. Cut in butter and
shortening until mealy. Combine milk and
egg, and stir into flour until dough holds
together in a ball. Chill one hour.*

*Melt 2 tablespoons butter in a skillet.
Sauté onion until limp. Remove from heat.*

Preheat oven to 375 degrees.

*Mix together mashed potatoes, egg,
flour, salt, pepper, and grated onion. Mix
until smooth, adding more flour if necessary
to make potatoes hold together like bread
dough.*

*On a lightly floured surface, roll out
chilled pastry to ¹/₈-inch thick. Cut into
6-inch circles.*

*Onto the center of each pastry circle,
place a scant ¹/₄ cup of the mashed potato
mixture, topping it with a teaspoon of the
sautéed onions. Wrap the dough up around
the potato mixture, pinching it together at
the top.*

*Place with sealed side up on a lightly
oiled baking sheet. Bake 20–25 minutes,
until well browned. Makes 10–12 large
knishes.*

*Knish Nosh: 101–02 Queens Boulevard, For-
est Hills, N.Y.; (718) 897-5554.*

(buckwheat groats) or cabbage if it's kosher; occasionally liver, if dietary laws are relaxed.

At Knish Nosh ("nosh" is Yiddish for snack), the entire menu consists of knishes, three varieties only: liver, kasha, or potato. Business is almost all take-out, although three window tables, each with a capacity of two, allow you to nosh with a view of the boulevard. Customers stream out the doors with bags full of knishes from 9 A.M. to 7:30 at night; and despite the fact that Knish Nosh does not offer mail-order service, our counter man boasted that "these knishes travel round the world; people carry knishes wherever they go."

The corner restaurant smells like a Jewish grandmother's kitchen on Sunday, and its cooking is a true taste of immigrant Eastern European heritage, yet the counter staff is American urban black. That's what you call melting-pot America!

Our own favorite recipe for knishes are made with souped-up mashed potatoes, but don't be shy about experimenting with any leftovers: sweet potatoes, roasts (ground up), or potato and cheese combinations.

Kansas City Quiche

If you like English muffins, you must now make a decision: Keep reading, and run the risk of irrevocably altering your muffin-eating life; or ignore these words, and maintain the bland and boring status quo.

Are you still with us? Good. We're going to talk about majestic English muffins—the biggest, and in our not-so-humble opinion, the best in the land. If you are a fanatic on the subject, or if you live in Kansas City, you may already know about them: Wolferman's English muffins. They come in such flavors as light wheat, cheddar cheese, cinnamon-raisin, blueberry, and original, but it is not their flavorings that make them spectacular. It is their size.

A Wolferman's muffin is approximately twice as tall as an ordinary muffin. It weighs one-quarter pound. Pull it into halves and you have mountain peaks and gorges rather than nooks and crannies. Toast the halves and instead of getting a couple of hard round tiles, you get two monumental loaves of multi-textured muffin: crusty charred tips at the very top, a stratum of dried, porous crunch just below, then the chewy, steamy center leading down to the sandy-surfaced bottom. They're so thick, some people *bake* rather than toast them.

Once you have sunk your teeth into such a muffin, you cannot

KANSAS CITY QUICHE

4 strips bacon
3 Wolferman's English muffins
butter to taste
1 egg
⅓ cup cream
pinch nutmeg
pinch cayenne pepper
¼ teaspoon salt
½ pound Gruyere Swiss cheese, grated

Fry bacon until crisp and drain on paper towel.

Pull muffins in half. Toast medium-brown. Butter to taste.

Beat egg with cream, nutmeg, cayenne, and salt. Pour over grated cheese in a bowl. Mix well.

Spread egg and cheese mixture over muffins. Crumble bits of bacon on top. Place under broiler, at least six inches from heat source, for 1–2 minutes. When cheese melts and top begins to show brown flecks, whisk the muffins out. Watch closely; do not allow cheese to burn. Serve immediately. Serves 6.

go back. You have tasted greatness, and now no scrawny garden-variety English muffin can ever satisfy your hunger.

Fortunately, with a little planning, muffin maniacs can always have a ready supply. Wolferman's muffins (which are freezeable) are sold in many gourmet stores; they are also available by mail. In fact, Wolferman's has a mail-order catalog featuring not only muffins, but specially designed muffin-splitters, complete breakfast kits, "Bountiful Brunch Baskets" (everything but the fresh fruit), and our personal favorite muffin topping, Honey Apricot Spread. The toll-free number for mail orders is 1-800-255-0169; the address is One Muffin Lane, North Kansas City, Mo. 64116.

Tripe à la Frank

NEW YORK—West 14th Street in New York City is a rugged place, especially in the morning when the meat men are at work. Big guys dig hooks into haunches of slaughtered cows to heft them from curbside trucks into butcher shops that line the street. The air smells of raw meat; the sidewalk is bloody.

This is the Gansevoort meat market, which supplies some of New York's grocery stores and best restaurants with their steaks and chops. The day starts early here—very early, shortly after midnight. By afternoon, the street is quiet and nearly all the shops and warehouses are closed, secure behind gates and metal curtains. Then as night falls, cars begin arriving and parking near the north side of the street just east of 10th Avenue.

They have come to Frank's, a bar and grill that opens every night for dinner at 5:30 P.M. Perhaps we should say reopens every night, because Frank's serves customers from the market all morning, every morning. It is the gathering place for the Gansevoort butchers and for the truckers who haul "swinging beef" into the city. They come for a short-order breakfast of bacon and eggs, or "coffee and." This out-of-the-way restaurant has been their hangout since the early 1900s, when Frank Poggi first fired up his stove and spread sawdust on the floor.

They still use sawdust on the floor at Frank's—it makes for easy sweeping up; but between the time the market crowd leaves and the dinner customers arrive, the old stuff is swept away and a fresh sprinkle garnishes the weathered surface. Tables are covered with soft linens. Lights are lowered. The steam table toward the back of the restaurant is curtained off. And the plate-lunch menu is replaced by a roster of some of the finest meat-and-potatoes meals New York has to offer.

TRIPE À LA FRANK

3–4 pounds honeycomb tripe
I large Spanish onion, minced (about I cup)
2 large carrots, diced
3 ribs celery, chopped
I clove garlic, minced
4 tablespoons butter
¼ cup olive oil
¼ teaspoon ground cumin
I cup dry white wine
I cup Italian plum tomatoes
spice bag as follows, tied in cheesecloth:
  I veal knuckle, cut in pieces by butcher;
  3 bay leaves; I teaspoon rosemary;
  ¼ teaspoon thyme; 6 peppercorns

Cut tripe in ¼-inch strips and boil in water 10–15 minutes. Strain, rinse in cold water. Set aside.

In heavy saucepan or dutch oven, sauté onions, carrots, celery, and garlic in butter and olive oil. When onion is translucent, add cumin, wine, tomatoes, and spice bag. Bring to boil. Add tripe. Simmer gently six full hours, or until tripe is fall-apart tender. Add salt and pepper to taste. Discard spice bag.

Serves 4–6 as main course; 8–10 as hors d'oeuvre.

Frank's: 431 W. 14th St., New York, N.Y.; (212) 243-1349.

Prices are high. A shell steak can run about $20, but this beef is selected by George Molinari, Frank Poggi's son-in-law and Frank's proprietor, from the primest prime meat the market has to offer. Frank's veal chop weighs more than a pound. The skirt steak is significantly larger than its broad oval plate. Prime rib is the most succulent hill of protein through which you will ever plunge a knife.

In addition to four-star steak and chops, Frank's specializes in "variety meats"—mammoth slabs of cream-tender calves' liver, sautéed sweetbreads, cognac-sauced veal kidneys, and a tripe dish that has become a legend among Frank's loyal clientele.

We'll be honest: We wouldn't voluntarily order tripe in a restaurant, or buy it at the supermarket. It looks yucky raw, and it takes some effort to cook, and hey, it's the lining of a cow's stomach, for crying out loud!

But wait. Please. Listen to us—as we listened to George Molinari when he convinced us to try a plate of tripe à la Frank. Tripe isn't as bad as it looks in the butcher's case, not even as bad as it smells when you cook it. In fact, it can be a sweet and succulent plate of food. Tripe à la Frank is not everybody's cup of tea, to be sure, but if you are an adventurous eater, we highly recommend it—as a momumental main course, or an extraordinary appetizer for a special meal. We have reduced Frank's recipe to home kitchen proportions.

Silver Spoon Wings

GEORGETOWN, Conn.—Chicken wings used to be poor relations of breasts, drumsticks, and thighs. Along with backs and necks, they were often relegated to the stockpot for making broth, or they were gnawed as second-class food by those who couldn't afford the meatier pieces.

Thanks mostly to Buffalo, New York, wings' fortunes have risen in the last few years. Buffalo chicken wings, once the exclusive specialty of local taverns and pizzerias, have taken flight and traveled across the land. They are now immensely popular munchies in restaurants and pubs, and even in people's homes.

We suspect that the reason for wings' ascension is that they are fun to eat. They are finger food. They go great with drinks. They are easy to chew and lick while standing up and carrying on a conversation, or while sitting back in an easy chair concentrating on a favorite television show. Sure, they're messy, but that is part of their sloppy appeal—just be sure to provide plenty of napkins.

Classic Buffalo wings are extremely spicy. First they are washed

SILVER SPOON WINGS

½ cup sugar

½ cup water

½ cup dark soy sauce

¼ cup pineapple juice

2 tablespoons vegetable oil

1 teaspoon grated fresh ginger

½ teaspoon garlic powder

2 to 3 pounds chicken wings, cut at the joints, tips discarded

Combine sugar, water, soy sauce, pineapple juice, oil, ginger, and garlic powder. Stir until sugar is dissolved. Pour over chicken wings in bowl small enough so that all are covered. Cover and refrigerate. Marinate at least one full day (two is preferable), stirring occasionally.

Preheat oven to 350 degrees. Lift wings from marinade and place on cookie sheet. Bake 40 minutes, or until tender, basting twice with remaining marinade. Can be eaten hot or cold.

Makes hors d'oeuvres for 6–8.

and patted dry. Then they get cut in three, yielding a mini-drumstick and a bow-shaped section. (The tips are discarded.) They get marinated about 30 minutes in a mixture of two parts melted butter to one part red hot sauce (a formula that varies depending on how hot you like them). Then they are fried 5–6 minutes in 365-degree oil, drained, sprinkled with paprika, and served immediately. In Buffalo, wings are always accompanied by celery sticks and a cup of blue cheese dressing suitable for cooling the palate.

If you don't want them hot, you can do almost anything else you like with wings. The great thing about them is that compared with other parts of the chicken, wings are mostly surface, with only minimal amounts of meat. If you like crunchy skin, interesting sauce, or exotic seasoning, wings are the perfect medium. Their essential character is created by the way the skin is seasoned and the wings are cooked.

Our favorite wings are quite plain. In fact, what we like most about them is that they are drippingly chickeny, not pepper-hot, with chewy mahogany-roasted skin and luscious shreds of moist meat inside.

We discovered these wonderful wings practically around the corner from our house at a gourmet shop called The Silver Spoon. Alas, The Silver Spoon has since closed it doors . . . but not before owner Connie Spitzmiller shared her recipe for her wonderful chicken wings. She calls them "Cantonese-style" wings, but to us, they're a reminder of the cheerful little shop in Connecticut where we first tasted them.

Smoked Salmon Salad Spread

FORKS, Wash.—Nearly everything we Americans eat has roots somewhere else: Russian Tartars were chowing down on hamburger-like patties hundreds of years before Ronald McDonald was even a gleam in Ray Kroc's eyes; hot dogs can trace an impressive genealogy to Germany and Austria; even mom's apple pie was beloved by the English long before pilgrims set off for the New World.

If you want to find a dish that is purely American, travel to the Olympic Peninsula of Washington, where salmon is king. Plenty of countries around the world enjoy salmon, and many enjoy it smoked. But only America—the Pacific Northwest to be exact—has perfected the art of cold-smoking salmon over alder wood.

The process was evolved over several millennia by Kwakiutl

Indians. The point of smoking was to preserve the fish so it would last throughout the winter. In the spring and summer they feasted on freshly caught salmon, roasted over blazing wood fires that imparted a virile smack to the rich pink meat; or they lightly smoked the fish, so that is was moist and luscious with a subtle wood perfume. For winter, they hung fish for a long stay in the smokehouse, infusing it with smoke but not actually cooking it with heat from a fire. This "cold smoke" technique fully dehydrated the fish, thereby preventing spoilage. The result was a chewy, flavorful pad of protein that would keep for months.

Although scarcer than a few centuries ago, when the rivers of the Olympic Peninsula are said to have brimmed with sockeye and chinook, salmon is still a staple of Pacific Northwest cookery. You can get it poached, steamed, or broiled in many fine restaurants; but for adventurous eaters in search of regional Americana, the significant way to have salmon is to have it smoked.

SMOKED SALMON
SALAD SPREAD

1 6¹/₂-ounce can smoked salmon, drained
¹/₃ cup finely chopped celery
¹/₃ cup finely chopped onion
¹/₂ teaspoon lemon juice
¹/₂ cup mayonnaise
salt and pepper to taste

Mix all ingredients. Cover and refrigerate.

Spread on bread or crackers.

Yield: hors d'oeuvres for 4–6, or two big sandwiches.

Smokehouse Restaurant: Highway 101 north of Forks, Wash.; (206) 374-6258.

Our favorite place to go is the Smokehouse, a rustic building along Route 101 with an Indian totem pole decorating the cedar boards in front, and a cannery-smokehouse out back. Stephen Torgesen, owner of the restaurant and the cannery, does all the smoking himself, using locally caught or Alaskan fish to produce salmon that is sold by the whole slab or packed in cans. (Mail-order information can be obtained by writing Slathar's Smokehouse Cannery, RR 1, Box 5050, Forks, Wash. 98331.)

The restaurant is a cheerful place, no fancier than a coffee shop with its black Naugahyde booths, pine paneling, and Formica tables. Upstairs, there is a Salmon Room for cocktails, and a butcher's case is well stocked with "salmon gift packs" to take (or mail) home.

The menu offers all kinds of seafood, including grilled oysters, local halibut, tiny shrimp, clams, crab, scallops, cod, perch, and prawns. Or you can eat steak or prime rib. Of course, it is salmon we recommend—either brushed with butter and charbroiled or straight from the smokehouse out back. It doesn't get much better than this.

The last time we returned from a trip out West, we brought home several cans of Smokehouse smoked salmon, along with a few recipes. One of the simplest is Stephen Torgesen's smoked salmon salad spread—suitable for sandwiches and hors d'oeuvres, or for stuffing tomatoes or celery. It's exactly like tuna salad (and every bit as easy to make), but smoky fish gives it a fetching tang. If you cannot find smoked salmon in your supermarket, we recommend you order some from Forks. It is entirely possible to use ordinary unsmoked tuna or salmon in this ultrabasic recipe, but then the taste is only ultrabasic.

3

Soups

Bowl of the Wife of Kit Carson

MORRISON, Colo.—Hungry, but a little low on cash? No problem if you are in the vicinity of Morrison, Colorado (on the southwest side of Denver). Simply catch yourself a few beavers, skin them, and bring the pelts to The Fort. Beaver pelts are accepted in lieu of currency as payment for meals. Credit cards are OK, too.

Payment in pelt makes sense at The Fort, as do the Southern Cheyenne calico costumes of the waitresses, and the five-inch Green River knives you get to slice your steak (beef or buffalo). Built twenty-six years ago as a re-creation of a fur trader's fort, the red adobe restaurant attempts to create a romanticized taste of frontier history—and succeeds deliciously well.

The Fort is outfitted with working black powder cannons, a couple of capacious fireplaces and an open-air campfire, and rugged wood tables and chairs set across a floor made of congealed dirt and beef blood. There is also a canvas tepee in the courtyard in which couples can dine seated on buffalo rugs, serenaded by owner Sam Arnold playing the saw. From outside, the view of Denver is dazzling. Inside, the vittles are unique.

The cuisine of The Fort is Wild Western, duded up for modern American palates. Frankly, we doubt if any cowpokes or ranchers or land barons ever dined this well. Even the drink list adds fashionable coolers such as daiquiris and piña coladas to historical exotica that ranges from "the hailstorm" (mint julep in a pint mason jar) to the "Santa Fe Original Gin Cock Tail," and Chimaja whiskey flavored with wild mountain parsley.

Hors d'oeuvres can be as familiar as guacamole and chips or as weird as buffalo tongue (a nineteenth-century delicacy featured on menus of the finest restaurants in New York and Europe). The tongue is served along with "prairie butter" (buffalo marrow) and boudies (a lean buffalo sausage) on what the menu calls a "Historian's Platter" of appetizers. One can also begin a meal with bite-size, peanut butter-stuffed jalapeño peppers, Rocky Mountain oysters (sliced, fried sheep's testicles), or a relatively tame shrimp and avocado cocktail.

Of course, there are all kinds of steaks to eat—sirloins, pepper-stuffed sirloins, strip steaks, prime rib, even a nearly fatless "Texas longhorn" cut. You can eat buffalo or elk or lamb chops, or a brace of quail or trout broiled Taos Indian-style—topped with bacon and mint.

The best-known dish served at The Fort is "Bowl of the Wife of Kit Carson." Technically, the true name for this lusty soup/stew (known to regulars at The Fort as the "K.C. bowl") is "caldo

BOWL OF THE WIFE OF KIT CARSON

8 cups chicken broth

2 cups bite-size chicken or turkey chunks
    (cooked)

2 cups cooked garbanzo beans

1 to 4 hot jalapeño peppers, minced (to
    taste)

2 cups cooked rice

2 teaspoons dried oregano

1 avocado, sliced into thin pieces

1½ cups cubed or coarsely grated Muenster
    cheese

Bring broth to boil in large suacepan.
Add chicken, beans, peppers, rice, and
oregano. Simmer 3–5 minutes.

Pour soup into four wide serving bowls.
Top with avocado and cheese just before
serving.

Makes 6 meal-size servings.

The Fort, 19192 Highway 8 (at Junction
with Highway 285), Morrison, Colo.;
(303) 697-4771.

tlalpeño," but Sam Arnold says that Kit Carson's granddaughter, Miss Leona Wood, told him that she ate it as a youngster. Many years ago when he first opened The Fort, he named it for her grandmother.

True Bowl of the Wife of Kit Carson requires smoked peppers called chile chipotles, sold by the can in Mexican supermarkets in the West. If you cannot get chile chipotle peppers, you can come close to the real thing by following San Arnold's recipe (which we adapted from his recipe book, "Frying Pans West") but substituting a quarter to a half a chopped hot jalapeño pepper per person.

Southern New England Clam Chowder

NOANK, Conn.—As mud season ends and summer sun warms the New England shore, lobster pounds and clam shacks swing their shutters open. It is time to eat outdoors again. Seaside patios are swept; picnic tables get new coats of paint. Hibernating kitchens come to life as boiling pots are set to simmer.

May is a delicious time of year to eat one's way up the coast. Breakfast on warm muffins and cider, or pancakes served with the spring's yield of maple syrup. Then mosey along the back roads and coastal byways, sampling stuffed quahogs and fritters, fried clams and clamcakes, lobster rolls, lobster pie, and just plain lobster. Because summer crowds haven't yet arrived, travelers have their pick of country inns, where the nights are still cool enough to require a glowing fire in every room, and two quilts on the bed.

Our favorite way to get warm is a bowl of chowder: clam chowder, fish chowder, corn chowder (you'll find that inland), or chowderlike seafood stew, which is a simple broth made with milk or cream and fish or oysters, but without any vegetables. Chowders and stews, in their myriad forms, are definitive Yankee food. They are hale and stark, economical eats for a climate where the down-east wind blows cold.

A vast amount of hot air is expended over the subject of clam chowder, specifically over the issue of tomatoes. True chowder, any Yankee chef will tell you, is a simple-milk or cream brew, made with salt pork, potatoes, and clams, but without even a hint of tomatoes. "Manhattan" clam chowder, which one irate Rhode Island chef described to us as "yesterday's vegetable soup with clams thrown in," is tomato-based and spicy. Simple enough, except for the small fact that several of Rhode Island's most esteemed chowderdromes sell a creamy pink-shaded chowder that is true to neither definition.

SOUTHERN NEW ENGLAND CLAM CHOWDER

4 ounces salt pork
1 teaspoon sliced garlic
1 tablespoon finely minced onion
1 tablespoon flour
2 cups clam broth
1 cup water
¼ cup finely chopped celery
¼ cup finely chopped carrot
¼ cup fresh parsley, chopped
8 ounces chopped steamed clams
1 bay leaf
¼ teaspoon rosemary
½ teaspoon thyme
1 teaspoon sugar
1 teaspoon salt
¼ teaspoon white pepper
¼ teaspoon cooking sherry
1 tablespoon butter
1½ cups raw diced potatoes

Cut salt pork into cubes and cook in a small saucepan until all the fat is rendered. Discard pieces of pork. Sauté garlic in rendered fat until browned. Discard garlic. Add onions and sauté until transparent. Gradually sprinkle in flour, stirring. Cook 1 minute, continuing to stir. Remove from heat and set aside.

Place clam broth and water in a large kettle over medium heat. When it begins to simmer, whisk in onion and flour mixture. Add remaining ingredients. Simmer gently 30 minutes. Cover, and place in refrigerator 24 hours to allow flavors to meld. Heat to serve.

Yield: 1 quart.

Abbott's Lobster in the Rough, 117 Pearl St., Noank, Conn.; (203) 536-7719.

Furthermore, one of the most savory varieties to be found in chowder houses along the southern New England coast is made with neither cream nor tomatoes. It is a bracing clam juice-based broth, made with a few finely chopped vegetables and plenty of fresh clams. This briny pearlescent stuff, according to chowder authority Carolyn Wyman of New Haven, is true Rhode Island chowder.

Fine. The only problem we have with that definition is that the best Rhode Island chowder we ever ate was in Connecticut. So why don't we just forget about the regional fine points and focus on this superior chowder, the specialty of a seaside lobster restaurant called Abbott's, in the tiny fishing village of Noank.

There is no prettier place than Abbott's to savor a full shore dinner, served in a completely casual, eat-in-the-rough style. Customers arrive by car or boat, and they eat their freshly steamed lobsters off cardboard plates at picnic tables strewn about the lawn and pier. The view is the Noank harbor, with its passing sailboats and fishermen's trawlers, and an occasional gull screeching overhead.

Abbott's renowned chowder, according to owners Ruth and Jerry Mears, "is the product of the hard work and genius of our predecessors, the late Ernie Abbott and his wife Doris. About thirty years ago, they spent a significant portion of their life in their home kitchen trying out variants of the recipe. Today's chowder is the fruit of their long and patient labors. It has grown to have a tremendous following of loyal, fanatical clam chowder lovers . . . and woe to those who even contemplate change in this mystical mixture!"

Ruth and Jerry obtain their clam juice when they steam their fresh clams, which is the only way to do it absolutely true and right. If that's too much trouble, you can use bottled clam juice. On occasion, we have even resorted to *canned* minced clams, although the folks at Abbott's would be horrified by anything other than clams straight from their shells.

Slumgullion

NEWPORT, Ore.—There are branches of Mo's up and down the Oregon coast from Coos Bay to Lincoln City. All sorts of restaurants, stores, and food stands sell Mo's famous clam chowder. But to experience the full glory of Mo's, it is best to go to Newport, where Mo's was born a half a century ago.

Mo's is on the Newport waterfront. Or perhaps we should say

SLUMGULLION

6 slices bacon

½ cup coarsely chopped onion

2 cups clam broth

3 medium potatoes, peeled and diced
   (3 cups' worth)

dash Tabasco sauce

1 teaspoon coarsely ground black pepper

3 cups milk

1 cup evaporated milk

1½ cups clams, chopped (fresh clams
   preferred!)

2 cups small cooked shrimp

salt to taste

Fry bacon over medium heat in large saucepan until crisp. Remove to paper towel and reserve. When cool enough to handle, break into bite-size pieces. Pour off all but 2 tablespoons of the bacon fat from the saucepan.

Sauté onion in fat until transparent. Stir in clam broth. Add potatoes. Bring to low rolling boil and cook until potatoes are fork tender and ready to fall apart on their own, about 10 minutes. Add Tabasco sauce and pepper.

Heat milk and cream. Add to potatoes, along with clams. When clams are warm (only a few minutes), stir in shrimp. Salt to taste. Use reserved bacon to garnish individual servings of chowder, if desired.

Serves 4–6 as main course, 8 as appetizer.

Mo's Annex, 657 S.W. Bay Boulevard, Newport, Ore.; (503) 265-7512.

Mo's *are* on the waterfront, because there are two of them, across the street from each other—Mo's Restaurant and Mo's Annex. They are surrounded by a dockside sprawl of fish markets, seafood packing companies, piers where boats unload the day's catch, and stores that advertise they will smoke any fish, meat, or fowl you bring in.

Menus at both Mo's are similar, issued on disposable newsprint. The "Restaurant" tends to offer a slightly larger variety of dinners, including grilled things (oysters, salmon, halibut) and fried things (fish and chips, clam strips, onion rings); the "Annex" specializes in casseroles and stews. Both dole out clam chowder by the individual cup or bowl or family-style for folks who like to serve themselves. No meal at either place costs more than $5.95, including chowder or salad and hot bread.

Although the menu at the Restaurant is slightly larger, we like eating at the Annex better. What a view! The bright-red eating shed is perched above Yaquina Bay, allowing diners to look out over the water and the commercial fleet berthed at the dock, and to watch sport fishermen cleaning their day's catch. In the distance, sailboats skim across the bay.

The cuisine of Mo's (Annex and Restaurant) is traditional (as opposed to nouvelle) fish cookery. They serve none of the spartan, unadorned seafood dishes that seem to be fashionable these days; indeed, what we like best at the Annex are its defiantly old-fashioned luxury casseroles, in which fish gets cosseted in cheese, cream, sauce, crumbs, etc. Scalloped oysters, for instance, are a sumptuous baked-together comfort-food combination of butter, cream, crackers, and oysters from Mo's own oyster beds. You can also get your oysters "barbecued"—shelled, sauced, smothered with cheese, and baked. Mo's makes a lush cioppino (fisherman's stew) thick with tomato sauce, a cheesy shrimp casserole, and a unique version of Hangtown fry, in which oysters or shrimp are combined with eggs, green onions, and bacon.

The chowder that made Mo's famous is not all that different from most clam chowders one finds along the Oregon coast—thick and creamy, stocked with pieces of clam, with a faint smoky taste. We like this chowder; but what we like even more is the oddly named chowder variation that Mo's makes, listed on the menu in the category of seafood stews as *slumgullion*. Slumgullion is a clam chowder given a special marine sweetness by adding shrimp. It's a terrific combination, and with a salad and a hunk of bread, a royal supper.

HEART OF ARTICHOKE SOUP

6–8 large globe artichokes
1/2 teaspoon salt
1/4 teaspoon pepper
2 cloves garlic, crushed
2 tablespoons vegetable oil
2 tablespoons lemon juice
2 cups chicken stock
1 small onion, diced
1 cup cream
salt and pepper to taste

Trim stems off artichokes so they stand securely on their bottoms. Cut 3/4 inch off the top of each artichoke and remove any tough bottom leaves.

Under cold running water, force the leaves apart and cut out the small sharp-edged leaves and prickly choke in the center with a grapefruit knife or paring knife. Press the leaves back together.

To 2 inches of boiling water in a vegetable steamer, add salt, pepper, garlic, vegetable oil, and lemon juice. Place artichokes top-down in a colander or top of steamer. Cover and steam 30–40 minutes until tender but not mushy.

Remove leaves. Julienne 8–10 leaves and set aside. (The remaining leaves can be served chilled with hollandaise or anchovy mayonnaise.)

Purée artichoke hearts, adding chicken stock to blender.

Bring stock and diced onion to boil and simmer 5 minutes. Stir in cream and thoroughly warm soup (but do not boil). Add salt and pepper to taste.

Garnish each serving with julienned artichoke leaves. Makes 4 servings.

Duarte's, 202 Stage Road, Pescadero, Calif.; (415) 879-0464.

Heart of Artichoke Soup

PESCADERO, Calif.—"Mr. Duarte, please tell us how to make such delicious artichoke soup."

"First, you start with an artichoke patch."

Ronald Duarte wasn't kidding. The farmland around Pescadero is thick with the thistle-topped stalks of artichoke plants. In fact, Pescadero isn't far from Castroville, which lays claim to the title of "Artichoke Capital of the World" (and boasts a restaurant called The Giant Artichoke, with a menu that includes not only boiled and fried artichokes, but even artichoke cake!). The Duarte family have their own patch; at their café on the main street of Pescadero, they make maximum use of the garden's yield.

Fat-leafed artichokes such as these are delicious every which way, whether simply steamed or elaborately stuffed (with fennel sausage—yum!). Their garden tang is especially welcome at breakfast, when omelettes are wrapped around mountains of pale green chunks of heart, steamed to toothsome tenderness and seasoned with garlic, salt, and pepper. Artichoke soup is served along with every dinner.

Ronald Duarte's artichoke specialties are merely a small portion of a menu built on California's bounty from the land and sea. Depending on the time of year and how the fish are running, you can dine on the finest-textured local seafood—sand dabs or rex sole. If you are an oyster lover, you haven't lived until you've tasted Duarte's Pigeon Point oysters, baked in pools of garlic butter.

The best meals we have eaten at Duarte's are reminiscent more of some great mythical mom's home cooking than restaurant fare: pork chops served with homemade applesauce and chunky mashed potatoes; pot roast; beef stew; roast turkey with sage dressing. Even the house salad—a perfunctory gesture in so many restaurants—is a bounty of beets, onions, carrots, tomatoes, and lettuce that all taste as if they were pulled, picked, or plucked from a nearby garden.

For serious feasting, we recommend a visit on Friday or Saturday night, when the kitchen brews a grand version of San Francisco cioppino, a symphonic red-sauced fisherman's stew made with clams, prawns, mussels, cod, and Dungeness crab. Cioppino is served with sourdough bread; second helpings of the stew are included in the price of dinner.

All this fine food tastes even better because of the hometown feel about Duarte's. It is an unpretentious tavern, where locals come to eat at mismatched tables and chairs in a knotty pine-paneled dining room. When it's crowded, as it usually is at mealtimes, strangers share tables. Geezers hold court; babies squall; towns-folk trade gossip; and travelers are made to feel right at home.

That's the way it has been since Ronald's grandfather Frank Duarte opened for business in 1894.

Cream of Mushroom Soup

READING, Pa.—Inscribed in the little black book of many a traveling epicure, Joe's of Reading, Pennsylvania, has specialized in mushrooms for more than fifty years.

When Joe's opened for business in 1916, it was a bar where workingmen came for mugs of beer and twenty-cent bowls of wild mushroom soup. The place was named for its owner, Joe Czarnecki; the soup was made by Joe's wife, Magdalena. Just as they had learned to do in Poland, Joe and Magdalena foraged for their mushrooms in pine forests and fields around Reading, then hung them on clotheslines behind the bar to dry.

Mushrooms have been a Czarnecki family obsession ever since, and Joe's humble tavern has become one of the most unusual restaurants in America. It is a temple of mushroom cookery, where each meal is created as a celebration of mushrooms—purchased, imported, or gathered by the Czarneckis.

When Joe's son Joe, Jr., took over the business in 1947, he added tables and expanded the menu. By the late 1950s, word about Joe's had begun to spread, and connoisseurs made pilgrimages to Reading to taste not only the wild mushroom soup, but exotic dishes based on rare varieties such as cepes and morels, slippery jacks, woodblewits, and russulas.

Joe's son Jack, along with his wife, Heidi, has been running the restaurant since 1974. Despite its inconspicuous neighborhood location, it is anything but a corner tavern. "Joe's?" said the local cop from whom we asked directions, "Joe's is gourmet dining."

The wine list is extensive (and expensive), meals are elegantly served from a rolling cart, fresh flowers decorate each table, and a chandelier glimmers overhead. This restaurant is fancy, but in a comfortable sort of way. It still has the feel of a family business—Jack and Heidi's place, where the proprietors stroll through the dining room, eager to share their love of mushrooms with customers.

Cream-sauced, marinated, stuffed with veal, or paired with snails or venison, many of Joe's mushrooms are local, from the fungus-friendly soil of southeastern Pennsylvania. (There is a Mushroom Museum just south of Reading in Kennett Square.)

CREAM OF MUSHROOM SOUP

8 tablespoons butter

6 tablespoons sifted flour

2 tablespoons chopped onions

1½ to 2 pounds fresh domestic mushrooms, cleaned

2 tablespoons water

1½ cups heavy cream

½ teaspoon dried savory

2 teaspoons sugar

1 teaspoon soy sauce

salt to taste

Melt 6 tablespoons of the butter in sauté pan and gradually stir in sifted flour. Cook over low heat, stirring, 5 minutes. Set aside.

Cook onions in remaining 2 tablespoons of butter in a separate saucepan. When onions are transparent, add mushrooms and water. Cover and lower heat. Simmer gently 30 minutes, stirring 2 or 3 times.

Remove lid from onions and mushrooms; stir in cream and all remaining seasonings except salt. Bring to simmer.

Stir in flour-butter mixture to thicken. Salt to taste. Serve immediately. Makes 4 small but filling servings.

Joe's, 7th & Laurel, Reading, Pa.; (215) 373-6794.

Other, rarer varieties are imported from across the country and around the world. Jack and Heidi still enjoy foraging for oddities that never make it to the supermarket, such as "chicken of the woods," "puffballs," and "inky caps."

If you are an amateur mushroom hunter or professional mycologist looking for novel recipes, or if you just want some new ideas for the mushrooms you can buy at the supermarket, have a look at *Joe's Book of Mushroom Cookery,* published by Atheneum.

Written by Jack Czarnecki, *Joe's Book of Mushroom Cookery* is a whole world of cooking based on the mushroom-centered menu of the restaurant. It contains recipes for soups, sauces, side dishes, and main courses made from the increasing diversity of mushrooms available in grocery stores and specialty markets. In addition, the book contains a fascinating chapter of recipes for "very wild mushrooms" aimed at pick-'em-yourselfers. Those recipes, of course, are prefaced by a warning emphasizing that you better know what you're doing before you go out to pick and eat your own. If you're so inclined, the book includes a list of clubs for mushroom hunters around the country.

Many of the recipes are for quite sophisticated meals, and some call for mushrooms not readily available in ordinary stores. But one recipe we relish from *Joe's Book of Mushroom Cookery* is as simple and easy as can be. Jack calls it "domestic" cream of mushroom soup. It uses ordinary supermarket mushrooms, and it does taste domestic—oh-so-homey, a superluxurious surprise if one has grown too accustomed to the cream of mushroom soup that comes condensed in cans.

Don't be concerned about what seems like such a small amount of liquid in this soup. As the mushrooms simmer, they give up their own powerful juices to form the basis of the soup.

Chicken Corn Soup

BROWNSTOWN, Pa.—We don't often recommend eateries with outdoor toilets, but we promise you won't mind the facilities at the Brownstown Restaurant. Although outside, they are heated, and they have modern plumbing. Still, there is something undeniably old-fashioned about this former stage stop on Route 772 in Pennsylvania Dutch country.

Its original tavern license, hung on a wall behind the bar, goes back to 1892, when the Brownstown was a stop on the stagecoach route to Harrisburg. Drivers changed horses here, and travelers refreshed themselves with a hot meal.

CHICKEN CORN SOUP

6 cups chicken broth
1 small onion, chopped
4 ounces medium egg noodles
1 cup corn kernels (if using frozen kernels, defrost them, but do not cook)
¾ cup lightly crushed corn kernels (about 1½ cups before crushing; you can crush with mortar and pestle)
1 cup cooked chicken, shredded
1 bay leaf
1 teaspoon salt
¼ teaspoon white pepper
3 hard-boiled eggs, chopped

Bring chicken broth to simmer in 3–4 quart stockpot. Add chopped onion and noodles. As noodles begin to soften (2–3 minutes), stir in corn kernels and crushed corn.

When broth returns to simmer, add chicken, bay leaf, salt, and pepper.

Continue simmering. When noodles are soft, remove bay leaf. Pour soup into serving bowls and stir about half a chopped egg into each individual serving. Makes 6 meal-size soups.

Brownstown Restaurant, Route 772, Brownstown, Pa.; (717) 656-9077.

In the 1920s it was known as Bill Hart's Brownstown Inn. The Lancaster-Reading trolley stopped nearby, and riders would visit the inn for ten-cent ham sandwiches and secret-recipe homemade root beer.

Today Frank and Arlene Slabach operate the premises as the Brownstown Restaurant. Specialty of the house: Pennsylvania Dutch cooking.

Dieters, go elsewhere. Come to Brownstown only if you are ready to roll up your sleeves and dig into multicourse, multicalorie meals designed to feed hardworking people.

When we first stopped in, it was morning. The wooden building had a welcoming old-hotel feel about it. The front room was occupied by locals sipping coffee and eating crumble-top brown sugar coffee cake. They sat at oilcloth tables beneath slowly spinning overhead fans. On the walls were displays of nostalgic memorabilia, including bottles full of patent medicine, antique auto advertisements, an ancient portrait of Abe Lincoln, and a pickle jar three feet tall.

We ordered a few blocks of coffee cake, accompanied by slabs of scrapple, Pennsylvania's favorite breakfast meat. For those accustomed to bacon or ham or sausage, scrapple is something else: tender, griddle-fried slices from a loaf made of pork and cornmeal. "Don't you just love it?" asked Candy, our waitress. With mouths too full to answer, we nodded yes.

When Candy saw we were enjoying ourselves, she started to tell us about some of the Brownstown's other Pennsylvania Dutch specialties, including chicken and waffles, oyster pie, roast pork with filling (filling is souped-up mashed potatoes), and beef rivel soup—a meaty broth thick with itty-bitty dumplings.

She told us that the best time to eat at the Brownstown Restaurant is for dinner, especially on Sunday, when the back room is opened up. There they've got fancier wallpaper and wood paneling, and families gather 'round for olympic-class all-you-can-eat feasting. The tables groan with bowls full of food from the robust Pennsylvania Dutch repertoire, incuding baked ham and roasted chicken, mashed potatoes, filling, buttered noodles, dried corn, baked beans, lettuce with hot bacon dressing, chow chow, red beet eggs, applesauce, and, of course, pies for dessert.

Best known for their fabulous way with pies (raisin, shoo-fly, buttermilk, etc.), Pennsylvania cooks are also masters of the soup and stew pots. Some of what they make is spicy, especially the Philadelphia specialty called pepper pot. Some, like beef or chicken rivel soup, is bland. None are thin or wimpy.

Many of the best soups and stews are combinations of a favorite Lancaster Country trio of ingredients: chicken, noodles, and corn. Our personal favorite is one called chicken corn soup, a sunny-hued comfort meal that happens to be a great way to use up leftover chicken meat.

The Brownstown version of chicken corn soup, given to us by the Slabachs, is so thick with goodies that there is scarcely room for the liquid. It comes in a bowl loaded with chicken, whole corn kernels, wide egg noodles, crushed corn kernels, and chopped-up hard-boiled eggs. We have adapted the recipe for home kitchens, and recommend serving it as a simple hot lunch, with a few pickled beets on the side for a typically Pennsylvania Dutch color accent.

DINER SPLIT PEA SOUP

I pound yellow split peas
¹/₄ pound salt pork, diced
¹/₂ cup diced onion
I¹/₂ quarts water
I cracked ham bone (get from butcher);
   or ham hock
I bay leaf
¹/₂ teaspoon pepper
3 tablespoons butter
2 tablespoons flour
2 cups milk
¹/₂ pound ham, cut into tiny cubes

Soak peas in water overnight, or bring to boil 2 minutes and let cool in water I hour.

In a deep stock pot, sauté salt pork over low heat until crisp, about 20 minutes. Remove pork with slotted spoon and discard. Sauté onion until soft.

Drain peas and put into stockpot with onions. Cover with water (about 4 quarts). Add ham bone, bay leaf, and pepper. Simmer gently, partially covered, 2 hours, or until peas are tender.

Remove bay leaf and ham bone. Use a strainer to remove peas. Purée peas in food processor or push through fine sieve until puréed, then return them to liquid.

Melt butter in saucepan over low heat. Sprinkle in flour, stirring constantly. Cook 2–3 minutes, stirring. Stir in milk to form a thick, creamy liquid. Stir this liquid into soup. Add cubes of ham to soup. Simmer soup gently 15 minutes, stirring frequently. Serves 8–10.

Carman's Diner, Route 12, Remsen, N.Y.; (315) 831-9993.

Diner Split Pea Soup

REMSEN, N.Y.—Awhile ago we received a postcard from a Marilyn, whose signed last name was not legible, and who included no return address on her card. Whoever you are, Marilyn, we thank you for writing; and we especially appreciate your suggestion.

"As I eat my way across the Northeast," she wrote, "I have found a diner you should check out—Carman's, up towards the Adirondacks: *great* home-baked fresh berry pies, cookies (oatmeal and chocolate chip), springy bread, beautiful blueberry muffins." The next time we traveled the New York State Thruway, we detoured at Utica and headed up Route 12 toward the mountains.

Carman's turned out to be a classic diner in every respect. It is a rather homely place by the side of the road, its silver and green exterior smudged by age and road grime. The inside is faded pink Formica and stainless steel. The ceiling has yellowed over time. The counter stools squeak when you swivel on them. The seats in the booths have a few wayward springs that will get you where it hurts if you don't choose your position with caution. Yessir, this place has character!

It also has some fine homemade food. You can see that fact the moment you enter, because spread out on the counter, right up front, are lovely loaves of freshly baked bread. Nearby are the muffins, doughnuts, and cookies. There are big cinnamon rolls, some laced with raisins, others with slivers of apple. In the morning, Carman's smells like a bakery.

The rest of the menu is pure diner. Breakfast, built around those good baked goods, is available from six in the morning to nine at night. Lunchtime daily specials include fare such as meat loaf, chili, and macaroni and cheese. You can get a sandwich made on the diner's firm-bodied, fresh-flavored bread. Pie (also homemade) is served in truck stop-size slices. We especially liked the apple pie—a homely, lumpy-crusted behemoth loaded with sweet and spicy chunks of fruit. We got it à la mode, accompanied by strong cups of coffee.

The dish we liked best at Carman's, and the one that most vividly evokes the classic hash house atmosphere of the venerable old diner, is split pea soup. It is thick and porky, generously loaded with chunks of ham, accompanied by a crusty Carman's homemade dinner roll. Here is how we duplicate Diner Split Pea Soup at home.

Tortilla Soup

BEL AIR, Calif.—As travelers who always go by car, we are confronted every night with the problem of where to stay. No matter how pretty the scenery or how delicious the regional food, motel rooms are always a downer at the end of the day.

The first few nights are fine; but after ten days on the road and ten different motels, you run out of jokes about stringy shag rugs and paintings-on-velvet and televisions chained to cinderblock walls. A motel dweller's ears become supersensitive to the sound of a noisy ice machine or the sight of a plastic cup wrapped in a baggy or a sash across the toilet seat. One more rubbery bedspread, and you'll scream.

It was just such motelmania that led us to the Bel Air Hotel. Although we are not rich and famous like most people who stay at the Bel Air, we contend that one's ability to survive weeks on the road is bolstered by an occasional dose of luxury. So we checked in to the most luxurious accommodation in the West.

There are plenty of high-tone hotels in this part of Southern California. Bel Air, after all, is a whisper away from Beverly Hills. But Beverly Hills is for those who have made it and want the world to know. Bel Air (the town and the hotel) is for people so powerful and well known that they want seclusion.

A compound of pink stucco bungalows and Mediterranean villas on the verdant residential street known as Stone Canyon Road (where the average home sells for $6 million), the Bel Air was built in the 1920s. It has been a home away from home for movie stars going back to Garbo, including Grace Kelly and Gary Cooper. Howard Hughes used to hole up in a suite for months at a time. Rockefellers, Kennedys, and Fords have all strolled these eleven acres of landscaped bliss. The Reagans gathered here for daughter Patti's wedding.

Decor is West Coast couth. Not thick velvet drapes and Chippendale furniture as you would expect in a posh Eastern hotel, but pink chintz and white wicker. Bathtub fixtures are heavy gold. Soaps are fat hand-milled swans (the Bel Air logo). Dressing room chaises are covered in white terrycloth to match the complimentary robes.

Outside our room, in the foreground of the swan lake and splashing waterfall, was a clump of trees, their branches heavy with limes and lemons. Gardenias, jasmine, and orange blossoms perfumed the air. This was a lifestyle we ordinary mortals know only by watching "Dynasty."

Having come for a night of pampering, we made dinner our first

TORTILLA SOUP

3 tablespoons corn oil

4 corn tortillas, quartered

2 cloves garlic, minced

2 medium onions, chopped

4 tomatoes, skinned and chopped

1 tablespoon ground cumin

1/2 or 1 jalapeño pepper (depending on how hot you want it)

8 cups chicken stock

1/4 cup fresh cilantro

GARNISHES:

crisp fried strips of tortilla

grated cheddar cheese

cooked julienne of chicken

diced avocado

chopped cilantro

Heat oil in 4-quart stockpot and fry quartered tortillas crisp.

Add garlic and onions and cook until onions are soft. Add remaining ingredients, bring to boil, and simmer 20–25 minutes. Add salt and pepper if desired.

Serve with garnishes in separate bowls. Serves 6.

The Bel Air Hotel, 701 Stone Canyon Road, Los Angeles, Calif.; (213) 472-1211.

order of business. Under the direction of Chef Joseph Venezia, the Bel Air's kitchen is an earnest one, honoring culinary tradition (for the Bel Air's long-standing regulars), yet offering some of the finest new California cooking. We began dinner with lemon grass consommé and tortilla soup, both made with herbs from the Bel Air's extensive herb garden. Then on to pink grilled tuna with pickled ginger and char-grilled honey-cured squab. For dessert: strawberries as large as a baby's fist, dipped in bittersweet chocolate; and champagne-thyme sherbet.

We paid our bill, then strolled along a winding stream, beneath an arcade overgrown with red-flowering trumpet vines. Alone in paradise!

Suddenly we heard footsteps running up behind us. We were about to be mugged! We turned to face the attacker. It was the host of the Bel Air dining room, flushed and panting. "Was everything all right?" he asked, crestfallen that we had left without personally assuring him the meal was satisfactory. How's that for attentive service?

We have adapted Chef Venezia's tortilla soup recipe for home kitchens. Fresh cilantro (coriander leaves) is an important part of the soup's zest, but they can be replaced by parsley if you cannot get the breathy herb.

Truck Stop Corn Chowder

WELLS RIVER, Vt.—Judith and Evan Jones know more about food and cooking than anybody we've ever met. Together they wrote *The Book of Bread*; Evan is the author of *American Food*, this country's definitive gastronomic history; as an editor at Knopf, Judith is responsible for books by Julia Child and M.F.K. Fisher.

Awhile back, we got a postcard from Judith and Evan, saying that they were returning to New York from their home in Vermont, and they had stopped at a wonderful restaurant they were sure we'd like. They said it was a big, family-run place with "lots of clatter and joshing among local regulars," as well as "mammoth helpings, trucker's specials, and ten kinds of pie."

We couldn't resist following their tip. We were curious about what kind of place might interest the eminent Evan and Judith Jones when they are on the road; and we wondered why they thought this particular restaurant was so recommendable to us. So the next time we headed into northern New England, we pulled off I-91 at Exit 17, parked in the lot of the P & H Truck Stop, and strolled into the Keep On Truckin' Cafe.

Those roving Joneses had hit a bull's-eye. This place is a gear-

TRUCK-STOP CORN CHOWDER

⅓ pound salt pork, diced

1 onion, diced (about ⅓ cup)

2 cups water

2 medium potatoes, peeled and diced
    (about 12 ounces)

2 ripe tomatoes, peeled, seeded and diced
    (10 ounces)

1½ cups milk

1½ cups cream

3 cups corn kernels (about 6 ears)

2 tablespoons butter

pepper to taste

In a large stockpot, fry salt pork over medium heat until it begins to crisp. Add onion and fry until translucent, about 3 minutes. Add 2 cups water and potatoes. Cover and simmer until potatoes are tender, about 10–15 minutes.

Stir in tomatoes, milk, cream, corn, and butter. Heat to lowest possible simmer (do not boil!), then lower heat and keep warm over low heat 5 minutes.

Add pepper to taste. (The salt pork should make it salty enough.)

Makes 6–8 servings (2 quarts).

Keep on Truckin' Cafe, P & H Truck Stop, Exit 17 off I-91 at Route 302, Wells River, Vt.; (802) 429-2141.

jammer's delight, from the wallpaper pattern of Macks, Peterbilts, and K-Whoppers to the fourteen dollar (linen included) bunkhouse rooms upstairs, complete with shower and lounge privileges. Next to the cash register, a bulletin board was thumbtacked with notes from deadheaders who needed loads heading west, and shippers looking for a reefer (refrigerated truck) going down to Florida.

The very first thing you see when you walk in is bread—shelves of homemade loaves. Dozens of pies are displayed on their own shelves in the big, wide-open dining room. And a blackboard lists two-fisted daily specials such as pot roast and chowder and sandwiches made on rough-hewn slabs of sturdy toast (from those homemade loaves).

The menu, encased in plastic and emblazoned with a crude drawing of a truck bursting through a wall, is a roster of truck stop grub, familiar except for the fact that everything is listed in French as well as English to accommodate drivers from Quebec.

The cuisine of the Keep On Truckin' Cafe has a regional accent as well. At breakfast, pancakes and French toast are served with pure Vermont maple syrup ("sirop d'erable pur" on the bilingual menu). Among the pies and puddings are down-east favorites such as Grapenut pudding, blueberry, and maple cream. And there is almost always a chowder of the day on the blackboard menu. The day we stopped for lunch, it was corn chowder hearty enough to be a meal unto itself.

So with a tip of the hat to the Keep On Truckin' Cafe, as well as Evan and Judith Jones, here is our own recipe for corn chowder, a time-honored specialty of Yankee farmhouse cooks.

Scandinavian Fruit Soup

BRIDGEPORT, Conn.—Politics is the specialty of the house at the restaurant named Bloodroot. Look at the menu, chalked onto a blackboard above the kitchen window, and you begin to see exactly where its owners stand. No red meat is listed on the board, no chicken, no fish. Those who conceived Bloodroot say that they are ethical vegetarians, meaning that they want nothing to do with the exploitation of animals as human feed.

Now look around at the dining room, and you learn more about the Bloodroot doctrine. The wall is covered with pictures of women, famous and unsung. To the left is a bookstore, devoted primarily to works by, for, and about women. Background music is tapes of women singing. "We are here," wrote the Bloodroot Collective in the acknowledgments to their book, *The Second Sea-*

SCANDINAVIAN FRUIT SOUP

1½ cups dried apricots

1 cup dried prunes

2 cups dried apples

2 whole sticks cinnamon

one-half lemon

1 teaspoon ground cardamom

⅓ cup quick-cooking tapioca

¼ cup raisins

¼ cup currants

1 teaspoon salt

sour cream as garnish

Dice apricots, prunes, and apples. Turn into a stainless steel pot and cover with 10 cups water. Let stand 30 minutes.

Add cinnamon, one-half lemon (squeeze it, but throw in the rind, too), cardamom, and tapioca. Bring to a boil, stirring frequently, scraping the bottom of the pot to prevent the tapioca from sticking. Simmer, stirring frequently, for 10 minutes. Turn off heat.

Add raisins, currants, and salt. Let soup cool, then chill in refrigerator.

If you want the soup thinner when you serve it, dilute with apple juice. Serve garnished with sour cream. Makes 6–8 servings.

Bloodroot, 85 Ferris St., Bridgeport, Conn.; (203) 576-9168.

sonal Political Palate, "because we want to make a women's space."

Everything about Bloodroot is unusual, including its setting, in a modest, well-tended residential neighborhood in the city of Bridgeport. The shingle-sided building that houses the restaurant hugs the shore of Long Island Sound, but this is not the shoreline of the wealthy. Instead, the view is of oil tanks in Bridgeport Harbor. It's a soothing vista, nonetheless, with gulls overhead, and masts of berthed boats bobbing in the distance.

There is nothing stingy or health-nutty about Bloodroot's vegetarian cuisine. Far from sprouts and raw veggies, the dishes served forth have a hearty peasant quality: rough-grained breads, thick-packed soups, dumplings, pasta, and cheese. In a strange way, perhaps because the restaurant is so focused on a celebration of the feminine spirit, the meals remind us of mom's home cooking.

You are greeted at the front door by a woman who asks if you have eaten here before. Not an idle question, because if you have not, getting your food can be somewhat confusing. There are no waiters at Bloodroot, which substitutes a democratic cafeteria system in which customers serve themselves. Pay first, deal directly with the cook, and when the food is ready, your name is called. After dinner, bus your own table. And of course, there is no tipping. That would be elitist!

This method, of course, is a political statement, and not everyone's idea of a gracious way to dine. But it's efficient, and it can be fun, as diners strike up conversations with others waiting to eat, or browse in the adjoining bookstore. It adds up to a very cozy, communal feel among staff and customers.

The menu at Bloodroot changes with the seasons and is amazing for its scope. If you are a recent convert to vegetarianism, or have ever tried to cook for a guest who doesn't eat meat, you know how difficult it can seem to come up with a variety of tastes. Bloodroot borrows from ethnic cuisines all over the world, dishing out surprises and innovations at every meal.

In the autumn, the menu is a festival of wild mushrooms, mincemeat baked apples, and roasted sunchokes; spring specialties include pasta with artichoke asparagus sauce and maple rhubarb tofu mousse.

One of the hot-weather refreshers is chilled Scandinavian fruit soup. Bloodroot lists it on the spring menu because it can be made before fresh fruits are available in the market. We like it any time of year, especially as a simple, filling meal in the heat of the summer, dolloped with sour cream. The soup is quite thick; leftovers are terrific as a topping for French toast or warm pound cake.

Shrimp Soup Orleans

SEATTLE—What'll you have? Name your pleasure. If it's got anything to do with eating, seafood in particular, raw on ice or cooked and ready to eat, the public market at the foot of Pike Street is likely to have it.

Seattle's Pike Place Market is the oldest and best open-air city market in the United States. It is a patchwork-quilt bazaar of stalls housing greengrocers and fishmongers, ethnic groceries of every stripe, useless souvenirs, antiques, flea market ephemera, and restaurants dishing out everything from Indonesian sate to tea and crumpets.

Although urban renewal has upgraded the market and its surroundings, it remains a shoulder-jostling Alice in Wonderland madhouse, effervescent with the authentic sounds, sights, and smells of Seattle's waterfront culture. You cannot walk through the main arcade, past the fruits and vegetables and fish stands, without vendors yelling at you to buy. And you do buy, because this produce is the Northwest's best. Some of the Pacific seafood on display is seldom seen anywhere else: salmon smoked over alder wood (an old Indian technique); fresh Dungeness crab: Quilcene and Canterbury oysters; black cod.

Pike Place Market is a grazer's paradise, where strollers can indulge their whim for fresh fruit, warm cinnamon rolls or oven-hot bread, and freshly opened oysters. For the oysters, our favorite place to belly up is Emmett Watson's Oyster Bar at the north end of the market. Emmett's boasts a sunny courtyard and a scattering of tables that provide the perfect setting for an easy hour of beer and Quilcenes on the half shell.

The last time we whiled away a blissful afternoon in just that fashion, there was a crisis on the grassy hill above the patio. The Oyster Bar's adopted cat had gone into the overgrowth and given birth to a litter of kittens. It was October, the nights were cold, and everyone at Emmett's was worried how the newborns would fare. Cardboard boxes were carried up to serve as shelter; but the commotion scared the mother cat, and the kittens scattered on the hill. Customers and oyster shuckers joined in a kitten hunt until the whole litter was found and reunited . . . in a warm box snugged close to the oyster bar.

The good deed called for another few dozen oysters and cups of chowder all around.

As befits an oyster bar, Emmett Watson's menu is a short one: steamer clams, seviche, smoked trout with homemade dill mayonnaise, smoked salmon with sweet and sour mustard. Soups are

SHRIMP SOUP ORLEANS

12 ounces tomato juice
4 cups chicken stock
1/3 cup white wine
1/2 cup diced tomatoes
1/3 cup chopped onion
1/2 cup chopped celery
1/4 teaspoon coarse ground black pepper
1 1/2 teaspoons finely minced garlic
1 teaspoon sweet basil
1/4 teaspoon tarragon
1/8 teaspoon paprika
1 bay leaf
5–10 drops Tabasco sauce, to taste
1 pound small shrimp, raw—out of shell

Combine all ingredients except shrimp in stockpot and bring to boil. Reduce heat to simmer. Add shrimp 5 minutes before serving. As soon as they are pink and firm, soup is ready. Serve with French bread.

Serves 4.

Emmett Watson's Oyster Bar, 1916 Pike Place, Seattle; (206) 622-7721.

served with chunks of brittle-crusted French bread on the side. If there is a chill in the air (as there so often is in Seattle), the way to blunt it is with shrimp soup Orleans, a specialty of Lois and Sam Bryant, proprietors of the bar.

Lois told us that she keeps the soup simmering all day long at the oyster bar, adding the shrimp when a bowl is ordered (if they linger in the simmering soup, they toughen). She also advised that she likes to use the soup for poaching fish, and suggests adding clams (in the shell, well scrubbed) or white fish fillets to the recipe five to ten minutes before you are ready to serve it. (We have reduced Sam and Lois's recipe to home kitchen proportions.)

4
Breads

THROWED ROLLS

I teaspoon sugar
I package dry active yeast
¼ cup tepid water (105–110 degrees)
I cup warm milk
¼ cup melted butter
¼ cup sugar
I egg beaten (at room temperature)
I teaspoon salt
4 cups all-purpose flour

Combine sugar and yeast in tepid water. Let stand 5–10 minutes until yeast begins to foam.

Thoroughly mix milk, butter, sugar, egg, and salt in large bowl. Stir in the yeast mixture and 3½ cups of flour, adding a bit more if necessary to make a soft, pliable dough.

Turn dough out on floured board and let rest while you clean and butter bowl. Knead dough gently 4–5 minutes, adding flour if necessary, until dough is smooth and silky. Return to bowl, cover with plastic wrap, and let rise in warm place until doubled in size.

Butter a 12-cup muffin tin.

Punch down dough. Pinch off pieces about 1½ inches in diameter (enough to fill one-half of muffin cup), and roll into smooth spheres. Place two such pieces in each prepared muffin cup. (It should be a tight fit.) Cover dough loosely with plastic wrap for 45 minutes. Preheat oven to 350 degrees.

Bake rolls 20–25 minutes, or until light brown. Serve as soon as they are cool enough to throw. Makes 12 throwed rolls.

Lambert's Cafe, 2109 E. Malone, Sikeston, Mo.; (314) 471-4261.

Throwed Rolls

SIKESTON, Mo.—Heads up! Here it comes: You've got one second, maybe two, to look up from the table once the Lambert's roll boy calls to you, before he begins throwing rolls your way. They come sailing across the dining room one at a time, high over the heads of other tables who have already gotten theirs.

Careful! As soon as you catch that roll, put it down. It's hot, so you want to let it rest before you bite. But pretty soon, before you have a chance to tear it open and let some steam escape, along comes Ol' Norm Lambert with his bucketful of sorghum molasses and a ladle. He whisks your roll off the table, pulls it open, and dollops sweet sorghum inside.

Now, the roll is impossible: hot and dripping sticky amber goo, oozing all over the oilcloth-covered table (at this early point during dinner, there aren't yet any plates). But somehow you manage to heft the roll and the sorghum to your mouth—and it's swell.

So you're eating your icky-sticky-yummy roll and drinking lemonade or iced tea from a one-quart fruit jar, and along comes the okra lady. She's got a bowl full of crisp, deep-fried okra, and she asks if you'd like some. Sure! But where is she going to put it? No problem. She spoons out a heap smack dab on the tablecloth, cushioned only by a paper napkin. Eat it like popcorn, with your fingers.

A couple more throwed rolls, and a pile of okra, and you're ready for dinner. That, you will be happy to know, comes on a plate! But there's sure nothing fancy about it. This is down-home eating: catfish or smothered steaks, fried chicken or country ham with white beans and turnip greens. Our favorite listing from the Lambert's menu is the one they call a "pie pan of beans"—accompanied by fried bologna, corn bread, a King Edward cigar, and a stick of Big Red chewing gum.

Just because dinner has arrived doesn't mean the folks at Lambert's give you any peace. They'll still be throwing rolls throughout the meal. If you ordered beans, they'll get replenished by a roving bean man from his bucket. There's red pepper relish, too, which the relish person heaps on your beans if you desire.

For dessert, choose cobbler or coconut cream pie. The menu says, "We serve the largest slab of pie in the United States." We don't doubt it.

What else is there to say about Lambert's Cafe, "Home of the Throwed Roll"? Well, there are the mule pictures—dozens of them: beauty photographs, oil paintings, and goofy cartoons of mules, all over the walls. Finally, a statistic: If the 924,180 rolls that

Lambert's bakes every year were laid side by side, they would be 73 miles long.

Our own recipe for throwed rolls, based on the twin-domed, five-inch Lambert's beauties, is a simple one that uses yeast to leaven the dough. These rolls are light enough so that dinner guests can't complain if they get beaned when you serve.

Sweet Potato Biscuits

ATLANTA—Let's talk about biscuits. Southern biscuits. Buttermilk biscuits, so hot that you can grab one but not hold it longer than it takes to move from tray to plate. The top is a perfect circle, burnished gold, oven-crisp. The bottom is a darker disk, thicker from contact with the baking sheet. And the columnar side is snow white, as tender as sifted flour.

It's a two-handed job: Grab the top and bottom, give a gentle tug, and it pulls apart like a warm cloud. A haze of buttermilk-scented steam rises from each ragged half. Now quickly grab pats of butter, ease them on, ever so meekly, and watch the cleaved biscuit drink in the fast-melting yellow emulsion.

Honey? Jam? Sorghum molasses? Red-eye gravy? Yes, yes, yes, yes. Everything is good on biscuits. And biscuits are delicious plain, without even butter.

They are the staff of Southern gastronomy, essential with fried chicken or country ham, at breakfast, and in any decent lunch or supper breadbasket.

There is nothing complicated about making a really good biscuit. All you need are flour, buttermilk, shortening, and baking powder—plus know-how.

Know-how is the tricky part, best learned by watching a veteran biscuit maker. One secret of Southern cooks is their flour. Ordinary bread flour is fine, but low-gluten flours made with soft winter wheat yield the fluffiest biscuits. (Both Martha White and White Lily brands, sold throughout the South, are ideal.)

To make classic Southern biscuits, begin by preheating the oven to 400 degrees. Mix 2 cups of flour with 2 teaspoons of baking powder, 1 teaspoon of salt, and ½ teaspoon of baking soda. Cut ¼ cup of lard or solid vegetable shortening into the flour, rubbing by hand until crumbly. Form a well in the flour and pour in ¾ cup of cold buttermilk. Mix only enough to blend. Knead three or four times.

Roll the dough out on a floured board to 1-inch thick. Using a floured drinking glass, cut out 2-inch biscuits and lay them on a heavy, lightly greased baking sheet. Bake 10–12 minutes at 400 degrees until the tops are light brown. You will get about 10 2-inch biscuits.

One of our favorite places to eat biscuits, as well as cracklin' corn bread, hush puppies, and Southern foods of every kind, is in Atlanta, at a tearoom named Mary Mac's.

Mary Mac's is a bustling place, especially at lunch, when you line up, write your own order, and eat fast. Among the specialties on the daily-printed pastel menu are such Dixie delights as turnip green pot likker (the seaweed-hued brew dredged from the pot after greens are boiled with fatback), Brunswick stew with barbecue, and a nutty pudding named Carter custard, after the Georgia peanut farmer who made it to the White House.

If you do not know about the South's love affair with vegetables, you will be shocked by the enormous choice at Mary Mac's. Squash soufflè, field peas with ham hock, candied yams, steamed whole okra, stewed tomatoes, lady peas with salt pork, turnip greens, collard greens, potatoes cooked with cheese: These are a few of the choices from Section Two of each day's menu. Section One lists entrées such as country steak, chicken pan pie, and the most delicious fried chicken in Georgia; but many people come to Mary Mac's for a "fresh vegetable luncheon"—four items selected from Section Two.

Every meal at Mary Mac's is accompanied by hot, homemade breads—muffins, yeast rolls, hoecakes, and—of course—buttermilk biscuits.

Not long ago, Margaret Lupo (Mary Mac) wrote a book called *Southern Cooking From Mary Mac's Tea Room*, in which we found recipes for most of the dishes we remember best from her restaurant, plus this fabulous variation of the biscuit theme. Serve them on the side of ham, at lunch or dinner.

SWEET POTATO BISCUITS

2 eggs
1/2 cup sugar
I cup cooked, mashed sweet potato
   (about 3/4 pound, uncooked)
2 tablespoons butter, softened
3 tablespoons solid vegetable shortening
I teaspoon salt
4 teaspoons baking powder
2 cups all-purpose flour

Preheat oven to 350 degrees.

In a large mixing bowl, beat eggs with sugar. Add mashed sweet potato and mix well. Mix in butter, shortening, salt, and baking powder. Add flour, 1/2 cup at a time, mixing after each addition. Dough will be sticky.

Turn dough out on lightly floured board. Flour hands and knead gently 3–4 times. Roll out to 1/2-inch thickness. Cut with 2-inch biscuit cutter or lightly floured rim of drinking glass. Place on ungreased baking sheet. Bake 15 minutes.

Yield: 20–24 biscuits.

Mary Mac's Tea Room, 224 Ponce de Leon Ave. N.E., Atlanta, Ga. 30308; (404) 875-4337.

BEATEN BISCUITS

2 cups flour
1 teaspoon salt
1 teaspoon baking powder
1/4 cup lard or solid vegetable shortening
6 tablespoons ice-cold milk
6 tablespoons ice water

TRADITIONAL METHOD: *Combine flour, salt, and baking powder in a large bowl. Cut in lard until mixture resembles meal. Stir in an equal mix of milk and ice water— just enough to form a stiff dough. Turn dough out on lightly floured board and beat with a rolling pin, hammer, or wooden mallet approximately 500 times (30 full minutes). Each time the dough flattens out, fold it over and continue beating. Roll dough out to 1/2-inch thickness. Proceed as below . . .*

FOOD PROCESSOR METHOD: *In the bowl of a food processor, combine flour, salt, and baking powder. Cut in lard with a few quick pulses until mixture resembles coarse crumbs. With motor running add mixed milk and ice water. Process until mixture forms a ball, then continue processing 2 full minutes longer. Roll dough onto lightly floured board in 1/4-inch thick rectangle. Fold over once to form two layers.*

Preheat oven to 350 degrees.

Cut beaten, flattened dough into 1-inch circles, using plain or fluted cutter. Place on lightly greased baking sheet. Prick each biscuit three times with triple-tined fork to form a nine-hole square. Bake 20–25 minutes. Finished biscuits will be ivory-colored.

Makes 20–24 beaten biscuits.

Sally Bell's Kitchen, 708 W. Grace St., Richmond, Va.; (804) 644-2838.

Beaten Biscuits

RICHMOND, Va.—You cannot eat at Sally Bell's. The red brick house across from Richmond Metropolitan Hospital is a take-out bakery. There are some very nice lawns nearby (at the Virginia Museum of Fine Arts in particular) that look right for picnics; or if you are a passer-through, as we were, you might have to eat in your car.

Front seats are an excellent place to eat Sally Bell's food, because the specialty of the house is box lunch: tidy meals perfectly suited for dining with minimal amenities in make-do circumstances.

Lunch is sold in a white cardboard box inscribed with Sally Bell's nostalgic logo, a cameo silhouette of a colonial dame. The contents of the box include a sandwich, a cup of salad, half a deviled egg, a cheese wafer, and dessert.

Sandwiches are made of chicken salad or Smithfield ham, or tea-time spreads such as olive and mayonnaise or cream cheese and nut, or pimiento cheese. The bread is homemade, thin-sliced and delicate. Naturally, its crusts have been removed.

The deviled egg is lush. Potato salad is bright with crisp bits of cucumber and onion. The cheese wafer is a heartwarmingly old-fashioned little cracker tile with half a pecan on top. For dessert, choose among upside-down devil's food cupcakes (on which only the top is unfrosted), yellow cake with caramel or chocolate icing, or a variety of powder sugar-dusted fruit tarts.

It is a body- and soul-satisfying meal. The only frustration is that those of us who are merely driving through town cannot avail ourselves of the fabulous array of cakes, breads, buns, and muffins lined up on Sally Bell's shelves—most of which call for a home kitchen, a table, a fork, and a leisurely pot of coffee for full enjoyment.

There is one extra item we did nab to take with us on our journey: a bag of beaten biscuits. They are one of Sally Bell's specialties, and have been since the bakery opened in 1926. In fact, beaten biscuits go way back to colonial gastronomy. Unlike soft, fluffy American-style biscuits, these are biscuits in the English sense of the word: hard and crisp, what most of us would call a cracker. They go great with soup, or as a munchie to accompany cold cuts (country-cured ham in particular).

Traditionally, beaten biscuits are a royal pain in the neck to make. To get the proper fragile, silken texture, the batter is beaten five hundred times on a tree stump with the blunt end of a hatchet! A food processor—as suggested in the second method here— makes them as easy as any ordinary quick bread.

BLUEBERRY GINGERBREAD

1/2 cup solid vegetable shortening

I cup sugar

I egg

2 cups flour

1/2 teaspoon ginger

I teaspoon cinnamon

1/2 teaspoon salt

I teaspoon baking soda

I cup buttermilk

3 tablespoons molasses

I1/2 cups blueberries, washed and dried

3 tablespoons sugar

Preheat oven to 350 degrees. Grease and flour a 9-by-9-inch pan.

Cream shortening and sugar. Beat in egg.

Sift together flour, ginger, cinnamon, and salt.

Dissolve baking soda in buttermilk.

Alternately add flour mixture and buttermilk to creamed mixture. Beat in molasses. Fold in blueberries.

Pour batter into prepared pan. Sprinkle with sugar. Bake one hour, or until sharp knife inserted comes out clean.

Serve slightly warm or at room temperature. (Keeps well 2–3 days.) Makes 9 servings.

Helen's, 32 Main St., Machias, Maine; (208) 255-6506.

Blueberry Gingerbread

MACHIAS, Maine—Late summer/early autumn is the perfect time for an eating trip along the coast of Maine. Clam shacks and lobster pounds abound, on wharfs and fishing piers and in little seaside villages. We reckon there are times we have driven up the shore without eating lunch or supper indoors for days: There are so many picnic-table eateries near the ocean, where the casual delights of a paper-plate-and-cardboard-tray meal are enhanced by the perfume of saltwater breezes.

There is one gastronomic stop you must make, especially in the fall, if you are heading way up the coast. It is the town of Machias, the best place we know to enjoy a taste of Maine's favorite fruit: the blueberry.

Machias regularly hosts the state's blueberry festival, a three-day bash that features cooking and eating contests devoted to the sweet little berries that are North America's alone. In Maine, they are ripe for picking by the end of August.

To the connoisseur, not all blueberries are alike. In this part of the country, folks are careful to make a distinction between "high-bush" blueberries, which grow in abundance up and down the East Coast, and "lowbush" blues, which are unique to Maine. You can easily tell the difference just by looking. Highbush berries are chalky blue and nearly as large as a marble. Lowbush berries are purple and tiny. They grow wild, but because their shrubs are tangled, they are much harder to harvest than the big blueberries from farther south.

Lowbush blueberries taste better. They have more character, they are sweeter and juicier, and their tiny size makes them more fun to roll around on the tongue—whether you pop them into your mouth plain, or spoon them up from a dish of heavy cream, or heft a forkful from a slice of pie.

No curious eater will have trouble finding a place to eat blueberries along the coast, but there is one restaurant in Machias that is worth a special berry-eating trip, especially this time of year. It's Helen's, a Main Street café that has been a town favorite since the 1940s.

One can breakfast at Helen's on hot muffins from the bakery downstairs (blueberry, as well as several other varieties), and lunch on traditional shoreline meals such as fried clams, broiled halibut, scallops, and shrimp. The dessert list includes a vast choice of turnovers, brownies, cakes, and cookies from which to choose, but it is berries—blue, boysen, straw, and rasp—for which Helen's bakery is renowned.

Choose between two varieties of blueberry pie—a conventional gooey-centered double-cruster, and the seasonal specialty known as the "down Maine" pie, for which a combination of cooked and uncooked wild blues is ladled into a crust and topped with whipped cream.

Pies like these are easy to make (if you get good berries, and if you can make a good crust). So instead of sharing a recipe for pie, we've got one for something different and unusually delicious. It is a gingerbread chock full of berries—a marvelous conjunction of sweet and spicy flavors. The recipe is based on one we brought home from Maine, courtesy of the state Department of Agriculture. Of course, they recommend using only wild lowbush Maine blueberries. It's better that way, no doubt; but if you use ordinary highbush berries, we won't tell.

Basil and Cheese Hot Breadsticks

GEARHART, Ore.—The seaside village of Gearhart was the boyhood summer home of James Beard. We spent some time with the greatest of all modern American chefs in the last few years of his life, when he often reminisced about his childhood, his mother's boardinghouse, and the delicious Oregon meals that educated his palate.

There must be something in the ocean-scented air that encourages culinary achievement, because a short while after James Beard died, we renewed a friendship with a woman named Candy Anderson—a college pal of Michael's—also from Gearhart, and one of the best cooks we have ever met.

Candy grew up surrounded by food. "My earliest memories," she told us, "are of women in white, bent over grease-spattered grills and smoking-hot French fryers, waving spatulas in their hands. I can still see my grandma up to her elbows in flour, making one of her many daily batches of biscuits."

That was 1952, when her uncle Bill ran a drive-in restaurant in Portland named Flanagan's. It was famous for the pies and cakes her great-aunt Auntie used to bake, and for the green rivers (lime sodas) and banana splits made by soda jerk Bill Strike. Candy's childhood was serenaded by the chatter of carhops, and her nights were lighted by the 50-foot red-and-blue neon sign that made Flanagan's a regional landmark. "Truly the stuff dreams were made of," she recalls, telling how all the roadhouse food was made from scratch, its honest kitchen leaving her with a taste for innocent and uncomplicated food.

BASIL AND CHEESE HOT BREADSTICKS

1½ cups warm (110 degrees) water

1 package yeast

1 teaspoon sugar

1½ teaspoons salt

1 teaspoon coarsely ground black pepper

2 tablespoons dried basil

1 tablespoon olive oil

½ cup grated Kasari (or Parmesan or Romano) cheese

6 cloves garlic, pressed, mashed or finely diced

5 dashes Tabasco sauce

3½ cups white flour

Dissolve yeast and sugar in water in large bowl.

When yeast is foamy, add all remaining ingredients, reserving a half cup of flour for kneading. Stir well. Turn dough out on floured board and knead until smooth and springy, about 6 minutes, adding flour as necessary to make dough workable.

Divide dough into 4 equal parts and roll each quarter out to ¼-inch thick. Cut each flattened piece into about 10 equal strips. Between palms or on board, roll and twist each strip into a rounded stick, 5–6 inches long.

Place rolled sticks on lightly greased baking sheets. Cover and let rise in warm (but not hot) place 30 minutes, until increased in size but not doubled.

Preheat oven to 350 degrees.

Bake breadsticks 20–25 minutes, or until light brown, switching baking sheets if necessary to make sure all get done evenly. Do not allow sticks to become dark brown.

When sticks are done, turn off oven, open door, but leave them inside 30 minutes, allowing them to crisp without further browning.

Makes about 3 dozen breadsticks.

Then Candy got married, and her Oregon-educated palate took a postgraduate degree in Italian home cooking from her mother-in-law, Sally Haley Russo. Sally introduced Candy to recipes for pizza rustica, braciola, and innumerable of-the-people dishes that don't even have names or written recipes.

Her mother-in-law also taught her photography, leading to a combined interest in photographing food. Now when you ask Candy for a recipe, she doesn't just give you the formula; it is accompanied by a gorgeous color picture of the finished dish. "It is the only way I have of capturing the beauty of food permanently," she told us. "Also, I'm a hopeless collector, so it gives me a great excuse to buy old mixing bowls, antique serving dishes, and all kinds of kitchen paraphernalia to use in my food photography."

She works in a kitchen bedecked with colanders and copper bowls, canning jars and colored bottles, with a window view of a garden and greenhouse. Her jams and chutneys are made with garden produce; she packs her own albacore tuna in the summer; with her husband, Mike, she makes wine in the fall. And there is always fresh baked bread on the table. "For me," she told us, "food is more than just a hobby. It's an integral part of my life."

Walnut Pineapple Corn Bread

USQUEPAUGH, R.I.—Don't blink as you drive along Route 138 through South County, Rhode Island. If you do, you might miss the village of Usquepaugh, and one of the most scenic gastronomic sites in the East.

Kenyon's Grist Mill, built 102 years ago alongside Queens River Mill Pond and waterfall, is a vision of rural tranquility. The wooden building, settled comfortably with age, still houses a mill in which whole grains are ground between huge wheels of rough-textured granite.

The grain is fed onto a stationary bedstone where it is crushed by a revolving 2½-ton "runner stone," then deposited into a barrel from which Kenyon's packs it into one- or three-pound boxes. It is an awesome sight to see the mammoth stone turning, and the meal come spilling out—yielding flours just as fine as you need to make New England specialties such as cornmeal johnnycakes, Indian pudding, and Anadama bread. Watch the miller as the great granite wheel turns. He actually keeps his nose to the grindstone—or at least puts it there often—in order to detect the smell of granite rubbing granite, an indication that the stones are running too close together.

For years, Kenyon's has hosted the Rhode Island Johnnycake Festival in late October, a village fair at which locals sell home-baked goods and garden preserves. The millers operate a wagon at the festival, doling out clam cakes and chowder along with their renowned lace-textured johnnycakes.

Year around, the grist mill keeps grinding, offering regular tours (actually no more than informal strolls through the primitive factory) in the summer. Across the street, a gift shop sells Queens River jellies, relishes, canned chowders, kitchen items, and knick-knacks.

Any time of the year, as long as someone is at the mill, you can stop by and purchase Kenyon's meals and flours. They come packed in two-color boxes that look like antiques borrowed from the shelves of a 1940s farm wife's kitchen. "Your food dollar doesn't buy a lot of unnecessary advertising, packaging, and 'premiums' with us," a pledge on the box advises. "It buys good old-fashioned food! And these days that's a bargain!"

Of course, Kenyon's sells whole wheat flour, and sifted whole wheat flour—which is here still called "Graham flour" (after its nineteenth-century champion, Sylvester Graham). They grind white or yellow cornmeal, special johnnycake meal (extra fine white cornmeal), rye meal, scotch oat flour, and buckwheat flour. And you can purchase miller's bran (the husks of the grain) by the ten-ounce bag.

In addition to selling straight meals, Kenyon's mixes ready-to-go blends: buckwheat pancake mix, clam cake and fritter mix, and corn muffin mix. We are especially fond of the brown bread mix, which is a perfect blend of Graham flour, rye, and cornmeal.

The last time we went to Usquepaugh to buy some meal, Mr. Drumm gave us a luscious recipe for walnut and pineapple corn bread, made with his yellow cornmeal. We have tried it with super-market cornmeal and it works perfectly well, but if you want that genuine Rhode Island taste, use the stone-ground stuff (which Kenyon's is happy to mail).

WALNUT PINEAPPLE CORN BREAD

1 cup yellow cornmeal
1½ cups sifted flour
4 teaspoons baking powder
1 teaspoon salt
2 eggs, beaten
¼ cup light vegetable oil
½ cup crushed, well-drained pineapple
  (one 8-ounce can)
½ cup pineapple jam
1 cup plus 2 tablespoons milk
1 cup chopped walnuts

Preheat oven to 375 degrees. Butter a loaf pan (approximately 9 by 5 inches).

Sift together cornmeal, sifted flour, baking powder, and salt.

Beat eggs, oil, pineapple, jam, and milk together. Stir wet ingredients into dry, mixing only enough to moisten. Do not overbeat! Fold in walnuts. Pour into prepared loaf pan and bake 1 hour. Let cool on rack 10 minutes. Turn out of pan onto rack to cool completely. Store wrapped.

Kenyon Cornmeal Co., Usquepaugh, R.I. 02892; (401) 783-4054. A mail-order list of meals and mixes is available.

Quivering Jalapeño Corn Bread

HARRISON, Ark.—The Rockhouse is a quaint kind of place. As barbecues go, it is rather genteel. It looks like a rock house cabin from the outside. Inside, the floors are gleaming polished wood, and the paneled walls are hung with impressive full-size quilts. Tables are covered with red checked oilcloth. And there is actually a cute printed menu (decorated with cartoons of cavorting pigs), listing many items other than barbecue, including fish and steaks broiled over hickory and a variety of "gourmet burgers" topped with "natural cheeses."

It is barbecue that draws the customers, particularly on weekend evenings when the fires are hot and the ribs are crusty.

They are loin back pork ribs, sold by the rack or half-rack, their meat fairly glowing with baked-in spice. Only a gentle tug is required to pull succulent strips of pork clean off their bone. There are other kinds of barbecue, too—beef brisket, sliced pork loin, ham, chicken, and Polish sausage—but it is ribs you want to eat.

The other thing to order is onion rings. They are quite an amazing creation: individual giant-size *O*'s with a fresh-fried crunch and a distinctive tang to their faintly sour, buttermilky batter. If onion rings are too tame or ordinary for your taste, the Rockhouse offers a whole roster of deep fried things, including dill pickles and jalapeño peppers.

Other regional specialties to enjoy at the Rockhouse: barbecued salad, which is the Ozark version of a chef's salad, made here with three kinds of meat; beverages served in one-pint Mason jars; pit-cooked beans laced with shreds of ham and onion. And then there is corn bread. Luscious, steamy, jalapeño-hottened corn bread. It is dished out in big squares on plates, and it is so quiveringly moist that you are best off eating it with utensils, like spoonbread.

The recipe here is our own version of Rockhouse-style corn bread. It goes with any meaty meal, or with catfish in lieu of hushpuppies, or with a dinner-size salad.

QUIVERING JALAPEÑO CORN BREAD

1¼ cups yellow cornmeal
½ cup white flour
2 teaspoons baking powder
1 teaspoon baking soda
1½ teaspoons salt
2 eggs
1 cup buttermilk
½ cup sour cream
1 6-ounce can cream-style corn
4 tablespoons butter, melted
1 3-ounce can chili peppers, drained and
    diced
½ cup grated sharp cheese

Preheat oven to 350 degrees.

Generously grease a 10-inch, ovenproof skillet.

Combine cornmeal, flour, baking powder, baking soda, and salt.

Combine eggs, buttermilk, sour cream, and creamed corn. Stir in melted butter and diced peppers. (Use hot jalapeños for very hot bread; mild chilies otherwise.)

Combine cornmeal mixture and buttermilk mixture. Pour into prepared skillet. Top with grated cheese. Bake one hour or until top is dark golden brown.

Rockhouse Bar-B-Que, 416 South Pine (Highway 7), Harrison, Ark.;
(501) 741-1787.

SPOON BREAD

3 cups milk
1¼ cups white cornmeal
4 eggs, well beaten
2 tablespoons butter, melted
1¾ teaspoons baking powder
1 teaspoon salt

Bring milk to rapid boil. Stir in cornmeal. Cook over low heat, stirring constantly to prevent scorching, for about three minutes until very thick. Remove from heat. Allow to cool. When cold, mixture will be very stiff.

Preheat oven to 375 degrees. Generously butter two 1-quart casseroles, or one 1½- to 2-quart casserole.

Use an electric mixer to beat in all remaining ingredients. Beat for a full 15 minutes. Pour into prepared casserole(s). Bake 40 minutes if using one casserole; 30 minutes if using two smaller ones. When done, it will be puffed and lightly browned.

Serves 4–6.

Boone Tavern: Main at Prospect (Kentucky Highway 25), Berea, Ky.; (606) 986-9358.

Spoon Bread

BEREA, Ky.—Nobody pays tuition to attend Berea College. Since it opened 132 years ago, all the students have worked their way through.

The Boone Tavern Hotel, which began as a guest house for visitors to the college, is a great place to see—and savor—the unique nature of a Berea education. Its rooms and lobby are furnished with walnut and cherry reproduction antique furniture made by students in the woodcraft program. Decorative touches are supplied by student weavers. The registration desk and the dining room are staffed almost entirely by students in the hotel management program.

In the beginning, most Berea students were Appalachian. Now they come from around the world, so if you dine at the Boone Tavern, you might just as easily be served by a boy or girl from Zimbabwe as from Zebulon (North Carolina). The dining experience remains distinctively Southern—graciously paced and quite formal (jacket is required for dinner). Don't worry, though, if you are allergic to fancy-pants restaurants and snooty service: The staff is mostly kids, and their good cheer gives the formality a happy family feeling—like Sunday dinner at the home of a grandparent who is a stickler for good manners.

There is lots of service at a Boone Tavern meal. Student waiters swarm through the dining room, offering dinner rolls, cleaning plates, bringing new courses, checking to make sure customers are happy. While not all the food they serve is totally delicious (there are students in the kitchen, too!), it is impossible not to enjoy their earnest efforts at making dinner a grand event.

The feast always begins with a relish tray, presented by a waiter who doles out whichever ones you choose: watermelon pickles, marinated carrots, etc. He (or she) is followed by another member of the staff carrying a hot bowl full of spoon bread. Quickly, clean your plate of relishes, because you want to spend some quality time with this spoon bread. It is the one dish that Boone Tavern dinner guests remember best: a classic, unadorned cornmeal soufflé, hot and fluffy, faintly granular, just a wee bit buttery, delicious with nearly any meaty main course.

What follows the spoon bread is a menu of classic Kentucky cookery. One of the aims of the college is to sustain and celebrate mountain culture, but in the case of the dining room, that does not imply a menu of Ma and Pa Kettle vittles such as hog jowls, baked beans, and scalded mush balls. The cuisine of the Boone Tavern is more refined than that. In fact, some of it is elaborate, such as the chicken flakes "Elsinore," a creamy Dixie belle of a meal served in a nest of potatoes. You can eat honey-cured ham in sweet lemon sauce or native turkey with fresh cranberry relish. And to end the meal, the kitchen offers impressive sweet-tooth regionalia such as Jefferson Davis pie (à la mode with homemade French vanilla custard ice cream).

Three cookbooks featuring most of the Boone Tavern recipes are available in the gift shop, but as we said, it is the spoon bread that leaves the lingering impression on one's taste buds. Remember, it is a last-minute dish, and should be served soon after it emerges from the oven—straight from the casserole, with a spoon. You may want to serve honey on the side to drizzle on the bread.

Triple Layer Spoon Bread

TRIPLE LAYER SPOON BREAD

1 cup cornmeal, white or yellow
½ cup whole wheat flour
½ cup white flour
2 teaspoons baking powder
½ teaspoon salt
1 egg, beaten
¼ cup honey or sorghum
¼ cup light vegetable oil
3 cups milk

Preheat oven to 350 degrees. Generously grease a 2-quart casserole.

Combine meal, flours, baking powder, and salt.

Combine egg, honey, vegetable oil, and milk. Stir into flour mixture. Pour into prepared casserole.

Bake uncovered 60 minutes, until top springs back. (It will still be jiggly.) Serves 6.

War Eagle Mill, Highway 98, 13 miles east of Rogers, Ark.; (501) 789-5343.

ROGERS, Ark.—Powered by an eighteen-foot redwood waterwheel, the War Eagle Mill uses stone buhrs to grind wheat and corn. The triple set of buhrs turns slowly, so that the grain is never heated up (as it is by high-speed modern steel roller mills). The result is whole-grain flour and cornmeal that contain all the natural germ, oil, and bran: nothing added, nothing taken out.

You can see the grist mill working every Saturday and Sunday in the riverside community of War Eagle, southeast of Rogers. Visitors are welcome to bring their own corn and wheat and have it ground by milleress Zoe Medlin Caywood.

Zoe's father, Jewell A. Medlin, built the mill in 1973, the fourth time a grist mill had been constructed on this spot along the War Eagle River. The first one flooded out in 1848; the second was destroyed by Confederate troops to prevent its capture by the Yankees; the third burned down in 1924.

The scenery is bucolic: pastures and grazing cows, and a steady-moving river dotted with canoeists and fishermen. On the top floor of the three-story building, the mill hosts a restaurant called the Bean Palace. Here you can sit down to breakfast of whole-grain buckwheat cakes and sausage, cracked wheat cereal, biscuits and sorghum molasses, or good old-fashioned grits.

Lunch at the Bean Palace is honest Ozark cooking. What fun it is to dip a steamy wedge of cornbread into an individual pot of pork and beans. Our smoked ham was served on tender slabs of whole-grain bread in country high style, on a blue-marbled graniteware dish. Iced tea was brought to the table in individual mason jars.

Just below the Bean Palace, on the second floor of the mill, visitors browse through a modest country store stocked with local crafts and grains from the mill. We carried away a handsome cherrywood "stirrer"—perfect for quickly mixing muffin or biscuit batter—and a giant-size, tomato-red graniteware pan suitable for fruit cobblers.

When we are at home, we shop at the War Eagle Mill through its mail-order catalog, which features vittles such as biscuit mix, hush puppy mix, fish fry coating, plus a complete variety of stone-ground flours and meals. To sweeten breads and biscuits, the catalog offers half-pint canning jars of muscadine jelly, apply cherry butter, blackberry preserves, Arkansas sorghum, and raw clover honey.

When our stone-ground flour arrives in the mail, we often turn to the *War Eagle Mill Whole Grain Cookbook* for inspiration. Written by Zoe Medlin, it is a treasury of health-conscious cookery. Naturally, there are oodles of recipes for breads and baking; there are even some down-home main courses such as cornmeal and bean pie or polenta cheese squares. Although only sixty-two pages long, Ms. Medlin's pamphlet reveals the wide range of possibilities available to cooks who want to go back to basics—everything from cornmeal mush to peach-topped whole wheat crepes.

One of the most fascinating corn bread recipes we have cooked is this spoon bread from the War Eagle cookbook. Although its ingredients are mixed thoroughly together, they separate as it cooks into a layered pudding, custard-like on top, bready below. Like most Southern spoon bread, it is more a country-style corn-flavored soufflé than the bread most of us bake in a loaf pan. Serve it straight from the casserole with a spoon, and eat it with utensils. It stiffens when it cools, so it is best eaten warm from the oven.

Apple Muffins

MADISON, Wis.—A good muffin ought to be served hot (not cooled, not even warm) from the oven. It will be unutterably tender, so gentle-bodied that the slightest tug renders ragged halves. Butter is its only complement, butter soft enough so it can be eased harmlessly onto the steamy, fruit-streaked landscape, where it will immediately melt.

Like biscuits, bagels, and beignets, muffins are usually considered breakfast food. In fact, culinary historians believe that muffins were invented to serve on the morning of bread-baking day—a quick and thrifty way to use up sour milk and save time while serious kneading and rising were going on in the kitchen.

APPLE MUFFINS

4 tablespoons softened butter
1/4 cup brown sugar
1/2 cup granulated sugar
1 egg
1 cup buttermilk
1 3/4 cups flour
4 1/2 teaspoons cinnamon
1 teaspoon baking soda
1/4 teaspoon salt
1 large red Delicious apple (or other eating
    apple), peeled and cut into 1/2-inch
    chunks
1/3 cup brown sugar

Preheat oven to 400 degrees. Grease a
12-hole, full-size muffin tin, including the
area between the cavities.

Cream butter and sugars until fluffy. Mix
in egg. Quickly fold in buttermilk; do not
overmix or batter will curdle.

In separate bowl, mix flour, cinnamon,
baking soda, and salt. Add gradually to
sugar-egg mixture, making sure there are
no lumps, but mixing no more than
necessary. Fold in apple chunks.

Fill each cavity in muffin tin nearly to the
top. Sprinkle extra brown sugar on top.
Bake 15 minutes.

Yield: 12 muffins.

Quivey's Grove, 6261 Nesbitt Road,
Madison, Wis.; (608) 273-4900.

Many cookbooks list them as a New England specialty, and while it is true that most of the good breakfast houses north of Connecticut specialize in muffins, they are by no means exclusively Yankee. Nor are they limited to morning meals.

Mr. and Mrs. Gregg Burmeister, who traveled around America with a copy of our *Roadfood* in their glove compartment, directed us to some swell Midwestern muffins in Madison, Wisconsin, at a restaurant named Quivey's Grove. "Like a visit to grandma's," is how the Burmeisters described this 1855 stone house with its five antique-filled dining rooms and menu of wholesome Midwestern food that is dedicated to Wisconsin's pioneers.

Cider-marinated pork loin, for instance, is called pork Brigham, in honor of Ebeneezer Brigham, the county's first postmaster. Pan-fried rainbow trout ("fish Phoenix") commemorates the Dutch immigrants who went down with the steamer Phoenix in Lake Michigan in 1847. Schurz schnitzel is named in remembrance of Secretary of the Interior Carl Schurz. It is all honest fare—beef, lamb, pork, or freshwater fish, accompanied by satisfying things such as mashed potatoes, fried apples, or sweet and sour cabbage.

The Burmeisters concluded their rave review of Quivey's Grove with the warning: "There is just no stopping with one of their strawberry, apple, or cranberry orange muffins." We agree, and we came away from Quivey's Grove with a recipe. Properly poured into muffin tins (almost to the top), they are heavyweight beauties, their canopy tops double-wide and crusted with a sparkling halo of brown sugar.

Peabody Vanilla Muffins

MEMPHIS, Tenn.—It is 10:55 A.M. A long red carpet is rolled from the bank of elevators into the lobby of the Peabody Hotel. It stretches all the way to the mighty marble fountain in the center. A crowd gathers along the carpet path, around the fountain, and in the mezzanine looking down. Cameras are poised.

Eleven o'clock, precisely. The anticipatory hush is blasted by a grand orchestral rendition of "Stars and Stripes Forever." The elevator doors open. Out march five mallard ducks, led by their uniformed trainer, Edward D. Pembroke. They waddle and quack along the carpet, completely out of step with John Philip Sousa, and plunge into the fountain. Here they will frolic until five o'clock, when Mr. Pembroke, personal chaperone of the Peabody duck corps since 1940, will lead them back up the penthouse elevator—to the strains of "The King Cotton March."

PEABODY VANILLA MUFFINS

2 cups flour
I cup sugar
2 teaspoons baking powder
1/4 teaspoon salt
2 tablespoons butter, melted and cooled
I cup milk
I egg
1 1/2 teaspoons vanilla extract

Preheat oven to 400 degrees.
Grease muffin tins well.
Sift flour with sugar, baking powder, and salt into large bowl.
Add melted butter to milk and egg. Beat to mix well. Add vanilla.
Make a well in the center of the flour mixture. Pour milk mixture in all at once. Stir with fork, only until all ingredients are moistened. Do not beat or overmix.
Quickly spoon batter into muffin tins, filling each slightly more than half-full.
Bake 15 minutes if using gem muffin pans; 18–20 minutes for full-size muffin pans. Remove from tins immediately and serve hot.
Yield: 12 3-inch muffins or 30 gem muffins.

Peabody Hotel, 149 Union Ave., Memphis, Tenn.; 1-800-PEABODY.

This noisy ceremony takes place every day at the Peabody Hotel, where marching ducks, Southern hospitality, and delicious bite-sized vanilla muffins are all part of a tradition that has endured for 116 years.

The lobby—ducks and all—is known in local lore as the place where the Mississippi Delta begins. Since it opened in 1869, the Peabody has been the social mecca of cotton country, host of countless King Cotton Balls, attended by local gentry in their finest attire. The hotel's first guests were always sure to arrive in silks, but were often splattered with mud from their mule cart ride to get here through the unpaved streets of Memphis.

Modern generations know the Peabody for its Skyway and Plantation Roof, from which Tommy Dorsey and Paul Whiteman broadcasted live in the 1940s. From this vantage point atop the hotel, nighttime revelers still enjoy a kingly view of the city that is the heart and soul of the mid-South.

For years the Peabody dining rooms—on the Skyway Roof and downstairs—offered the finest in Southern cooking: not the sleeves-up cuisine of grits and barbecue and catfish, but the higher-toned cookery of the antebellum South. Here was the place to savor shrimp from the Gulf, two-year-old Tennessee country ham, and Mississippi black bottom pie.

After a long postwar decline, the Peabody was recently renovated back to bandbox perfection. Its restaurant (called Dux) serves a full roster of regional American and Continental gourmet food, including the tastiest fillet of pan-blackened redfish we have eaten anywhere outside New Orleans.

But we want to talk about one small item that hasn't changed at all over the years. Whether fortunes are up or down, the Peabody Hotel has always served vanilla muffins. These sweet and chewy morsels have become one of the legendary breadstuffs of the South.

During the Depression in the 1930s, vanilla muffins were a complimentary accompaniment to a five-cent cup of coffee. Today, they are presented in the breakfast breadbasket and at brunch.

Whether made in miniature pans or full-sized muffin tins, it is imperative that vanilla muffins be served warm, preferably straight from the oven. Accompany them with spreadably soft butter.

IPPY'S STAFF OF LIFE BREAD

1¾ cups milk

4 tablespoons butter

⅔ cup honey

1½ teaspoons salt

½ cup oatmeal (not instant)

1 package yeast

⅓ cup bran

3 tablespoons wheat germ

3¾ to 4¼ cups white flour

¼ cup white sugar

¼ cup dark brown sugar

1 teaspoon cinnamon

Heat milk and butter. As it warms, add honey and salt. When it comes to a boil, remove from heat and stir in oatmeal. Let cool until tepid (no more than 110 degrees), about 1½ hours.

Pour into mixing bowl. Stir in yeast. Stir in bran and wheat germ. Stir in 3¾ cups flour, small amounts at a time. Turn dough out on floured board and let rest while you clean and lightly butter bowl.

Knead dough 8–10 minutes. Add flour if needed to keep dough workable. It should be quite resilient.

Return dough to bowl. Cover and let rise in warm place until double in size, about 2 hours.

Mix together sugars and cinnamon. Butter a 9-by-5-inch bread pan.

On a lightly floured board, punch the dough down to a flat oval. Sprinkle half the cinnamon-sugar mixture over oval and roll it up tightly. Flatten it into an oval again by punching. Sprinkle on remaining cinnamon sugar, and roll the dough up, perpendicular to the first roll.

Ippy's Staff of Life Bread

WEST REDDING, Conn.—Normally, we tip readers off to great places to eat. Here is one you cannot visit unless you get an invitation. We're referring to the home of our friend Ippy. And the reason we are going to talk about Ippy is that she makes the best bread on earth.

It is an off-white loaf, swirled with moist veins of cinnamon brown sugar. Billowy tender with a rich brown crust, it invites you to slice it very thick, then just barely toast it. The surfaces get faintly crisp, but the inside of the slice stays moist, and the thick mahogany-colored veins of sugar drip and ooze as you tear off chunks. You need no butter or condiment for a slice of Ippy's bread. It's a perfect solo.

She makes it nearly every week, six loaves at a time, one or two to bring to friends (still warm from the oven, if we're lucky), the others to keep for breakfast and tea-time snacks.

Ippy calls it Grandma K's bread, because it was her Grandma Klonis, from upstate New York near the Chazy River, who taught her how to make it. Grandma Klonis is a health-conscious person. "She grows her own carrots," Ippy told us. "And she has her own compost heap." When Grandma K lived in New York City, she sold her bread at a bakery on 57th Street, where she used to call it "Staff of Life Bread."

Like most heirloom recipes, this one has evolved through the years. Grandma K used to sprinkle each loaf with soy flour just before she finished kneading, but Ippy, who doesn't like the taste of soy, cut it out. The original Staff of Life Bread also had raisins mixed with the cinnamon sugar, but Ippy's daughter, Pilar, doesn't like raisins, so they got thrown out of the recipe, too. Once you make Ippy's bread a few times, you will probably think of a few twists that will make the hand-me-down recipe your own.

Ippy, by the way, is a nickname that has stuck since she was fifteen years old and she came to school in Connecticut from Chile. "The Girl From Ipanema" was a popular song at the time. Although Ipanema is in Brazil, not Chile, she does look like the girl in the song—"tall and tan and young and lovely"; and so she became the girl from Ipanema, a.k.a. Ippy.

Place loaf into prepared bread pan, lightly covered with a cloth. Let rise one hour.

Heat oven to 350 degrees. Bake 25 minutes, then cover loaf securely with aluminum foil. Bake 30 minutes more. Remove from oven. Cool in pan 15 minutes. Remove from pan and cool thoroughly on rack before slicing. Makes I loaf.

OLD-FASHIONED EGG MUFFINS

2 cups all-purpose flour
¼ cup non-fat dry milk
2½ teaspoons baking powder
I teaspoon salt
⅓ cup sugar
4 eggs, beaten
½ cup light salad oil
¼ cup water

Preheat oven to 400 degrees. Generously grease muffin tin (12 holes) or line each hole with baking cups.

Mix flour, dry milk, baking powder, salt, and sugar.

Mix eggs, salad oil, and water.

Combine dry and liquid ingredients, mixing only enough to blend (a few lumps are OK).

Spoon into prepared muffin tins, filling each about two-thirds.

Bake 12–15 minutes, or until sharp knife inserted in muffin comes out clean. Serve warm.

Makes 12 muffins.

Cole Farms, Route 100, Gray, Maine; (207) 657-4714.

Old-Fashioned Egg Muffins

GRAY, Maine—Most summer visitors to Maine stick close to the ocean. But there is another, year-round Maine. It is not quite so picturesque, nor is it as famous for its food; but it is fascinating country to explore, and it has some four-star roadside restaurants. We are talking about inland Maine, a less-traveled Down East landscape dotted with towns that have oddly international names like South Paris, East Peru, Poland, Naples, and Denmark.

We love to eat our way through this part of the state because its cafés and lunchrooms are treasuries of true New England cookery, with little compromise to please out-of-towner tastes.

Coming from the south up the Maine Turnpike, the first good place to get off and eat is in the village of Gray. The last time we exited the highway and headed along Route 100, we passed an old lady on a front porch spinning wool: How's that for color? A local radio station was playing country-western music; nearly every farm had stables, with horse trailers parked in its driveway. Stores advertised tack equipment and cowboy clothes. Half the vehicles on the road were pickups.

The place local people congregate to eat is a restaurant called Cole Farms. It is a big café, four or five rooms strung together, then partitioned with a kind of chicken wire fence, so that even though the space is sprawling, each booth seems cozy.

You would never call Cole Farms picturesque. Decor is a cavalier mix of varnished pine with Formica. Place settings are marked by paper mats that ask "Did You Know?" and feature trivia questions.

The plainness of the setting is perfect for highlighting the honesty of the food. The menu, for instance, lists two kinds of soup: Campbell's or Cole Farms', the latter selling for ten cents more per cup. It also lists "Mashed Potatoes—When Available." The waitress explained that Cole Farms does not use instant spuds, so when one batch of real mashed potatoes is gone, customers must wait until more are mashed. The mayonnaise on our BLT was unmistakably homemade.

But it isn't just the food's authenticity that makes Cole Farms distinctive; it's character, too. Many house specialties are uniquely, stubbornly Yankee. The menu lists five kinds of pudding (no mousse whatsoever), including New England favorites like Indian (cornmeal) and Grape-Nut. You can make a meal of baked beans, with or without hot dogs, or of "American chop suey"—a dowdy dish that some New England boarding school alumni may remember with horror. Corn or fish chowder is always on the menu, as are super-clammy clam cakes served with freshly made tartar sauce.

When Cole Farms opens at 5 A.M., most customers come for muffins. They are available with fillings such as blueberry, apple, bran, even oatmeal; or you can get them absolutely plain—a purposeful breakfast breadstuff that Warren Cole told us is known simply as "old-fashioned egg muffins." We love them—warm and eggy, served hot directly from the oven, augmented with a pat of butter and a blob of honey.

We reduced Cole Farms' recipe from an eight-dozen yield to proportions for twelve. They are just barely sweet, and quite stark all alone; if you don't want them quite so plain, fold in a cup of sweet berries or chopped apples before spooning the batter into muffin tins.

5
Salads

Black-Eyed Pea Salad

THAYER, Mo.—It is hard not to like a restaurant that begins lunch hour by clanging a bell.

At Nettie's the call sounds every day at 11 A.M. A horde of hungry loiterers grab trays and slide their way along the line.

Nettie's is a cafeteria, which makes it doubly delectable in our book. We were tipped off to it by Judy Novak of Milpitas, California, who told us that the prime time to come is Sunday, when the array of tempting home cooking is most spectacular. Sorry to say, we missed the Sunday feast, but our weekday lunch was memorable.

Nettie's baked chicken is so limber it cannot be lifted from the plate without all the meat sliding off its bones. To accompany this sunny plate of food, we selected a bowl of dumplings in chicken broth. For dipping in the broth, a pair of warm dinner rolls exactly filled the bill. What a tender-spirited meal!

But it wasn't all gentleness and soft things to eat. Fried chicken was a handful and a mouthful—brittle-crusted, meaty, saturated with the punch of black pepper. There was zingy spinach, too, cooked the way collard greens are cooked in a traditional Southern kitchen, served wallowing in a pool of potent pot likker.

As in so many good cafeterias, the choice of salads was tremendous. There were leafy things, creamy slaws, multicolored gelatins, marinated vegetables, and cool, sweet macaroni.

The salad that left the best impression was a wide-awake combination of black-eyed peas, chopped scallions, and diced red peppers in a sugary marinade. It was tart, sweet, sour, and—because of the peas—substantial. At first bite, it wasn't really a knock-out. But as we oinked our way through the fried chicken, baked chicken, dumplings, as well as a smothered steak with mashed potatoes on the side and two slices of still-warm coconut meringue pie, our forks kept going back to the black-eyed peas. By the time we left Nettie's, we knew this was the recipe by which we wanted to remember lunch.

Nettie's is not by any means a grand restaurant. The tables are Formica; and the decor is a modest assortment of barnboard and old-timey knickknacks. There are several dining rooms, including a big one in back where the local Rotary Club meets. It is not exactly Michelin three-star material.

Keep your Michelin. Nettie's is the kind of roadside experience that makes happy travelers. To get to the town of Thayer, one must do some serious meandering. The prettiest way to find it is to head down Route 19 through the Mark Twain National Forest toward the Ozarks. Just before crossing into Arkansas, you come upon the

BLACK-EYED PEA SALAD

2 cups fresh or frozen black-eyed peas (or
    about 1 cup dried)
1/2 pound chunk of salt pork, scored
1 clove garlic, halved
1 cup chicken stock, plus water
1/2 cup olive oil
1/3 cup red wine vinegar
1 tablespoon sugar
2 red peppers, diced
1 bunch scallions, thinly sliced
1/4 cup chopped parsley

In a large stockpot, combine the peas,
salt pork, and garlic clove with chicken
stock and enough cold water to cover everything. Bring to boil. Cover and reduce heat
to simmer. Cook 30–40 minutes, stirring
occasionally, until peas are tender but not
mushy. (If using dried black-eyed peas, soak
them overnight, covered with water. Then
cook them, partially covered, 1 hour.)

Drain peas, removing salt pork and garlic
clove.

Combine oil, vinegar, and sugar. Pour
over warm peas. Stir in red pepper, scallions, and parsley. Chill. Serve with
cornbread.

Makes 4–6 servings.

Nettie's, junction of Routes 63 & 142,
Thayer, Mo.; (417) 264-7900. (There is a
branch of Nettie's in Mountain Home,
Ark.)

shopping center that Judy Novak had written about. And there is
Nettie's. If it's just before eleven o'clock, there will likely be a small
group of townspeople gathered around waiting for the bell to ring
for lunch.

If you are anywhere nearby, we recommend you find it. It is a
straight taste of America.

Cinnamon Apple Jellied Salad

PITTSBURGH—Pittsburgh is a city of neighborhoods and neigh-
borhood restaurants of every ethnic persuasion, from Samreney's
Cedars of Lebanon Middle Eastern lounge in Oakland to Born
Free in Shadyside, where the specialty is African cuisine. Among
the not-to-be-missed eating experiences are a "mystery sandwich"
(whatever the kitchen has on hand) and an Iron City beer at
Chiodo's Tavern in Homestead, a butter-basted steak at The
Colony in Greentree, and all-night breakfast at Ritter's Diner in
Oakland.

Of all the interesting things to eat, there are two Pittsburgh
meals that no adventurous eater ought to miss. The first is
chipped-chopped (pronounced "chip-chopped") ham. This is a
strictly western Pennsylvania foodstuff that is served just like the
lowliest junk food from the dime-store deli or convenience-store
counter: processed ham shaved tissue-thin and piled inside a burger bun or between two slices of spongy white bread. Phil
Langdon, roadside archeologist nonpareil and author of *Orange
Roofs and Golden Arches,* was the first to clue us in to the delicacy,
which he said connoisseurs prefer served warmed in a frying pan
with melted cheese inside the sandwich. After a meal of chipped-
chopped ham, Phil suggested a drive along a country road in
search of a more obscure western Pennsylvania specialty, goat's
milk fudge.

Back downtown, you will find us at the Tick Tock Coffee Shop in
the basement of Kaufmann's Department Store, enjoying another
only-in-Pittsburgh meal. For this gem of a restaurant, we have
"Taste of America" reader Patty Rowe of Riverside, California, to
thank. Patty had read a column in which we wrote about our search
for the best hamburger—in Los Angeles, Connecticut, Colorado,
and Texas. "I have tried, sampled, and enjoyed hamburgers all over
the country," Patty informed us. "Most are pretty much the same.
But the best I ever tasted is at the Tick Tock in Kaufmann's, in
America's number one city, Pittsburgh."

Yes, indeed, this Tick Tock burger is a dandy—charbroiled to a

CINNAMON APPLE JELLIED SALAD

³/₄ cup red cinnamon candies
1 6-ounce package lemon gelatin
2 cups sweetened applesauce
*2 3-ounce packages cream cheese, soft-
     ened to room temperature*
¹/₃ cup mayonnaise
¹/₂ cup chopped pecans
¹/₂ cup chopped celery

*Melt cinnamon candy in 1 cup very hot
water, stirring over low heat for 5 minutes.
Remove from heat and add lemon gelatin,
stirring until completely dissolved. Stir in
applesauce.*

*Pour half of gelatin mixture into an 8-
inch square pan (make sure pan is 2 to 3
inches deep). Chill until firm (about 30 minutes), letting remainder of gelatin stand at
room temperature.*

*Beat cream cheese and mayonnaise
together until fluffy. Fold in nuts and celery.*

*When first mixture is firm, spread top
with cream cheese mixture. Pour remaining
gelatin on top of cream cheese and return
to refrigerator until set.*

Serves 8.

*Tick Tock Coffee Shop at Kaufmann's, 5th
and Smithfield, Pittsburgh, Pa.;
(412) 232-2682.*

glistening crusty crunch on the outside, yet thick enough to still be moist and rose-pink in its center, served inside a big homemade bun.

Excellent hamburgers are not the only thing the Tick Tock has to offer. In fact, the oozingly drippy, two-fisted burgers are a bit of an oddity on the otherwise ladylike menu of soups and salads, dainty cream-sauced dishes of chicken and turkey, and fluffy cakes and chiffon pies.

Mid-morning, you can come for homemade muffins, but-terscotch rolls, German apple bread, blueberry pancakes, or steamy pecan waffles. By lunch, a blackboard is set up outside the dining room listing all the day's specialties—most of them fancy desserts such as pecan stick torte, silk 'n' satin pie, chocolate port wine cake, and a variety of homemade ice creams.

Among the specialties of the house are molded salads—elabo-rate concoctions such as jellied beet velvet cream, and this spicy variation of Waldorf salad, the recipe for which was derived from a book of Kaufmann's favorite recipes available at the Tick Tock cash register.

Canlis Salad

SEATTLE—In case you didn't notice, the revolution has suc-ceeded. Old ways are a thing of the past.

We are referring to the culinary revolution, an upheaval of eat-ing habits that began in the 1960s. It was a revolution founded on gourmet aspirations and nutrition mania, championed by Julia Child and the granola generation. A quarter-century later, almost everyone is a bit of a gourmet, and health food is no longer the sole concern of long-haired eccentrics.

As American's cooking changed, so did our concept of a fine and fancy restaurant. Old-fashioned luxury went out of fashion. Nouvelle gourmets, who wander the restaurant scene looking for even more exotic kicks, no longer consider it chic to go to a posh dining room with a view of the city and eat steak and drink martinis and have a hot fudge coconut snowball for dessert. That's for tourists!

Tourists we are; and tourists we will gladly be whenever we visit Seattle. Because Canlis, although out of style by any definition of modern cookery, is a haven for traditionalists who cherish pre-revolutionary luxury.

First there is the setting: magnificent! Perched high on the banks of Lake Union, the building is a dramatic showpiece of 1950s-vintage architectural modernity. Its cantilevered all-glass

CANLIS SALAD

1 large head romaine lettuce, washed and
    sliced into 1-inch pieces
2 tomatoes, peeled and cut into bite-size
    wedges
1/4 cup chopped green onions
1 cup freshly grated Romano cheese
1 cup cooked crisp bacon, chopped fine
2 tablespoons chopped fresh mint
1/4 teaspoon oregano

DRESSING
juice of 1 lemon
1/2 teaspoon freshly ground pepper
1 egg, coddled in boiling water 30 seconds
1/2 cup olive oil
1/2 cup croutons

Place all salad ingredients in a large
bowl, in order given, reserving 1/4 cup of the
Romano cheese.

In a separate bowl, whisk lemon juice,
pepper, and coddled egg. Slowly add olive
oil, whisking constantly. Pour over salad and
toss thoroughly. Top with croutons and
reserved 1/4 cup Romano cheese.

Serves 4.

Canlis, 2576 Aurora N., Seattle, Wash.;
(206) 283-3313.

panoramic wall provides a startling view, at dusk, of seaplanes landing, and after dark, of Seattle's shimmering lights along the shore.

Accommodations are plush: banquettes and chairs upholstered in textured fabric with strands of gold woven among the fibers. The vast open space of the dining room creates a rugged Northwest ambience, which is tempered by "less-is-more" Oriental decor. Waitresses are Japanese, dressed in kimonos; some barely speak English.

A good measure of the creamy Canlis ambience is created by its clientele. You will find no yuppies or epicurean camp-followers here. These are all people able and willing to pay dearly for the familiar, the tried and true. Yes, it costs plenty to dine in the bastion of swank cuisine—at least fifty dollars for two. Men wear jackets and ties. Ladies wear diamonds and furs. Whoever you are, you can expect the staff to treat you as if you were rich. For years, a rumor has circulated around town that undesirable or uncouth types are discreetly given a card by the valet on their way out requesting PLEASE DO NOT COME BACK TO CANLIS. We trust the rumor is not true, but it does give you an idea of the lofty status Canlis holds in Seattle folklore.

What about the food? No surprises. This is the place to enjoy a ritual Big Deal Meal. That means blue-ribbon steaks, the best money can buy, broiled over charcoal. Or big lamb chops. Or perhaps swordfish or the Hawaiian dolphin known as mahi mahi (a fish, not a mammal). On the side you want plates of shoestring potatoes or onion rings: They're delish.

For starters, you definitely want a Canlis salad. This is a Canlis trademark, its elaborate tableside construction evocative of all the good old ways for which the restaurant stands. It is like a Caesar salad, but minted and enriched and dazzlingly jazzy. When we make it at home, it is dinner by itself.

Orange Salad

HARTFORD, Conn.—Among the tall tales of gastronomic folklore, one of our favorite whoppers is the explanation for why the Normans conquered Sicily in the eleventh century. It seems there was a prince of Salerno who sent a gift box of locally grown oranges to the duke of Normandy. The duke liked the fruit so much he mounted up and lead his army south to take the orange trees of southern Italy for himself.

Sicily is citrus heaven, perfumed by lemons, oranges, tangerines, citrons, and grapefruit. Figs and grapes and pomegran-

ORANGE SALAD

1 clove garlic

1 anchovy filet

1 egg yolk

1 teaspoon prepared hot mustard

½ cup olive oil

6 seedless eating oranges, peeled and cut
   into bite-size chunks

1 medium red onion, peeled and sliced
   super thin

½ cup fresh coriander

salt and pepper

croutons (optional)

*Using a fork or spoon in a heavy salad
bowl, mash together garlic and anchovy
until they are pulpy. Mix in egg yolk, mustard, and olive oil.*

*Add oranges, onion, and coriander. Toss.
Add salt and pepper to taste. Top with
croutons if desired. Serves 4.*

*Carbone's, 588 Franklin Ave., Hartford,
Conn.; (203) 249-9646.*

ates are staples of the classic Sicilian table. Despite that sunny harvest, few Americans think of southern Italian food as anything beyond pasta and pizza, or perhaps seafood with tomato sauce.

Our own education in the nuances of southern Italian cuisine—beyond the familiar Neapolitan dishes—came not from traveling to Italy, but from eating our way up and down Franklin Avenue in Hartford—one of America's great enclaves of ethnic restaurants.

Here are scores of Italian bakeries, coffee houses, social clubs that are also cafés, and restaurants of every rung up and down the socioeconomic ladder. Whether you crave a mountain of spaghetti and meatballs at bargain prices or an elegant feast of lobster "fra diavolo" topped off with espresso and a shot of anisette liqueur, you will find it on Franklin Avenue.

The snazziest and the best-known (and the best) of all the avenue's restaurants is an establishment called Carbone's. For years, Carbone's has been Hartford's grand place to eat—a magnet for the city's politicians and high rollers, and a special-occasion place for ordinary citizens who want a night out on the town with pomp and flourishes.

Dazzling tableside preparation is a house specialty. Dinner is punctuated by dramatic interludes as a staff skilled in pyrotechnical cuisine sets up rolling carts and burners to assemble pasta sauces on the spot, or to whip up a spectacular flaming spinach salad, or to ignite fancy coffees for dessert.

Beyond the flash, the important thing to know about Carbone's is that the food tastes wonderful. Even quiet, nonflaming dishes leave indelible memories: shrimp "Gaetano" awash in garlic butter; "vitello amore" (which roughly translates as "veal love") in its intoxicating gravy laced with Frangelico liqueur; peppery fettucini carbonara.

One of the dishes for which Carbone's is renowned is called Sicilian orange salad. Indeed, it is so well known by regular customers that it isn't listed on the menu. But connoisseurs know that it is one of the things this place does best. It, too, is a tableside production number, beginning vaguely like Caesar salad, but then veering away from cheese and romaine lettuce to incorporate the Sicilian citrus bounty.

The specific elements of the recipe are wide open to interpretation. Experiment; do it your way. If you hate anchovies, cut them out. If you like another herb more than coriander, give it a try. The essential character of the dish is the contrast of sweet orange segments with a tangy salad dressing.

Crab Louie

OLEMA, Calif.—Pearlescent crabmeat, plump and succulent; or bouncy, firm-fleshed prawns; or slivers and chunks of pink meat torn from inside the shell of a sweet and salty lobster: No sauce or condiment can improve upon these natural oceanic wonders.

But there is one salad dressing that, made properly, is their match. Its name is Louie. Among fanciers of West Coast shellfish, even those who are purists and insist on savoring unadulterated marine meat, Louie has a host of friends.

Louie is loved because it is quiet. It is an orchestration of minor notes, hints of texture, mere suggestions of other flavors, all working to amplify the goodness of the shellfish star they cosset. Because it is really nothing more than mayonnaise accented with a few dashes of chili, onion, pepper, etc., it is a snap to prepare; serious Louie aficionados, however, insist that the mayo must be made from scratch.

No one seems to know who Louie was or if his name ought to be spelled Louis (both ways are common on menus), or where and when he invented his immortal dressing. Historians do agree that it was a West Coast creation, most likely around the turn of the century. The St. Francis Hotel in San Francisco is often given credit. We have also seen it claimed by Portland and Seattle.

Because the seafoods it complements are expensive, Louie is usually found on the menus of pricey restaurants. But one of our favorite places for crab or shrimp Louie is an anything-but-fancy eatery known as Jerry's Farmhouse.

Jerry's is located in the town of Olema ("population 60," boasts the menu) at the gateway to the Point Reyes National Seashore, a long strip of pine forests and uncrowded beaches. It is a big, shingle-sided barn of a restaurant with a casual sprinkling of tables and chairs in its mazelike dining area.

A real down-home kind of place, with a menu that goes all the way from a grilled cheese sandwich to a rib-eye steak, with sturdy-crusted apple pie for dessert, Jerry's is a slice of Americana—and an honest taste of simple California seafood.

Local oysters, either raw or pan-fried, are the specialty of the house. Or you can dine on prawns, halibut, sole, or rock cod. Dinners are accompanied by clam chowder and fleece-white baking powder biscuits, served with little cups of honey and homemade strawberry preserves. Shrimp or crab Louie (or half-and-half), its mayonnaise binder lightly lumpy with relish and a dollup of Thousand Island dressing, is served with hot French bread.

Our own recipe for Louie dressing is a wee bit fancier than

CRAB LOUIE

1 cup mayonnaise
2 tablespoons chili sauce
2 tablespoons grated onion
1 tablespoon sweet-pickle relish
1/3 cup minced green olives
dash of cayenne pepper
1/2 cup whipped cream
salt to taste
6 large iceberg lettuce leaves
1 pound fresh crabmeat, flaked
2 ripe tomatoes, cut into six wedges each
3 hard-boiled eggs, quartered

Mix mayonnaise with chili sauce, onion, relish, olives, and cayenne pepper. Fold in whipped cream. Add salt to taste.

Arrange iceberg lettuce leaves on 4–6 plates, depending on size of portions desired. Place crabmeat atop lettuce. Dollop generously with dressing. Garnish with tomato wedges and hard-boiled eggs.
Makes 4–6 servings.

Jerry's Farmhouse, 10005 State Route No. 1, Olema, Calif.; (415) 663-1264.

Jerry's, and we do try to make our mayonnaise fresh. But we won't tell if you use mayo from a jar, nor is it a crime to fiddle with the recipe; there are as many different versions as there are chefs. The only unbreakable rule about making Crab Louie is that the crab-meat must be fresh. Dungeness crab is best; lump crabmeat from the mid-Atlantic coast is fine; even king crab, although stringy-textured, is acceptable.

If no fresh crabmeat is available, cooked shrimp or lobster is equally at home dabbed with a dollop of Louie.

Cold Curried Shrimp

LOVE'S COVE, Maine—Not many modern cooks live in a place where they can swap recipes across the back fence with neighbors. Anyway, who has time?

We know one person who takes the time to share her recipes along with a good measure of conversation: Karyl Bannister of Maine, who writes a newsletter called *Cook and Tell*. Karyl's monthly publication, written in her 1850s farmhouse overlooking Love's Cove, is a treasury of homespun philosophy, culinary nostalgia, local color, and whatever other topics the season inspires. The good gab is always wrapped around four pages of recipes for what Karyl calls "nonfiction cooking."

The eight small pages of *Cook and Tell* are divided into all kinds of categories: the Chocolate Chit Chat column, one part titled "Now Playing in a Kitchen Near You," a box of "Personals" to people who have written in with special recipe problems, a cookie contest, an occasional lost-and-found recipe section, and a "shop and tell" of recommended books and products. It is all *very* informal; we especially enjoyed the June 1984 issue, for which the *n* on Karyl's typewriter went on the blink and she had to add a note (headlined "Nonentity," in pencil) announcing, "We have rux out of x's uxtil the xest issue."

The most distinctive feature of this newsletter is that despite its being Karyl Bannister's forum, soapbox, true confession, and personal diary, it also belongs to her readers. The richly packed pages are an effervescent dialogue between publisher and subscriber. They write in to report how well the recipes worked and how many people they served and what they did with leftovers. And Karyl answers them with more recipes, snappy comebacks, and occasional open calls to help her solve gastronomic riddles.

One fascinating colloquy recently took place over an old-fashioned, now vanished ingredient called baking ammonia, a leavener

COLD CURRIED SHRIMP

ASPIC

1½ envelopes unflavored gelatin
¼ cup cold water
1 cup chicken bouillon, boiling hot
salt to taste
2 tablespoons Major Grey's Indian chutney,
  chopped
¾ cup orange juice
1 tablespoon lime juice

Soften gelatin in cold water. Add hot bouillon, salt, and chutney, stirring until gelatin is dissolved. Add orange juice and lime juice. Stir thoroughly, then pour into 2½-cup ring mold rinsed in cold water. Chill, unmold, and fill center with curried shrimp. (There will be extra shrimp to serve on the side.)

SHRIMP

1 cup cooked shrimp, cleaned and cut up
½ cup chopped celery
¼ cup capers
1 hard-boiled egg, chopped
2 tablespoons chopped onion
1 cup mayonnaise mixed with 1 tablespoon
  curry powder

Combine all ingredients.
Serves 4.

Subscriptions to Cook and Tell are available from Cook & Tell, Love's Cove, West Southport, Maine 04576.

called for in a recipe sent in by a reader. Karyl investigated, and reported that baking ammonia predates baking powder, and is no longer available in groceries. But you can get it at the pharmacy—in one-pound batches. Karyl bought a pound and sold it by the ounce to readers so they could try the "wondrously delicate butter cookies" it makes.

Who are the approximately five hundred people who subscribe? A recent tabulation listed one mayor, two cookbook authors, two newspaper publishers, four clergymen, two poets, the eleventh-generation descendant of Miles Standish, one purveyor of frog legs, and one jazz musician among the faithful. Karyl describes them as "people who like to read as well as feed."

None of the recipes in *Cook and Tell* are highfalutin. Indeed, some are real goofy: like corn dogs and choco-scotch clusters and turtle candies (each of which, by the way, was quite wonderful). Most are interesting variations of familiar themes. Guided by recipes in *Cook and Tell*, we have cooked a show-stopper Mexican pork roast and scrumptious roast beef bathed in beer, and we have baked a delicious—albeit utterly eccentric—"apple pie in a paper bag."

Karyl learned how to make cold curried shrimp (printed as part of a "garden party" menu) from her mother-in-law. "It's a teeny bit tony," she said, "but we always love it."

Carrot Salad

LAKEWOOD, Ohio—Miller's Dining Room has style. But it is not stylish. And we doubt if its distinctive way of serving dinner will set any trends. It has been doing things pretty much the same since 1949.

That was when fire destroyed Cleveland's old Central Market, and Mrs. Ruby Miller, who had worked there in the family butcher shop, joined with her husband, John, himself the son of a butcher at the West Side Market, to open a restaurant on Detroit Avenue in Lakewood, just west of the city. Their motto was, "A Place for the Family."

Those words are still inscribed above the entryway to Miller's Dining Room, now run by the Millers' daughter, Doris Urbansky, with her husband, Tom, and their daughter, Carol.

If we had to be marooned on a desert island with only one restaurant, Miller's Dining Room just might be the choice. We love this place, and always plot any trip through northern Ohio so that we pass through Cleveland at lunch or dinnertime.

CARROT SALAD

4 cups shredded fresh carrots
2 tablespoons sugar
I teaspoon salt
2 cups diced celery
I cup raisins
³/₄ cup mayonnaise

   Mix shredded carrots with sugar and salt and let stand I hour.

   Place carrot mixture in colander or large strainer. Add celery and raisins, mix together, and let stand 30 minutes.

   Stir in mayonnaise and mix well. Let stand in strainer over sink 15–20 minutes, so extra mayonnaise can drain.

   Serve in scoops on leaves of lettuce. Refrigerate to store. Makes 6–8 servings.

Miller's Dining Room, 16707 Detroit Ave., Lakewood, Ohio; (216) 221-5811.

No matter when we eat at Miller's, the experience reminds us of Thanksgiving, as Norman Rockwell painted it. It is a place for families—multigenerational groups skip, walk, and wheel their way inside. Wallpaper is muted blue; tables are set with fresh flowers and white linen. At dinner, each customer is given a finger bowl at the conclusion of the meal. There is nothing pretentious about any of these niceties. They are simply nice—a decent, civilized way to serve a meal.

The food is Midwestern American. Chicken à la king—made from cream and chicken and fresh green peppers and mushrooms—is served in baskets of deep-fried potato shreds. Roast turkey is sided by fluffy hills of whipped potatoes, running rivulets of melting butter. Ham puffs are accented by steaming heaps of spiced escalloped apples.

The only problem is that by the time entrées arrive, you may be full. As soon as customers are seated, they are approached by one of Miller's roll girls, carrying her battered metal tray heaped high with corn sticks, cloverleaf rolls, and swirling cinnamon buns sticky with caramelized sugar. Help yourself, and help yourself again the next time she comes around. These rolls—hot out of the oven—are sensational; and there are always more.

In addition to the roll girl, Miller's way of doing things includes a salad girl. She approaches with a tray of only-in-Ohio variety, many of them molded salads. (We have long maintained that Ohio is the Jell-O capital of America; this tray is proof.) Here are fruits and nuts and coconut suspended in jiggly rainbows of gelatin that Busby Berkeley would have been proud of if he had been a salad-maker.

Cherry cream imperial, a stupendous combination of sour cream, cherry gelatin, and cherries, and plenty of whipped cream, is served on dainty leaves of lettuce. There is Waldorf salad, its hard texture softened with miniature marshmallows. Or Harvard beets—teeny-weeny cubes bathed in orange sauce. Or bean salad that is snapping fresh.

One of the less show-offy salads always on the tray is made of shredded carrots. Variations of carrot salad are popular throughout the Midwest and South. It used to be Lesson No. 1 in many home-ec classes; and we know gourmets who make fun of its simplicity. But we confess that we never let the salad girl pass without grabbing a bowl. At Miller's it contains fresh mayonnaise, which makes all the difference; but even with mayo from a jar, we hold deep affection for carrot salad as a friendly kitchen classic. If you want to jazz it up, add a handful of chopped nuts or health-foody seeds, apple slivers or—for a more substantial salad—tiny cubes of cooked ham.

Herbed Buttermilk Dressing and Molded Tomato Salad

WINNETKA, Ill.—"We just roast food," is how Harry Klingeman describes the secret of the Indian Trail. They certainly do a good job of it; since Harry's parents, Harvey and Clara Klingeman, opened their thirty-seat eatery in 1934, this family-run restaurant has earned a reputation as one of Chicagoland's old reliables.

The Klingemans have made a few changes in the last fifty years. New dining rooms were add, the kitchen expanded; the Indian Trail now seats three hundred. And now the Winnetka voted down Prohibition (just a few years ago), you can get a drink with dinner. When Henry took over from his parents, he even opened up a beer garden for fair-weather meals, and has modernized the menu to include sandwiches and light entrées.

But some things never change—like freshly baked, hot spice muffins and dinner rolls with every meal. Or the item listed on the menu with the charming old-fashioned name of "guest luncheon"—made-from-scratch turkey fricassee, served sprinkled with chow mein noodles and sliced toasted almonds. Talk about comfort food! Or a staggeringly delicious hazelnut rum roll lined with real whipped cream. And in-season blueberry pie, rhubarb tart, or fresh melon salad with poppy seed dressing.

Many Winnetka families (Michael's included) have been dining at the Indian Trail for three generations. (In fact, little sister Ellen Stern used to wheel her red wagon full of rhubarb from the back-yard garden to the restaurant's kitchen and sell it for fifty cents a wagonload—a practice health department regulations now no doubt forbid.)

When the Klingemans started their business in the midst of the Depression, the culinary pickin's north of Chicago were scarce. A few Italian restaurants up in Highwood, a diner or two, the grand old Hearthstone in Hubbard Woods—that was about it. Now you can find flashy modern cuisine all over the North Shore, plain and exotic menus of every stripe. But we never go back home without at least one square meal at the Indian Trail.

"In the early days," Clara Klingeman remembered, "we never worked from recipes. That meant taste, taste, and taste." She recalls one year when they were experimenting with a new kind of cake and brought samples out to the lobby to solicit the opinions of customers waiting to be seated. "Customers bring us new recipes all the time. Waitresses come up with ideas, too. We try them, and everyone who works here tries them. Sometimes, they work out!"

Although it is the dinner rolls that greet you, and the meat and potatoes that satisfy, and the desserts that send you into orbit, no Indian Trail fan fails to mention the distinctive salad dressings when describing what makes a meal so special. For head lettuce, there is thick beige gorgonzola or ultrafarmy poppyseed; and seafood salads or tomato aspic can be had with pillowy buttermilk dressing, for which Harry Klingeman gave us the recipe. We have reduced and adapted it for home kitchens, and included a recipe for molded tomato salads, on which the buttermilk dressing is just about perfect. (It also makes a great dip for raw vegetables.)

HERBED BUTTERMILK DRESSING

I cup buttermilk
I cup mayonnaise
1½ teaspoons finely chopped parsley
½ teaspoon salt
½ teaspoon dried chives
¼ teaspoon dried oregano
¼ teaspoon dried basil
¼ teaspoon dried tarragon
I clove garlic, finely minced
¼ teaspoon black pepper
1½ teaspoons lemon juice

Combine all ingredients and mix well. Makes I pint. Refrigerate to store.

MOLDED TOMATO SALAD

3½ cups tomato juice
I onion, grated (about ⅓ cup)
2 teaspoons sugar
½ teaspoon celery salt
¼ teaspoon black pepper
I teaspoon vinegar
1½ envelopes unflavored gelatin dissolved in
    ¼ cup water
2 tablespoons lemon juice

Bring all ingredients except gelatin and lemon juice to a simmer for 5 minutes. Remove from heat and immediately add softened gelatin. Stir until clear. Add lemon juice. Pour into 4 lightly oiled I-cup molds. Chill until set. Serve on lettuce leaves with herbed buttermilk dressing. Makes 4 servings.

Indian Trail, 507 Chestnut St., Winnetka, Ill,; (312) 446-1703.

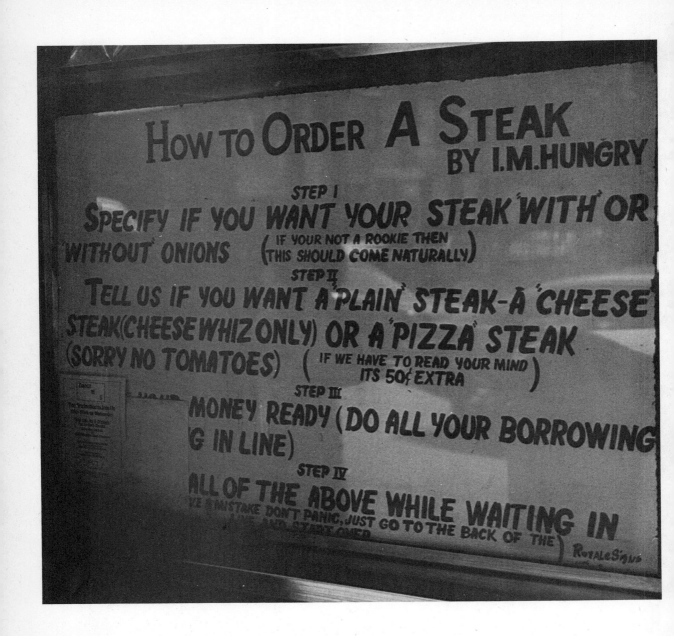

6

Beef, Lamb, and Pork

PLANKED STEAK

To do it right, you need a solid kiln-dried oak plank. Boards specially made for planking food have grooves or a decorative cutout to hold juices. The board should not be painted, lacquered or in any way sullied. A new board must be rubbed with vegetable or olive oil and baked at 225 degrees for one full hour before it is ready to use. If you don't want to bother with wood, a fine planked meal can be made on any oven-proof platter (although plank aficionados claim the wood lends special savor to meat or fish).

Because whitefish is hard to find away from the Great Lakes, our recipe is for planked steak. But the same principles can be applied to any broilable food: trout, chops, etc. No matter what you decide to plank, your choice should be cooked almost completely before getting planked.

1 4-pound steak, about 1½ inches thick
4–5 cups mashed potatoes, seasoned to taste

Planked Steak

HARBOR SPRINGS, Mich.—Of all the distinctly American ways to serve a meal, none is quite so grand as planking it. Everything—main course, potatoes, vegetables—is spread out on a seasoned hardwood board and served together.

Although any entrée can be planked, the method suggests top-of-the-line provender: a heavy, blood-rare porterhouse-for-four or a couple of thick filets of just-caught Great Lakes whitefish look mighty pretty centered on a slab of kiln-dried oak, especially when the board is festooned with bouquets of beans, peas, mushrooms, and stuffed tomatoes, all surrounded by a piped-on wall of duchess potatoes, stout enough to keep the juices shored inside. A meal such as this is one of the glories of American cookery.

At least it used to be. Once a popular way to present a feast, planking has disappeared from the repertoire of most cooks. Cookbooks from seventy-five years ago are filled with ideas for planked dinner, including chicken, lobster with oysters, lamb chops, and shad with creamed roe.

We don't know how the idea got started, and we doubt if it will ever be so popular again; but we do know one fine restaurant where planked whitefish and planked prime rib have been the specialties of the house for more than half a century: Juilleret's of Harbor Springs, Michigan.

2 egg yolks
4 tablespoons butter, melted
1 pound mushrooms, sliced and sautéed in
    butter until tender
cherry tomatoes
parsley

Broil steak on both sides until nearly
done. Remove from broiler.

Make duchess potatoes by beating
mashed potatoes with egg yolks and butter.
Load into pastry tube.

Pipe a wall of potatoes around the edge
of a well-oiled plank or ovenproof platter,
leaving no spaces and trying to leave only
enough room in center for steak. Place
steak in center, and fill moat between steak
and potatoes with sautéed mushrooms and
cherry tomatoes.

Broil until potatoes begin to brown, 4–5
minutes.

Garnish with parsley and serve
immediately directly from plank. Serves 4.

Juilleret's, 130 State, Harbor Springs, Mich.;
(616) 526-2821.

Long before Juilleret's planked its first meal, it was a boat livery
and makeshift ice-cream parlor, the sodas served on a wooden
board set across two sawhorses. No sundaes were served, however,
as they had not yet been invented. Juilleret's opened for business in
1895—two years before the first sundae was made (in Two Rivers,
Wisconsin). After Prohibition was repealed in 1933, Juilleret's
became the restaurant it is today.

What a scene! Noisy, informal, boisterous, it is a summer place,
crowded with vacationing families of every age. Adults holler conversations booth to booth, teenagers stroll through the soda fountain in bunches, babies gurgle and cry. Through the happy
pandemonium, sweet-smelling platters of planked whitefish are
paraded from the kitchen to the tables.

The whitefish planks come in all sizes, for one to ten people.
Succulent, snowy-meat fillets are piled in the center, speckled with
spice, surrounded by the Great Wall of Spuds, strewn with
tomatoes, lemons, and pools of melting butter. A loaf of good hot
bread and a trip to Juilleret's unsurpassed farmland salad bar come
on the side. For dessert, the man behind the soda fountain will set
you up with such nostalgic concoctions as a rainbow thun-
dercloud, a tin roof, or a hand-whipped velvet. All are fashioned
from ice cream and toppings made on the premises.

Juilleret's is a national treasure.

Granny's Beef Stew

COLORADO SPRINGS, Colo.—If we were asked to plan the curriculum at some mythical University of Gastronomic History (UGH for short?), our Department of Hamburgerology would include a full semester's course on the evolution of Conway's Red Top Restaurants in Colorado Springs.

Conway's is the place with the motto that reads "One's a Meal." These colossi are *real* whoppers: half a foot across, served on broad-domed buns, accompanied by shoestring French fries and titanic pitchers of soda.

Their history goes back to 1944, when Norb Conway went to work for a new hamburger joint known as the Red Top. Norb and his wife, Phyllis, took over the business in 1962, employing their ten children, including even those too short to reach the counter, who were stood on boxes so they could reach the sink and wash dishes.

It was a real family operation. Grandma Esther (Phyllis's mom) contributed her recipes for soup, stew, and pie; and as the children grew, Conway's Red Top grew with them. Soon there were three locations in Colorado Springs, each managed by a Conway. Currently ten of the Conways' grandchildren are employed in the family business.

The family nature of the Red Tops is as much a part of their charm as the giant hamburgers. You know when you eat here that it is being run by people with a strong sense of pride in what they are doing. The Red Tops aren't really much more than hamburger shops, with the kind of quick service and low prices one expects, but there is something delightfully old-fashioned about the honest menu, homemade food, and genuine hospitality.

Longtime fans of Conway's remember Norb (who died in 1983) as the soul of the operation, whistling while he cooked, and greeting out-of-state customers by name when they returned each year for their summer in Colorado Springs. "Going to the Red Top," Phyllis reminisces about those good old days, "was like having a family dinner without the work."

Hamburgers are the stars of the show. Panavision-wide but not gourmet-thick, they are happy lunch-counter patties, with enough oily smack to imprint the bun with their savor. They are sold whole or half, topped with regular cheese (Velveeta) or zestier jalapeño cheese, or served as a "Hickory Dickery Top" infused with smoke flavor and smothered with chopped onions and barbecue sauce.

As the motto promises, one is a meal, especially if accompanied by fries and a large soda. But it would be a shame to visit the Red

GRANNY'S BEEF STEW

2 pounds lean stewing beef, cut into large
    chunks
1½ tablespoons flour
2 tablespoons vegetable shortening
2 cups boiling water
1 tablespoon Worcestershire sauce
2 teaspoons garlic powder
1 teaspoon salt
1½ teaspoons pepper
1 large onion, chopped (about 1 cup)
2 to 3 medium potatoes, cut in 1-inch
    squares (2–3 cups)
4 large carrots, quartered lengthwise and
    cut into 1-inch lengths
3 medium tomatoes, peeled and cut bite-
    size
1 cup stewed canned tomatoes

Roll beef in flour. In heavy pot with cover,
melt shortening over medium-high heat and
brown beef, a few pieces at a time, setting
aside browned pieces. When all are richly
browned, return them to pot.

Standing back to avoid the splatters,
pour in boiling water. Add Worcestershire,
garlic powder, salt, and pepper. Lower heat,
cover, simmer 2 to 2½ hours, or until meat
is very tender.

Add onion, potatoes, carrots, and
tomatoes. Cook 30 minutes more, until
potatoes are tender.

May be served immediately, but this stew
tastes best when refrigerated overnight and
reheated.

Makes 6 servings.

Conway's Red Top, 1520 S. Nevada,
Colorado Springs, Colo.; (303) 633-2444.
(Additional locations at 3589 N. Carefree
and 390 N. Circle Drive.)

Top without a taste of the soups and stews that are still made from
Grandma Esther's original recipes. The navy bean soup, for example, is a stout brew with a profound, long-simmered flavor redolent
of hickory-smoked ham and spice. With its accompanying sourdough roll, it is hearty enough to be a filling lunch (with a minuscule price tag).

The beef stew is another classic, hours in the making so all the
juices of the beef and vegetables have a chance to mellow and
blend and soften. There is nothing exotic about our home kitchen
adaptation of Granny's recipe, but if you are looking for the classic,
comfort-food beef stew, this is it.

This Is It Meat Loaf

HOUSTON, Texas—Fifteen years ago, when we first hit the road in search of good things to eat, we used to hear tales about a certain café in Pennsylvania, not far from the turnpike, that served the most delicious meat loaf in the world. Truckers and traveling men sang hosannas when they recalled the loaf's lush texture, its spicy crust, the swirls of mashed potatoes that came alongside, and the warm apple pie that always followed it for dessert. Unfortunately for us, the stories always lacked specific directions to find the great meat loaf café.

We never did come across it. Even today, every time we pass through Pennsylvania, we search the back roads and small towns with a glimmer of hope that one day we will walk into a little roadhouse somewhere near the highway and see a blackboard menu that lists nothing but meat loaf, mashed potatoes, and apple pie.

Meat loaf can do funny things to a person. Although it is a common food, it has an unparalleled capacity to command loyalty and inspire rhapsodic foodlore. At its best, meat loaf can satisfy in a soulful way what no dolled-up food could ever match.

Let us be honest, though: Meat loaf is not always wonderful. If it's all filler, if it's too dry or too fat or gristly gray, it can be a ghastly meal reminiscent of the worst institutional cuisine.

Because it can be (and often is) so bad, there are many people who never order meat loaf in a restaurant. There are others, like ourselves, who always order it, ever optimistic we will hit upon a loaf that measures up to the legend of the one in Pennsylvania we never found.

That is why we were thrilled when Tim Brookover, an infallible guide to Houston good eats, told us about the This Is It Bar and Grill, a down-home restaurant in a down-at-the-heels neighborhood. Tim said that every meal at This Is It is an extraordinary experience—a stroll along a short cafeteria line that always features galaxies of soulful Southern-style vegetables such as collard greens, green beans, squash casseroles, and yams, plus corn bread and hot rolls. For main courses, This Is It makes standards like pot roast, baked chicken, pork chops, and—every Thursday night—meat loaf.

What a fine loaf it is! It's the all-beef (no pork or veal) variety—high-spiced, succulent, and moist, with stick-to-the-ribs pleasure in every bite.

The fun of the loaf is amplified by its surroundings. Despite the collection of beer signs that illuminates the dining room, This Is It is *not* a bar; in fact you can't even get a beer with dinner. Iced tea is

THIS IS IT MEAT LOAF

1 pound ground beef
1/2 pound ground pork
1/2 pound ground veal
2 eggs, beaten
3/4 cup finely chopped onion
1 tablespoon Worcestershire sauce
1 1/2 teaspoons dry mustard
1 teaspoon salt
1/2 teaspoon pepper
1 1/2 cups dry bread crumbs
3/4 cup tomato juice
6 strips bacon
1 8-ounce can tomato sauce

Preheat oven to 350 degrees.

Mix meats, eggs, onion, Worcestershire, mustard, salt, pepper, bread crumbs, and tomato juice together. Mix with hands, "fluffing" loaf rather than compressing it. You want a mixture that you can mold into a bomb-shaped loaf.

Mold into loaf 8–10 inches long, 4 inches high, on shallow casserole or baking dish (with a rim to hold drippings). Cover top with bacon strips, laid on in a diagonal pattern. Pour tomato sauce evenly over loaf. Bake 1 hour and 15 minutes. Bacon, which will have blackened, may be removed if desired before serving.

Serves 6–8.

This Is It Bar and Grill, 239 W. Gray, Houston, Texas; (713) 523-5319.

the house drink, served in jumbo tumblers. Decor is pure funk: sports trophies, a couple of televisions to watch, and a radio blaring.

A meal at This Is It is ridiculously inexpensive; you can hardly spend more than five dollars for a full dinner. The way we see it, the honest price is part of what makes meat loaf such a likable thing to eat.

When we asked the people at This Is It for their meat loaf recipe, we were happy to discover that it is a lot like the loaf that we have evolved over the years. We usually like to lighten it a bit by substituting a half-pound each of ground pork and veal for half the beef. It may not be perfection, but it'll do until we find that place in Pennsylvania.

Max's White Meat Loaf

SAN FRANCISCO—It used to be that a diner was a lowly place to eat. It was known as a greasy spoon, a hash house or—in trucker lingo—a choke and puke. Diners were fluorescent-lit dives where the city's fallen angels went for a cup of mud (coffee) and a sinker (a doughnut); where night hawks and wandering hobos wiled away the wee hours. As for food at diners, it was strictly for the crude of palate—heavy on the starch, grease, and gristle.

You still might find an occasional diner like that if you scour the fringes of cities in the Northeast; we even know of a few rare and treasured back-road diners where they actually serve good food. But mostly, the great authentic diner has vanished from the land.

If you are feeling a twinge of nostalgia for that naughty stainless steel and neon ambience; if you crave to indulge yourself in an evening's entertainment in which the theme is grade-B movie gastronomy, we recommend a trip to San Francisco, where the all-American diner has been reborn.

Max's Diner is a fantasy come to life. It is diner as dinner theater. Although it is not in any way like any real diner you have ever seen, everything about it is meant to evoke nostalgic thoughts of blue-plate specials.

The primary difference between Max's and real diners is the food. Max's food is much better. Indeed, Max's food, although not pretentious, is consistently first class. Turkey (for hot turkey sandwiches with mashed potatoes and cranberry-applesauce, or for turkey dinners with dressing, spuds, and succotash) is cut fresh from an expertly roasted bird. The mashed potatoes are exquisite, served in a volcano shape, with "crater gravy" spilling down the

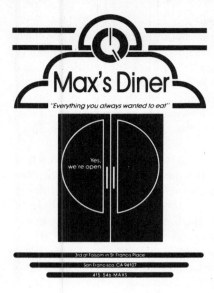

Max's Diner

"Everything you always wanted to eat"

Yes,
we're open

3rd at Folsom in St. Francis Place

San Francisco, CA 94107

415 546 MAXS

MAX'S WHITE MEAT LOAF

1 pound ground white turkey meat (raw)

⅓ pound ground veal

¼ cup minced celery

¼ cup minced onion

¾ cup white bread crumbs

¼ cup milk

1 egg

1 teaspoon salt

½ teaspoon white pepper

1 teaspoon minced garlic (1 large clove)

   Preheat oven to 350 degrees.

   Mix all ingredients well. Form into loaf and set in a 8-by-4-inch loaf pan. Bake 1 hour, 15 minutes.

   Serves 6.

Max's Diner, 311 3rd St., San Francisco, Calif.; (415) 546-6297.

side. There are three kinds of hash (sausage, corned beef, or pastrami-chicken); and you can choose between normal-size hamburgers and basketfuls of little White Castle-style "sliders." For dessert, there is a long list of pastries, cakes, pies, homemade ice creams, and sauces "made in New York," the menu says, "by a certified chocoholic who refuses therapy."

Aside from the good food, Max's differs from real diners in its cleanliness and polite manners. It sparkles. It is big and streamlined, with comfortable booths (and of course a counter, too). Waitresses, in crisp black and white uniforms, do not sport tattoos (at least none are evident) or chew gum or sass the customers.

The dining areas are a veritable museum of pop cuisine, including heroic pictures of diners on the wall, thick white dinner plates plainly labeled MEAT LOAF PLATE, and stacks of Bazooka bubble gum boxes at the takeout counter (meals conclude with a complimentary block of Bazooka for each customer). The menu warns, "We reserve the right to refuse service to anyone using the word *nouvelle*." Checks promise "More Calories for Your Money." And the house motto is "Everything You Always Wanted to Eat."

Max's is fun. It is a spoof, a gustatory game of wish fulfillment, serving 1980s versions of yesterday's square meals.

There are two kinds of meat loaf listed in a section of Max's menu headlined "The Food of the '50s—Ready-to-Serve 'Blue Plates'": regular dark beefy loaf, with mushroom gravy; and all-white loaf, made with turkey and veal. The white one was a treat; and the people at Max's were nice enough to share its recipe. Serve it with mashed potatoes, gravy, and an appropriately sallow vegetable—succotash, canned green beans, or carrot-and-pea combo.

Brisket Roast

SAN DIEGO—Like neighborhood restaurants, grocery stores can be fascinating opportunities to taste a city's personality. Browsing through the aisles of the Fiesta in Houston, or Treasure Island on Chicago's Lake Shore Drive, or Byerly's in Minneapolis, you are savoring the real stuff of American life. In these special places, ordinary groceries are supplemented by regional delicacies (and vast arrays of nonedibles, too) that travelers might never find back home.

One of our favorite cities to go marketing is San Diego, where the old Farmer's Bazaar and the new Irvine Ranch Farmer's Market, both downtown, represent twin poles of grocery-gastronomy.

Located in unrenovated San Diego, surrounded by wholesale fruit and vegetable dealers, the Bazaar is a genuine "mercado," where the produce is sold from individual booths at bargain prices, and the inventory of things to eat is supplemented by miscellany such as souvenir clocks and Latino records (upstairs), even a pool and game room to keep young folks happy while their parents elbow their way through the crowds.

You've got to be fussy when you shop the Bazaar. Feel those melons to find the perfectly ripe one. Sort through the peppers (we counted five separate varieties of chilis for sale) to select those without blemishes. Haggle with the fishmonger in back to get the brightest and freshest red snapper, seemingly large enough to feed all the San Diego Padres.

When you get hungry marketing, head outward to the circumference of the Bazaar, where food stands sell snacks suitable for taking to little indoor picnic tables. The off-the-cuff cuisine isn't only Mexican (although the tacos, hot tamales, and ricewater drinks are swell); it has all the wide-ranging ethnicity you would expect in this port city. Here is Italian food listed on Korean-language menus; Oriental wild rice soup, described on its hand-written sign as topped with heaps of "graded cheese." There are even some ultrahealthful vegetarian drinks made-to-order from carrots, beets, and celery smooshed into a juicer. And those who like weird taste sensations can avail themselves of salted dried plums rolled in hot chili powder.

If all that round-the-world fare is too funky for your palate, head over to the spanking-clean branch of the Irvine Market in the nouvelle mall called Horton Place. Here, too, the inventory is boggling—whole aisles of baby vegetables, four different colors of bell pepper, a bakery (try the chocolate-covered croissants), a cheese room, and a fruit stand featuring hollowed-out pineapples stuffed

BRISKET ROAST

1 brisket roast, 4 to 6 pounds when trimmed
1 can condensed cream of mushroom soup
1 package dry onion soup mix

Preheat oven to 325 degrees. Using three to four layers of heavy-duty aluminum foil, securely wrap the roast, spreading the condensed soup and dry soup over its surface before sealing the foil. Seal it very well, and neatly—you will want to unwrap it later and save the juice inside.

Bake 45 minutes per pound.

Unwrap roast, being careful to save all the gravy. Transfer meat to serving dish. Pour gravy into gravy boat.

Slice brisket against the grain. Top slices with gravy from inside the foil.

Serves 6–8

Irvine Ranch Farmer's Market, Horton Plaza, San Diego, Calif.; (619) 696-7766.

Farmer's Bazaar, 205 7th Ave., San Diego, Calif.

with chunks of melon and ripe berries.

If prices at the Irvine Market seem higher than at the Farmer's Bazaar, it's because Irvine's food is all flawless. Not a bruise will you find on the apples or avocados. The butcher case, filled with everything from T-bone steaks to English bangers, is so impeccably neat that you're almost afraid to select anything, lest you disturb the beautifully symmetrical display.

Since we were passing through (and therefore kitchenless) the last time we shopped, we contented ourselves merely to browse, sipping just-pressed coconut-pineapple drinks and snatching handfuls of recipe cards that the butcher gives away. Among our prizes was this Irvine Market oh-so-easy recipe for fall-apart-tender brisket roast.

Creole Daube

NEW ORLEANS—Casamento's, a favorite local oyster bar for more than fifty years, closes every year between June and September; and it closes each afternoon between 1:30 and 5:30. When it is open, there's hardly any room for customers. It is tiny, two small dining rooms with maybe a few dozen chairs, plus room for a couple of stand-up oyster eaters at the bar.

Floors and counters are decorated with lovely flower and scroll tiles like a pretty—but modest—home kitchen. The oyster bar is worn from years of use.

The menu is small and uninventive. Most people come to eat raw or fried oysters, fish or shrimp, spaghetti and meatballs, or soft-shell crabs in the spring.

What a simple place! And yet, despite its modesty, Casamento's is one of the great New Orleans restaurants.

When Joe Casamento built it in 1919, he had been in America only three years. He heardly spoke English. Magazine Street was an unpaved dirt road. Oysters on the half shell sold for fifteen cents a dozen.

Mr. Casamento died in 1979, but his son-in-law, Vernon Gerdes, maintains the family feeling and honest menu that has made Casamento's a landmark of Creole cooking.

The most famous dish in the house is an oyster loaf. It's like a po'boy sandwich—New Orleans's version of a hero, sub, grinder, hoagie—but even bigger. To make an oyster loaf, first they fry the oysters. And let us tell you, you have never tasted an oyster quite so delicious, so briny-sweet, so crackle-crusted. When we asked Mr. Gerdes what made them special, he told us that the method was

CREOLE DAUBE

6 garlic cloves
½ cup water
1 cup chopped onions
2 cups whole tomatoes
1 cup tomato paste
1 cup tomato sauce
1 teaspoon ground black pepper
1 tablespoon salt
2–3 pounds boneless chuck roast
⅓ cup sugar
12–14 ounces spaghetti
olive oil

Place garlic in blender with water. Blend until thoroughly pulverized. Add onions and tomatoes, and blend. Add tomato paste and sauce, pepper, and salt. Pour into a pan large enough to hold the roast.

Bring to boil and reduce heat to low simmer. Add roast. Cover. Simmer 3½ hours, stirring every half hour to keep roast from scorching on bottom.

Remove roast. Add sugar to sauce in pan and simmer another half hour.

Boil spaghetti in salted water until tender. Drain and add enough olive oil to keep it from being sticky.

Arrange spaghetti on a plate, top with slices of roast, then top roast with gravy. Serves 4 to 6.

Casamento's, 4330 Magazine, New Orleans, La.; (504) 895-9761.

"too simple to call a recipe." The oysters are freshly shucked, dipped in corn flour, then dropped into open iron pots of pure lard. "Everything is fried by feel and sound," he said. "It requires a lot of personal attention and experience."

The fried oysters are then loaded into an entire loaf of bread. It is unsliced white, cut lengthwise, scooped out and toasted, its bland, yeasty tenderness a perfect foil for the sharp oceanic bite of the oysters. It is a feast for two.

In addition to its exalted reputation for oysters and other Gulf seafood, Casamento's is a reminder of the strong Italian influence in Creole cookery. Many customers come for spaghetti, or a fascinating sweet-and-savory dish that has had a definitive influence on the taste of Creole cooking—the meat and gravy known as *daube*.

The recipe Mr. Gerdes gave us is just as his father-in-law Joe Casamento made it since he came from Ustica, Italy, in 1916. We have reduced the proportions for home kitchens.

Chimichangas

TUCSON, Ariz.—There is scarcely room on the plate for the beans, guacamole, and sour cream around this behemoth chimichanga, venting wisps of cumin-scented steam. It is a blimp, the ultimate customized burrito, specialty of the house at El Charro, America's oldest Mexican restaurant.

Chimichangas, or "chimis," as they are known by their close friends, were invented in Tucson in the 1950s. They have since become popular all across the United States.

Out-of-state versions can be good. But like Kentucky fried chicken and New York cheesecake, they are never quite as good as the real thing, enjoyed in its natural habitat. Arizona chimichangas—Tucson chimis in particular—are majestic: jumbo flour tortillas fried around a pocket of superior fillings that range from chili meat and chicken to "frijoles con queso" (beans and cheese) and "chorizo y huevo" (sausage and egg).

South of the border you might find a "chivichanga," which is a fried burrito; but it will likely be a modest little roll-up. A true chimichanga is a hefty dude, a burrito elegante. Born in Arizona, it isn't really Mexican at all. The chimichanga, which roughly translates as thingamabob, is second cousin, once removed, of true Mexican food.

In fact, most of what we gringos enjoy as Mexican food isn't purely Mexican. It is a hybrid from both sides of the border: Tex-

CHIMICHANGAS

2 cloves garlic, minced

2 medium onions, diced

2 tomatoes, diced

1 teaspoon ground cumin

1 tablespoon vegetable oil

2 cups cooked chicken, shredded

1 4-ounce can mild green chilies (peeled, chopped, and seeded)

1 teaspoon salt

8–10 flour tortillas

1½ cups Monterey Jack or sharp cheddar cheese, grated

vegetable shortening for frying

Combine garlic, onion, tomato, and cumin in bowl.

Heat 1 tablespoon vegetable oil in frying pan, add tomato mixture, and cook over medium heat for 3 minutes. Lower heat and simmer 7 minutes more, uncovered. Strain off any liquid and combine tomato mixture with chicken, chilies, and salt.

If your tortillas are not fresh and pliable, sandwich them two or three at a time within a well-wrung-out, damp dish towel in a warm oven to steam for one minute.

In the center of each tortilla, place two heaping tablespoons of chicken mix, topped with a heaping tablespoon of cheese. Fold one side of tortilla to cover filling; fold in adjacent sides, then the final flap. If it doesn't hold together, secure it with a toothpick.

Mex from cowboy country; or New Mexican-Mex (that's the fire-hot stuff); or Arizona/California-Mex. The cuisine of Tucson is derived from the relatively mild food of Sonora, due south. It is based on wafer-thin tortillas, oozy cheese, shredded chicken, and "carne seca" (dried beef).

Other than their chimichangas, Tucson's Mexican restaurants are known for magnificent tostadas—a.k.a. Mexican pizzas. Each disk is a husky corn tortilla, baked to a fragrant crisp, its broad surface a mottled field of patches that are alternately brittle and soft. Tostadas are topped with a sprinkle of ingredients: chili or guacamole or cheese. They are served on a tall pedestal, ashy cornmeal edges extending beyond the circumference of the platter.

Our favorite place in town to eat tostadas and chimichangas is El Charro, a whitewashed cottage in El Presidio, Tucson's historic district.

When Monica Flinn opened El Charro in 1922, Arizona had been a state only ten years. Her legacy is continued today by Carlotta Flores, Mrs. Flinn's niece, who told us that in the early days when a customer walked in, Monica took the order, then rushed to a nearby grocery store to buy ingredients, returning through a back door to the kitchen to cook the meal.

It is still an extremely personal operation, with a porch for outdoor dining, hung with plants and pottery. The inside is packed with souvenirs and Mexican artifacts. Nice stuff, but what grabs the eye is the dining room, which is decorated entirely—wall to wall, floor to ceiling—with El Charro calendars dating back to 1946.

These calendars are not merely ways to tell what day it is. Each is a four-color rendering that looks like a frozen frame from a daytime soap opera written by Cheech and Chong and cast with body builders dressed in loincloths. Sun gods with bulging muscles carry swooning damsels to the tops of ancient pyramids. Bathing maidens and their horses frolic by a stream. Caballeros ride into the sun. Spurned lovers weep. The pictures are almost as dramatic as El Charro's stunning plates of food.

Heat 1½ inches of vegetable shortening to 350 degrees in skillet. Place chimichangas flap-side down and fry until golden brown. Turn, and fry other side. Drain on paper towels and place in low oven to keep warm until all are done.

Serve garnished with chili sauce, surrounded by sour cream, guacamole, lettuce, and tomato.

Yield: 8–10 chimichangas, to serve 4–6.

El Charro, 311 N. Court Ave., Tucson, Ariz.; (602) 622-5465.

Sour Cream Enchiladas Coloradas

MESILLA VILLAGE, N.M.—Four-by-four inches wide and a couple inches high, the sopaipillas at La Posta look overinflated. The outsides of these quick-cooked bread pillows are brittle crisp. Their insides are webbed mazes of gossamer dough. They come with a pitcher of honey. Tear off a crusty ribbon and pour a blob inside as floury vapors escape. Then get the steamy pouf to your mouth before the honey oozes off in your lap.

Sopaipillas are the traditional breadstuff that come with most native New Mexico meals—which is one reason we think this state is one heck of a fine place to eat. Every time we visit, its restaurants take our breath away. Of all America's diverse regional cuisines, New Mexican is probably the most exotic, and along with Cajun cookery, the most sharply defined. (It is certainly the spiciest!) As for sopaipillas, there are good ones—featherweight, crisp, hot out of the fry kettle; and there are gross ones. Some of the best are served at La Posta.

The setting for these A-1 sopaipillas, and other excellent native feasts, is stunningly Southwestern. The village of Mesilla dates back to the 1500s, when Coronado and Juan de Oñate made it a way station on their expeditions up from Mexico. After the war of 1845, its allegiance wavered as the shallow Rio Grande (the border between the United States and Mexico) shifted course many times, putting it on both sides of the line of demarcation.

The Rio Grande conclusively maneuvered to the west in the 1850s, making Mesilla *New* Mexican. It then became a layover on the overland mail route. That is when La Posta was built as a stagecoach stop. After the Civil War (when Mesilla served as the Confederate capital of the Territory of Arizona), the town became a haunt for frontier characters such as Billy the Kid, Kit Carson, and Judge Roy Bean.

Today, Mesilla is a state monument, preserved as it was a century ago. Adobe homes and shops surround the plaza where the Gadsden Treaty (annexing New Mexico) was signed in 1853. It is a favorite destination for travelers, who come to buy turquoise jewelry and souvenirs, and to eat the good food at La Posta.

The restaurant's lobby is a boisterous place, especially if the parrot in the cage near the tank of pirañas happens to be in a conversational mood. Eating here is an informal affair. The restaurant is fun for families, its tables topped with red vinyl cloths that are easy to wipe clean when you drip hot sauce or honey. Thick adobe walls give La Posta a cool, secluded atmosphere, even on a hot summer day.

SOUR CREAM ENCHILADAS COLORADAS

½ cup vegetable oil

12 corn tortillas

2–3 cups enchilada sauce (hot or mild, to taste)

2½ cups grated sharp cheese

½ cup chopped onion

4 eggs, fried sunny-side up (optional)

1 cup sour cream

shredded lettuce as garnish

Heat oil in skillet and fry tortillas one by one, cooking only long enough to soften them, about 15 seconds. (Do not fry crisp.) Drain. Quickly dip each tortilla in red sauce, place on serving plate, then sprinkle with cheese and onion. Continue in layer-cake style, until each plate is topped with three tortillas and three layers of cheese and onion. Top with extra sauce, if desired. Dollop sour cream on the side. Crown each stack with a fried egg, if desired. Serve garnished with lettuce.

Serves 4.

La Posta, Mesilla Village, N.M.; (505) 524-3524.

The food is authentic: rich guacamole, chunky with avocados; chilies rellenos stuffed with cream cheese and fried golden brown; tacos filled with finely seasoned beef; enchiladas with the savor of freshly fried corn tortillas and sauce made with native chili peppers. And, of course, the super sopaipillas.

La Posta's recipes are simple classics of the New Mexican kitchen. Their excellence depends on the quality of ingredients. These enchiladas with red sauce (that's what "coloradas" means) can be made with any tortillas and sauce; but if you make your own, or buy the best in a specialty store, they soar.

Indonesian Lamb Roast

SAN FRANCISCO—We love every Trader Vic's we have ever been to. Some are better than others; some serve food that isn't terrific; but the *idea* of Trader Vic's—the concept—never fails to be fun.

Among trend-following gourmets, "the Trader," with his Polynesian cuisine and baroque rum potations, is considered hopelessly unchic. There are few restaurants anywhere further from the cutting edge of modern gastronomy.

Indeed, that is one reason Trader Vic's fans enjoy the place so much: It is old reliable. You know what to expect when you walk past the Tiki god faces at the entryway: a nice, relaxing pu-pu platter, then specialties such as lamb curry with yogurt or Chinese oven-baked chicken. However strange or foreign it may sound, a Trader Vic's meal will never be furiously spiced or totally unfamiliar. In their translation from the original Tahitian, Hawaiian, or Chinese, the Trader's dishes are always neutered of their danger, tempered to suit meat-and-potatoes palates.

The atmosphere is reassuring, too. The Pacific isle theme, including bamboo chairs, colored lights, fishnet wall hangings, and occasional faraway thumping drums on the house sound system, is like an old Hollywood movie: corny, unreal, unabashed.

We especially like to visit Trader Vic's when we are weary at the end of a hard day. That is when those tall, bright rum drinks look good, and when the kitchen's tamed exotica tastes especially soothing. And then the Muzak-like drums and decor help lull one into uncaring bliss.

Remember: We are not saying that all the food at every Trader Vic's is delicious. To be honest, we have had some less-than-wonderful things to eat at a few of the branches.

That is why we are writing this column: to alert travelers to the extraordinary excellence of the Trader Vic's in San Francisco. It is

INDONESIAN LAMB ROAST

1/3 cup celery, finely chopped
1/3 cup onion, finely chopped
1 clove garlic, minced
3/4 cup peanut oil
1/4 cup red wine vinegar
2 teaspoons A-1 Steak Sauce
2 dashes Tabasco sauce
3 tablespoons honey
1 teaspoon dried oregano
3 tablespoons curry powder
2 bay leaves
1/2 cup Dijon mustard
juice and rind of 1 large lemon
12 loin lamb chops or 2 racks, trimmed of
    fat

Sauté celery, onions, and garlic in oil. Add all other ingredients except lamb. Simmer briefly. Chill.

Marinate meat in mixture 4 hours in refrigerator. Preheat oven to 400 degrees. Drain meat but reserve marinade. Wrap bones with foil, leaving meat exposed. Arrange in greased, shallow baking pan. Brush meat with marinade. Bake 10–15 minutes for rare chops, 20–30 minutes for racks. Turn once and baste frequently while cooking. To crisp meat, finish under broiler 1–2 minutes.

Serves 4–6.

Trader Vic's, 20 Cosmo Place, San Francisco, Calif.; (415) 776-2232.

the flagship of the chain, across the bay from the original, which opened in 1934 in Oakland as a beer joint named Hinky Dink's. There is nothing obviously different about the San Francisco branch. The menu is the same hodgepodge of recipes borrowed from around the world; the decor is like a scene from a Cecil B. De Mille adventure movie.

But this Trader Vic's stands out for two reasons. First, it is swanky. The clientele who are honored with a table in the clubby Captain's Cabin dining room are not tourists; they are old-money San Francisco. The service is as suave as you'll find in any Continental restaurant.

Second, the food is prepared by experts. It is good enough to remind you that Trader Vic Bergeron really was an innovative culinary adventurer in his day, gathering recipes from exotic lands and introducing them to America. Since then, the reputation of Polynesian food has sunk out of sight. No food critic takes it seriously. At Trader Vic's in San Francisco, however, it is still a pretty wonderful thing to eat. Try this Trader Vic's recipe for lamb roast, and see if you don't agree.

Ham-Stuffed Apples

DAHLONEGA, Ga.—Tongues are shocked by a first taste of country ham. Nothing like the mild pink oval in a supermarket can, country ham is brick-red, momentously salty, packed with flavor. A top-quality ham is so fine-grained it appears dry, but when a knife glides through, peeling off a parchment-thin slice, it beads with moisture.

Genuine country hams are hung in burlap and packed with salt for months. The older and moldier they get, the more they are prized by connoisseurs, who relish the gamy character that blooms as the salt seeps in and cures the meat.

The wallop of country ham explains why so many Southern ham recipes highlight, and at the same time s-t-r-e-t-c-h, the flavor. Ham biscuits, stuffed with ham cut into translucent scarlet sheaves, muffle the salinity between fluffy pastry pillows made from soft winter wheat.

Southern cooks know to complement the sting of their ham with sweet side dishes: a mound of buttered crabmeat fresh from the Virginia shore, kernel-dotted corncakes, fried apples, candied yams. One of the best things to do with whole hams is to baste them with Coca-Cola as they bake. "You need two bottles at the stove," a lady from Mobile told us, "one for the ham, one for the

HAM-STUFFED APPLES

4 large baking apples, unpeeled
I cup baked ham, diced (either country
    ham or canned cooked ham)
¼ cup raisins
¼ cup chopped pecans
2 tablespoons white sugar
2 tablespoons butter, melted

GLAZE:
4 tablespoons water
4 tablespoons dark brown sugar
I teaspoon dry mustard
I teaspoon cider vinegar
I teaspoon cornstarch
⅛ teaspoon ground cloves

Preheat oven to 350 degrees.
Scoop out apples, leaving the shell
approximately ⅓-inch thick to hold stuffing.
Coarsely chop the apple you have scooped
out, removing any seeds or core.
Wrap apples halfway up with a piece of
aluminum foil, crumpling and shaping foil
to fit close to skin.
Mix I cup of the chopped apple with
ham, raisins, pecans, sugar, and butter. Fill
apple cavities with stuffing. Place apples in
uncovered baking dish.
Mix all glaze ingredients in a small
saucepan. Bring to boil, stirring. Remove
from heat. Spoon glaze over apples.
Bakes 45 minutes. Gently remove foil
wrappers.
Serves 4.

Smith House, 202 S. Chestatee,
Dahlonega, Ga.; (404) 864-3566.

cook." After hours of steady basting, the ham emerges from the oven with a dazzling mahogany glaze over meat that glows with cola-nut sweetness.

Few ham-centered meals have so distinctly Southern a flavor as ham-stuffed apples: pink chunks mixed with raisins, pecans, and butter-sopped brown sugar, the whole luscious mess packed inside a baked apple underneath a clove-mustard glaze. We discovered this hearty delicacy at a hotel called the Smith House, in Dahlonega, Georgia—a beacon for travelers who like to eat in a big way.

You cannot make a dinner reservation at the Smith House; service is strictly first-come, first-served. On weekends, the place is packed. What an elbow-to-elbow celebration of good food! Tables are communal, shared by families, local folks, and strangers. The basic act of eating is turned into a party, with everybody passing platters back and forth, chattering happily about the unbelievably delicious food.

Pay one price and eat your fill. There is no menu to look at; there are no choices to make. Everything the kitchen has prepared that day is brought to the table in large serving dishes. Count on fried chicken, supplemented by Brunswick stew or catfish and hush puppies; plenty of Southern-style vegetables, including brandied chestnut soufflé, turnip greens, and fried okra; and always warm breads: cracklin' corn bread, blueberry lemon muffins, angel biscuits. The food keeps coming until all have had their fill.

This unique establishment goes back to Georgia's gold rush, which attracted prospectors from all over America. One was an already-wealthy Vermonter named Captain Frank Hall, who staked a claim just east of the public square . . . and struck a fabulously rich lode.

Dahlonega authorities, so the legend goes, would not allow their town's heart to be stripped open. The ornery Yankee declared that if he couldn't have his pay dirt, neither would anybody else. So he promptly built an ostentatious mansion, complete with carriage house and servants' quarters, smack on top of the vein.

In 1922, long after Captain Hall's feud with Dahlonega ended, Henry and Bessie Smith bought the house to run it as an inn, where for $1.50, travelers got a room and three square meals a day. Mrs. Smith was a sensational cook, and word spread fast about her fried chicken, country ham, and platters of fresh vegetables. By 1946, when Fred and Thelma Welch took over the kitchen, the Smith House was known for its family-style feeds.

Forty years later, the rooms have been modernized, but the food on the tables in the dining room is old-fashioned north Georgia cooking, just like it's always been. To our knowledge, nobody has yet mined Captain Hall's gold.

Stuffed Cabbage

INDIANAPOLIS—Funny, Shapiro's doesn't *look* Jewish—at least not like the familiar Jewish delicatessens in New York or Miami or Los Angeles. It looks like a modern, Midwestern, cafeteria-style restaurant, with ample parking outside and a spacious interior dining room with plastic chairs and Formica tables. Instead of the platoon of crabby old Jewish men who traditionally staff deli counters in the East, the servers here are a heterogeneous group of men and women—some young, some black, some rather pleasant.

If we hadn't been tipped off by passionate Shapiro's fans from around the country, we might have driven right past. They told us that despite Shapiro's modernization into a somewhat anonymous-looking eatery, it is still the finest delicatessen in town, and one of the best in the Midwest.

Perhaps even those superlatives are understatements. We would

STUFFED CABBAGE

2 medium-size heads cabbage

1 pound lean ground chuck

1/2 cup finely chopped onion

1 rib celery, finely chopped

1 egg, beaten

3 slices white bread soaked in 1/3 cup red wine

1/4 cup tomato juice

1 cup cooked rice

1 teaspoon salt

1/2 teaspoon black pepper

2 cups stewed tomatoes

1/2 cup tomato purée

I cup water
½ cup brown sugar
juice of I lemon
6 gingersnap cookies (about 2 inches in
    diameter)
½ cup golden raisins

Core cabbage and blanch in a large pot
of boiling water until leaves begin to loosen.

Combine ground chuck, onion, celery,
and egg. Mix in wet bread (bare hands are
the best tools for this). Add tomato juice
and rice, salt, and pepper.

Carefully peel off cabbage leaves and roll
each around 1–2 tablespoons of the meat
mixture, tucking in the sides so it holds
together. Repeat until all the beef is
wrapped. (There should be 18–20 packets.)
Chop remaining cabbage leaves and reserve
4 cups' worth.

Prepare sauce: In a large stock pot, heat
stewed tomatoes, purée, water, brown
sugar, and lemon juice. Crumble
gingersnaps and stir into mixture. Stir in
raisins and chopped cabbage leaves. (Taste;
add salt and pepper if desired.) Carefully
add stuffed cabbage packets to sauce.
Cover well and cook over medium-low heat
I hour, 15 minutes. Check occasionally and
add ¼–½ cup tomato juice to sauce if it
seems to be drying out.

Serves 6.

Shapiro's, 808 S. Meridian St., Indianapolis,
Ind.; (317) 631-4041.

stack Shapiro's corned beef sandwich against any corned beef
sandwich, anywhere. The meat is lean but not too lean—succulent
enough so each rosy slice, rimmed with a thin halo of smudgy
spice, glistens underneath the fluorescent lights of the dining
room. Butter-tender slices are piled high and heavy inside slabs of
rye bread that has a shiny, hard, sour crust and a tan interior redolent of yeast and rye flour richness. Slather on the mustard, crunch
into a dill pickle to set your tastebuds tingling, and this sandwich
will take you straight to deli heaven.

Get some *latkes* (potato pancakes), too. They are double-thick,
lush, and starchy: great companions to a hot lunch of short ribs or
stuffed peppers. And soup: Bean, lentil, split pea, and chowder are
daily specials. You can always order chicken soup with rice or with
matzoh balls. Then there is dessert—preferably a slice of cheesecake with a cup of coffee.

When we asked Brian Shapiro (great-grandson of founder
Louis Shapiro) for a recipe, he suggested a customer favorite,
stuffed cabbage. We have reduced his recipe for 120 to home portions, and adapted it to home kitchens. There are many ingredients and it takes some time, but it is a classic palate-pleaser of the
Jewish kitchen. Don't forget the gingersnap cookies—they are
what make stuffed cabbage so distinctive!

Salt Pork and Milk Gravy

BERLIN, Vt.—The Wayside Restaurant is as pure and true a taste of Vermont as we have ever found on one menu.

When you drive past the Wayside on Route 302 just south of Montpelier, it does not appear to be anything special: a plain brick rectangle, mustard-yellow, surrounded by a parking lot, with an American flag flying high on a pole out front.

Inside it's modern and comfortable—a wide, wood-paneled café with easy listenin' on the radio and a couple of counters and rows of booths bustling with locals.

There is nothing precious about the menu; the kitchen isn't trying to prove its regional character to anyone. In fact, it is entirely possible to come for a hamburger or a BLT or a plate of scrambled eggs. Of course, those are not the meals that have endeared the Wayside Restaurant to us.

Instead, we recommend dishes such as milk oyster stew or fish chowder, oven-broiled haddock or fresh native perch, hot blueberry muffins or pancakes with real maple syrup. This is maple country, and so it is not surprising to find an ice cream sundae dripping with amber syrup or—our favorite dessert—a slice of maple cream pie in which a toffee-thick layer of maple filling is topped with a lightweight ribbon of whipped cream.

Most days, the kitchen offers hash. On occasion it is red flannel hash, made from a traditional New England boiled dinner of corned beef, potatoes, carrots, and beets (whose juices dye it the color of a farmer's long johns). It is served mounded high in a boat-shaped dish—a damp mass of stick-to-the-ribs, north-country comfort food. On the side you get a basketful of freshly baked dinner rolls.

Just as hash is a parsimonious way of stretching yesterday's dinner into today, so "American chop suey" is another favorite Yankee way of getting the most out of one's larder—by combining ground beef with macaroni and tomato sauce, turning it into a one-dish meal. On the Wayside menu, this dowdy dinner is known as the "Vermont Special."

The most old-fashioned dish of all offered by the Wayside kitchen is a plate of salt pork and milk gravy. Like hash and American chop suey, it is a meal reminiscent of frugal farmhouse cookery.

You see, way back when, most farm cellars held a pork barrel in which slabs of salt pork were kept in brine. The pork (or occasionally the brine itself) was used to season stews, vegetables, chowders, and main courses of beef or venison. But on those occasions when there was no meat, no vegetables, nothing from which to construct a chowder, inventive Yankee cooks figured out ways to turn the salt pork itself into a satisfying meal.

We've *never* seen salt pork and milk gravy served in any other restaurant. It is some trouble to make; and most customers, we reckon, wouldn't recognize salt pork as a fitting main course. But in this part of Vermont, there are enough old-timers around to know just how delicious it can be; and so it is on the menu of the Wayside Restaurant once a week.

SALT PORK AND MILK GRAVY

²/₃ pound slab of salt pork
2 tablespoons butter
¼ cup yellow cornmeal
¼ cup plus 2 tablespoons flour
1 cup cream
½ cup milk
pepper to taste

Slice pork into pieces slightly less than ½-inch thick. Place in skillet full of water. Bring to boil and simmer 3 to 5 minutes. Drain. Rinse salt pork in cold water. Pat dry.

Over medium heat, melt butter in large skillet.

Combine cornmeal and ¼ cup flour. Dip slices of salt pork in mixture, then fry in butter. Use tongs to turn slices often as they fry, cooking 6 to 8 minutes until they are brittle crisp and golden-brown. Remove from skillet and drain on paper towels.

Remove all but 2 to 3 tablespoons of fat from skillet. Over medium heat, gradually sprinkle in remaining flour, stirring constantly, scraping bottom of skillet as you stir. When smooth, slowly stir in cream and milk. Lower heat. Cook and stir 5 minutes, until thick and smooth. Add pepper to taste.

To serve, spoon gravy over salt pork.

Makes 4 servings.

Wayside Restaurant, Route 302 (Barre-Montpelier Road), Berlin, Vt.; (802) 223-6611.

7

Fish

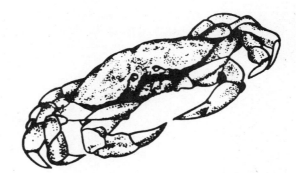

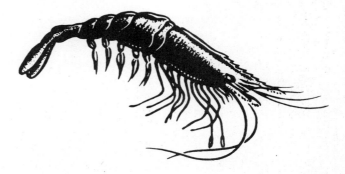

FOURTH OF JULY SALMON

I 4–6 pound salmon, cleaned and dressed
I teaspoon salt
I lemon, sliced thin

Preheat oven to 425 degrees.

Rinse fish in cold water and pat dry. Salt the inside cavity, then insert about half the lemon slices.

Wrap salmon with remaining lemon slices in 2–3 layers of aluminum foil. Secure foil well, but leave some room around the fish inside. Your goal is to allow the fish to cook in its natural juices, while keeping those juices inside.

Place fish on a baking pan with a rim (to catch stray leaks). Bakes 45 minutes.

When removing the fish from the oven, carefully unwrap it, taking care not to let it fall to pieces. Gently roll it onto its serving platter.

To carve, make an incision down the center. Peel back the skin. Cut downward from the top side, then slide the knife underneath and gingerly ease each section to be served from the bones. Use a large spoon and fork to keep the pieces intact as you lift them.

Fourth of July Salmon

OGUNQUIT, Maine—When America was young, New England's rivers swarmed with salmon that swam upstream to spawn each summer. The event was cause for celebration, in the form of an early harvest that climaxed on the Fourth of July.

Potatoes, planted on St. Patrick's Day, were small and tender by midsummer; young peas were ready to be shelled; strawberries were beginning to ripen on the bush. These became the ingredients for an Independence Day banquet that was popular throughout New England: salmon in egg sauce, green peas, buttered new potatoes, and strawberry shortcake.

This seasonal feast has become rare in modern times, except in tradition-conscious private homes and at a few venerable restaurants, such as Boston's Union Oyster House and the Ogunquit Lobster Pound in Maine. When it comes to Independence Day eating, most people think of frankfurters. Far be it from us to impugn the all-American hot dog. But don't you think it is an inspired idea to honor history by rediscovering the joys of this patriotic meal?

The customary method is to poach or steam the salmon. It is also possible to grill salmon steaks over an open fire; or as we

EGG SAUCE

4 tablespoons butter

4 tablespoons flour

2 cups hot milk

2 hard-boiled eggs, coarsely chopped

1 tablespoon capers

Salt and pepper to taste

3 tablespoons chopped parsley

Melt butter in saucepan over low heat; blend in flour, stirring constantly, 4–5 minutes until it bubbles slightly. Gradually add milk, stirring until sauce thickens. Let simmer one minute. Add chopped eggs, capers, and seasoning to taste, then parsley. Pour over individual servings of salmon.

Serves 6.

Ogunquit Lobster Pound, Route 1, Ogunquit, Maine; (207) 646-2516.

suggest below, to bake the whole fish. The topping should be a simple white sauce enriched with hard-boiled eggs. Strawberry shortcake—served on a biscuit, not sweet cake—makes the meal a classic.

If you happen to be traveling through Maine in the summer, you can enjoy this meal at the Ogunquit Lobster Pound north of Ogunquit Center. The Pound is an enchanting place to eat salmon, whole lobster, lobster stew, and fresh berry pies and tarts. There is a gracious indoor dining room with a big fireplace and rough-hewn beams; and there are picnic tables outside in a grove of mature pine trees. Pick your own lobster from the pound; and while away the wait in a lazy swing-for-two hanging from a tall branch.

If you want to make Fourth of July Salmon the historic way, you need a fish poacher or large roasting pan with a rack. Make a court-bouillon by simmering 3–4 quarts of water with chopped onion, peppercorns, an aromatic *bouquet garni* of cloves and bay leaves, and a couple of cups of white wine. Poach the fish in this stock about 6–8 minutes per pound. The oven-baked method we suggest is less authentic . . . and much less fuss.

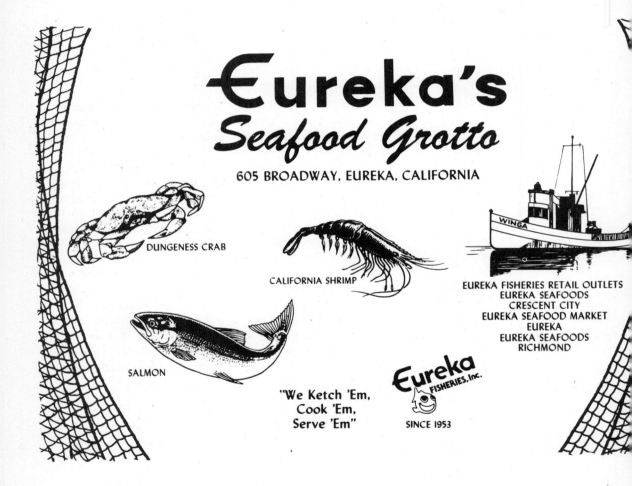

Eureka's
Seafood Grotto

605 BROADWAY, EUREKA, CALIFORNIA

DUNGENESS CRAB

CALIFORNIA SHRIMP

SALMON

EUREKA FISHERIES RETAIL OUTLETS
EUREKA SEAFOODS
CRESCENT CITY
EUREKA SEAFOOD MARKET
EUREKA
EUREKA SEAFOODS
RICHMOND

"We Ketch 'Em,
Cook 'Em,
Serve 'Em"

Eureka
FISHERIES, Inc.

SINCE 1953

BARBECUED SALMON

2 pounds salmon steaks, ¾-inch thick

¼ cup soy sauce

¼ cup teriyaki sauce

¼ cup white wine

1 tablespoon sugar

3 tablespoons peanut oil

2 cloves garlic, pressed

1 teaspon ground ginger

¼ teaspoon onion powder

½ teaspoon ground black pepper

Combine all ingredients in shallow pan and marinate salmon steaks for at least 30 minutes.

If broiling steaks, place on rack 6 inches from heat source. Broil 5 minutes. Baste with marinade, turn, broil 4–5 minutes more. If using outdoor grill, brush grill with oil so steaks don't stick, and broil 4–6 minutes per side, using marinade to baste.

Serves 4.

Seafood Grotto, 605 Broadway, Eureka, Calif.; (707) 443-2075.

Barbecued Salmon

EUREKA, Calif.—WE KETCH 'EM, COOK 'EM, SERVE 'EM, brags the sign outside the Seafood Grotto. This restaurant on the coast of northern California is owned by Eureka Fisheries, the biggest processor of seafood (except for tuna) in the West—about forty million pounds of fish per year. Behind the dining room they also operate one heck of a retail fish market, which sells a harvest of Northwest seafood that includes ready-to-eat hunks of smoked salmon and albacore tuna, as well as whole and picked crab, cod and cod ckeeks. Up front, near the cash register, exotic fish (strictly decoration) swim in a large aquarium.

If you suspect that the Seafood Grotto is a good place to eat seafood, you are right. However, what we like even more than its cuisine is its informality. It is an honest kind of place. You wouldn't call it picturesque. Tables are set with disposable placemats and paper napkins. The menu is plastic-laminated. The china is heavy duty, and your thick coffee cup will be filled as soon as you hit your seat. Waitresses, clad in black nylon café uniforms and orthopedic-soled shoes, are fast and ingratiatingly fresh. Get a window seat, and the view outside is of trucks rumbling past on Broadway.

There is nothing romantic about a meal here. It makes us think of dining in the company cafeteria (of a fish-packing firm). Prices are low (under five dollars for lunch, about ten dollars for dinner); and although the variety of seafood available is vast, the kitchen has no epicurean aspirations. At noon, most customers come for a cup of chowder or bowl of cole slaw and a quick plate of clams or oysters or fillet of rockfish or grilled rex sole, then it's back to work—probably at a job in some way related to the town's fishing business.

The chowder is Northwest style—thick, creamy, and abundantly clammy. It is sold by the cup, bowl, large bowl (a satisfying meal), and by the pint or quart (to go). On the Formica table you will find a bowl full of garlic croutons, which are nice to sprinkle on top.

Heading the long roster of local seafood is Dungeness crab, served in big, creamy-white chunks on a bed of ice or mixed with dressing into a giant-size crab Louie (or combination shrimp and crab Louie). You can get hefty Pacific oysters, too—chilled, grilled, or deep-fried.

Among local flatfish, the Grotto lists the delicate little sweeties known as sand dabs, rex and petrale sole, broiled salmon steaks or fillets. Most are available with wine sauce or egg sauce, but what we remember most fondly is a simple and unadorned slab of petrale sole, filleted and grilled to moist perfection.

As we paid our bill at the Seafood Grotto, we noticed a small spiral-bound cookbook for sale: *The Seafood Cookbook*, put together by a group called the Commercial Fishermen's Wives of Humboldt. (Eureka is on Humboldt Bay.) It is a collection of humble recipes, from shrimp balls and tuna burgers to instructions for cleaning and cooking cracked crab. One whole chapter is devoted to salmon cookery, including this simple and delicious recipe for marinated barbecued salmon, contributed by Fredi S. Fleener.

PRAWN SAUTÉ CHARDONNAY

8 large mushrooms
12 prawns
2 tablespoons flour
6 tablespoons butter
4 scallions, chopped
pinch of salt
pinch of pepper
pinch of dried basil
½ cup chardonnay or dry white wine
1 teaspoon chopped parsley
juice of ½ lemon

Wash mushrooms well. Drain. Slice thick.

Peel, butterfly, and devein raw shrimp. Dust with flour.

Heat large skillet to medium temperature and add 4 tablespoons butter. When butter is hot but not smoking, add shrimp. Sauté 2 minutes. Add scallions, mushrooms, salt, pepper, and basil. Stir well and cook 2 minutes more.

Add wine and simmer 2 minutes.

Remove from heat. Stir in remaining butter, chopped parsley, and lemon juice.

Serve immediately with boiled rice and green vegetables.

Makes 2 servings

Tadich Grill, 240 California St., San Francisco, Calif.; (415) 391-2373.

Prawn Sauté Chardonnay

SAN FRANCISCO—They don't make them like Tadich's any more. Look at the china plates: sturdy dishware, nothing fancy, thin green lines around the edge. They're classic eating-hall issue. Look at the hunk of sourdough bread that comes with dinner. Broad hatch marks crisscross its leathery crust; and the inside is chewy, punchy. It's lusty bread, not for sissies.

Now look at the menu, printed and dated every morning. "No personal checks or credit cards accepted," it announces. Dollars, honest American dollars, are the currency of Tadich Grill. The menu is mammoth, packed with preparations that remind you of eating in simpler days, when a good restaurant could lavish its attention on high-quality food rather than waste time on elaborate presentations.

For example, you can come to this very high-class establishment for a meal of bacon and eggs, or corned beef hash. And although the vast majority of customers eat seafood, the menu also lists some of the most delicious charcoal-broiled steaks and chops we have ever plunged a knife through: calves liver steak with bacon and onions; sirloin steak smothered with mushrooms; lamb chops or pork chops. Side these corny cuts of meat with exemplary potatoes—crisp shoestrings or a straw mat of hashed browns, buttery soft beneath their brittle crust, flecked with parsley.

We are in heaven picking our way through a brimming menu such as this . . . and we haven't even told you about the fish. Fish is Tadich's specialty, listed on the menu under a disclaimer advising that the choice is "subject to season, weather, and fishing conditions." The roster is categorized thus: charcoal-broiled, poached, pan-fried, sautéed, deep-fried, or baked. Plus cold prawn or crab Louie salad, hot milk oyster stew and clam chowder, and San Francisco's definitive cioppino—halibut, swordfish, scallops, shrimp, crab, and cherrystone clams in a peppery tomato sauce, served with toasted garlic bread on the side.

For dessert, one can get Monterey Jack cheese, melon, or even chocolate mousse, but we like to conclude a Tadich meal with old favorites such as eggy bland rice custard pudding, a chocolate sundae, or a big baked apple. They aren't the most chichi desserts around, but like all the food at Tadich's, they sure put a smile on your face.

Tadich wasn't always a dressy grill. It started as a coffee stand set up in 1849 by three Yugoslavians to serve the harbor of Yerba Buena (San Francisco's first name). Earthquakes and city development hastened a few moves, expansion, and change, but it has always been a very American restaurant, always run by Yugoslavians. John Tadich started work in 1871 and took over in 1887. In 1913, Tom Buich began working here; eventually he bought the place in 1929. It is still a Buich family business.

Although it has been in its present location only since 1967, Tadich Grill surrounds diners with icons of San Francisco's long-standing grill tradition: snowy linen at the tables, white-aproned waiters, fine polished woodwork everywhere. Single diners are made comfortable at a long mahogany counter, where the noisy mess-hall ambience gives the meal an extra shot of local color.

Some of the most delicious Tadich meals are unique to the West Coast: pan-fried sand dabs or rex sole; charcoal-broiled Pacific red snapper; kippered Alaskan cod with butter sauce. For this recipe from Tadich chef John Canepa, all you need are extremely large shrimp (less than fifteen per pound). On the West Coast they're called prawns.

Shrimp de Jonghe

CHICAGO—Shrimp de Jonghe is one of the gastronomic glories of Chicago, yet it is virtually unknown everywhere else. For us, no trip through the Midwest is really right unless we have the opportunity to plunge our forks into a hot casserole laden with shrimp and a heap of the most wondrous bread crumbs on this earth— sopped with butter, sherry, and garlic.

We knew it was unique to this city, but it wasn't until we got to talking with James Ward, restaurant critic for Chicago's Channel 7 (ABC), that we had any idea how an ocean seafood dish with a Belgian name ever came to be a Chicago specialty.

Mr. Ward, who proudly asserts "I never et a shrimp de Jonghe I didn't like," told us it was invented by a Belgian family named de Jonghe who immigrated in the 1890s and ran a restaurant on the South Side of Chicago during the Columbian Exposition of 1892.

Then they moved downtown to Monroe Street and opened de Jonghe's Hotel and Restaurant.

Until it was closed in the 1930s for violating Prohibition, de Jonghe's was one of Chicago's premier eateries, celebrated for the winning ways of its chef, Emil Zehr. No one seems to know whether it was chef Emil or proprietor Henri de Jonghe who invented the magnificent casserole that now bears the family name. Whoever did it deserves credit for a meal that has become one of the outstanding luxuries of Chicago cooking—along with chicken Vesuvio (another local oddity with a no-doubt fascinating genealogy).

Other parts of the country have dishes that are similar. Scampi is a garlicky variation, but it is usually served on noodles, which call for serious fork-twirling. Genuine de Jonghe, which is nothing but shrimp and moist, odoriferous bread crumbs, is so elementary it can be eaten with a spoon; that simplicity is what makes it such a sensuous pleasure. It's the butter in the bread crumbs that makes de Jonghe so delish.

Our own version is based on a recipe that has been passed around the city for years. The classic formula calls for a single clove of minced garlic, which is probably a good starting point. Being garlic gluttons, we like to double that amount.

Despite its swanky nature, it is an easy dish to make; its goodness depends on the quality of shrimp you use. Go to a fish market and get big, plump ones. Boil them just before making the casseroles. They are an expensive ingredient, but believe us: This is one of the winningest meals your tongue can ever know.

Because it is so oozingly rich, shrimp de Jonghe doesn't demand much in the way of side dishes. We suggest serving it with nothing more than a simple salad or a minimally seasoned green vegetable on the side.

SHRIMP DE JONGHE

12 tablespoons butter (1½ sticks); softened
1 teaspoon salt
1 to 2 cloves garlic, finely minced (to taste)
1 cup bread crumbs (dry)
⅓ cup minced parsley
½ cup dry sherry
dash of cayenne pepper
dash of paprika
2 pounds large shrimp

Cream together butter, salt, and garlic. Mix in bread crumbs, parsley, sherry, pepper, and paprika.

Peel and devein shrimp. Toss into simmering water and cook just a few minutes, only until they turn pink. Rinse with cold water and drain.

Preheat oven to 375 degrees. Butter 4 to 6 individual ovenproof casserole dishes (or one wide dish).

Divide shrimp among casserole dishes. Mound crumb mixture on top. Bake 20 minutes, or until crumbs are golden brown and sizzling.

Serves 4 to 6.

Crab Baked in a Ramekin

CARRBORO, N.C.—"Romanticism is back," advises the newsletter of The Fearrington House, a country restaurant southwest of Chapel Hill. The elegant white-columned house, built by dairy farmer Jesse Fearrington in the 1920s, is the soul of gracious Southern living, with a menu of truly elegant Carolina specialties.

The Fearrington House is the center of a small, planned village that includes a gourmet food market (in what used to be the granary), a pottery shed (the old milk barn), and a post office (formerly the blacksmith's shop). The setting is American country at its most beguiling. From the restaurant's dining rooms, you look out on flowering crab apple trees, rosebushes, snapdragons, rows of herbs and vegetables, and a two-acre field of daffodils.

Inside, the rooms are perfumed by fresh roses; the tables set with elaborate patterned fabrics. In the evening, it is a place for lovers. To watch the sun set over rolling fields, to sip a mint cooler (bedecked with mint leaves from the garden), and to linger on the wide slate veranda in a heavy wooden rocker: What a rhapsody of Southern charm!

At lunch, sun streams in the windows and through vaulted skylights in an upstairs lounge that holds an antique bar and giant flower box with flowers and a living tree.

The Fearrington House menu is an eloquent expression of culinary tradition, from coastal specialties such as crumb-fried shrimp and parsley-dusted flounder to lemon frost pie. Unlike the cliché of Southern food as little more than grits and barbecue, this food is refined, suitable for white-glove dining. One is tempted to call it nouvelle Dixie cooking.

Many of The Fearrington House specialties were originally formulated by highly esteemed Southern cook Edna Lewis (author of *A Taste of Country Cooking*). Although Edna has moved on, her mark on the kitchen is indelible. Nowhere else will you find buttermilk biscuits like these—devoid of baking powder's bite and of sugar's sweetness; hardly more than a puff of flour with a wispy sour tang. Edna's chocolate soufflé is a gravity-defying wonder, garnished with warm chocolate sauce and whipped cream laced with bittersweet chocolate shavings.

This kitchen wows you from soup to nuts. A salad plate of black-eyed peas and summer savory is brilliantly seasoned with chervil. Potato salad is made with breathy dilled mayonnaise. Panned quail is served with a syrup made from freshly pressed white grape juice. Ham biscuits are accompanied by honeycup mustard. Even the simplest green salad is extraordinarily Southern, its tender leaves of Bibb lettuce garnished with toasted pecans.

The menu changes with the seasons. Spring dinner might begin with an appetizer of oysters broiled with buttered bread crumbs, and move on to sautéed baby trout. In the summer, vidalia onions are paired with leeks and bathed with tarragon-scented vinaigrette. Seasonal vegetables and fruits are picked in the morning to be served that night. In the autumn, roast pork loin is accompanied by fried apples and fresh zucchini strips. At Sunday brunch, buttermilk pancakes are served with country sausage, honey-maple syrup on the side.

Jennie Fitch restored The Fearrington House with her husband, R.B. (nobody, including Jennie, calls him by any name other than his initials). She sent us her own family recipe for one of the specialties of the house, crab baked in a ramekin. She told us that it was handed down by her mother, Nell Elder, and that The Fearrington House kitchen makes it with fresh crabs shipped from the North Carolina coast. Fresh crabmeat is expensive, but freshness is what makes this dish so delicious. These measurements stretch 1½ pounds to make six meal-sized servings.

CRAB BAKED IN A RAMEKIN

1½ pounds fresh lump crabmeat,
   thoroughly free of shell
¾ cup chopped celery
1½ teaspoons lemon juice
½ teaspoon salt
½ cup mayonnaise
2 tablespoons melted butter
1 cup dry bread crumbs
2 chopped hard-boiled eggs
1½ teaspoons Grey Poupon mustard
1½ teaspoons Worcestershire sauce
dash cayenne pepper
1½ cups fresh bread crumbs

Preheat oven to 400 degrees. Combine all ingredients except fresh bread crumbs and divide among six lightly buttered 8-ounce ramekins. Cover lightly with bread crumbs and top with thin dots of butter. Bake 12–15 minutes, until crumbs are golden brown.

Serves 6.

The Fearrington House, U.S. 15-501, Carrboro, N.C. (eight miles south of Chapel Hill); (919) 967-7770.

HISTORY OF JAKE'S

ake's Famous Crawfish descended from two early-day bar restaurants — Mueller and Meyer, founded in 1892 at 18th and Washington, and the Quelle,. a crawfish house founded by Baron Schlenk, at 2nd and Stark. In 1908 Mueller and Meyer moved to a new location at 12th and Stark and sold out to John Rometsch, who developed the business into a soft drink parlor during Oregon's prohibition era. In 1909, the Quelle lost its lease and went out of business. Jake Freiman, an old Quelle waiter, joined John Rometsch as a partner and added crawfish to the restaurant. Jake became a favorite with both customers and employees and in 1920, the restaurant was named "Jake's famous Crawfish" in his honor.

The paintings and decorations of Jake's certainly tell part of the restaurant's history. Many have been handed down through the years or collected especially for Jake's. The chandeliers came from the old Knapp House, built in 1881. The oak buffets, now serving as our back bar, were shipped around Cape Horn in 1880 for a total freight cost of $10.00. The painting above the first small booth in the carpeted dining room shows the construction of the Portland Hotel. It was painted between 1883-1888 by F.C.R. Groth. The hotel remained partially constructed during this time of business depression. In 1888 a group of Portland investors raised money for the completion of the hotel. It was opened in 1890 and represented an investment of about one million dollars. Every president of the United States stayed in the hotel at one time or another until it was torn down in 1952. Of interest also is the large painting on the center wall of the same dining room, believed to be Mt. Hood. It was painted by James Everett Stuart, an itinerant artist, born in Dover, Maine, in 1852, and was hung in the Los Angeles Museum of History and Art for a number of years.

S.W. TWELFTH & STARK STREETS · PORTLAND, OREGON

Dungeness Crab Cakes

PORTLAND, Ore.—You will know what Jake's is all about as soon as you set foot in the door. There in the front of the dining room is a blackboard with several dozen types of seafood chalked on. This is Jake's "fresh board," an inventory of which straight-from-the-market fish the kitchen has that particular day.

Many items will be familiar to any seafood dilettante: bay shrimp, little neck clams, silver salmon, albacore tuna. Others are rare: kumamoto oysters, opaka, New Zealand pompano, broiled marlin. Nearly half the entries on the board are set apart with an asterisk, indicating they are local products. Among them are celebrated regional delicacies such as Dungeness crab, petrale sole, and chinook salmon. Here, too, are some surprises: Dover sole is listed as a local product, as are crawfish.

It isn't only the inventory of fish that makes Jake's a Northwest eating experience without peer. Look beyond the blackboard at the dining rooms. This is a grand place, nearly a century old, outfitted in belle epoch gold-flocked wallpaper and antique chandeliers, its tables draped with thick white cloths, its high-backed wood booths dark with age. Above the booths and tables hang painted tableaux of Oregon scenery and wildlife, as well as moments of local history.

Although fine, Jake's is not fancy. Waiters in their white jackets are casual and efficient, without pomp. You can come to this restaurant for a quick business lunch as simple as a crab and cheddar sandwich or a hangtown fry (a fried oyster omelette). Many customers patronize Jake's for no reason other than to hang out at the bar, or to sip beer and fork down golden mantle oysters by the dozen.

For out-of-towners like ourselves, the most outstanding thing about Jake's is its character. The ancient wood booths, the daily printed "fresh sheet" (a reprise of the blackboard) enclosed in the regular menu, the loaf of hard-crusted sourdough bread set upon the table: These are a taste of Portland virtually unsullied by food trends and fashions. There are other restaurants in town that are very good, serve fresh fish, and offer innovative menus; but none resonates with the regional veracity of Jake's.

Although it has been called Jake's Famous Crawfish since 1920, when waiter Jake Freiman added the customarily Cajun (but in fact local) crustacean to the menu, Jake's great meals are not crawfish pie and etouffee. Eat oysters on the half shell, crab any time it is listed on the fresh sheet, baked scallops, pan fried petrale sole, or salmon. Drink local wine, and top things off with a serving of Oregon "three berry cobbler."

DUNGENESS CRAB CAKES

1 pound crabmeat, picked clean
4 slices crustless white bread, in bite-size
    pieces
2 tablespoons diced sweet onion
1 rib celery, diced
1 teaspoon white pepper
1/2 teaspoon dry mustard
1 teaspoon salt
2 eggs, beaten
2 tablespoons mayonnaise
2 tablespoons cream
2 tablespoons minced parsley
1 cup unseasoned bread crumbs
butter for frying

Mix together all ingredients (except butter and bread crumbs) and form into six hamburger-like patties. Gently bread each patty. They will want to fall apart, so handle very carefully.

Melt butter in large frying pan over medium-high heat. Fry patties until crisp and golden brown on both sides. Careful when flipping! Serve immediately.

Makes 4–6 servings.

Jake's Famous Crawfish, 401 S.W. Twelfth, Portland, Ore.; (503) 226-1419.

The best meal we ate at Jake's was a couple of chinook salmon steaks broiled over charcoal—heavy, moist and gorgeous pink. On the side we shared crab cakes—fresh Dungeness crab mixed with cream and a jot of spice to form ethereal patties totally unlike the hot, devilish crab cakes of the East. One needn't use Dungeness crab in the recipe we offer for these ultrafragile cakes; but fresh (not canned) crabmeat *does* make all the difference.

Deviled Crab à la Sam

SAN FRANCISCO—Enter through old-fashioned saloon doors, and you are guided to a high-walled private booth. Pull back the curtain, and there is your table, draped with a starchy white cloth. On the cloth is a loaf of the most outstanding brittle-crusted sourdough bread in town.

Surrounded by the luster of mahogany walls, you are left alone with your dining partner and the loaf of bread. By the time the waiter peeks through the curtain to take your order, the white cloth is strewn with crumbs.

This is the restaurant we dream about, hungrily, whenever we anticipate a trip to San Francisco. While the rest of America has only recently discovered California cuisine, Sam's Grill has been perfecting it for 121 years. In a city famous for trendsetting grill cookery, Sam's is still the best of the lot.

It is a quirky establishment, the way venerable oldsters are entitled to be. Open only on weekdays, only until 8:30 P.M., it caters to a loyal clientele of people who work downtown and come every day for lunch, or for an early dinner before heading home. At noon, it is mobbed with successful-looking types jockeying for a table, or crowding three-deep against the bar. Reservations are not accepted. Whoever you are, you wait.

A uniquely San Francisco blend of elegance and informality, Sam's is outfitted with yards of thick white linen and brass hooks for coats. Although this isn't Sam's original location (that was in the Old California Market), its old-time look is genuine; there is nothing affected about it.

Once you get a table, it is an immensely comfortable place to eat. The staff of formally dressed waiters are anything but stiff; they are consummate professionals, not even blinking when they bring a second loaf of bread to a certain greedy twosome who pocketed their loaf to take with them on the trip north up the coast.

Sam's is a taste of fine restaurant dining the way it must have been a hundred years ago. How deliciously romantic it is to have

DEVILED CRAB À LA SAM

2 stalks celery (without leaves), diced
1 medium onion, diced
1 green pepper, diced
1/4 pound butter (one stick)
1 cup flour
3 cups scalded milk
2 teaspoons dry mustard
1 tablespoon Worcestershire sauce
dash of Tabasco
1/4 cup sherry wine
1 1/4 pounds crabmeat (fresh or frozen)
6 tablespoons Parmesan cheese
6 tablespoons butter

Preheat oven to 400 degrees.

In a large saucepan, cook celery, onion, and pepper in butter over low heat until soft. Slowly sprinkle in flour, a little at a time, stirring constantly, until fully incorporated into a smooth roux. Slowly add scalded milk, blending well. Cook for 10 minutes over low heat, stirring occasionally until thick and smooth. Add dry mustard, Worcestershire, Tabasco, sherry, and crabmeat. Bring to boil; remove from fire immediately.

Pour into 3-quart casserole dish. Top with Parmesan cheese and dot with butter. Bake uncovered for 30 minutes, or until golden brown and bubbly.

Serves 6–8.

Sam's Grill, 374 Bush St., San Francisco, Calif.; (415) 421-0594.

one's own private booth. (It can also be a little disconcerting the first time a waiter's head bobs in between the curtains to see that everything is going well.)

For all the fancy, formal trappings, Sam's menu is simplicity itself, printed every morning at ten, after a trip to the fish and produce markets to find what's fresh. The kitchen turns out a huge roster of straightforward American food, including two dozen specials and almost one hundred à la carte selections every day. It is possible to order charcoal-grilled steaks and chops, or short ribs of beef with horseradish sauce, or just bacon and eggs; but nearly everybody comes to Sam's for the seafood.

As is characteristic of so much new California cuisine, most of Sam's seafood is plainly cooked, to underscore its natural flavors. This is the place to sample Pacific rarities that never make it East, like genuine Hangtown fry (an omelette made with tiny Olympia oysters from the Northwest); rex and petrale sole grilled over charcoal; and the unbelievably delicate local fish called sand dabs—about a half-dozen sweet little filets sautéed in lemon butter.

One whole portion of each day's menu is devoted to "casseroles à la Sam," almost all of them made with fresh Dungeness crabmeat from the northern coast. There are crab creole and crab curry, crab au gratin and creamed crab with noodles. But the corker, a Sam's specialty since the beginning, is the one called deviled crab à la Sam.

This sunny-hued casserole of cream and crab and sherry is not nearly as devilish as its name implies. It is a fairly mild dish, tweaked with mustard—comfortable party food. It is as easy to make as it is to eat. The only trick is patience. Slowly add the flour to make the roux. And take your time blending in the milk.

Sam's of course, uses fresh crabmeat. We tested our variation of Sam's recipe with fresh and frozen meat, and found that frozen is almost as good. Serve it on rice or toast points, or plain with hard-crusted French bread and an avocado salad on the side.

Ginger Sherry Crab Legs Andrea

BANDON, Ore.—Are you ready for the creamiest, most succulent seafood dinner you have ever eaten? Here it comes: ginger sherry crab legs Andrea. What a dish! It combines extravagant ingredients without any fuss or bother to make a meal that is nothing less than bliss.

Andrea Gatov of Andrea's Old Town Cafe gave us the recipe awhile ago because we had eaten in her restaurant, liked it a lot, and asked her to share something with our readers. We put the recipe in a stack of things to be done, and there it sat for a few weeks while we nonchalantly went about our normal life. Then the day came to test it.

The recipe worked perfectly; but it didn't merely work; it made us swoon. It knocked us for a loop. It dazed us with deliciousness. It made us pause and give thanks to Andrea for bringing such pleasure into the world. We added it to our permanent file of wonderful things to serve to special quests on special occasions.

We have never eaten this miracle dinner at Andrea's Cafe because we have only been to Andrea's for breakfast. That is a special meal, too, from brawny Viennese coffee to slow-cooked oatmeal with gratifying oat oomph. Bran muffins are moist and steamy. Hot croissants are accompanied by a crock of smoke-flavored pear butter. We also managed to sample a slab of Andrea's locally renowned cheesecake—uncut dairy opulence.

The Cafe is an enchanting storefront in Bandon-by-the-Sea, a fishing and cranberry-growing village on the south coast between Port Orford and Coos Bay. Located in "Old Town," a neighborhood of crafts stores, art galleries, and bookshops, Andrea's has a homey, unorthodox atmosphere: greenery on shelves and suspended from the ceiling, background music from a radio tuned to NPR, and a collection of Japanese kimonos hanging about the place. (They are for sale.)

Andrea describes herself as an experimental chef. She likes to cook Creole, African, Italian, French, Israeli, and classical American cuisine. Her specialty is local seafood, in particular a garlic seafood stew made with a stock she concocts by simmering prawn shells, onion, celery, parsley, and thyme. "That one is really redolent of the ocean," she beamed. "I also raise my own lamb," she told us. "And I have at least thirty cheesecake recipes."

We told her we wanted a recipe with the flavor of the Oregon coast, which is why she gave us one that uses Dungeness crab legs. You cannot always find them in other regions of the country, but that's all right, because Andrea said that the recipe works equally

GINGER SHERRY CRAB LEGS ANDREA

4-inch length of ginger root, peeled and
    finely chopped (totaling about 1/3 cup
    chopped ginger)
1½ cups cream sherry
1½ cups salted butter (3 sticks)
6 large cloves garlic, finely chopped
1½ pounds picked Dungeness crabmeat
    (from upper portion of legs) or 1½
    pounds sea scallops
1½ cups light cream or half-and-half
parsley and paprika as garnish

Marinate ginger in cream sherry at least two hours.

Melt butter in large frying pan over medium heat. Sauté garlic, but do not brown. Add crabmeat or scallops and sauté for one minute, turning lightly so meat doesn't break up. Add sherry and ginger and bring to boil for one minute. Remove crabmeat or scallops and set aside.

Add cream to frying pan and bring to hard boil, stirring frequently, until reduced to a rich, creamy sauce. Return crab legs or scallops to sauce to reheat.

Serve, garnished with chopped parsley and paprika.

Serves 6.

Andrea's Old Town Café, 160 Baltimore, Old Town, Bandon, Ore.;
(503) 347-3022.

well with large sea scallops. We have tried it both ways, and in fact prefer the scallops because it can be some work picking the meat from the crab legs. And scallops, at their best, are even more tender and luxurious.

Oyster Stew

PORTLAND, Ore.—The oyster business was booming in mid-nineteenth century America, on both the East and West coasts. Supplies seemed endless; there were dozens of varieties ready for the taking.

That was when sailor Meinert Wachsmuth got shipwrecked in the Annie Doyle on Yaquina Bay, Oregon. It was 1865—the accidental beginning of a tradition of good oyster eating in Portland.

After his unexpected landing, Mr. Wachsmuth decided that his sailing days were over. He went to work for an oyster company in San Francisco, where he fathered a son named Louis. A few years later, he moved north to the oyster beds of Shoalwater Bay. In 1907, the Wachsmuths began their own oyster business: the Oregon Oyster Co. After Meinert retired, Louis acquired Yaquina Bay and its oyster beds, the very same place where his father ran aground a half-century before.

Louis began his restaurant as a sideline to the wholesale oyster trade, selling nothing more than raw oyster cocktails over an old wooden bar. He added oyster stew to the menu, and soon he moved his office to a location where he could actually seat people at tables. His "oyster house" flourished. The sidewalk on Ankeny Street was stacked with boxes of live crabs, oysters, and shrimp; the tables inside were packed with customers who came to feast on oyster cocktails and stews.

You still might share a table with strangers when you come to eat at Dan and Louis Oyster Bar, surrounded by decades worth of Wachsmuth family memorabilia. Beer steins, antiques, decorative plates, model ships, rope riggings, and nautical souvenirs from around the world are hung throughout a dining room that resembles the cabin of a sailing ship.

The menu, which invites diners to "Eat 'em Alive" and to visit the still-flourishing oyster beds upstream from Newport, is shaped like an oyster, gnarled around the edges. It is a small menu, limited almost exclusively to shellfish, including fried shrimp or scallops and chopped geoduck (say "gooey duck") clams. You can eat crab Louis salads or shrimp and crab cocktails, even creamed crab or shrimp on toast.

OYSTER STEW

3 cups milk
½ teaspoon salt
dash of pepper
½ teaspoon seasoned salt
3 tablespoons butter
2 cups shucked oysters
4 pats butter
chopped parsley as garnish

Heat milk over boiling water in top of double boiler. Lower heat. Add salt, pepper, and seasoned salt. Add butter and stir until melted.

Add oysters and their liquor. Cook over gently simmering water 30 minutes, stirring occasionally.

Skim oysters out of milk and portion into 4 serving bowls, with enough of the liquid so they don't dry out. Cover bowls and keep warm.

Let milk cook 15 minutes longer over simmering water, then ladle over oysters. Top each serving with a pat of butter and chopped parsley. Serve with plain crackers on the side. Makes 4 servings.

Dan & Louis Oyster Bar, 208 S.W. Ankeny St., Portland, Ore.; (503) 227-5906.

When it's cold outside, few dishes are as comforting as a bowl of oyster stew. Here they sell theirs made with either diced Pacific oysters (large and bland) or cocktail-size Yaquina Bays (zesty and oceanic). You can get a normally apportioned serving or pay extra and get the stew loaded with a double dose of oysters.

No matter how it is ordered, the most striking thing about the stew is its simplicity. There is nothing more to it than milk and butter, a bit of seasoning, and the oysters. And warmth. The buttery warmth, coddling the oysters in their milky brew, is what makes this simple preparation unimprovable. Of course, it is possible to lace it with a quarter-cup of dry sherry, if desired. Add the sherry in the last ten minutes, after the oysters have been removed from the milk.

The flavor of oyster stew depends on the type of oysters it contains, as well as their freshness. The more of the oysters' natural juice you use, the brinier the stew will be.

Pan Roast

NEW YORK—Because New York likes to set trends, its traditions tend to get forgotten. Nowadays, when gourmets eat out in Manhattan, they will probably go to a restaurant specializing in Tex-Mex, Creole, or California cooking. Food from all over the country is very popular in New York.

But we'll let you in on a secret: The regional American meals served in New York are second-rate. Detached from its Southwestern roots, a chicken-fried steak is a sad cut of cow indeed. Barbecue served without a Southern accent doesn't have any soul. And when you transfer a pretty plate of precious baby vegetables from its rightful home on the West Coast to a table in the Big Apple, it tends to look awfully wimpy.

When we visit New York, we like to eat real New York food. That might include a visit to Chinatown or Little Italy, but more likely you will find us at a Jewish delicatessen on the Lower East Side, or in a no-frills steak house in the Gansevoort meat market, or in the very heart of the city, underground, at the Grand Central Oyster Bar.

The Oyster Bar may be the most New York restaurant of all. Attached to Grand Central Terminal, it is a huge, multiroom place with a high vaulted tile ceiling that bounces noise so hard through the dining area you practically have to shout to be heard by the person sitting next to you.

The menu, printed every day, lists both plain and exotic seafood from around the world, including sometimes as many as a dozen different kinds of oysters imported from all three American coasts. Prices are very high (raw oysters are often more than one dollar each) . . . but the service is terrible, and the accommodations are uncomfortable.

But seriously, folks, this *is* New York City. If the Oyster Bar were quiet and polite, it just wouldn't seem right. And besides, those oysters for which you suffer through the commotion and brusque treatment are impeccable, opened just seconds before they are slapped down before you. And you can be sure that any other kind of fish you order will be absolutely fresh.

Although one can sit at a table and be served by waiters, just like in an ordinary restaurant, we believe the experience of the Oyster Bar is fullest at the counter opposite the oyster shuckers. Here you watch the men work their magic, opening dozens lightning fast. Most get sent away raw, for eating on the half-shell, but some get tossed into stews and pan roasts, which are the signature dishes of the Oyster Bar.

A pan roast is true New York food, heir to a long mid-Atlantic tradition of luxurious but uncomplicated seafood cookery, the primary principle of which is the coddling of shellfish in warm cream. It is a meal in a bowl, one of the supreme comfort foods for adults. It is a forthright dish, and it can be prepared fast (if you have the ingredients on hand). At the Oyster Bar, it takes them about two minutes, total, to whip up a pan roast.

Our recipe, based on one in *The Grand Central Oyster Bar and Restaurant Seafood Cookbook*, is for an oyster pan roast, but nearly any kind of shellfish will work fine. For the oysters, you can substitute about one-third pound shrimp (raw, peeled, deveined), one-fourth pound lobster meat (cooked), a dozen tiny bay scallops (raw), or a half-dozen shucked small clams (raw).

PAN ROAST

6 to 8 large oysters, freshly opened, with
    their juice
2 tablespoons clam juice
2 tablespoons butter
1 tablespoon chili sauce
1 teaspoon Worcestershire sauce
dash of celery salt
½ cup cream
1 slice thick dry toast
½ teaspoon paprika

Combine oysters with their liquor, clam juice, 1 tablespoon of the butter, chili sauce, Worcestershire, and celery salt in top of double boiler over boiling water.

Whisk vigorously (without hurting oysters) for 1 minute until the oysters' petticoats begin to ruffle (edges start to curl). Add cream. Stir over boiling water 1 minute more.

Place toast in wide soup bowl. Pour pan roast over toast. Dot with remaining tablespoon of butter. Sprinkle with paprika. Serve immediately.

Makes 1 serving.

Grand Central Oyster Bar, 42nd and Vanderbilt Ave., New York, N.Y.; (212) 490-6650.

BUSTERs = SOUL
FOOD RESTURANT
NOW OPEN
SOFE DRINKS
GOOD SERVED

Celery Cream Broil Oysters

BROOKLYN, N.Y.—Here is a restaurant that is a living museum of New York food.

By "New York food," we do not mean modern, upwardly mobile, high-fashion cuisine; nor are we referring to the delis and ethnic eateries that are so plentiful (and so good) in New York. We are referring to a bygone style of eating, to the elegant belle epoque cuisine once served by ritzy restaurants such as Rector's and Delmonico's to high-roller omnivores such as Diamond Jim Brady and his buxom pal, Lillian Russell.

Gage & Tollner opened for business in 1879, outfitted in the haute monde taste of the times. Its mirrored dining room is a cozy vault of cherry wood wainscoting and burgundy velvet tapestries. Brass gaslights still hang in chandeliers overhead, and although electrical fixtures supplement their soft, romantic glow, Gage & Tollner proudly boasts of its ability to keep business going even during blackouts.

Tables are covered with white linen, and the waiter corps is dressed in long aprons, their jackets emblazoned with military-style emblems indicating how long they have served. A star equals five years; an eagle, twenty five. One head waiter lasted sixty-one years!

The menu is a nostalgic roster of long-forgotten dishes once popular in the luxurious eating establishments of the mid-Atlantic coast. You can order golden buck and Yorkshire buck (first cousins to Welsh rarebit); a mutton chop (mutton, not callow lamb) cooked over anthracite coal; or fried chicken with corn fritters and maple syrup.

The potato list alone suggests a dozen different ways, starting with boiled, baked, and French fried, going all the way to grilled or candied sweets. In between is a most wonderful item called "hashed browns in cream"—a silver serving dish holding a crisp-crusted cake of buttery hashed-browned spuds up to its waist in warm cream.

Among the vegetables are such antique preparations as grilled, fried, or stewed tomatoes, and even a dish of spaghetti au gratin.

How comforting it is to sit in this oasis of yesterday's majesty and dine on lobster cream stew or deviled crabmeat or chicken Maryland with bacon and cream sauce. Meals are accompanied by baskets of New York breads: large oyster crackers, raisin-pumpernickel rolls, soda cracker disks, caraway-seeded rye. They arrive warm, wrapped in soft white napkins.

Gage & Tollner is primarily a seafood house, offering lobster,

Gage & Tollner.

Prix-Fixe Menu

Choice of:

Clams Casino

or

Clam or Fish Chowder

All cooked to order:

Shrimp Scampi

Broiled Coho Salmon

Smoked Cornish Hen

Soft Shell Crabs

Petite Filet Mignon with Bernaise Sauce

Choice of:

Potato

Baked or Hash Brown

or

Mixed Green Salad

Caramel Custard, Ice Ceam or Fresh Strawberries

Coffe or Tea

$15.50 per person

Our full a la carte menu is always available

CELERY CREAM BROIL OYSTERS

10 large oysters
½ cup chopped celery
1 cup heavy cream
dash of celery salt
2 pieces toast, cut into triangles, crusts removed
parsley for garnish

Clean and open oysters. Remove from shell, reserving their liquor.

Blanch celery in boiling water a few seconds.

Heat cream in saucepan until reduced by one-third. Add celery salt. (Add any additional seasonings at this point.)

Warm oysters in their liquor over low heat until their edges curl. Place in serving dish. Sprinkle with celery. Add reduced cream.

Serve over toast points, garnished with parsley.

Makes 1 serving.

Gage & Tollner; 372 Fulton St., Brooklyn, N.Y.; (718) 875-5181.

clams, oysters, scallops, and flatfish prepared in a startling number of ways. We counted sixteen different styles of clams and ten things to do with scallops. Most are elementary preparations, the freshly opened shellfish merely coddled in warm cream, butter, sherry, cornmeal crumbs, or a felicitous combination thereof.

Among the nine oyster dishes, celery cream broil oysters best expresses the sumptuous character of Gage & Tollner's cookery. It has been on the menu here since the beginning, when Rutherford B. Hayes was president and the streets of Brooklyn were clogged with horse-and-carriages . . . and the Brooklyn Bridge was only in the planning stages. The dish cost fifty cents then, twenty times that much today, and it is simplicity itself, a minimal recipe entirely dependent on the full oceanic flavor of the oysters and the sweetness of heavy cream. If such luxurious blandness is just too plain for your taste, the dish can be perked up with a few tablespoons of chili sauce, a shake of Tabasco, and a teaspoon of Worcestershire.

To do it in the high style of Gage & Tollner, the finished oysters should be presented in a silver serving dish and eaten off fine china. And for that old-fashioned New York touch, follow them with a dessert of whipped cream and sponge cake with a cherry on top, called charlotte russe.

Door County Fish Boil

FISH CREEK, Wisc.—Door County has its own way of cooking fish in the summertime. They call it a fish boil; it is a rowdy nightly event at inns and beachfront parties all along the peninsula between Green Bay and Lake Michigan's western shore.

Many locals refer to the ceremony as an Icelandic fish boil, because the tradition goes back to Icelandic fishermen who settled here last century. They used to entertain their families on the beach by building massive bonfires and boiling up their catch each evening.

The fish boil has become part of Door County culture, although it is virtually unknown outside this one finger of the Wisconsin shore north of Sturgeon Bay. Among locals and vacationers, it is a picnic with a sense of place and history, a meal that has come to symbolize Wisconsin's rich culinary heritage. Hand-scrawled signs advertising impromptu fish boils line the road each summer in small towns like Egg Harbor, White Fish Bay, and Ephraim; some of the nightly cookouts are so popular that you have to make reservations weeks in advance.

DOOR COUNTY FISH BOIL

12 small red potatoes
1½ pounds small onions
cheesecloth
8 quarts water
1 pound salt
2–3 pounds 1-inch thick fish steaks (cod,
    haddock, halibut, lake trout, tuna,
    whitefish, or salmon)
1 cup butter, melted
lemon wedges

Scrub but do not peel potatoes. Cut a thin slice from each end. Tie them loosly in a cheesecloth bag. Peel onions (but don't cut them) and tie them in a second cheesecloth bag.

Bring 8 quarts of water to boil over high heat. Slowly add ½ pound of salt so as not to lower boil, then add the bag with potatoes in it. Partially cover, and boil 12 minutes. Add the bag of onions. Boil 6 minutes more.

Wrap fish securely in cheesecloth, allowing enough space between steaks for water to circulate easily. Add fish to pot with remaining salt. Cook 10 minutes, skimming fish oils from surface of water. (Do not try the "kerosene overboil" technique at home unless you have an experienced Master Boiler on hand to supervise.)

Lift out all ingredients, portion onto plates, and drizzle with melted butter. Accompany fish, onions, and potatoes with cole slaw and bread; garnish with lemon wedges. And serve cherry pie for dessert. Serves 6.

White Gull Inn, Fish Creek, Wis.; (414) 868-3517.

At the White Gull Inn, a clapboard hotel in the village of Fish Creek, the Master Boiler suspends two kettles over an oak wood fire each Wednesday, Friday, Saturday, and Sunday night throughout the summer. Whitefish is cooked using the time-honored technique: Fish steaks and new potatoes, along with pounds of salt, are boiled together unti the fish is perfectly cooked.

The fun comes when the Master Boiler deems everything ready to eat. He tosses kerosene onto the flames. The fire licks up and the water boils furiously. The show has a purpose: The "overboil" skims fish oil off the surface, so the steaks come out clean and sweet.

Fish and potatoes are then drizzled with melted butter. On the side, the White Gull serves cole claw and a trio of breads (including orange date nut and pumpkin). Dessert at a fish boil is always cherry pie.

If you do not have a genuine fish boil kettle, it is easy to devise one using a big pot and cheesecloth. Although it can be done indoors on a stove, the fun is cooking over a wood fire outside; for that, you need a kettle with a handle, and a rig to hang it over the fire. The measurements, suggested by the White Gull Inn, are for a fish boil to feed six people. (Yes, a pound of salt is required—to elevate the boiling point of the water and to keep the fish steaks intact; don't worry, though: they absorb minimum salt flavor.)

8
Chicken and Turkey

Vermont Chicken Pie

WESTON, Vermont—Eccentric and off the beaten path, country stores are legacies from an era long before boutiques and shopping malls. The good ones have merchandise impossible to find anywhere else.

If, for instance, you are in the market for a goosedown pillow, or a pillow filled with English hops (alleged to induce sound sleep), or red flannel long johns with the trap door in back, we've got just the place for you: the Vermont Country Store in Weston, in the southern part of the state.

Here is where to stock up on "bag balm" for rubbing on sore udders, plain white enamel breadboxes, all-natural mattress ticking (the material that predates shiny satinette), and reconditioned, like-new, twenty-five-year-old Electrolux vacuum cleaners that look like the Hindenburg.

Penny candies from red-hot Atomic fireballs to horehound drops (known as "slugs") occupy the front of the store. Stroll back, around the warm pot-bellied stove, and you hit the serious foodstuffs section. These shelves hold an amazing array of Down East groceries, including Jacob's cattle beans for genuine New England baked beans and stone-ground meals from the store's mill in nearby Rockingham.

When was the last time you considered a steamy bowl of "lumberjack mush" for breakfast? Here it is, "for children and older folks who want a soft cereal with high nutritious value." You can also buy bags of samp—the cracked wheat and corn cereal that the Pilgrims learned to eat soon after landing. Groats, porridge, grits, buckwheat flour, and superfine white cornmeal for johnnycakes: Come and get 'em.

In a basket among the beans, grains, and weird cereals are a spill of Common Crackers, offered as samples. They are plain, hard, and primitive-looking, the kind of cracker that is customarily kept in a wooden cracker barrel.

Invented in 1828 by Charles and Timothy Cross in Montpelier, Vermont, and called cracker because it could easily be cracked in half, the Common Cracker used to be essential for "building" a serious chowder in the time when chowders were like layered casseroles of crackers, potatoes, salt pork, and fish. Crackers were used to make cracker pudding, mock mince pie, and turkey stuffing. Or they were simply split, buttered, and toasted.

As much as they are part of Yankee folklife, genuine Common Crackers had become extinct until the Vermont Country Store began making them again in 1981. Specialty stores around the

VERMONT CHICKEN PIE

5 tablespoons butter
⅓ cup flour
3 cups warm chicken stock
¼ teaspoon white pepper
¼ teaspoon thyme
salt to taste
4 cups cooked chicken meat, cut into bite-
　size pieces
3 tablespoons dry sherry
2 to 2½ cups Bisquick
⅔ cup milk

Melt butter in large pot. Whisk in flour
and cook over medium heat 5 minutes,
whisking constantly. Gradually add warm
stock, whisking constantly. Stir and simmer
about 20 minutes, until it is gravy-thick.
Add pepper and thyme; salt to taste. Add
chicken and simmer until chicken is heated
through. Stir in sherry. Pour into 2-quart
casserole.

Preheat oven to 450 degrees. Beat 2
cups Bisquick and milk, adding more
Bisquick if necessary to make a manage-
able dough. Turn onto floured board.
Knead until smooth, about 30 seconds. Roll
out large enough to fully cover top of
chicken in casserole. Cut to fit, using scraps
to make a dough design on surface of crust.
Bake until golden brown, 10–12 minutes.
Serves 4–6.

The Bryant House, Route 100, Weston, Vt.;
(802) 824-6287.

country now carry Common Crackers, but if you cannot find them, they can be mail-ordered (as can pillows, vacuum cleaners, samp, and bean pots) from: The Vermont Country Store, Weston, Vt. 05161; (802) 824-3184.

There is only one restaurant we know that offers milk and crackers every day at lunch. It is the Bryant House, next to (and part of) the Vermont Country Store. Like the store, the Bryant House is a treasure trove of bygone ways, its menu listing such favorites as baked beans and brown bread, Indian pudding, butternut squash bisque, and Common Cracker crumb haddock. They were kind enough to send us the recipe for one of Vermont's traditional comfort meals, chicken pie.

Chicken and Dumplings

YACHATS, Ore.—Beulah's Sea View Inn is due for remodeling. They will probably throw out the sculpted rug, the weathered café chairs, the avocado-green and gold plastic tablecloths, the tired wood paneling. And they ought to do something about the sea shell display case below the cash register, too: displays of shells such as these are quite passé.

There is little doubt in our minds that Beulah's will modernize, and that it ought to; but it will be a sad day. This town dining room with its panoramic picture window above the bay in Yachats (pronounced ya-*hots*) is like an old pair of shoes: homely but so comfortable. Beulah's has personality.

We knew it was worth investigating when we got a letter from our Oregon friend Paul Pintarich, an otherwise hard-boiled guy, who rhapsodized thusly: "Beulah's shines like a well-worn jewel in the tiara of the coast's finest eating establishments. Where the Sasquatch pad down softly to the sea, Beulah regulars burp down huge meals featuring chicken-n-dumplings, homemade tomato preserves, and scones, for crying out loud."

To understand Beulah's charms is to know something about Oregon's character. It is a sane and reliable restaurant, without airs. No one eats here for any reason other than to have a square meal, or maybe, on a special occasion, to have a drink in the lounge and a twirl around the dance floor. The supper club atmosphere in the area adjacent to the dining room is conservative and comfortable.

Every place is set with a paper mat, silverware, and a coffee cup. Meals begin with soup and salad, both pretty boring, served in little plastic bowls. If you don't like iceberg lettuce, you can opt for a "molded salad" (a block of pretty gelatin) with a blob of mayonnaise on top. Good eating begins when they bring the bran muffins and tomato preserves—both homemade. Then comes dinner. The menu lists a full variety of steaks and chops; but it is poultry that makes Beulah's kitchen sing.

"Oregon turkey dinner" is the real thing, with all the trimmings—spicy dressing, real mashed potatoes, whole berry cranberry sauce. It is all good, except for a heavy fried cornbread ball (a.k.a. corn fritter) that is served covered with a sweet red sauce the consistency of mucilage.

The great thing to eat at Beulah's—the dish that made this place famous, and that is a specialty at family-style restaurants up and down the Oregon coast—is chicken and dumplings. It is one hearty meal: lofty clods of biscuit dough heaped into a deep plate

CHICKEN AND DUMPLINGS

1 4-pound chicken, cut up
2 teaspoons salt
½ teaspoon pepper
1 cup diced celery
½ cup chopped onion
3 tablespoons flour
1½ cups cooled broth (reserved from cooked chicken)
¾ cup milk

DUMPLINGS:
2 cups sifted flour
3 teaspoons baking powder
1 teaspoon salt
1 teaspoon sugar
4 tablespoons solid vegetable shortening
¾ cup milk

Cover chicken parts with hot water in large saucepan. Add salt, pepper, celery, and onion. Cover, simmer gently until tender (about an hour), skimming the top frequently. Strain chicken pieces, celery, and onion from broth, and cool broth. When cool, skim off fat and discard.

Blend flour with 2–3 tablespoons of the cooled broth. Stir in remaining broth (1½ cups, total), then cook and stir in saucepan over medium heat until thick. Add salt and pepper to taste, if desired. Stir in milk. Set aside.

Preheat oven to 425 degrees.

Make dumplings: Sift together flour, baking powder, salt, and sugar. Cut in shortening until mixture is like cornmeal. Add milk, mixing only enough to blend. Pat dough out on floured board to ½-inch thick. Cut into biscuits about 2 inches in diameter.

Place chicken pieces, celery, and onion in a 3–4 quart casserole, pour in gravy, then top with biscuits, nestled close together.

Bake 20–30 minutes, or until biscuits are light brown.

Serves 4–6.

Beulah's Sea View Inn, Highway 101, Yachats, Ore.; (503) 547-3215.

STRONGBOW TURKEY TETRAZZINI

8 ounces thin spaghetti, cooked firm, lightly buttered

8 slices (½ pound) bacon, cut into 1-inch strips

½ cup chopped onion

½ cup chopped bell pepper

1 cup sliced fresh mushrooms

3 tablespoons flour

¼ teaspoon salt

¼ teaspoon white pepper

2 cups turkey broth (chicken broth may be substituted)

3 cups diced cooked turkey

1 10-ounce package frozen peas, cooked until defrosted

1 4-ounce jar pimientos, chopped

¾ cup toasted slivered almonds

½ cup grated Parmesan cheese

with about half a chicken (bones, skin, and all), gravy, and parsley. It is a uniquely Oregonian way of making chicken and dumplings—a bracing meal when it is cold and rainy outside.

Strongbow Turkey Tetrazzini

VALPARAISO, Ind.—Heoh, heoh, heoh, the holidays are coming; and the only thing we have to say about that is yedle, yedle, yedle.

Just in case you aren't multilingual, we ought to tell you that we are talking turkey. "Heoh, heoh, heoh," when gobbled, means "let's all get together." "Yedle, yedle, yedle" is what turkeys say when they like the food.

We learned turkey language at the Strongbow Inn of Valparaiso, Indiana, where a brochure deciphering the gobbler's language is published. Turkey is the specialty of the house at the Strongbow, as it has been since 1940. The Strongbow story begins a few years before that, in 1937, when an Indiana woman named Bess Thrun started a turkey farm in order to supplement her husband's university professor salary. Mrs. Thrun knew nothing about turkeys, except that there was money to be made raising them; and besides, she wanted to live in the country rather than downtown Valparaiso.

So the Thruns bought a farm, one-hundred hens, and a dozen toms. Their turkey dynasty was begun. But in 1939, U.S. Highway 30 was rerouted clean through the middle of the Thruns's farm. Never one to be discouraged, Mrs. Thrun opened a motel, filling station, and twenty-eight-seat diner for passersby. She cooked one bird a day back then, alternating kitchen duties with her jobs as motel clerk and gas jockey.

The restaurant grew and was named Strongbow Inn in honor of a Potawatomi Indian chief who once lived hereabouts. In the early days, it was a self-sufficient operation, the turkeys raised, butchered, and cleaned on premises. Now federal inspection laws require Strongbow turkeys to be shipped to packinghouses for slaughter, then returned to the farm. They remain highly prized; customers from coast to coast pay top dollar to have them airshipped for Christmas.

The menu at the Strongbow has grown beyond turkey, but it's the birds—and all their proper fixings—that make dining here so special. No shortcuts are taken in this kitchen. Meals begin with fluffy yeast rolls, accompanied by a quarter-stick of butter. Wet your whistle with turkey soup-consommé made from scratch, laced with a few tender noodles. Or how about turkey paté, like glorified

Cook spaghetti, set aside.

In a 2-quart saucepan, cook bacon until crisp. Remove from pan and drain on paper towels.

Cook onion and green pepper in bacon fat until tender but not brown. Remove with slotted spoon and set aside. Cook mushrooms in bacon fat until tender. Remove with slotted spoon.

Sprinkle flour into fat, stirring constantly as it bubbles and thickens. Stir in salt and pepper, then add broth, continuing to stir gently until smooth. Add onion, pepper, mushrooms, turkey, peas, and pimiento.

Spread cooked and buttered spaghetti over the bottom of a shallow buttered casserole, approximately 12 inches by 8 inches. Sprinkle bacon over spaghetti, then cover with turkey mixture. Top with almonds, then Parmesan cheese. Place under broiler until cheese begins to brown, 5–7 minutes.

Serves 8.

Strongbow Inn, U.S. Highway 30, Valparaiso, Ind.; (219) 462-3311.

chopped chicken liver—loud, strong, topped with bits of sweet chopped onion.

For a main course, you can get the basic, unimprovable turkey dinner: white meat atop a mound of sage-scented dressing, sided by mashed potatoes, topped with giblet gravy, accented with a dish of tart cranberry sauce.

Or there are turkey pies, their hand-formed crusts containing all-turkey (no vegetable) hash of light and dark meat. Or a whole drumstick on a plate, or turkey salad, or turkey wings. At lunch on Thursdays, Strongbow offers a simple and delicious "leftovers" dish called Potawatomi roll-ups: crepes filled with turkey breast meat, dolloped with warm cranberry relish.

Mrs. Thrun's daughter, Caroline ("Chuggie") Adams, gave us another great recipe for the next day's turkey. Although not served at the restaurant, it has been a family favorite for years: turkey tetrazzini.

Tetrazzini sounds Italian, but it is as American as the warm apple pie that the Strongbow serves for dessert. Invented as chicken tetrazzini in San Francisco early in the 1900s, it is a winning combination of pasta, poultry, and Parmesan cheese. According to James Beard, it was named to honor opera star Luisa Tetrazzini, who had "astounding girth as well as a thrilling voice."

Chicken Jelly

BALTIMORE—One day recently we were chatting with the editor of a cooking magazine, and as editors are wont to do, she was predicting the future. "Gelatin," she prognosticated, "is coming back."

"Jello-O?" we questioned with glee, being devotees of elaborate, ultra-customized gelatin salads festooned with coconut, marshmallows, Mandarin oranges, nuts, seeds, cheese, etc.

"No, not Jello-O," she explained, reminding us that Jell-O, like Kleenex and Band-Aids, is a trademarked brand name. "Not bright-colored, sticky-sweet desserts. I mean subtle-flavored aspics, made from scratch, with plain gelatin and interesting stock."

Perhaps she was right; but even if nouvelle gelatin isn't the next big food trend, we know just the place to go to enjoy a taste of it. And it is hardly an avant-garde restaurant.

The Woman's Industrial Exchange Restaurant in Baltimore is so far out of fashion, it's back in fashion. Aspic never lost favor in this downtown lunchroom that first opened for business back in 1882.

The last time we were there, we had an inspired lunch of what the menu called "chicken jelly" (a.k.a. chicken aspic), accompanied by deviled eggs and freshly made mayonnaise, and a plate of oven-warm baking powder biscuits.

The front room of the Woman's Exchange is an outlet for ladies' handwork such as shawls, embroidered pillows, doll clothes, and hand-knit sweaters (at low, low prices). "Whenever you purchase any of the merchandise," a sign advises, "you receive good value and are aiding a very deserving woman."

The dining room in back is a time machine into the genteel past: black-and-white tile floor, long red banquette, cream-colored walls hung with soothing pictures of birds and flowers. Waitresses, in their crisp blue uniforms, are the type who fret if you don't clean the plate. When we left half of a deviled egg, our waitress insisted on wrapping it up so we could have it with us later, for an afternoon snack.

The menu is from-scratch good food, some of it as nostalgic as the chicken jelly. Croquettes are a frequent lunch special, as is floating island dessert. There are regional meals, too, such as Baltimore crabcakes, made with great hunks of sweet meat; and breakfast of biscuits and country ham. The dessert list features towering meringue pies, mocha cake, yellow cake, and devil's food cake (with white icing).

And when you leave, you will notice a wide variety of jams, jellies, and preserves for sale by the cash register. They are the work of deserving women, too, packed in mismatched, miscellaneous jars the way grandma used to do it.

Our own recipe for chicken jelly is a bit more substantial than the one we ate at the Woman's Exchange. Theirs was clear stock only; we include plenty of chicken chunks as well. The flavor of chicken jelly depends on the chicken stock you use. Canned broth is fine (although quite salty), but if you can make your own stock by simmering a couple pounds of chicken backs, necks, bones, etc., with celery, a bay leaf, peppercorns, and a halved onion for about five hours, the jelly will have a much more chicken-like flavor. If using canned broth, eliminate the salt from this recipe.

CHICKEN JELLY

2 packages plain gelatin
1/3 cup cold water
1 1/2 cups boiling chicken stock
1 teaspoon salt (only if using saltless broth)
1/4 teaspoon paprika
2 cups diced, cooked skinless chicken
1/2 cup finely diced celery
2 tablespoons chopped pimientos
2 tablespoons pickle relish

Soak gelatin in cold water until thoroughly softened. Add boiling stock, salt (if necessary), and paprika, stirring vigorously until gelatin is dissolved. Cool in refrigerator until thick (but do not allow to fully set—you want it thick enough so that solid ingredients will "float" rather than sink).

Stir in all remaining ingredients. Pour into moistened mold, large enough to hold 4–5 cups liquid. Refrigerate 5–6 hours. Unmold. Serve on lettuce leaves, with deviled eggs and mayonnaise.

Makes 4–6 servings.

Woman's Industrial Exchange Restaurant, 333 No. Charles St., Baltimore, Md.; (301) 685-4388.

9
Casseroles

HOT TAMALE PIE

TAMALES:

3 dozen corn husks (or parchment paper
   cut into 8-by-5-inch rectangles)
½ pound finely ground meat
1 clove garlic, minced
1 tablespoon bacon fat
½ cup beef broth
3 to 4 tablespoons chili powder
1 teaspoon salt
1½ cups warm water
3 cups finely ground yellow cornmeal
1 cup lard
1 teaspoon salt

   Soak corn husks in hot water until
pliable, about 1 hour. (If using parchment,
no need to soak it.)

   Brown meat with garlic in bacon fat. Add
broth, chili powder, and salt. Simmer
uncovered, adding more broth if necessary
to make a thick, moist sauce (about 1 cup).

   Combine 1½ cups warm water with
cornmeal. Let stand. Cream lard with salt
until fluffy. Add cornmeal mixture and beat
well.

   Combine cornmeal mixture and meat.
Spread in husks, leaving a one-inch edge,
untouched by filling. Roll the husk to form a
tight wrapper around the filling. Tie each
end with a string (or twist tie).

   Stand tamales upright on a rack above
one inch of water in a pot tall and narrow
enough to keep them from tipping over.
Cover loosely and steam 45 minutes.

   Yield: 3 dozen tamales.

Hot Tamale Pie

GREENVILLE, Miss.—At Doe's Eat Place in Greenville, you can buy tamales to go packed in coffee cans; and at night, when Doe's opens its dining room, you can get a few to tease your tongue before digging into a steak dinner the likes of which you will taste nowhere else.

You would never guess by looking at it that Doe's is one of the best restaurants in America. It is—let us be kind—an unprepossessing place. Actually, it is a dump, a dilapidated ex-grocery store on the wrong side of town, with "Doe's" painted in big black letters across its white cinderblock wall.

The back room is the kitchen, which doubles as the main dining room. Tables are surrounded by shelves of mismatched plates and the clatter of the waitresses mixing salads and frying potatoes. If you decide you want steak, tell your waitress the cut you like and the poundage you desire, and she will go to the meat locker and fetch a likely raw cut for your approval. It gets sent up front to be broiled.

Dig in to your plate of hot tamales, then aim your knife and fork at the T-bone set before you, charred in the broiler and served in a puddle of natural juice alongside a hill of skillet-cooked French fries.

There may be two or three other steak houses in this country that serve cuts of meat on a par with Doe's, but none provide the happy party feeling of these oilcloth-covered tables in the back room of an old grocery store. Prime beef is a luxury money can buy; the character of Doe's Eat Place is priceless.

Inspired by a recipe given us by Doe Signa, our tamale pie can be customized by replacing the beef with cooked and shredded pork, or sharp cheese and chopped nuts, or any well-seasoned, finely chopped cooked meat. We like it best with beef tamales, and any simple chili with beans. We don't give exact measurements, as the pie is flexible, and can be made in any size you like.

HOT TAMALE PIE:

   *Preheat oven to 350 degrees. Butter a
shallow casserole. Carefully remove tamales
from husks and layer on the bottom of the
casserole. Top with chili, then a generous
sprinkle of scallions (including tops), then a
layer of grated sharp cheddar cheese. Bake
20–25 minutes, until cheese begins to
brown.*

*Doe's Eat Place, 502 Nelson, Greenville,
Miss.; (601) 334-3315.*

Golden Noodle Bake

INDIANAPOLIS—There is something special about department store eateries. They feel safe, insulated; they are oases of civility, distanced from the chaos of the city by the orderly access routes of escalators and elevators. Even the most modern of them seem nostalgic, conjuring up thoughts of genteel ladies in white gloves and gay hats trading conversation over dainty bisques, crustless sandwiches, and sunshine cake.

Of all the department stores in which we have eaten, the one we like most is the Tea Room in the L.S. Ayres Department Store in downtown Indianapolis. The store is eighty-two years old; the Tea Room has been the highlight of the eighth floor since 1929.

It is an awesome room, built in ocean-liner scale with a tall ceiling and elaborate chandeliers, the vast space measured by massive classic columns. It is the size of a large gymnasium, but thick curtains on the two-story windows and a luxuriant carpet soften the lunchtime commotion to a low bustle.

As you come away from the elevators and face the magnificent vista, you see a mannequin in a spotlight, wearing the fashion of the moment. Near the mannequin is an open treasure chest containing small wrapped packages; gifts "for good little girls and boys who have lunch at the tea room."

If you are in a hurry, you can dine cafeteria-style on the right side of the room and be in and out in ten or fifteen minutes. Even those who request table service, however, do not come to the Tea Room for a dragged-out meal. There is a spirit of celerity about this grand old dining room. Shoppers and working people come to eat, and maybe to talk, but seldom to linger.

Tables are real wood with an aged patina. Waitresses are real, too—real professionals in black uniforms and white aprons who get the job done fast. Despite their speed and bustle, there is a calming quality about these ladies. You know they know how to take good care of a customer.

GOLDEN NOODLE BAKE

1 pound egg noodles, ½-inch wide
4 tablespoons butter
⅓ cup chopped onion
½ cup cottage cheese
½ cup sour cream
1 egg, beaten
2 tablespoons sugar
½ teaspoon salt
pepper to taste
½ cup cornflakes
8 strips bacon, fried to taste

Cook egg noodles in boiling salted water until just tender, 5 to 10 minutes.

As noodles cook, sauté onion in butter until translucent (but not brown). Remove from heat.

Butter a 2-quart casserole. Preheat oven to 350 degrees.

Drain noodles when tender, then toss in large bowl with sautéed onions and butter.

Mix cottage cheese, sour cream, and egg. Stir in sugar, salt, and pepper. Mix well with noodles. Empty noodles into casserole and bake, uncovered, 20 minutes. Sprinkle on cornflakes and bake 5 to 8 minutes more, until cornflakes are toasty brown.

Top each serving of noodle bake with 2 strips bacon.

Serves 4.

L.S. Ayres Tea Room, 8th Floor, L.S. Ayres Department Store, 1 Washingon St., Indianapolis, Ind.; (317) 262-4411.

Food is what really puts the L.S. Ayres Tea Room on the good-eats map of America. Here is classic department store lunch in all its splendor—from individual chicken pot pies (with real mashed potatoes on the side) to strawberry angel food ice cream sandwiches. Oh, sure, you can eat lo-cal plates and salads, even quiche if you must; but the treasures of this kitchen—known and loved by generations of customers—are old-fashioned specialties such as roast pork with spiced apples and sage dressing, or chicken velvet soup, or "pumpkin fingers" (cream cheese on pumpkin bread), or ice cream pie dolloped with real, swoonfully delicious butterscotch sauce.

Perhaps the best-known of all the Tea Room's lunches is Golden Noodle Bake—a casserole perfect for soothing frazzled shoppers' nerves, or for any time one craves a bowl of gentle comfort food. Here is how we make it at home.

Austrian Ravioli

OKLAHOMA CITY—"We called it goulash when we were growing up," explained Jim Geist, whose family runs the Lady Classen Cafeteria. "We have been serving it here for as long as I can remember. One day a man from Europe came in, ate a plate of goulash, then told us that it was exactly what they serve in Austria. That's how Austrian ravioli got its name."

Jim's story makes perfect sense . . . except for the small fact that Austrian ravioli, as served by the Lady Classen Cafeteria, bears no resemblance to ravioli, and little resemblance to any dish we have ever seen attributed to Austria. Indeed, what it most resembles is American chop suey—the odd New England specialty that (despite its name) has nothing whatsoever to do with Chinese food.

Before this gets any more confusing, let us tell you exactly what Austrian ravioli is: elbow macaroni, ground beef, tomato sauce, and peas. We suspect that this popular, all-purpose meat and macaroni dish has innumerable local variations; and that many families have their own special way of making it. One friend says he grew up with a similar dish called noodleburger casserole. Another knows it as slumgullion.

Whatever you call it, Austrian ravioli is one of those mundane foods that we Americans love to call by an exotic name. For example, we once spent days searching the southern Midwest for a dish we had heard referred to as "Arkansas wedding cake" . . . only to learn that this rare specialty was in fact Missourians' smart-aleck name for ordinary white bread. If you are in the Northeast, don't expect mashed potatoes, giblet gravy, and cranberry sauce if you order "Cape Cod turkey": that's the local sobriquet for codfish balls. And out West, you'd better be an adventurous eater if you order Rocky Mountain oysters. These "oysters" are in fact sliced and sautéed (or deep-fried) testicles of sheep.

We cannot plumb the logic of how Austrian ravioli got to be called ravioli, but we certainly recommend you try a plate of it at the Lady Classen Cafeteria if you are ever in Oklahoma City.

Most Lady Classen food is classic Southwestern fare: pan-fried catfish and hushpuppies, baked chicken and cornmeal mush, baked ham and potato royale. Entrées are complemented by homemade breads, individual Jell-O molds, vast varieties of vegetables, and shelves' worth of pies, cakes, cobblers, and puddings.

The dining room in this shopping center cafeteria is extraordinarily gracious, decorated in a Colonial style complete with brass chandeliers (kept at candlelight level), mahogany and cherrywood china cupboards, and a serpentine red brick wall reminiscent of

AUSTRIAN RAVIOLI

8 ounces elbow macaroni
1 cup canned stewed tomatoes, drained
1 cup tomato suace
1 clove garlic, mashed
2 tablespoons olive oil
³/₄ pound ground beef
³/₄ cup cooked peas
salt to taste
1 cup grated cheddar cheese

Boil macaroni in boiling salted water until tender—about 7 minutes. Drain and mix together with tomatoes and tomato sauce in a large bowl.

Sauté garlic clove in olive oil over medium heat until it begins to brown. Remove clove from oil and cook meat, stirring constantly to keep it loose.

Add meat to macaroni mixture. Stir in peas, salt to taste, and grated cheddar cheese.

Serves 4.

Lady Classen Cafeteria, 6903 N. May Ave., Oklahoma City, Okla.; (405) 843-6459.

Jeffersonian architecture. Whether you come for after-church turkey and all the fixings on Sunday afternoon, or a tuna skillet sandwich for Friday lunch, mealtime at the Lady Classen is a civilized experience.

If you aren't coming to Oklahoma City, here is our own version of the way Lady Classen cooks make this all-American meal. It is homely, inexpensive, uncouth . . . and really delicious. We think of it as comfort food of the first order. The easy recipe can be augmented however you please: with corn niblets, ground cooked sausage, pearl onions, etc. It is important, however, to use elbow macaroni; other kinds of noodles don't mix as neatly with their companion ingredients.

10

Vegetables and Side Dishes

Candied Apples

SEVIERVILLE, Tenn.—Drive a spell along Route 339 after you have turned off of Dolly Parton Parkway (Sevierville is Dolly's girlhood home), and you will begin to wonder if Gladys Breeden's restaurant really does exist. Through fields and hollers and over gentle hills, you are penetrating the Tennessee countryside and seeing arcadian America the way no main road ever shows it.

When you begin to feel lost—and you will—you might find a man on his front porch, just sitting. He'll give directions, but not by route number and stoplights. "Right at the bridge, left at the second blacktop. When you get to Howard's Grocery, you know you're on your way."

Finally, the narrow road leads to a pale green cinderblock building that is Gladys Breeden's home and restaurant. Turn off the car's engine, and as dust settles, you are bowled over by the silence. Roosters crow in some distant barn. A frog croaks. A zephyr rustles leaves in the field across the way.

The restaurant is all alone. There are no other businesses for miles, and Gladys has never advertised. But people take the trouble to find this place, because the food is good and the prices are low, and most of all, because the "ambience"—as a restaurant critic might call it—is a soul-stirring taste of country ways.

The dining room contains a counter with nine stools and exactly three Formica tables—mismatched, with assorted kitchen chairs. Gladys sits at one with a lad who appears to be her kin. When we walked in the door, Gladys told us to grab a plate and dig in.

We didn't see any plates. A counter customer pointed to a kitchen cabinet. We opened it and saw a stack of battered china. "Take a couple big ones!" he laughed, which we did. Then we turned to the stove and "dipped our own"—mountainese for help yourself.

Simmering on Gladys Breeden's old kitchen stove are pots and pans and platters of everything she's cooked that day: fried chicken, pork chops, barbecued ribs, country steak and gravy, hominy, mashed potatoes, creamed corn, macaroni and cheese, greens, boiled cabbage, snap beans, and about a half-dozen other vegetables and stewed fruits. Around the stove are serving tables set with baskets full of biscuits, dinner rolls, and cornbread wedges. And there are three or four lattice-top fruit pies. And fried pies. And peach cobbler. And banana cream pie.

Pile a plate with everything you like (except dessert, for which you'll make a second trip), then find a place to eat. When you've had your fill, you carry your plate back to the sink, pay Gladys five

CANDIED APPLES

8 tablespoons butter
4–6 Delicious apples, cored but not peeled,
  cut into six wedges each
1 cup sugar

  Melt butter in heavy saucepan over medium heat. Add apples, tossing and stirring to coat thoroughly. Sprinkle sugar on top of apples.
  Bring to simmer, stir gently, and lower heat. Stir occasionally, but do not mash or break up apples. Simmer very gently thirty minutes, spooning off excess juice as it bubbles up. Serve warm.
  Makes 6–8 small servings.

Gladys Breeden's, Wilhoite Road off Route 339, Sevierville, Tenn.; (615) 453-7490.

ONIONS AND POTATOES

2 large red onions, sliced thin
2 large potatoes, cut into ¼-inch sticks
oil for deep frying

  Soak onions in cold water 15 minutes, separating rings. Blot totally dry.
  Soak potato sticks in cold water 15 minutes. Blot totally dry.
  Heat 2 inches of oil in deep fryer to 380 degrees. Fry potatoes, a handful at a time, making sure they don't stick together, 3–5 minutes until light brown. Remove from oil and drain on paper towels. Continue frying potatoes until all are done. Make sure temperature of oil stays at 370–380 degrees. Keep cooked potatoes warm in a 275-degree oven on a baking sheet lined with paper towels.

dollars, and walk out into the clean mountain air, refreshed by a meal like no other in America.

While we were eating, Gladys showed us a picture taken by the tourism bureau to attract people to Tennessee. It was shot in Nashville, in a photo studio decorated to look just like her restaurant, only prettied up with gingham curtains, unstained pots and pans, and FTD flower arrangements on each table. And Gladys is wearing a lovely dress. "I've worn pants for thirty years!" she laughed, telling us how they wanted to spruce up her as well as her restaurant for the picture. It is a very nice picture indeed. But we like the real thing—a bit disheveled, totally honest, and Gladys in pants.

When we asked her to share a recipe, she explained that all she does is cook "old-timey food," and gave us this simple formula for one of the distinctive side dishes always set on her stove, a Tennessee mountain cook's classic. Its supersweetness is the perfect counterpoint for fried chicken or country ham.

Onions and Potatoes

BEVERLY HILLS, Calif.—Local patrons of the Grill on the Alley say they like it because it is a restaurant that reminds them of New York.

The last time we arrived on the West Coast, we headed straight to the Grill because the way we see it, this place is pure L.A.

Years ago there were places like the Grill in the East: the forthright eateries of Manhattan's "Steak Row" off 3rd Avenue in the East 40s, where honest food was served in comfortable (but never fancy) surroundings. They were considered masculine restaurants because their menus were almost entirely red meat and potatoes, and because they were places where businessmen met over martinis and sirloin steaks.

How times have changed! New York's steak houses have priced themselves beyond the reach of ordinary men's wallets. Few men demand meat every day. And the business lunch has become the province of women as well as men. More apropos, the best New York steak houses are now located in Los Angeles. The newest and highest-tone of them is the Grill on the Alley in Beverly Hills, just off Rodeo Drive.

As New Yorky as it may be in its original philosophy (listed on the menu as "quality without compromise"), the Grill offers an eating experience that is strictly Tinseltown.

Where else does a seeming majority of customers arrive in Mer-

When all potatoes are cooked, fry onions, a few at a time, until golden brown. They will take only 2–3 minutes per batch, so watch carefully. Drain on paper towels; keep warm on a separate baking sheet in the oven.

Serve immediately when onions are finished. Salt potatoes and place on plate. Top potatoes with fried onions. Salt onions to taste.

Serves 2–4, depending on size of portions.

Grill on the Alley, 9560 Dayton Way, Beverly Hills, Calif.; (213) 276-0615.

cedes-Benzes and Rolls-Royces? The talk inside is nearly all movie talk. Agents sit with casting directors; movie stars join producers at the bar; and white-jacketed waiters—many of whom you've seen playing bit parts in TV shows and commercials—chatter among themselves about casting calls and backstage goings-on.

The scene is fun, but it's the menu we like best. It is printed every day, a long roster of steaks and chops, California seafood, freshwater fish, Dungeness crab from up north, eastern oysters, a superb Cobb salad, and such ordinary (but extraordinarily good) desserts as apple pie and hot fudge sundaes.

It is an ingenuous list of food, not an unnecessary adjective anywhere—a reflection of the kitchen's forthright approach to cooking. You can even come to the Grill for a supper of ham and eggs or, if it's after 10:30 P.M., Welsh rabbit as good as at Musso's.

If you like potatoes, you'll find happiness in a Grill booth, because the list of what they do with them is an honor roll of great dishes from the Starch Hall of Fame. Even the plain baked potato is fabulous—a giant, served with its steamy white insides erupting from its chewy tan skin. There are O'Briens, shoestrings, Lyonnaise, hashed browns, and French fries . . . and a combo plate that brings us to our knees every time.

The combo is simple. "Fried potatoes and onions" is what the menu says. But my, what good ones! The onions are batterless, thin and wispy. The potatoes are skinny sticks, mostly crunch with only a slim core of tender white fluff inside. The delicate onions are heaped on top of the potatoes so your first fistfuls are lacy. The deeper you go, the spuddier it gets.

Vegetables and Side Dishes

COUNTRY SIMPLE YELLOW SQUASH

4 yellow summer squashes, 8 inches long
8 tablespoons butter
1 teaspoon Accent
1 to 1½ cups evaporated milk

Wash squashes and snip ends off. Steam over briskly boiling water until barely tender (but not mushy), 4–5 minutes.

Preheat oven to 350 degrees.

Lay squashes in pan just large enough to hold them. Cut a deep plug about the diameter of a 50-cent piece in the top of each and divide butter equally among holes, piling it up as needed. Sprinkle squashes with Accent. Pour enough evaporated milk into pan so it is ½-inch deep.

Bake 25 minutes.

Spoon evaporated milk from pan into holes of squashes, and serve directly from pan.

Makes 4 large servings.

Branch Ranch: Branch-Forbes Exit off I-4, north ¾ mile to sign, turn right on Thonotosassa Rd.; (813) 752-1957.

Country Simple Yellow Squash

PLANT CITY, Fla.—There is no more dramatic restaurant success story than that of Mrs. Mary Branch, who began serving meals to paying guests in the TV room of her family home thirty years ago. Her makeshift eatery became known to an ever increasing circle of friends; as new people crowded in for dinner, Mrs. Branch enlarged her place, calling it the Branch Ranch.

Today the Branch Ranch is a sprawling eating complex that can serve a thousand people in a day. In its reception room, where throngs wait for a precious weekend table, the walls are plastered with a million calling cards of customers who have come from around the world to partake of the legendary Florida feasts.

And yet, for all the noise and commotion, despite the silly "IQ Test" pegboard set on tables to amuse the kids, this place is for real. There are few restaurants in the South or anywhere in the United States that offer such an unadulterated taste of true country cooking.

The meal begins with a relish tray—pickled beets and tangy bread-and-butter pickles that would do any farm cook proud. Chewy buttermilk biscuits, warm from the oven, are accompanied by bitter orange marmalade and jam made with whole, tender-textured strawberries. Everything is made from scratch, the kind of blue-ribbon stuff you cannot buy in supermarkets or even in gourmet stores.

The main courses are country ham or fried chicken or steak, and they're all just fine. But the best part of a Branch Ranch meal is the arrival of the tower of side dishes. The stack of pans is a yard high: candied sweet potatoes, scalloped eggplant, pole beans, white potatoes, yellow squash, and dumpling-topped chicken pot pie. These, we repeat, are merely the side dishes! And of course there are more biscuits, too.

Serve yourself, family style; or designate one person at the table to dish out the food, just as Dad does at home for Sunday dinner. For dessert, tradition demands peach cobbler, or white cake topped with grated coconut. And if you like those pickles or homemade jams, we suggest you buy some to take home with you. Believe us when we tell you that after you eat relishes here in Plant City, no store-bought ones will ever taste the same again.

Surrounded by the orange groves and unspoiled farmland east of Tampa, the Branch Ranch remains one of America's great rural restaurants. Size and popularity have done nothing to diminish its glow.

Restaurant manager Andy Anderson told us that yellow squash

has been on the vegetable roster since the beginning in 1956, with the exception of a few days last year when they couldn't get it fresh. It's an elementary recipe; no fancy flourishes will improve its quiet goodness.

BELLE MEADE BUFFET SQUASH

4 to 5 cups summer squash, cleaned and
    cut
½ medium onion, chopped fine
6 tablespoons margarine
¼ cup sugar
½ teaspoon salt
¼ teaspoon white pepper
¾ cup breadcrumbs

Boil squash in salted water 3 to 5 minutes, until tender. Drain well and mash, but do not pulverize.

Preheat oven to 400 degrees.

Sauté onion in margarine until limp. Add to mashed squash. Add sugar, salt, and pepper. Pour into greased baking dish. Bakes 20 minutes. Top with breadcrumbs. Return to oven and continue baking 5 to 7 minutes until breadcrumbs begin to brown.

Serves 4 to 6.

Belle Meade Buffet, Belle Meade Plaza, Nashville, Tenn.; (615) 298-5571.

Belle Meade Buffet Squash

NASHVILLE, Tenn.—"Please study menus and make selections as quickly as possible," instructs the sign at the beginning of the line at the Belle Meade Buffet. To whet appetites, the entrance to the cafeteria is decorated with enormous four-color photographs of food—glamour shots that show dew glistening on ripe tomatoes, steam rising from slabs of prime rib, butter melting onto steaming hot biscuits.

We try hard, we *do* try hard to study the menu and make our selections quickly, as requested. But it is hopeless. The moment we reach the beginning of the buffet line, we become stupid. "May I he'p you?" asks the server in her Tennessee accent. Then it happens: Our minds go blank. Our jaws drop open. Our hands grow too numb to even point at what we want.

Can you recognize the symptoms? Yes, we confess: We suffer from the eater's disorder known as cafeteria anxiety. It never fails to happen when we visit the Belle Meade—as we always do whenever we are within a hundred miles of Nashville.

The problem is that no matter how firm our selections are when we first join the line out in the lobby, we are always flummoxed and flabbergasted as soon as the line curves around and we are faced with the sight of the actual buffet itself. Here is a vista of vittles to make food lovers weep for joy. How can we possibly choose *x, y,* and *z* (catfish, hush puppies, and chess pie), and by choosing them, not choose *a, b,* and *c* (fried chicken, seasoned greens, and lemon meringue pie in a graham cracker crust)?

It's especially bad for us New Englanders, since so much of the spread is food that we *never* get back home. Food that we dream about. Food that we crave. And here it all is, cooked to perfection. From jalapeño cornbread and eighteen different salads to pistachio cake and peach cobbler: There are far, far too many things we yearn to eat to fit them all on a single tray, or even two.

So we muddle through the line in a kind of anxious daze, usually winding up with ridiculously unbalanced meals. Jane will likely have two pies, a cake, a pudding, a chicken-fried steak, fried chicken, and roast beef. On Michael's tray, you might find six

Southern-style vegetables, a mountain of biscuits, and three congealed salads (Jell-O).

Once the bill is toted up at the end of the line (it is virtually impossible for two people to spend more than ten dollars for dinner), a Belle Meade waiter whisks the trays to a table in the dining room.

It is a brightly lighted room. Just as the serving line moves fast, people eat fast, too. That's another thing we like about this place: nobody dawdles. Since the whole meal is set out before you, there's no waiting between courses. And when you're done, you don't have to flag down the waiter for a check. Few people spend more than an hour at the Belle Meade, start to finish. That's our kind of meal!

Cafeteria dining such as this is one of the glories of Southern gastronomy. Even the cafeteria chains, such as Morrison's, Furr's, and the Picadilly, usually set out a mighty fine spread. But let us tell you, the Belle Meade is something special; it's a cut above.

Vegetables are especially noteworthy. They are cooked Southern-style, which means they're customized, superseasoned, and vigorously spiced. Cabbage gets stir-fried with bacon until it sops up the porky goodness. Whipped yams are flavored with vanilla, dotted with raisins, and streaked with marshmallow. And squash—as in this recipe given to us by Belle Meade owner William Ogburn—is transformed into something glorious by means of sugar, onions, and margarine. (Margarine, not butter; we tried it with butter, and it isn't the same.)

San Antonio Squash

AUSTIN, Tex.—"We don't serve all you can eat," reads the credo of Threadgill's Restaurant. "We serve more than you can eat."

No lie. Most hearty eaters will likely manage to finish the entire chicken-fried steak on their plate. It's virtually impossible to stop eating this tender, half-inch-thick slab of beef, hand breaded and fast-fried so it develops a crunchy, dark-brown, savory crust to pocket the meat. You might mop up all the good pan-drippin' gravy, too . . . but the going gets tough when you face the mashed potatoes that come alongside. This mound is approximately three normal servings' worth of genuine still-a-wee-bit-lumpy spuds, also flowing with gravy.

There are other vegetables, too: take your pick from among blackeyed peas, cheese-ballasted baked squash, creamed corn, stewed okra, turnip greens, hamhock and beans, etc. They're all

SAN ANTONIO SQUASH

4 cups sliced summer squash, sliced ¼-inch
  thick
2 tablespoons butter
1 tablespoon corn oil
⅓ cup chopped onion
1 clove garlic, minced
3 tablespoons flour
1½ cups warm milk
1 cup grated sharp Jack cheese
1–3 chopped jalapeño peppers, to taste

Preheat oven to 350 degrees. Butter an
8-inch square casserole.

Boil squash in water 2–3 minutes, until
slightly tender. Drain and spread in the
casserole.

Heat butter and oil in saucepan over
medium heat. Sauté onion until limp, about
3 minutes. Add garlic and sauté another 2
minutes. Whisk in flour, stirring constantly
over medium-low heat 2–3 minutes until
flour is very pale gold. Whisk in milk. Stir
constantly until thick and bubbly, about 3
minutes. Remove from heat. Stir in cheese.
Stir in jalapeños.

Pour sauce onto squash in casserole.
Bake uncovered 20 minutes.

Serves 4–6.

Threadgill's Restaurant, 6416 N. Lamar,
Austin, Tex.; (512) 451-5440.

served in gargantuan portions. And how about the block of corn-bread? And cobbler and pie and pudding: You don't want to miss any of these things, not if you like down-home cooking.

It may be a rare feat to polish off a Threadgill's meal. But what fun it is to try! Hey, Threadgill's is fun as soon as you walk in the door, even before the chow arrives. So before getting back to the food, let us tell you about the place.

It is a juke joint that was a gas station a half-century ago, and started serving beer after Prohibition. The floor is creaky wood; decor is mostly neon beer signs. The wall in the main taproom features a picture of the late Mr. Threadgill with Janis Joplin, who hung out here in the 1960s when his place was one of Austin's prime hootenanny parlors, frequented by pickers, yodlers, balladeers, and bluesmen. At any mealtime, ambience is boisterous in the extreme, with crowds surging into the various sprawling dining rooms as waiters push through carrying loaded plates.

Threadgill's kitchen turns out the only kind of food that would taste right in these surroundings. They call it "American food, Southern style." As much as we adore the chicken fried steak and the outstanding Creole meat loaf, it is Threadgill's vegetables that stir our souls. These are not frail veggies like one must eat on a diet. They are seriously cooked, highly seasoned, ultra-enriched, buttered, sweetened, and gooped-up vegetables, each as luscious as a slice of buttermilk pie (another not-to-be-missed specialty).

You can always come for a vegetable-only plate of five different kinds. On occasion, the blackboard lists an amazing "nine-veggie orgy" for $5.95. Among them is "San Antonio squash," the etymology of which remains a mystery. Frankly, we don't care how it got its name. What matters is that we know how to make it. Any time we want an authoritative vegetable dish with the spark of peppers and the wanton luxury of cheese sauce, here's the way we do it, inspired by the one-and-only Threadgill's.

Derby Dressing

DERBY, Iowa—There is no sign outside, but it is easy to find the Derby Restaurant once you find Derby, Iowa. Of the three buildings in town, it is the one that is not the Derby Opera House and not the Derby Post Office.

We pulled up Thursday at noon, led by a tip from Margaret and Allison Engel, authors of *Food Finds*, the nationwide guide to mail-order good eats. They know the Derby Restaurant because Allison lived on a nearby farm. "We would save up for weeks (calories, that is) before attempting a Derby feed," Margaret said. "It is a true groaning board, the best restaurant in Iowa."

We wondered if it was still in business. Derby's Main Street was ghostly quiet. A few cars and pickups and a couple of tractors were parked nearby, but there wasn't a sign of life other than a freckle-bellied puppy who scampered out of nowhere to greet us as we got out of the car.

When we opened the door to the Derby Restaurant, we were rendered speechless. Before us stretched a scene that we can only describe as Jane and Michael Stern's gastronomic holy grail—the kind of place we dream of finding.

In contrast to the street outside, the restaurant was noisy, even boisterous. There were big tables up front, shared by six or eight or ten—mothers, children, grannies, spinsters, farmers in overalls. Toward the back, there was more seating at long counters that faced each other across the wide, wood-floored room. And there was the food, all laid out in Tupperware bowls, electric skillets, pie plates, Pyrex casseroles, and Crockpots. The way it works is this: You pay four dollars, grab a plate, then help yourself.

First, though, you have to find someone to take the four dollars. The three sisters who run the place (who cook everything in their nearby home) are busy filling customers' glasses with tea, clearing places, and playing hostess. Finally, when you find one to take your money, she asks if you'll sign the guest book, points you to the food, then helps you find a seat somewhere, elbow to elbow with the folks of Derby.

It is hard to describe the ambience of the Derby Restaurant, because it is like no place else. The best thing about it is its mess-hall high spirits. Most conversations stretch from table to table and across the counters. It's like a town meeting, at which everybody knows everybody. And if you are a stranger, as we were, they'll be curious.

"Where're you from?" one farmer asked across two counters.

"Connecticut," we answered.

DERBY DRESSING

4 cups white bread torn into bite-size pieces
3/4 cup chicken stock
1/4 cup melted butter
1 teaspoon dried sage
3/4 teaspoon salt
1/2 teaspoon pepper

Preheat oven to 350 degrees. Combine all ingredients. Spread in 1-quart casserole. Cover dish with foil. Bake 1 hour. If crusty dressing is desired, remove foil after 30 minutes.

Serves 4–6.

The Derby Restaurant, Main Street, Derby, Iowa. (No phone.)

"It's a long way to come for a meal," the man's wife commented, with a large forkful of peanut butter pie on the way from her plate to her mouth.

"Yup," a nearby man laughed, watching the farmer's wife eat the pie with gusto. "But it sure is worth it!"

As for local color, there is plenty: pictures of the Derby High School graduating class of 1937; jars and jugs, baskets and knick-knacks that are old, but not quite antique; calendars of yesteryear; slow-spinning fans overhead. No inventory of decor, however, could convey the sense of community imparted by this truly folksy scene.

The food is farm-wife cooking: a happy hodgepodge of freshly baked breads, sweet rolls, and coffee cakes alongside pastel Jell-O molds and homey casseroles, vegetables galore, *real* mashed potatoes, four kinds of pie and a couple of cobblers, all anchored by serious main courses of baked chicken, ham, and roast beef.

One of the dishes we liked was an elementary one: chicken dressing, the recipe for which was given to us by the lady at the Crockpot where it was kept warm. Its secret, she explained, is sturdy homemade bread. It makes a great simple "second stuffing" to go with turkey, as a companion to a more elaborate one inside the bird.

Onion Rings

SPARTANBURG, S.C.—Brace yourself. Get calm. Take a deep breath. Now walk through the entrance to the Beacon Drive-In. You have stepped into a tornado. New customers push in behind you. The line ahead moves fast. From behind the counter, white-aproned waiters scream at you to hurry up and place your order. "Barbecue," you stammer. "Pork-a-Plenty, sliced, with slaw and onions."

And before the last syllable is out of your mouth, the server is yelling your order back to an immense open kitchen, where dozens of cooks chop and fry and assemble meals in what seems like total chaos and confusion. You breeze down the counter, beneath signs advising, "J.C. Says It's Fine to Pass in Line" and, "Place Your Money in Hand and Have Your Order in Mind so We Can Get You to the Ball Game on Time."

Now you have arrived at the drink station. This choice is easy. Although Pepsi, milk shakes, and lemonade are on the menu, nearly every Beacon customer orders tea. It is iced tea, Southern-style, meaning liberally presweetened, served in a gargantuan tumbler loaded with crushed ice. Forget about straws; the way to lap this tea up is with one's snout deep inside the cavernous cup.

Less than a minute has passed since the kitchen devoured your called-out order, and whammo! Here comes the food, exactly what you wanted, brought to you by whichever server yelled it out.

Now dig into some of the finest barbecue in a state where barbecue is king. Hickory-flavored ham is available as tender "inside slices," lean, with a subtle, smoky tingle; or as "outside meat" with a chewy, sharply seasoned crust. Both come bathed in a sauce that smacks of cloves and vinegar. On the side, if you get a Pork-a-Plenty plate, you want French fries, plus sweet relish slaw, and out-of-this-world fried onion rings.

The Beacon sells a ton of barbecue each day, but if pork with its accoutrements is not your dish, you may choose from a one hundred-item menu that includes fried chicken, catfish sandwiches, "pig's dinner fudge sundaes," and double chili cheeseburgers with bacon, lettuce, and tomato.

You can eat indoors at the Beacon, in one of several rooms equipped with televisions and iced tea dispensers (for seconds). And, of course, you can eat in your car. Car service at the Beacon is fast, although not quite as thrilling as a run through the line inside. If you are lucky, you'll get Thomas Byrd or Robert Evans as your curb attendant. They are Beacon veterans, having carried pork and onion rings to customers for over thirty years each.

The Beacon Drive-In opened for business on Thanksgiving Day in 1946, and it has since earned a reputation as a one-of-a-kind landmark for barbecue, burgers, iced tea, and lightning-fast service. Operated first by John White, now his sons, it is a restaurant with real personality, a taste of an American style of eating and serving that has been eclipsed nearly everywhere else by the sameness of franchised food.

If you dine in your car, one of the sights visible from the parking lot will be bags full of onions piled up against the drive-in wall in eight-foot-tall heaps. John White Jr. told us that the Beacon goes through a freight car full of onions every three weeks, almost all of them made into onion rings. The rings taste good, he told us, because they are dipped in a batter made with buttermilk before they're fried.

ONION RINGS

3 large Bermuda onions (about 3 pounds)
2 eggs, lightly beaten
2 cups buttermilk
2 cups flour
1 teaspoon baking soda
2 teaspoons salt
fat for deep frying
salt to taste

Peel, then slice onions into 1/4-inch slices and break up into individual rings. Soak in large bowl(s) filled with ice-cold water at least one hour, until fully chilled.

Beat eggs with buttermilk, then stir in flour, baking soda, and salt.

Heat fat to 350 degrees.

Remove a few onion rings from ice water and thoroughly pat dry. (If membrane separates from onion, remove it.) Dip in buttermilk batter, let excess drip off, and fry in fat, turning once, until golden brown. Do not crowd deep fryer. Drain rings on paper towels and keep warm in 200-degree oven.

Continue frying onion rings, a few at a time. Serve as soon as possible. Salt to taste before serving.

Serves 4–6.

Beacon Drive-In, 255 Reidville Road, Spartanburg, S.C.; (803) 585-9387.

Fried Okra

ABBEVILLE, Miss.—The formal name of the restaurant we are about to describe is Ruth & Jimmie's Sporting Goods & Cafe. You come here to buy a rod and reel, hip boots, or shells for your shotgun. You stock up on live bait from the buckets on the porch. You gas up at the pumps out front. You buy a pair of Lady Beverly pantyhose, a Hav-A-Hank for your breast pocket, or sack of White Lily flour for making biscuits.

The main reason we recommend a visit to Ruth & Jimmie's is lunch. Toward the back of the store, beyond the dry goods and hardware, past ammo and groceries, is a counter with 12 stools. It opens at 5:30 in the morning, and serves food until 7:30 at night. Midday is the choice time to come, when a short list of the day's meals is chalked on the blackboard.

The cuisine is country-style: fried steak smothered with gravy, ham and cooked apples, roast beef and creamed potatoes. There is always a big selection of vegetables such as black-eyed peas, squash casseroles, collard greens, and fried okra: Choose three to accompany any main course. There is corn bread for mopping up gravy, and fruit cobbler or mud-thick fudge pie for dessert.

The food is good. Honest vittles. Soul-satisfying in a way few highfalutin dinners ever are. But it is not the food that makes a Ruth & Jimmie's meal extraordinary. It is Ruth & Jimmie's. It is the pronounced tilt of the old wood frame "shotgun" building, its creaky floor, and the complex aroma of steak gravy mixed with the good smell of a hardware store that wafts across the ancient lunch counter.

The experience of eating here is unique to the deep South, to Mississippi in particular, where tradition reigns supreme. As you plow into a plate of smothered chicken and dressing at the back of this old country store, it is hard to believe that it is 1988 outside. Conversely, when you leave Ruth & Jimmie's, get back on the main road, and reenter a world of fast-food franchises, you might begin to wonder if this colorful legacy of rural life wasn't some Brigadoon-like fantasy.

It is real, we assure you. And Abbeville is a real town, with a population of 450. Ruth & Jimmie's, at the crossroads that constitutes the "business district," was built in the 1930s and started serving meals in 1973. Most of the lunch traffic is local folks supplemented by a loyal contingent from the University of Mississippi in nearby Oxford, as well as hunters in season, and occasional tourists visiting Ole Miss for events such as the annual William Faulkner Conference.

FRIED OKRA

1 pound fresh okra
2 cups vegetable oil
1 cup buttermilk
1 egg
2 cups all-purpose flour
1 teaspoon salt

Wash and trim okra. Slice into ¼-inch pieces.

Heat vegetable oil in deep fryer or skillet to about 350 degrees.

Mix buttermilk and egg. Mix flour and salt.

Dip okra pieces into buttermilk wash, then roll in flour.

Deep-fry okra until golden brown, about 3 minutes. Lift from oil with slotted spoon. Drain on paper towels and serve immediately.

Serves 4–6.

Ruth & Jimmie's, Route 7, Abbeville, Miss.; (601) 234-4312.

You won't spend more than a few dollars to eat here, but there are few culinary experiences anywhere in America as rich.

When we asked Jesse B. Davis, owner-manager of Ruth & Jimmie's, for a recipe, he gave us one for what he described as "the clear favorite of many, and probably the most distinctly regional" dish on his menu: fried okra. Some recipes call for rolling the okra in a mixture of cornmeal and flour. Mr. Davis uses only flour. We like to moisten it first in a buttermilk wash, as follows. The one suggestion we would add to this recipe is to make more than you think you're going to need. Fried okra is addictive, as easy to pop in your mouth as popcorn. Serve it as a side dish with any hot meal.

Hush Puppies

ST. CLOUD, Fla.—Attention, Walt Disney World visitors! If you are looking for a true taste of Florida, eat at The Catfish Place. One of many inconspicuous shops along the main highway in St. Cloud east of Orlando, this wood-panel and Formica roadhouse features a menu with a long list of regional delicacies, including turtle, gator tail, frog legs, snapper, shrimp, and—of course—catfish.

For oyster lovers, one side of the restaurant is occupied by a horseshoe-shaped raw bar, where the prices are low enough to down 'em by the dozen (about four dollars a dozen the last time we checked). In the vestibule, dividing the oyster bar from the dining room, the management maintains a lively salt-water aquarium. Other than the tank of exotic fish, decor is minimal: a few Floridian murals on the walls.

It is food, not atmosphere, that makes The Catfish Place so popular among locals and visitors. Portions are large, the fish is fresh, side dishes are superb, and the price is right. No meal, except steak, costs over ten dollars.

Catfish is sold as an all-you-can-eat dinner, including hash browns or French fries, cole slaw, and hush puppies. It is easy eating, without bones: The catfish are filleted in the kitchen, cut into thin strips, dipped in seasoned stone-ground cornmeal, and deep fried until golden brown. If you've never eaten catfish, or if you find whole, bone-in fish a bit scary, you can learn to love it here. These hassle-free crisp strips are mild, sweet, and moist.

For connoisseurs and adventurous eaters, the menu also lists catfish fingerlings: whole small fish with (edible) bones. And for culinary explorers who want to eat Florida foods they won't likely find back home, there is much, much more.

The "house special" dinner, for example, is a gargantuan feast

HUSH PUPPIES

oil for deep frying
¼ cup sugar
2 teaspoons baking powder
1 teaspoon salt
¼ teaspoon pepper
½ teaspoon garlic salt
⅔ cup chopped onion
1 egg, beaten
1¼ cups milk
1½ cups yellow cornmeal
1½ cups flour

Heat oil in deep fryer or deep skillet to 375 degrees.

Mix sugar, baking powder, salt, pepper, and garlic salt.

In a blender, mix onion, egg, and milk until they are milkshake consistency.

Whisk together the two mixtures and let sit until bubbles begin to form, about 5 minutes.

Mix cornmeal and flour and gradually whisk into liquid mixture. Batter should be thick, like drop-cookie dough.

Drop hush puppies by heaping teaspoons into hot oil. Fry only a few at a time. They will bounce to the surface in 2 minutes, be golden brown by 4–5 minutes. Remove from oil with slotted spoon and drain on paper towels.

Makes 30 hush puppies

The Catfish Place, 2324 13th St., St. Cloud, Fla.; (305) 892-5771.

featuring not only familiar fried foods such as oyster, catfish, scallops, and shrimp, but these strictly local items: turtle chunks, gator tail, and frog legs. Want to know how the weird things taste? The turtle, cut into small, boneless chunks, is strong, swampy, and mean. Gator tail has a rugged chaw, but a mild, veal-like flavor. The frog legs are plump and meaty, far more luscious than leapers we have eaten in any other region of the country. Our waitress explained that their goodness was due to the fact that "when it comes to frogs, Florida's legs are better than anybody else's."

Not all the food at The Catfish Place is fried. There is a substantial list of boiled and broiled seafood, including shrimp, red snapper, rock shrimp, and frog legs broiled in butter. But it is the fried food we recommend, especially those succulent strips of fried-crisp catfish.

No catfish dinner is complete without hush puppies; and the ones served at The Catfish Place are especially delicious—slightly sweet and oniony, small enough to pop in your mouth whole. But we'll let you in on a secret: We often make hush puppies at home even when we're not having catfish. They are great companions for a bowl of gumbo or New England clam chowder.

Copper Pennies

PENSACOLA, Fla.—Hopkins Boarding House has been high on our list of favorite restaurants for years. Any time we know of someone traveling along Florida's Gulf Coast, we recommend it in the strongest terms possible. But a funny thing happens every time we steer people its way. The travelers return and accuse us of not telling them just how *really* wonderful Hopkins is.

We have concluded that no mere superlatives can express the magic that happens when one eats in this special place. You see, it isn't the food—which is swell, in its unique deep South boarding-house way; nor is it the ambience, which is quaint and unaffected; nor the service, of which there is very little, since you reach for most of the food yourself; nor the scenery, which isn't much to see.

It is all the intangible things that make a meal here wonderful. Sit down among strangers who, as you eat, become friends. Help yourself, and when the serving bowls get low, more food is brought from the kitchen. And when you've had your fill, mosey out to the front porch and find yourself a rocking chair. Relax a spell, relishing the afterglow of a real down-home meal.

Arkie (Mrs. G.J.) Hopkins opened up her boardinghouse and dining room thirty-nine years ago. She had nine people for lunch. The next day she had seventeen. Today, you might have to wait to get a place at one of the broad tables in her tall-ceilinged dining room. When we first stopped by for a meal, about ten years ago, there was a fellow on the front porch who boasted to us that he had been living at the boardinghouse for a quarter century and hadn't once missed a meal—three squares a day!

Mrs. Hopkins's cooking, although profoundly regional, is not in any way bound by purist notions of tradition. Yes, of course, there is classic fried chicken on the table at most meals, as well as barbecue and drippingly delicious turnip greens and oven-hot biscuits. But you will also find blissfully calorific convenience-food wonders such as heavenly hash salad (made from mini-marshmallows, canned fruit cocktail, canned coconut, pecans, pineapple tidbits, and canned bing cherries).

As is true at so many Southern cafés and cafeterias, vegetables are the most memorable dishes produced by the Hopkins' kitchen. Sometimes they are fresh and simple: sweet corn, pole beans, or baby peas. There are always a few vegetable casseroles on the table: squash, rutabaga, and an oozingly luscious (and outrageously unfashionable) broccoli-rice combination stuck together with plenty of Cheese Whiz and canned cream of mushroom soup.

COPPER PENNIES

2 pounds carrots, peeled and cut into discs
1 medium green pepper
1 medium onion
1 can tomato soup
1/2 cup vegetable oil
2/3 cup sugar
3/4 cup cider vinegar
1 teaspoon dry mustard
1 teaspoon Worcestershire sauce
1 teaspoon salt
1/2 teaspoon pepper

Cook carrots in boiling water until tender (but not mushy). Drain.

Cut onion into rings. Cut pepper into rings, discarding seeds. Combine onion and peppers with cooked carrots in heat-proof bowl.

Combine all remaining ingredients in saucepan; slowly bring to simmer over medium heat. Remove from heat and pour over carrots, onions, and peppers. Cover and refrigerate overnight. Serve cold. (Will keep in refrigerator 2 to 3 weeks.)

Serves 8.

Hopkins Boarding House, 900 N. Spring St., Pensacola, Fla.; (904) 438-3979.

We don't want to get run out of town by the Nutrition Police, so we have chosen a recipe from the Hopkins repertoire that is relatively fresh and healthful. It does use one can of tomato soup (a no-no to serious gourmets), and it is quite sugary. But to lessen the sweetness, or to somehow substitute real tomatoes for a can of soup, would be a lie. Copper Pennies are a real taste of America. We're always proud to serve them—and guests never have any problems polishing them off!

Rice and Gravy

TALLASSEE, Ala.—Here is a page from our black book of little-known, way-out-of-the-way, outstanding American places: the Hotel Talisi. There is nothing quite like it.

Northeast of Montgomery, a good drive off the interstate, a little bit below Thurlow Dam and this side of the Tallapoosa River, the town of Tallassee is a mere dot on the map. It has one main street (Sistrunk), and one good place to eat and stay.

Accommodations at the hotel are modest, and priced accordingly. Room for one, including television and wall-to-wall carpeting, is $16. Room for two, with two twin beds, is $20.50 if you use both beds, $18.50 if you use only one.

The Hotel Talisi (derived from the same Indian name as "Tallassee") is a plain brick building with a simple sign hanging over the street corner, and a few nice pots of flowers near the entrance. It has no penthouse or elevators or health spa, no concierge or twenty-four-hour room service. What it does have is a working baby grand player piano in the lobby, reeling out tunes by Irving Berlin and Tommy Dorsey. And there is a pump organ near the staircase, too. That's about it for amenities.

What has drawn customers to the Hotel Talisi for more than a quarter-century is the dining room. Breakfast, lunch, and dinner are served Monday through Saturday; breakfast and dinner (until 3 P.M.) Sunday. Service is help-yourself, Southern-style from tables replenished throughout the meal by the kitchen staff. Pay one price—$5 on Sunday, $4.50 any other time—and eat all you want.

If you come on Sunday—the best, most cornucopian day—you may have to wait a spell for your turn to pile up a plate along the buffet tables. The groaning boards at the Hotel Talisi are a gastronomic Circe for hungry students from nearby Auburn University, families from Montgomery and Tuskegee and Phenix City, and a few savvy traveling chowhounds who know about the hotel by word of mouth.

The spread is a kaleidoscopic vista of classic Dixie cooking. Fried chicken is always the star attraction, supported by a second main course such as roast beef, sirloin tips, or pork loin. Side dishes are invariably luscious, from recklessly goopy macaroni and cheese to sweet potato soufflé streaked with marshmallows. There are supersweet squash soufflés, richly seasoned platters of rice and gravy, purple hulled peas, peppery casseroles of chicken and dressing, innumerable salads, relishes and watermelon pickles, hot rolls, biscuits, and muffins. For dessert, there is pie: chocolate custard, apple, or lemon icebox.

Mrs. Clyde Patterson (known to her friends simply as "Miz Clyde") is the lady responsible for all this good food. She and her husband, Dr. T.M. Patterson, have been running the hotel and its dining room since 1962. If you come for a meal, please give her our regards. Miz Clyde enjoys welcoming visitors from around the country . . . and showing them what Alabama hospitality is all about.

Our recipe for rice and gravy, inspired by the rice casserole at the Hotel Talisi, is very much like the "dirty rice" they serve farther south in Cajun country—almost rich enough to be a meal by itself.

RICE AND GRAVY

⅔ pound chicken gizzards
½ pound chicken livers
¼ cup vegetable oil
2 cloves garlic, minced
1 large onion, finely chopped
2 tablespoons flour
¼ cup chicken broth
3 cups boiled rice
1 to 2 teaspoons salt, to taste
1 teaspoon pepper
Chopped parsley as garnish

Grind gizzards and livers coarsely (like hamburger meat). (A food processor may be used, if one is careful to discard any large hunks of gristle after processing.) Sauté briefly in vegetable oil in large skillet over medium heat. As they begin to brown, add garlic and onion. When meat is browned and onion is translucent, whisk in flour. Cook, continuing to stir, 2 to 3 minutes. Stir in chicken broth, then rice. Add salt and pepper, adjusting seasoning to taste. Garnish with parsley and serve immediately.

Makes 6 side-dish servings.

Hotel Talisi, Sistrunk St., Tallassee, Ala.; (205) 283-2769.

Tea Room Spinach Delight

GALLATIN, Mo.—"I am confident you will like your visit here," wrote America's first motoring gourmet, Duncan Hines, back in 1936. "The McDonald Tea Room is amazing. Whenever I am in this section of the country, I always make a point of going here for dinner."

We do likewise, and suggest that travelers in search of genuine Americana follow Mr. Hines's lead. Virginia Rowell McDonald died in 1969, but her personality informs this oasis of ladylike cuisine in the farmland east of St. Joseph, Missouri.

Her hats—wide, flamboyant, feathery creations—are hung on the wall as decoration. Her china collection fills one of the back rooms. The color scheme is pink and black; the chairs are elegant wrought iron; the whole frills-and-flowers style of the place is feminine in a way that has long since vanished from the American restaurant scene.

"A love of the beautiful, cleanliness, and order are the dominant passions of my life," Mrs. McDonald once explained. "All three are very necessary attributes of a successful cook." Even today, eighteen years since she died, you get a feeling for her sense of propriety when you arrive. The Tea Room is a clean white building,

TEA ROOM SPINACH DELIGHT

*20 ounces fresh spinach, washed and
de-stemmed*
4 to 6 strips bacon
½ cup chopped onion
pepper to taste

*Into a large pot of boiling salted water,
add spinach bit by bit. Boil 3 to 4 minutes,
drain, and run spinach under cold water.
Chop coarsely.*

*Fry bacon in heavy skillet until medium-
crisp. Remove from fat, drain on paper
towels, and cut into bite-size pieces.*

*Remove all but 3 tablespoons bacon fat
from pan. Over medium-high heat, sauté
onion in fat until transparent. Add chopped
spinach, stirring constantly as leaves absorb
bacon fat. Remove from pan and add
bacon. Serve immediately.*

Serves 4.

*McDonald Tea Room, 211 W. Grand,
Gallatin, Mo.; (816) 663-2021.*

virtually gleaming in the sun, with flowers in the windows and a cozy little pathway leading to the front door.

When we walked in for lunch, the first thing we noticed was the smell: a yeasty, come-hither aroma of rolls fresh out of the oven. "Bread is the most important part of any meal," Mrs. McDonald wrote in a small pamphlet of recipes she printed in 1937. "Being Southern, I like hot bread."

Beyond the fresh-baked rolls that come with every meal, the menu is small and simple—Southern-accented classics such as country ham or fried chicken, as well as roast beef. If you don't want a hot meal, there is a salad bar set up with all sorts of greens, garnishes, and composed salads to heap on a plate.

We had fried chicken and ham, both of which were quite all right, but what we remember best are the rolls, the side dishes, and dessert. Along with each main course, we received a bowl full of buttered potatoes—plain boiled potatoes, glistening hot and fork-tender. And there was another bowl of what the waitress referred to as "spinach delight": a heap of limp green leaves enriched with bite-size pieces of bacon and sautéed onions. The spinach was an invigorating combination of ingredients with nostalgic appeal—the kind of decent yet rather luscious dish for which tearoom proprietors such as Mrs. McDonald were once renowned. Each customer received a silly salad, too: a scoop of cottage cheese set atop a pineapple ring, crowned with a maraschino cherry.

It has always been customary at the McDonald Tea Room to follow a meal with pie. "Men prefer this form of dessert," Mrs. McDonald wrote, explaining that the three necessary ingredients to a good pie were a flaky crust, smooth insides, and a stiff-standing meringue. All three were in resounding evidence in the slices of peanut butter cream pie we got at the climax of our lunch.

When we considered which recipe would best give a sense of the McDonald Tea Room, we thought about some of Mrs. McDonald's absolutely zany froufrou items such as pink pears, egg whites shaped into Easter lilies, or peaches fashioned into miniature faux-pumpkins for Halloween. She loved that kind of amusing presentation. But the Tea Room of 1987, while respectful of her legacy, is never quite so outrageous. So we are going to share our recipe for Spinach Delight, a dish that symbolizes the kind of forthright good food you will get if you visit Mrs. McDonald's grand old dining room today.

Tipsy Sweet Potato Pudding

LYNCHBURG, Tenn.—When we met Miss Mary Bobo, she was about to celebrate her one hundredth birthday. She was standing at the door of her boardinghouse, wishing Godspeed to each of twenty guests who had just enjoyed a midday family-style dinner of Southern fried chicken, mashed potatoes, hot biscuits, peach cobbler, and lemonade.

We walked onto Miss Mary's front porch and scanned the heat-baked streets of Lynchburg, Tennessee. It was easy to imagine what the town was like more than seventy years earlier, when Miss Mary began taking in boarders. It fact, if you took away the cars, you wouldn't see much evidence of progress at all.

That was 1980, and although she no longer took in overnight guests, dinner at Miss Mary's was a true taste of boardinghouse life. It had a special flavor that went way beyond delicious food.

The meal commenced with the ringing of a bell. Everybody sat down at once and dug into serving bowls mounded with country-style vittles. Platters flew back and forth across the table. Arms stretched in boardinghouse style to nab a second biscuit or corn-bread muffin.

Everyone ate fast, with gusto, which is just the way to do it in a boardinghouse. Nobody wasted time looking at a menu: We got what the kitchen made, like it or not. Nor was there any break between courses—all the food was on the table from the start. And if extra helpings were called for, Miss Mary's staff replaced the serving platters before anyone had a chance to ask.

The meal was a party at which strangers immediately became friends. We swapped travel stories with families from Oregon and Oklahoma, and got tips on some excellent pie stops from a Pennsylvania trucker who had come to Lynchburg to tour his favorite bottling plant—the Jack Daniel's distillery.

After we thanked Mary Bobo for the meal, we walked slowly to our car, turning back for last glimpses of the old lady who had run the house since 1908. It was a tableau of vanishing America: Mary on her porch, framed by great white columns, picket fence in the foreground, and the smell of biscuits lingering in the Tennessee air.

Mary Bobo died in 1983 and the boardinghouse closed. A year later, Lynne Tolley, who grew up in Lynchburg, reopened it. She hired back Miss Mary's cooks; she weeded the vegetable gardens that provide ingredients for summer casseroles; and she polished the brass bell that rings at one o'clock every afternoon to announce dinner's beginning.

TIPSY SWEET POTATO PUDDING

2 eggs

¾ cup sugar

2 cups raw sweet potatoes, grated (about 2 potatoes)

1 12-ounce can evaporated milk

½ cup milk

½ teaspoon ground cinnamon

½ teaspoon ground nutmeg

½ teaspoon salt

1 cup shredded sweetened coconut

4 tablespoons butter, melted

2 tablespoons Jack Daniel's whiskey

whipped cream as garnish

Preheat oven to 350 degrees. Generously butter a 1½-quart casserole dish.

Vigorously beat eggs and sugar together in large bowl. Stir in all remaining ingredients except whipped cream. Pour into prepared casserole dish and bake 1 hour, until barely firm.

Serve tepid, garnished with whipped cream.

Makes 6–8 servings.

Miss Mary Bobo's Boardinghouse, Lynchburg, Tenn.; (615) 759-7394. Dinner (midday) by reservation.

There are four dining rooms at Mary Bobo's, each presided over by a hostess who shows guests through the ropes. First, all the people at the table introduce themselves. Then people are on their own: Take what you want, pass the platter to the left—unless you are sitting at the round table downstairs. That one has a lazy Susan in its center, making it easier to concentrate on eating (as long as you are quick enough to grab what you want when it spins past).

Fried chicken cooked in iron skillets is always on the table, augmented by a second main course such as pork chops or turkey and dressing. There are biscuits, natch, and at least half a dozen vegetables. Extraordinary vegetables, Southern-style vegetables, make no mistake about it: cooked with fatback or hambone, sweetened or enriched. Carrots or cabbage luxuriate in casseroles oozing butter or cheese and topped with cracker crumbs; sweet corn straight off the cob is pan-cooked with thick-sliced bacon; okra is deep-fried to a brittle crisp; apples are sautéed with butter and sugar until they turn limp and caramelize.

The voluptuous meal concludes with yummies such as pecan icebox pie, meringue-topped raspberry pie, or tipsy sweet potato pudding. The only problem with the pudding is that in Lynchburg, it isn't legal. You see, Moore County, Tennessee, home of America's oldest distillery, is dry.

Anyway, the alcohol evaporates, and you hardly taste the hooch in this Mary Bobo boardinghouse recipe for Jack Daniel's-spiked pudding. It is a textured ambrosia—sweet, coconutty, and Southern to the soul.

FRENCH FRIED EGGPLANT

1 large eggplant
³/₄ cup flour
³/₄ cup milk
1 cup fine cracker meal
old cooking oil
seasoned salt to taste
cocktail sauce

Peel eggplant. Cut lengthwise into ¹/₂-inch strips. Dip strips in flour, then in milk, then roll in cracker meal.

Heat oil in deep fryer to 350 degrees. Fry sticks a few at a time, without crowding in oil, 8–10 minutes, until golden brown. Be sure oil temperature stays at 350 degrees.

Remove sticks from oil and drain on paper towels. Sprinkle with seasoned salt and serve with cocktail sauce.

Makes an hors d'oeuvre for 6–8.

Thomas's F & N Steak House, Route 8, Dayton, Ky.; (513) 261-6766.

French Fried Eggplant

DAYTON, Ky.—Despite wizened worryworts who warn us against the evils of red meat, there is still no meal quite as satisfying—or as joyously American—as a sizzling steak.

The cut we like best is the sirloin strip, known in different regions of the country as a New York or K.C. strip, or a shell steak. It is a glistening boneless crescent of char-crusted red meat about a foot long, four inches wide, and three fingers tall. If it has been broiled right, it has a pillowy plumpness. It looks heavy; you can see that it is packing a load of juice. And sure enough, as soon as the knife plunges through the darkened crust into the high meat mesa to remove a pink-centered triangle, the natural gravy begins to flow; and as the steak is surrounded by its oozing juices, you sop through them with forkfuls of starchy white potato.

Honestly now, can any pale piece of fish or bowl of rabbit-food veggies compete with the tastebud-tickling protein tang of such a hunk of meat? Of course it is much too luxurious to be everyday food, but there are occasions—happy celebration meals—when only a fine aged steak will do.

If you happen to be anywhere near Cincinnati when a serious beef craving strikes, we've got the place you want to know about: Thomas's F & N Steak House, just over the Ohio River in Dayton, Kentucky.

Established in 1929, Thomas's is a higgledy-piggledy roadhouse that looks as if it has expanded in random fits and starts for the last fifty-nine years. Its multiple dining rooms are loaded with memorabilia, souvenirs, antiques, and just plain junk. Photos from the 1950s share wall space with Victorian prints; there is a wooden cookstove in one room, a million statuettes in another; six fireplaces altogether. Booths are as large as a roomette, with the kind of spreading-out space demanded by a mighty meat meal.

Thomas's steaks are aged and cut on the premises. You have no doubt, at first bite, that they really are aged, with the heightened flavor smack that a couple weeks on the hook gives to beef. (It is possible to order nonaged beef if you prefer a callow cut of cow.) The menu also includes fish and lobster, baby back ribs, and barbecued chicken, but it is steak that has established the F & N as a landmark for carnivores: delmonicoes (rib-eyes), chopped steaks, chunked and skewered tenderloins, T-bones, two-pound porterhouses, filets mignons, and the ultimate New York strip—described on the menu as "man-size."

Meals are served with salad, potato, string beans, and a warm loaf of bread. The most memorable dish, other than the meat itself, is an extra-cost appetizer of French fried eggplant. Cut in thin strips, served with fiery horseradish-spiked cocktail sauce, these sticks are perfect munchies to accompany predinner drinks.

The recipe is inscribed on the F & N paper placemats. We took one home and now put it into action whenever we have some used cooking oil doing nothing. Old oil is essential, according to the F & N chef, because it has character. New oil, like a new steak, is pale and without pizzazz. So if you've just fried up some fish or chicken or potatoes, or even doughnuts, keep the oil hot, and try a batch of these puffy appetizers. Of course, they should be eaten immediately after frying.

MASHED POTATOES À LA RIVERSIDE

6 russet potatoes
6 tablespoons butter or margarine, cut into pieces
½ to ¾ cup warm milk
salt to taste

Peel potatoes and cut into large, equal-size pieces. Boil until tender enough to break apart with a fork, 25 to 30 minutes. Drain, leaving about ¼ cup of the potato water in the pot.

Add butter and beat with electric mixer until smooth. Gradually add milk, a little at a time, beating after each addition until potatoes are fluffy. Do not add too much milk or potatoes will get watery. Different potatoes require different amounts of milk. Add salt to taste.

Serve topped with an extra pat of butter. Makes 4 to 6 servings.

Mashed Potatoes à la Riverside

STOCKPORT, Ohio—Any real estate broker can tell you that there are three important factors to consider when looking at a piece of property: location, location, location.

By those criteria, you won't find a nicer restaurant than the Riverside, on Water Street at the foot of Main, eight feet away from the Muskingum River. Every seat in the house has a water view. The scene changes daily: boats passing through the locks; birds and water life; solid ice in the coldest months of winter. "Like escaping from the world for a while" is the way it was described to us by Frances Brandum, who bought the building with her daughter, Susan Moody, at a sheriff's sale in 1980.

They gutted it down to its hickory beams and designed a restaurant to resemble a riverboat dining room of the mid-nineteenth century, which is when the building was constructed. It was originally a warehouse for goods traveling the waterways. "More turkeys and hogs were shipped east through here than from any place in the country," Frances told us.

When the railroad was built in the 1890s, river traffic slowed. The warehouse became a general store, then a feed mill. Since Frances and Susan turned it into a restaurant, it has gained a reputation far and wide as one of the great home-cooking stops in southeastern Ohio. Stockport is a small town, miles from Interstates 70 and 77, yet the Riverside guest book lists names from across the country and the world, including the signatures of one couple who stopped in while traveling from New York to Denver on lightweight bicycles.

Many customers detour to Stockport on Sunday, when Frances and Susan set out a giant-size smorgasbord that includes their renowned baked chicken and biscuits and a salad bar that, in the

FIVE·WAYS TO GLORIFY MASHED POTATOES:

   —*Substitute ³/₄ cup sour cream for the milk.*

   —*Add only ¹/₄ cup of milk, along with ²/₃ cup of grated sharp cheddar cheese.*

   —*Mash potatoes with butter, and substitute 4 to 6 ounces creamy mild goat cheese for the milk.*

   —*Mash potatoes with butter and milk, then combine with an equal amount of boiled, mashed, and buttered carrots or turnips.*

   —*Mash potatoes with butter and milk, then combine with an equal amount of boiled, shredded cabbage and ¹/₂ diced onion. Fry the mixture over medium heat in butter in a large skillet, pressing down to flatten it into a cake. When brown, reduce heat and cook 5 minutes until cooked through. In English pubs, this combo is called "bubble and squeak."*

Riverside Family Restaurant, Water Street, Stockport, Ohio; (614) 559-2210.

summer, gets picked from the family garden. Other house specialties include their own farm-raised roast beef (from Susan's farm), barbecued ribs, and pork chops, New England-style boiled dinner, dinner rolls and breads baked from old family recipes, and elderberry pie made just the way Frances's Pennsylvania Dutch great-aunt Ida used to do it.

Although she cooks by touch and taste and memory, Frances was kind enough to write down several of her best recipes, including one for our favorite dish at the Riverside Restaurant: mashed potatoes. "Real potatoes," the menu promises, "cooked the way you like them." Yes, indeed. Fluffy, starchy, laced with the taste of butter and a splash of milk: Although made of simple ingredients, mashed potatoes such as these are exquisite food.

We never thought there was any way to improve on the basic formula, until we tried Frances's trick of including a bit of the water in which the potatoes were boiled. Conventional wisdom says potatoes should be moisture-free before mashing. But a bit of potato water is what makes these whipped-up ones so extraordinarily creamy.

Mashed potatoes are usually considered a side dish, and that's probably the way it ought to be, but allow us to suggest that a plate of butter-dripping hot whipped potatoes all by itself just might be the apex of comforting cuisine. Nor do they have to be dowdy. Consider a plate piled with nothing but pure white mashed spuds, a dot of black caviar on top. What could be more elegant?

If plain mashed (actually whipped) potatoes according to Frances Brandum's recipe aren't quite jazzy enough, we have added a few suggestions for giving them an extra shot of personality.

Haystack Potatoes

WALNUT, Iowa—The firefighters of Walnut were worried. It was 1960, and they were planning their annual supper, but nobody liked the idea that the nearest steakhouse was six miles out of town. What if there was a fire in Walnut while they were slicing through their T-bones? Six miles was too far away.

They went to Russ Lenhardt, owner of The Gardens, a sandwich-only tavern that Russ had been operating near the railroad stop in Walnut since 1946. Russ had taken over from his father, who started the business—as a steakhouse—in 1940. The firemen convinced him to borrow a grill and cook their steaks right in town.

The firemen's dinner was a great success. They loved the way

HAYSTACK POTATOES

Allow one potato per person. Preheat oven to 400 degrees. Wrap potatoes in foil and bake 1 hour. Turn off oven and let potatoes sit in oven another hour. Remove and cool (still in foil). Refrigerate 2–3 hours or overnight, until potatoes are fully chilled.

Remove potatoes from foil, peel off skin, and grate potatoes coarsely. Over medium heat, pour enough corn oil into a large frying pan or griddle to coat it. When oil is hot, empty grated potatoes onto griddle and gently spread potatoes into a thin, even pancake. Push in the loose edges with a spatula, but don't pat them down with a spatula, as that compresses them and makes them mushy. Sprinkle additional corn oil around edge of pancake. Season with salt and pepper as desired.

When golden brown, flip potatoes over. (You may want to cut the pancake into halves or quarters to facilitate flipping it.) Sprinkle a little more corn oil around edges and fry until golden brown. Serve immediately.

The Gardens, Pearl and Atlantic Streets, Walnut, Iowa; (712) 784-3940.

Russ cooked steaks. And Russ had a ball. "I decided," he recalled with characteristic understatement, "that the food business wouldn't be so bad after all."

Russ returned the borrowed grill and bought one—the smallest grill on the market, which was the only size that would fit his pint-sized kitchen. He and his wife, Lucy, started serving steak dinners to the citizens of Walnut and vicinity, weekends only (Thursday, Friday, Saturday).

The menu consisted of exactly one dinner: T-bone, French fries, and salad with Italian dressing. But Russ had a way with steaks, and the Lenhardts's restaurant, still called The Gardens, prospered. Sirloins and rib eyes were added to the repertoire, as were baked and hash brown potatoes, and a choice of salad dressing. Beyond that, nothing changed. To this day, The Gardens is just a steak house, weekends only, with Russ cooking all the steaks in his tiny kitchen on that original pint-sized grill.

It is the kind of restaurant that you would never find by accident, tucked away as it is on a side street in the hamlet of Walnut (population 897) alongside Route 80. We got to it one evening years ago when we tumbled into a nearby motel after a day of hard highway travel researching a book about truck drivers. We craved a gracious meal, but all we could see around the motel were truck-stop cafés—guaranteed greasy spoons.

The pamphlet-slim Walnut Yellow Pages didn't list any eateries that looked promising, and we had little hope when we asked the lady behind the motel desk for her suggestion of a really nice restaurant within fifty miles. "There is such a place," she grinned, directing us to The Gardens, just a few minutes away in town.

There was no sign outside, but we knew it was the right place because it was surrounded by cars and we could smell the aroma of steaks and hash brown potatoes sizzling on a grill.

The inside is booths and a bar, dark and tavern-like, with a dance floor and a jukebox. Little illuminated dioramas of Western farm life decorate the walls. There is still no written menu. Waitresses describe the cuts of meat available. On occasion, Russ peeks out from his kitchen to greet customers, most of whom are old friends.

After our first steak dinner at The Gardens—one of the simplest and most satisfying meals we have ever had on the road—we drove slowly back to the motel room, through rich black-dirt Iowa farmland. It was a clear night, and the stars were shining without any competition from city lights. We stopped the car and turned off the engine. Silence, except for the lowing of cows and an occasional piggy squeal. For a short while we fantasized about giving up everything, moving to a farm in Walnut, Iowa, and eating steak dinners at The Gardens every Friday night.

There are no great secrets to Russ Lenhardt's meals. He buys prime steak, aged two to three weeks, and he cooks it on the grill over medium heat until the outside is crusty brown, pocketing a heavy pillow of mineral-rich, juicy beef. As for the hash browns, known in some parts of the Midwest as "haystack potatoes," Russ makes his from potatoes that have already been baked. That means that any time you have a leftover baked potato, you have the makings for Russ Lenhardt's hash browns the next morning.

Zwiebelkuchen

MEQUON, Wis.—Boder's on-the-River is a landmark of Great Lakes gastronomy. It has been a family-run restaurant for four generations, going back to 1929, when John and Frieda Boder bought an old homestead in the country outside of Milwaukee and turned it into a rural lunch room.

Their specialty then was afternoon tea, served to city folks who came to enjoy not only the good food, but a visit to Border's bathing beach on the river or a stroll through the cornfields just outside the dining room.

The Boders' casual country place was known also for the animals the family kept around, including Tommy the Turkey, who was famous for peering into the dining room as customers ate, and Peter the Parrot, who was once accused of calling out "Hi, Fat!" to a neighbor. (Actually, he was saying "Hi, Jack" to the Boders' son.) Customers' children rode on a horse named Brownie or played with Charlie the St. Bernard. It was not unusual, after a cold spring rain, for dinner to be delayed because all the Boders' employees were outside rescuing baby ducklings from the cold. The little birds were brought inside and placed in the kitchens' slightly warm ovens until they were dry enough to be taken to the barn.

Today, Boder's isn't quite so eccentric or casual, but it remains a treasure trove of country cooking, and a favorite destination for Milwaukeeans in search of family-style dinners of grandmotherly goodness.

All meals are anchored by soul-satisfying bakery goodies such as pecan rolls, cherry muffins, and baking powder biscuits, as well as Boder's legendary oversized corn fritters, served with maple syrup. You begin by forking into a tray of demure garden relishes and macaroni salad, then continue on to steaks or chops or Lake Superior whitefish.

ZWIEBELKUCHEN

CRUST:

1 cup flour
¼ teaspoon salt
¼ teaspoon sugar
8 tablespoons butter, chilled
2 tablespoons milk

Sift flour, salt, and sugar into bowl. Cut in butter as for pie crust. Add milk, a tablespoon at a time, mixing only until dough holds together. Shape into ball, wrap in waxed paper, and chill 1 full hour.

Preheat oven to 425 degrees. Roll out dough and ease into lightly floured 9-inch pie plate. Flute edge. Chill 30 minutes. Line shell with foil. Bake 6 minutes, remove foil and bake 6–8 minutes more until light brown. Cool on rack. Turn oven to 375 degrees.

FILLING:

3 slices bacon cut into small pieces
1½ cups chopped onion
1 egg plus 1 yolk, beaten
⅓ cup sour cream
¼ teaspoon salt
dash of pepper
½ teaspoon chopped chives
⅛ teaspoon caraway seeds

Fry bacon until crisp. Remove from grease and drain on paper towel. Sauté onions in bacon grease until soft; remove with slotted spoon. Combine onions and bacon with all remaining ingredients except caraway seeds. Place mixture in crust. Sprinkle with caraway seeds. Bake until set, about 25 minutes. Serve warm.

Makes appetizers for 8.

Boder's on-the-River, 11919 N. River Rd., Mequon, Wis.; (414) 242-0335.

If you know the Midwestern palate, you know that dessert is the grand finale to any meaningful meal, especially on weekends. That goes double for Wisconsin, America's Dairyland, where cream is king. Boder's roster of desserts includes poppy seed chiffon torte, banana split ice cream pie, peanut swirl ice cream pie, and the stunning local specialty known as a schaum torte—featherweight meringue shells filled with ice cream and either strawberries or raspberries.

When we get homesick for the Midwest, we need only thumb through our pamphlet of *Favorite Recipes from Boder's on-the-River* that we picked up last time we were there. It is no mere list of recipes; it includes the whole history of the Boder family and their restaurant, including snapshots of their Model A Ford (named "Fritter"), of various Boders getting married, and of Chico the runaway horse. It is a family album—the best kind of cookbook—in which the recipes make sense because they are part of people's real lives. Among the appetizers, we found a recipe for zwiebelkuchen—a delicious onion pie reminiscent of quiche, but not nearly so eggy.

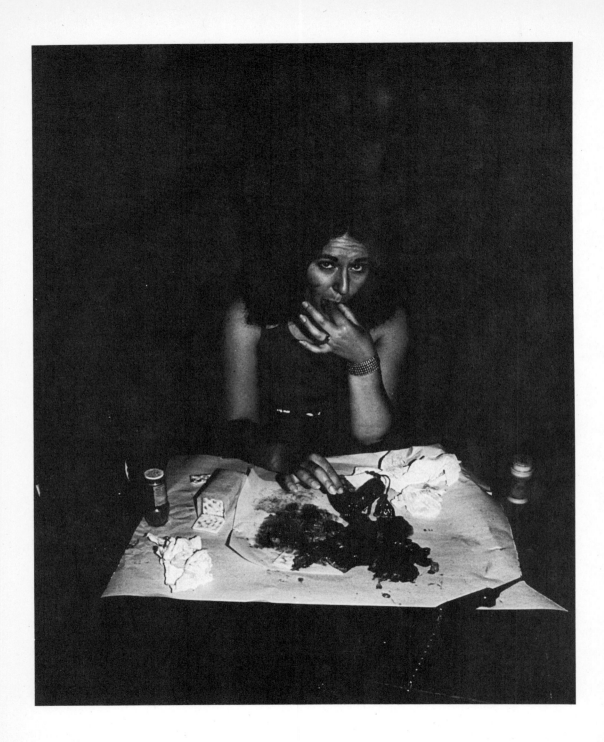

11

Condiments and Sauces

Sweet Onion Mustard

CLIFTON, N.J.—As we exited the Garden State Parkway, we asked the toll-taker for directions to Rutt's Hut. He knew just where it was. As our car lurched away, we called to him, "Is it worth the trip?"

"The beer's good!" he hollered back.

Maybe so, but it wasn't beer that led us to Rutt's Hut. It was a hot dog tip.

We were clued into this surly roadside weinerteria by the most unlikely of sources: Martha Stewart. Caterer extraordinaire, author of cookbooks about fine and fancy entertaining, known for chic cuisine and elegant soirees, Martha collared us at a party in Connecticut one night and said we better try the tube steaks at Rutt's Hut.

This we had to see. We could hardly imagine Martha Stewart eating a weiner, certainly not a weiner in a spongy bun, dripping with mustard. She's so cool, so refined, so feminine. People of her ilk don't eat weenies, do they?

Darned if Rutt's Hut wasn't the real thing—an all-American, get-down, roll-your-sleeves-up eating experience with a wild New Jersey accent.

Actually, the accent is Greek if you go to the stand-up part of the restaurant, where the orders are barked to an open kitchen with the same insouciance John Belushi used in his "cheeseburger–Pepsi" skits on "Saturday Night Live."

There is also a sit-down side of Rutt's: a big easygoing taproom with wood panel decor and a long menu of stalwart blue plate specials. Here customers quaff their beer with platters of chow such as chicken croquettes, stuffed cabbage, Jersey pork chops, and bean-heavy chili by the cup or bowl. Prices are low, and the cuisine, although not exactly highfalutin, is satisfying in a thick-neck sort of way.

It's the open half of the Hut that's really fun. There are no seats, just high counters with a view of the parking lot and Highway 21. A couple of scrawny potted plants are the only interior decoration. Customers stand and scarf their food while reading journals of classified auto ads that are strewn about. Signs say "Please Do Not Sit On Counter" and "Please Pay When Served." Although there is no background music per se, one's ears are serenaded by the rep-artee of the countermen, hollering out the euphonic language of the greasy spoon.

"Cheeseburger—dipped!" they call out, meaning that the bun gets sopped with gravy. "I got a dog working!" is the cry to hustle

SWEET ONION MUSTARD

4 tablespoons dry mustard

1/2 cup white vinegar

3 tablespoons sweet pickle juice

1 tablespoon sugar

1 teaspoon salt

3 egg yolks, beaten

3 tablespoons sweet pickle relish

1/2 cup finely diced sweet onion

Beat together mustard, vinegar, pickle juice, sugar, and salt. Cover and let stand 2–3 hours.

Place mixture in top of double boiler over simmering water. Whisk in egg yolks, and continue whisking 5 minutes, until mustard is thick and creamy. Stir in relish and onion. Cover and cool in refrigerator.

Yield: about 1 1/2 cups.

Rutt's Hut, 417 River Road, Clifton, N.J.; (201) 779-8615.

things along. "Twins!" seemed to be another frequent call, which we assume referred to a pair of hot dogs on a single plate.

The menu in this sassy part of Rutt's is limited to only a few weekend special sandwiches, plus the people's choice: hot dogs and hamburgers. The burgers are classic lunch counter patties: thin, chewy, slick enough to moisten the bun even if you don't get it dipped. Onion rings are excellent—fat hoops of sweet, crisp onion barely sheathed in brittle batter. You'd almost call them couth.

Hot dogs, as per Martha Stewart's recommendation, are the pièce de résistance. There is nothing intrinsically wonderful about the dogs themselves; they appear to be your basic tubes of mild pork and beef. But Rutt's trick is to deep-fry them. The skin is fissured by the high heat and gets all crackly and chewy, but the inside stays soft. So it's the texture that's the kick. These weiners are a wonderful chaw.

It's easy to make them at home in a large skillet. Simply fry your favorite brand of hot dogs in about a half-inch of corn oil at medium-high heat, turning frequently, until they are dark brown. Drain on paper towels.

Then, to give the dogs a true Rutt's Hut accent, top them with onion mustard, our own version of the snappy-sweet condiment set out on the Hut's counter.

A Man's Barbecue Sauce

AMARILLO, Texas—If you think the world has become unisexual, stop in at a joint named Beans and Things down Amarillo way. The walls are plastered with prints and paintings of John Wayne, and there is a good-sized bust of the Duke, too. Where John Wayne's mug is not, Marine Corps paraphernalia is: insignia, photos of bulldogs, and vast amounts of leatherneck mementos. On the remaining wall space is a display of barbed wire. Son, this is a man's restaurant, and don't you forget it.

The man is Wiley Alexander, who served as police chief of Amarillo for fifteen of his twenty-five years on the force. His sidekick at Beans and Things is his son-in-law James Peach, an ex-Marine wounded in Vietnam who, according to Wiley, will never get those leatherneck years out of his system. Ol' Wiley himself knows a thing or two about combat, having been with the Texas 36th Division when it hit the beaches of Salerno in World War II.

With backgrounds like that, these two could hardly be expected to serve watercress sandwiches and weak tea.

The fact is that all their surging maleness has found its logical

A MAN'S BARBEQUE SAUCE

2¼ cups catsup
2¼ cups water
2 teaspoons instant beef broth
1¼ teaspoons dry mustard
1 tablespoon chili powder
1 teaspoon black pepper
¼ teaspoon cayenne pepper
½ teaspoon garlic powder
½ teaspoon salt
2 teaspoons Worcestershire sauce
2 shakes Tabasco sauce
3 tablespoons brown sugar
½ teaspoon liquid smoke
1 tablespoon lemon juice

Bring everything to boil, reduce heat and simmer, stirring occasionally, 15 minutes. Cool to room temperature.

Makes 1 quart.

Beans and Things, 1700 Amarillo Blvd. E, Amarillo, Tex.; (806) 373-7383.

culinary expression in some of the finest barbecue and chili you will eat in Texas. A few years ago, while motoring through the Lone Star State, we just happened to stop in for a snack at Beans and Things. Within five minutes of digging into what was on our trays, we voted these vittles into our Southwestern good eats pantheon.

We didn't want to like Beans and Things as much as we did. Its modern façade made it look too much like a fast-food chain; and even the name seemed less authentic than other barbecue parlors we like, such as Bub Sweatman's, Shotgun Coleman's, or Lester's Pit. But there was no denying the excellence of the food. We were smitten, and we pledged undying allegiance.

Wiley Alexander didn't always want to run a barbecue. About ten years ago, when he retired from the police force, he bought a flower store and ran it with his daughter. Maybe he got antsy being around all those petunias, but something made him decide to leave the flowers behind. Eight years ago, he opened Beans and Things with his old squad-car partner. The partner bowed out early, which is when James Peach joined in. It was up to the two of them to come up with a perfect sauce for the meat.

Where did Wiley and Jim turn for advice? To Julia Child or Craig Claiborne? Not exactly. They called on Ray "Rip" Van Winkle, the old jailhouse cook at the Amarillo slammer, and Rip brought them a recipe book that he had saved from his Army days. The three men put their heads together and fussed around the kitchen until they all agreed the sauce was right. And the sauce became the basis of the Beans and Things menu. "It keeps them coming back," Wiley told us with characteristic understatement.

It is a sauce that tastes equally good on ribs and beef brisket, especially the smoky-crusted brisket they serve here—butter-tender, heavy with juice, the lush meat tangy with the flavor of the wood fire. We suspect the sauce also finds its way into the beans and maybe even into the chili. There isn't much more than that on this exemplary regional menu, except for coleslaw, cornbread, and a selection of hot jalapeño peppers on the salad bar.

Wiley Alexander's recipe arrived at our house in a box, accompanied by two surgical masks, which were supposed to be put on as soon as the sauce began to boil. "Do not breathe directly into the pot!" Wiley's directions warned. He also insisted that for proper results, all of the ingredients must be mixed by the light of a full moon, and the sauce must be stirred only clockwise.

We have adapted Wiley's recipe for home kitchens. It can be used to baste beef, pork, or chicken as it grills, or as a condiment for already cooked meat.

Chickasha Hot Sauce

CHICKASHA, Okla.—The meal you want to see at Jake's Rib is the one listed on the menu as "House Special for ???" It costs $16.95, and it consists of four meats and six side orders. Sounds like a good deal, right? You have no idea how good a deal it is.

For under twenty dollars, including a few bucks for iced tea or beer, Jake's kitchen sends forth enough vittles to feed four or six, maybe eight healthy eaters. The side dishes alone are an awe-inspiring sight: precarious piles of curlicue fried potatoes, at least a foot high; whopping heaps of "Okie fried" spuds (cheese-encased potato skins); troughs of pinto beans and of sandy crusted fried okra.

The meats, served in equally generous portions, are as handsome as meats can be: mighty ribs, crusted wih sizzling sauce the color of mahogany; heavy slices of smoke-scented, fall-apart pork; "sloppy Jake" (hacked pork) served like a magnificent potion, thick and glistening in a deep bowl; pepper-hot sausage links with crackling crisp skin and luscious insides. Even the bologna steak is a startling sight, sliced as thick as sirloin and charred on the grill. Iced tea is served in tumblers, beer in pitchers the size of a goldfish bowl.

We don't love Jake's Rib only because the meals are gigantic. They also happen to be delicious—powerful smoky Southwestern good eats.

The meats themselves are excellent, but what puts them over the top is the sauce. It comes to the table before anything else, served warm in a pitcher, either hot or mild. Then you get some white bread: fresh, soft, good ol' American supermarket white bread—the classic and proper companion of barbecue. So you dip the bread in the pitcher of sauce, let it soak real good (but not so good it gets sauce-logged and falls into the pitcher), and slurp it up to your mouth. This is truly one of America's superlative sauces—good to eat with nothing but white bread, fabulous when applied to any barbecued meat.

The folks responsible for all this good stuff are a couple named Ron and Marianne Eaton. They've made Jake's Rib a culinary landmark along I-44. It is a modern ranch-style restaurant with unclothed tables arranged around a big wood stove, and a large-screen television in the corner of the dining room. Nearly all the customers are locals who take Jake's for granted; but the waitresses were not surprised when we took pictures of the astounding portions of food they set down at our table. Newcomers, they explained, often take snapshots to amaze their friends back home

---

CHICKASHA HOT SAUCE

4 cups catsup

1½ cups molasses (dark)

¼ cup red wine vinegar

3 tablespoons Worcestershire sauce

2 teaspoons Tabasco sauce

¼ cup lemon juice

1 cup finely chopped onion

2 cloves garlic, finely chopped

¼ cup brown sugar

3 tablespoons dry mustard

1–3 teaspoons cayenne pepper (depending on how hot you want sauce)

Combine all ingredients in large stockpot with cover. Mix well. Add up to 2 cups water to create a sauce with a cream-like texture. Bring to boil, stirring constantly. Reduce heat, partially cover, and simmer very gently 1 hour, stirring frequently. Add a bit more water if sauce gets too thick.

Makes 1 quart sauce.

Jake's Rib, 100 Ponderosa, Chickasha, Okla.; (405) 222-2825.

with the wonders they have seen and eaten.

When we talked to Ron about how he got his sauce as good as it is, he told us that it is just a matter of tinkering and fiddling with spices, beginning with a commercial barbecue sauce base. Using his recommendations for molasses as a sweetener and cayenne pepper as a hottener, we went home and devised this facsimile—suitable for slathering on any barbecued beef, chicken, or pork.

Mustard Sauce

MIAMI BEACH, Fla.—When Joe Weiss moved to Florida in 1913, there was no place to eat in Miami Beach. Joe, a former waiter from New York, opened a restaurant in a small wood-frame house, where he and his wife cooked shore dinners for the sprinkling of tourists who came to visit. They served oysters, pompano, shrimp, yellowtail, and south Florida seafood of all variety—with the exception of stone crabs.

Although plentiful in the waters of Biscayne Bay, stone crabs were not popular food seventy-five years ago. For one thing, they are difficult to catch. They hide themselves in sand and mud; their claws pinch hard. And once captured, stone crabs have shells that are tough to crack.

But ten years after opening his restaurant, Joe put stone crabs on the menu. Business boomed. He moved to a larger white stucco building, renamed Joe's Stone Crab. Since then, Joe's restaurant has come to symbolize everything delicious and unique about old-fashioned Florida seafood meals. And stone crabs have become one of the scarcest local delicacies.

"They now sell by the karat," Damon Runyon once wrote, referring to their high price tag. He lamented that they were all gobbled up by visitors, leaving none for Florida natives. "A certificate of at least four years' residence in Dade County should be required of every person desiring stone crabs," he jokingly suggested.

In fact, the population of stone crabs diminished not so much because of all the people eating them, but because the harbor where they lived was dredged as Miami boomed in the 1920s. The crabs moved south to the Keys. In order to ensure their survival today, when a stone crab is caught, only one claw is broken off (claws are the only part worth eating). The crab is then thrown back in the water, where it will grow another claw large enough to be harvested in about two seasons' time.

As the fame of Joe's Stone Crab spread, Joe Weiss launched his own fleet of boats; the restaurant went through half a ton of crabs on a good day. Arthur Godfrey paid homage to the landmark restaurant innumerable times on his "Talent Scouts" television show. And Miami Beach grew up to the north of Joe's.

Joe's son Jesse took over the business; now Joe's granddaughter, Jo-Ann Sawitz, runs the place; and although the waiters all got new tuxedos a couple years ago, not much else has changed. Despite the high cost of stone crabs, Joe's is not a ritzy dining establishment. It still takes no reservations, so at any ordinary mealtime, everybody waits for a table. In rustic fish-house style, the white walls are decorated with photographs of Florida and Miami Beach that go back to the time when Joe's was young—you had to take a boat to get here from Miami. High ceilings make for a booming, hustle-bustle noise level in the dining room.

The menu is classic south Florida cooking, with a few special twists that Joe's fans have come to love over the years. Red snapper, mackerel, and pompano are as fresh and good and expertly prepared as you will find in any restaurant. Hash brown potatoes are the usual accompaniment, but many regulars know to order Joe's special cottage-fried sweet potatoes, a delectable companion to a large fillet of yellowtail and a side of cool coleslaw. For dessert, choose key lime pie or chunky apple pie with a wedge of cheddar cheese.

Stone crabs arrive cool, five or six claws to an order. Their color scheme—coral pink, tipped with ebony—is distinctly Floridian. The hard shells, of course, have been precracked in the kitchen, allowing for easy extraction of plump, succulent segments of meat with the long fork provided.

On the side, you have a choice of two dips: plain drawn butter or Joe's special mustard sauce. The tangy yellow sauce is an inspired complement for the moist, sweet meat of the stone crab, as well as for other varieties of crabmeat, lobster, or shrimp. Whenever we serve a chilled seafood cocktail, we offer it alongside traditional red cocktail sauce.

MUSTARD SAUCE

3½ teaspoons dry mustard
1 cup mayonnaise
2 teaspoons Worcestershire sauce
1 teaspoon A-1 sauce
1½ tablespoons light cream
⅛ teaspoon salt

Beat all ingredients three full minutes. Chill and serve.

Yield: 1 cup, enough dipping sauce for hors d'oeuvres for 4–6.

Joe's Stone Crab Restaurant, 227 Biscayne St., Miami Beach, Fla.; (305) 673-0365. (Note: Joe's is open only during stone crab season, between mid-October and mid-May.)

Dee's Tartar Sauce

WESTPORT, Wash.—If your dream of paradise is a meal of steel-gray, briny oysters on the half shell, a sizzling slab of fresh-caught fish, and a slice of warm wild berry pie, all perfumed by breezes off the Pacific Ocean, Washington's Olympic Peninsula is the place you want to go.

It has broad beaches facing west, their slate-colored sand strewn with bleached-white cedar logs. It has moss-draped rain forests,

DEE'S TARTAR SAUCE

1½ cups mayonnaise

¼ cup fresh parsley, chopped fine

1 tablespoon minced sweet onion

⅓ cup finely chopped medium-sour dill
   pickle

½ lemon, juice and chopped pulp (without
   peel)

1 tablespoon cider vinegar

1 tablespoon dill pickle juice

Stir parsley, onion, and dill pickle into
mayonnaise. Stir in lemon, vinegar, and
pickle juice. Refrigerate to store.

Dee's Restaurant, 203 S. Montesano St.,
Westport, Wash.; (206) 268-9737.

spectacular rock formations (at Ruby Beach in particular), and a small number of fascinating places to stay and eat all along Highway 101 as the coast road winds its way from Hoquiam and Humptulips up to the Strait of Juan de Fuca, then down Puget Sound (on the side opposite Seattle) to Olympia.

Gastronomic specialties of the region include a variety of oysters (including minuscule—but gigantically priced—Olympias), Dungeness crab starting in the fall, fine-textured petrale sole, fried razor clams, creamy seafood chowders, and salmon—either freshly caught or alder wood-smoked the way the coast Indians have done it for centuries. Berry bushes and cranberry bogs abound in this part of the country, making for some grand desserts, from cranberry cream pie at the Ark in Nahcotta to boysenberry pie at Three Crabs out toward Dungeness Spit.

One of the fine, undiscovered places to eat is a plain forty-seat café just south of the town of Westport. The type of paper-napkin place favored by locals more than tourists, it is called Dee's—known for fish, terrific breakfast, and superb clam chowder brewed by cook and owner Dave Zaichkin.

The price is right in this small, quick-service establishment; and the fish is *fresh!* Salmon, ling cod, sea bass, crab legs grilled in butter, and breakfast of eggs and almond-crusted fried razor clams: This is some good eating, Northwest-style.

Over slices of walnut pie and cups of coffee one winter afternoon, Dave clued us in to some of his fish cooking techniques. Fish fillets and razor clams are dipped in fine cracker meal. And they are seasoned with a secret-formula salt and pepper powder he concocts and uses as a flavoring for nearly everything he makes, from chowder to fish to beefsteaks. Then—and this, he told us, is the real reason his seafood tastes so great—he watches carefully as the fish cooks. "People almost always overcook seafood," he said, pulling crisp-crusted razor clams from their hot oil after only about a minute's cooking time on each side.

Another secret of Dee's good food is Dave's homemade tartar sauce. It is easy to make, and it's different. The use of dill pickles rather than sweet ones gives it a tang that contrasts beautifully with sweet-fleshed fish of any kind. Once we tried it, we never went back to store-bought again. We have reduced Dave's restaurant recipe to make two cups. Refrigerated and covered, it will keep well two to three weeks.

PEANUT SATAY SAUCE

1 cup peanut butter, smooth or chunky to
   taste
2 teaspoons crushed red pepper
2 cloves garlic, minced
3 tablespoons honey
1 teaspoon cayenne pepper
1/4 cup lime juice
1/4 cup dark soy sauce
1/4 cup peanut oil

Mix together peanut butter, crushed red peppers, garlic, honey, and cayenne pepper.

Mix in lime juice, then soy sauce, then peanut oil.

Let stand at room temperature 30 minutes to 1 hour before serving.

Yield: 2 cups sauce.

Bali Oriental Foods, 139 White St., Danbury, Conn.; (203) 743-9761.

Peanut Satay Sauce

DANBURY, Conn.—When we moved to the outskirts of Danbury, the first great restaurant we found was The Goulash Place, a small diner where locals went for home cooking, Hungarian-style. Then we happened upon a joint called Texas Taco, a Tex/Mex/hard rock café where torrid tacos were dished out at tables set with piles of 1950s *Life* and *Look* magazines.

We soon discovered that Danbury is also the home of our favorite chocolate candy: Chocolate Lace, the exquisite confection originated forty years ago by a Russian immigrant named Eugenia Tay. All the Chocolate Lace in the world is manufactured on a single rattletrap machine nicknamed "Veronica Lace" in the basement of a Danbury apartment building.

From goulash to Chocolate Lace, Danbury is a gold mine of fascinating foods—ethnic, old world, and new wave. What's best is its treasury of corner cafés—lunchrooms where you can dig into honest plates of Italian, Czech, German, Polish, Portuguese, Middle Eastern, or vegetarian cuisine.

Bali Oriental Foods is a grocery store specializing in products from Indonesia, Japan, Thailand, and the Philippines. It is the place to go if you need palm seeds, bean threads, rice sticks, lemon grass, or dried lily flowers.

The store was opened fifteen years ago by Dina and Bill Koegler, both from Indonesia. They named it Bali, Dina says, because "Bali is a magic place. Once you go there, you always want to return."

As you browse along the shelves of culinary exotica, the fragrance of grilling meat wafts forward from the back room. You hear stirring and chopping. Look beyond the counter and there you spy either Bill or Dina or both of them, turning out Indonesian boxed lunches. It is strictly a mom-and-pop operation.

The menu is small, and there is no place to eat inside Bali Oriental Foods. But at noon, locals line up to carry away plates of spicy chicken or cups of cloud ear soup or gigantic egg rolls loaded with curried beef. The mighty rolls, called "lumpia," are packed with a melange of snow peas, bamboo shoots, cabbage, and bean sprouts.

You never know exactly what will be on the menu at Bali Oriental Foods, and service isn't lightning fast, since each plate is cooked and assembled as ordered. We love it when Dina makes shrimp and green beans in coconut sauce, but the lunch we like the best is satay, which is the Indonesian term for barbecue. Bali's best satay is pork, chunked and skewered, then cooked until crusty, but still unbelievably succulent inside. It comes "rijsttafel style," the

Dutch/Indonesian term for a skewer of meat sided by a slew of extras such as hot-sauced hard-boiled eggs, stir-fry vegetables, or the luscious jerked beef called rendang padang.

To make the satay sing, there are sauces. Peanut satay sauce is spread across the meat. Thick, grainy, faintly sweet yet pepper-hot, sumptuous and satisfying, it is similar to what is served on cold noodles as an appetizer in Szechuan Chinese restaurants. Indonesian satays, which come in dozens of varieties, are always accompanied by a sauce like this.

In a tiny paper cup on the rijsttafel plate is a second sauce—the Koeglers' homemade sweet soy, a mahogany-colored syrup that they bottle and market under their own Marapi brand.

You don't have to make Chinese noodles or skewered barbecued pork to enjoy either of these sauces. They make ideal brush-ons for good old American grilled beef, lamb, poultry, or shrimp. Whenever we get a couple of lunches to go at Bali Oriental Foods, we always leave with bottles full for cooking at home.

When we cannot get to Danbury, we make our own peanut satay sauce, inspired by a recipe we found in Kathy Gunst's book *Condiments* (Putnam). Kathy's book of sauces, oils, and relishes contains tips on what to buy and how to use it, as well as recipes for everything from herbed mustard to coriander-cashew chutney.

This satay sauce is a study in yin-yang balance and contrast: hot and sweet, smooth and chunky. The sharpness of peppers is muffled by the gentleness of peanut butter, and honey contrasts with lime juice.

It is a sauce of a dozen uses. We brush it over barbecued meats, serve it as a dip for raw vegetables, or mix it with al dente spaghetti and chopped raw scallions.

Apple Butter

MIDDLEBURY, Ind.—We discovered the Essenhaus thanks to Mrs. William Burer of Cincinnati who wrote "although we live 188 miles away, we visit the restaurant four or five times a year." Mrs. Burer recommended it for groaning-board family-style dinners of chicken and roast beef, and for the fabulous selection of pies—raisin cream all year around, and fresh peach late in the summer.

Hats off to you, Mrs. Burer! We've oinked our way through a couple of gigantic feasts in the barnboard *Ess Kich* ("eating kitchen"), and have carried home basketsful of homemade breads and preserves, cookies, egg noodles, and scrumptious salad dressing from the Amish Country Kitchen.

APPLE BUTTER

4 cups pure apple cider
8 cups thinly sliced tart apples
1 cup sugar
1 cup dark corn syrup
1 teaspoon cinnamon
1/4 teaspoon allspice
1/4 teaspoon ground cloves

Over medium heat, boil cider until it is reduced by one-half. Add apples and simmer gently (uncovered) as mixture thickens, stirring occasionally. Simmer 1 hour, until apples are mushy and mixture is as thick as applesauce.

Stir in sugar, corn syrup, cinnamon, allspice, and cloves. Lower heat and simmer 10–15 minutes more, stirring constantly, until mixture is approximately as thick as applesauce. When it is proper consistency, spoon apple butter into a heat-proof container immediately (so it doesn't stick to the pan).

Makes about 1 quart.

Das Dutchman Essenhaus, U.S. 20, Middlebury, Ind.; (219) 825-9447.

Although decor is rustic—massive timbers, murals of country life, pot-bellied stoves—Das Dutchman Essenhaus is too big to seem quaint. It is a jumbo eating barn, complete with seven dining rooms (including the "Straw Shed," "Hay Mow," and "Cow Stall"). A foursome can even choose to dine in a small compartment shaped like an Amish buggy.

It's hokey, all right; but there is something ingenious about the straightforward appeal to tourist taste. And there is nothing phony about the food.

The mashed potatoes, for example, are real, made from locally grown spuds. The dressing that accompanies chicken dinners is homemade, as is the aromatic golden gravy, as are the breads and rolls and noodles and apple butter.

True to Amish tradition, everybody at the table helps themselves from communal serving bowls. When the bowls run low, more food is brought to the table. And it keeps coming for as long as anyone is still hungry.

The only thing that's limited is dessert: one per customer at each family-style meal. Choosing is tough, considering the dessert card lists twenty-four different pies. There's traditional shoofly, custard or cream, apple or Dutch apple, rich pumpkin, deep chocolate, tangy lemon, and peanut butter. Strawberry, blueberry, and peach pies are made from fresh fruits when they ripen. If pie is not your dish, they also offer ultra luxurious date pudding, an apple dumpling, and sundaes with homemade vanilla ice cream.

After a meal at Das Dutchman Essenhaus, it's fun to stroll through The Country Cupboard, a shop full of gifts, local crafts, wooden barrels and buckets, and jars full of jams, jellies, and salad dressings. Among the treasures we always bring home are jars of apple butter—a thick, spicy condiment that is on the Amish table at breakfast (for spreading on toast or muffins), lunch, and dinner (as a relish to accompany pork roast, ham, chicken, or almost any meat).

Apple butter makes a great souvenir of a visit to Amish country; but it's also a snap to make at home. Our recipe is for rather lumpy, country-style apple butter. If you prefer it smooth, run the apples and cider through a food mill before adding sugar and corn syrup. These measurements yield a little over a quart; but they can be doubled if you want extra: homemade apple butter makes a great little gift.

SALSA FRESCA

*10 fresh plum tomatoes, chopped fine (save
and add juice from chopping)
2 small yellow onions, chopped fine
½ cup chopped cilantro (fresh coriander)
5 serrano chilies (canned green chilies are
OK; or 2 to 3 jalapeño chilies if you like
hot salsa), seeded and chopped
Juice of 2 to 3 limes, to taste
1 to 2 teaspoons salt, to taste*

    *Mix all ingredients together. (If mixture
seems too dry, strain ½ to 1 cup of juice
from a can of plum tomatoes. But do not
use the kind of tomato juice you drink.)
Serve with chips, guacamole, or on the side
of any Mexican meal.*
    Serves 6 to 8.

*Benny's Burritos, 113 Greenwich Ave.,
New York, N.Y.; (212) 633-9210.*

Salsa Fresca

NEW YORK—Try to get a good burrito in the East. Try to get any decent Mexican food. Impossible, you say?

Eat at Benny's Burritos, we say.

This street-corner shop in New York's Greenwich Village, with its pink Formica luncheonette tables and collection of way-out 1950s lamps, is a small miracle: not just good, but *great* Mexican food. Open only a few months, it has already made the cognoscenti's map of New York City's hot spots.

Benny's burrito is the size of a plate, a foot-wide flour tortilla bundled around beans, rice, guacamole, gobs of sour cream, and chunks of fall-apart tender beef (or chicken).

The beans—black or pinto—are exquisite. They haven't turned to mush, yet they are fragile enough to yield a flood of vegetable vim at first bite. The rice you would happily eat by itself—a vegetarian meal. It is infused with tomato purée, onions, chili powder, and a jolt of this kitchen's favorite herb, cilantro. Chunks of avocado make the guacamole filling an opulent wonder. It is pale green, silky smooth, with an occasional crunch of onion. Get a bowlful to whet your appetite.

Beef or chicken fillings are real food: ample pieces delicately seasoned—nothing like the pulverized dog chow that passes for Tex-Mex in most New York area restaurants. Around the good stuff the tortilla is steamed supple, but remains hard enough to secure what's inside.

On top of this Mexican magnum opus, you get your choice from three salsas: verdes (green), rojas (red), or molé (fifty cents extra). Beg your waiter for some of each; or if you're part of a group, each get a different one. They all demand attention. The green is brilliant with the tang of tomatillos. Red is the color of cinnabar—grainy, complex, with a real chili pepper flavor. Molé is the strangest. Yes, you really taste chocolate, but isn't it exotic to have it without candy's sweetness? The profundity of cocoa is blended with the adult pleasure of toasted almonds, and the punch of three kinds of hot pepper. It is deep, deep red, darker than mahogany.

Co-owner Ken Sofer, a friend whose skillful cooking we have known for years, was concurrently moaning and boasting to us the other day about his chef, Liz Hagan, who insists the kitchen do everything by hand. "We remove all seeds from chili peppers," Ken explained, "so the salsas won't be too hot. And she won't allow a food processor for chopping tomatoes. She insists they look nicer hand-chopped."

She is right. The salsa fresca that comes with chips and

guacamole is gorgeous . . . and especially tasty. When Liz came out of the kitchen, we begged the recipe. There's nothing to it, really—except getting the right ingredients. Cilantro is essential, as are fresh plum tomatoes. If you don't have access to serrano chilies, chopped canned jalapeños will do. But add them cautiously: You don't want this sauce overwhelmingly hot. Its dominant quality is *freshness*, which is why it makes such a welcome complement for nearly any Mexican food, from plain tortilla chips to multilevel enchiladas.

12
Desserts

Blue Ribbon Pie Crust

WEST JEFFERSON, Ohio—The gas pumps outside Henry's Sohio aren't working any more. There isn't much activity in either of the garage bays, either. The EAT sign by the side of U.S. Route 40 has turned to monotone rust, and the big blue clock above the doorway is stuck at three. In fact, the door that leads into the café is permanently shut.

Don't let any of that stop you. Henry's Sohio, despite its forlorn appearance and its location on a stretch of highway that the Interstate (70) has made obsolete, is a bonanza for adventurous eaters in search of blue-ribbon roadfood.

We mean that literally. When you enter the dining room (via the garage), you can see the blue ribbons pinned up on the wood-paneled walls, and strung in rows along the pie case on the counter. They aren't all blue: A few reds and yellows hang among the first prizes. Madge Knox, who bakes the pies at Henry's Sohio, sometimes takes all the top prizes when she enters baking contests in county fairs.

It isn't likely you will spend much time admiring the ribbons, because behind the colorful silk festoonery in that counter pie case is an array of the most lovely slices of pie a hungry traveler could ever hope to find. They are what's really beautiful . . . in a homespun sort of way. Deep dark blue and blackberry fillings, vivid red strawberries, dusty rose rhubarb, tan and tawny apple chunks: All these mouth-watering good things ooze from inside pale crusts that look ready to shatter into tender flakes as soon as you poke them with a fork.

Madge makes a dozen and a half such pies every day. Most are fruit-filled, although a few creams (chocolate, butterscotch, etc.) are available, too. She has been baking pies—and winning ribbons—for about fifteen years. Although she doesn't remember exactly how she learned to do it, she recollects that the original recipes probably came from a local Mennonite cookbook and were then adapted and elevated to blue-ribbon status.

It is the pies that inscribe Henry's Sohio on the good eats map of America, but you can precede them with some fine roadside meals. The first time we stopped in, it was lunch hour; so we postponed our pie pleasures with a platter of diner-style meat loaf and a mega-caloric ploughman's lunch of ham and white beans served together in a trough, accompanied by a block of yellow cornbread.

As the blue ribbons foreshadowed, the pies were sensational—their fruit fillings vivid, crusts masterful. Indeed, it was the crusts for which we begged a recipe from Madge Knox. And the dear woman was kind enough to give it to us. Here is how to make perfect pie crusts, exactly the way Madge does.

Her recipe, which makes enough dough for 5–6 crusts, is impossible to scale down. However, Madge advises that these crusts, once formed into shells and wrapped well in freezer paper, freeze well, then can be defrosted, baked, and used for one-crust pies. If making two-crust pies, the dough may be refrigerated before being rolled out, but not frozen.

BLUE RIBBON PIE CRUST

5 cups all-purpose flour
I teaspoon salt
I teaspoon baking powder
2½ cups solid vegetable shortening
I teaspoon vinegar
I whole egg

Mix flour, salt, and baking powder. Cut in shortening until mixture is cornmeal-textured.

In a I-cup measure, beat together vinegar and egg. Then fill to I-cup mark with cold tap water.

Mix together flour and vinegar-egg-water mixtures. It will be soft and sticky.

Working on a very well-floured board, roll out a piece of the dough to approximately ⅛-inch thick and 2–3 inches wider than your pie pan. Put in lightly floured pie pans. Roll out equal-size circles for top crusts.

For pies requiring unbaked shells, crimp edge, chill 30–45 minutes, and follow recipe.

For pies requiring partially baked or prebaked crust, press a square of aluminum foil against the dough and bake in preheated 425 degree oven 6 minutes. Remove foil, bake 6 minutes more, until crust is light brown (for "partially baked crust"), or 12 minutes for a crust that will get cooled and filled.

Henry's Sohio, 6275 U.S. 40, West Jefferson, Ohio; (614) 879-9819.

Lemon Chess Pie

HARRODSBURG, Ky.—It is as sweet and luscious as a wedge of hard sauce packed into crust. Yet it is an austere dessert, monotone gold beneath its oven-burnished skin. It is called chess pie, and it is one of America's great regional delicacies, served throughout the mid-South.

Despite wide popularity in Kentucky, Tennessee, Virginia, and North Carolina, chess pie remains something of a culinary mystery. Nobody knows how it got its name. The likely story is that it came to the Southern colonies from England as "cheese pie," was misspelled, and lost its cheese along the way. One Kentucky cook we know claims that it was always served as finger food to visitors who came to play a game of chess. "Chess pie is for gentlemen," she told us. "It is a respectable pie."

Unlike oozy fruit-filled pies, this high-tone, Southern-accented beauty is especially neat to eat, often made in patty pans or as tiny tartlets suitable for stand-up parties and summer picnics. Its pantry ingredients—scarcely more than eggs, cream, and sugar—make it a year-round dessert, independent of seasonal fruits and berries.

Some cooks like to add cocoa to the amber filling for chocolate chess pie. Others substitute brown sugar for white and make butterscotch chess pie, or add a dash of vanilla. But we think the best way to have it is the way it is served at a restaurant called Murphy's on the River, a restaurant snuggled up against the banks of the Kentucky River in Harrodsburg.

Murphy's chess pie is a study of simplicity, its cream-and-sugar goodness heightened by a brilliant lemon kick. The heirloom recipe, passed down to Mrs. Dorothy Murphy by her grandmother, Lucretia Curd King, originally listed such cheerfully farmy ingredients as "pullet eggs," "four big handsful of sugar," "butter the size of a hen egg," and "milk to match." Mrs. Murphy brought the recipe up-to-date, but continues to make the chess pies for her restaurant in batches of two at a time, just the way her grandmother did.

At Murphy's on the River, the pie is customarily served as a grand finale to a down-home country meal of pan-fried catfish, enveloped in a fine-grained brittle crust. The fish is presented whole, then deftly boned by the waitress, who takes the skeleton away. And if you look around the dining room, you will see where the spirited-away skeletons wind up once they are cleaned and bleached. They are hung on the Murphy's "catfish tree," like a Christmas tree; only instead of ornaments, it is decorated with catfish skeletons.

LEMON CHESS PIE

2 whole eggs plus 4 yolks
1 cup granulated white sugar
4 tablespoons butter, melted
¼ cup heavy cream
1 tablespoon yellow cornmeal
1 tablespoon flour
4 tablespoons lemon juice
1 tablespoon grated lemon rind
1 9-inch unbaked pie crust

Preheat oven to 350 degrees.
Beat eggs, yolks, and sugar together at high speed for 2 minutes. Add butter and cream; beat again at high speed for 2 minutes. Add cornmeal, flour, lemon juice, and rind. Mix well. Pour into pie crust and bake 30 minutes.
Allow pie to cool to room temperature before serving. May be topped with a dab of whipped cream.

Murphy's at the River, U.S. 68 East, Harrodsburg, Ky.; (606) 734-9739.

PEANUT BUTTER PIE

PASTRY:
1½ cups sifted flour
½ teaspoon salt
2 tablespoons sugar
½ cup shortening
2½ to 3 tablespoons ice cold water

Sift together flour, salt, and sugar. Cut in shortening until it resembles cornmeal. Add water, 1 tablespoon at a time, tossing with fork until moist enough to hold together. Shape into a ball. Wrap in waxed paper. Refrigerate 1 hour.

We ought to assure anyone squeamish about dining among rattling rib cages that Murphy's on the River is not a ghoulish boneyard. In fact, it is an enchanting roadhouse, built around a log cabin that used to be a grocery store and blue-plate café on a bend of Highway 68 as the two-lane sweeps through bluegrass hills west of Lexington.

The river setting, near the crossing called the Brooklyn Bridge, is idyllic. The water is so close that when the river flooded a few Decembers ago, Murphy's on the River became Murphy's *in* the River, completely submerged. It took months of shoveling, scrubbing, and sanding to dig out, but now Mrs. Murphy's restaurant gleams—all wood-paneled walls and varnished floors, tables set with crocheted cloths, water served in souvenir glasses from the 1975 Kentucky Derby.

Her dessert menu is like home—only one choice each day. Peach cobbler maybe, or fresh rhubarb pie—or, if you are a lucky traveler, the old family favorite, lemon chess pie.

In a pie like this, with such few ingredients, what makes it sparkle is the quality of the cream, butter, and eggs. They don't have to be fresh off the farm—although, of course, that is the way Grandma King made hers: with warm-from-the-hen eggs and topmilk from the morning milking . . . and then she baked it in the oven of her woodburning stove.

The pie will fall into a slim circle as it cools. It should be served at room temperature, sliced quite thin.

Peanut Butter Pie

DALLAS—What is most fun about driving through Texas is its never-ending variety of places to eat. There are smokeshacks at the ends of dusty roads, barbecues attached to grocery stores, family-style boardinghouses, seafood stands along the Gulf Coast, and Indian reservation cafeterias in the west. Tacquerias, chili parlors, steak joints, and cafeterias: However you'd like to put on the feed bag, Texas highways and back roads offer choices galore.

Plain cafés are one of the state's great eating-out traditions, whether located in small towns or city neighborhoods. A café, Texas-style, is a modest place that specializes in plate lunch at low prices, sassy service, and local color of the sort you will never find in a fancier eatery that calls itself a restaurant.

One of the greatest of the city cafés is a minuscule cafeteria in Dallas known as Gennie's Bishop Grill. A forty-two-seat operation opened fifteen years ago, Gennie's has since become the standard

Preheat oven to 450 degrees. On a lightly floured board, roll out chilled pastry until large enough to line a 9-inch pie pan. Dust top lightly with flour and line pan. Prick all over with fork. Flute edges. Place in freezer 15–20 minutes. Bake 12–15 minutes. Cool.

PIE FILLING:

3 egg yolks
pinch of salt
2½ cups milk
¾ cup sugar
½ cup flour
1 teaspoon vanilla
½ cup smooth peanut butter
baked pie shell (from above recipe)
1 cup cream, whipped
½ cup roasted peanuts

Combine egg yolks, salt, and milk. Mix well. Place in heavy saucepan and cook over low heat, stirring until warm. Combine sugar and flour; gradually add to milk mixture, stirring constantly until thickened. Boil 1 minute. Remove from heat. Stir in vanilla and peanut butter. Let cool slightly.

Pour filling into cooled pie shell. Chill thoroughly. Garnish with whipped cream and roasted peanuts.

Gennie's Bishop Grill, 308 N. Bishop, Dallas, Texas; (214) 946-1752.

by which all other home-cooking restaurants in Dallas are measured. Gennie's daughter, Rosemarie, branched out and opened her own, larger café (called Rosemarie's) about a mile away, featuring the same from-scratch good food; but it is the original Grill, now run by Rosemarie's husband, Gus Hudson, that gives the truest taste of down-home "café society."

Decor? That consists of calling cards of happy customers, tacked up on the walls. And a formidable picture of the Dallas Cowboys. And clippings from newspapers that have praised the vittles and no-nonsense ambience. Gus once cheerfully described his place to us as "a dump," but a dump with great food.

"We try (at both places) to serve only the freshest and best food available at a price the working people can afford," Rosemarie said. That means shopping every day at the Farmer's Produce Market for vegetables to make soulfully seasoned turnip greens, pinto beans, acorn squash, and stuffed bell peppers. Hot yeast rolls are baked every day. And the Bishop Grill's chicken-fried steak, seasoned with paprika and black pepper, served under a mantle of cream gravy made with natural steak drippings, is one of the best in town.

Desserts are extra-special good—like everything else, made from scratch. We especially like strawberry pie in a flaky crust, and the vanilla wafer-layered banana pudding—or as it is known hereabouts, 'naner pudding. But the greatest dessert of all is one for which Rosemarie was generous enough to share her recipe: peanut butter pie. It's a real Texas treat suitable for after barbecue, or after a genuine café meal.

Shaker Lemon Pie

NEW HARMONY, Ind.—New Harmony is a lot like heaven. Here are peace and quiet and hot donuts in the morning. Here is the New Harmony Inn, a serene retreat on a tree-shaded lane in a village of less than a thousand people.

If you've been on the road awhile, staying in ordinary highway motels, as we had been when we found New Harmony, its charm is overwhelming. The southern Indiana countryside for miles around is farmland: no business or industry, no malls, no convenience stores, no chain restaurants. Just a lot of green landscape, two-lane roads, and family homes.

New Harmony was always a special place, founded in 1814 by followers of George Rapp, who wanted to create a utopia based on principles of celibacy and communal property. Ten years later, the Rappites left and Robert Owen began his own utopian experiment.

SHAKER LEMON PIE

3 lemons
2 cups granulated sugar
dough for 2-crusted 9-inch pie
5 eggs
2 tablespoons melted butter

Peel lemons, removing all pith, and slice as thin as possible. Remove seeds. Place in large bowl. You will have about 1½ cups of slices. Add sugar and gently mix until sugar is dissolved. Cover and let sit overnight.

Roll out pie dough and place bottom part in 9-inch pie pan. Preheat oven to 425 degrees.

Beat eggs until sunny yellow. Add butter and lemon-sugar mixture. Stir gently to mix well. Pour into crust. Cover with top crust. Crimp edges and cut vent holes in top.

Bake 45 to 50 minutes until pastry is golden brown. (If pastry is overbrowning after 30 minutes, cover with aluminum foil.) Let cool thoroughly on a rack, but rewarm slightly to serve.

Red Geranium Restaurant at the New Harmony Inn, North & Brewery, New Harmony, Ind.; (812) 682-4431.

Owen's idea of perfection was built on a belief that environment determines character. He and his four sons tried to make New Harmony an ideal place to work, live, and study. Foremost among their concerns was higher education; so it wasn't long before scientists and scholars from all across America were drawn to the little town on the Wabash River, which became known as the Athens of the West. It was here that the Smithsonian Institution had its beginnings.

Although the New Harmony social order didn't last long, the town enjoyed an "afterglow" that continued to inspire high-minded religious and philosophical activity. As recently as 1957, architect Philip Johnson designed a "roofless church" in accord with the idea that only the sky is large enough to embrace all of worshiping humanity.

Today, many of the Harmonists' original buildings still stand: dormitory number two, the cooper shop, the opera house, and several sturdy wood-frame homes. One of our favorite sites is New Harmony's great circular maze of shrubbery—built by the Harmonists as a walk-through symbol of life's complexities.

Despite its historical significance, New Harmony has maintained an ingratiating small-town feel. You can stroll from end to end, stop in at the bookstore if you want to read about local history, visit old buildings and new churches, or just find a bench by a pond and let your mind wander.

The place to stay—and eat—is the New Harmony Inn. In keeping with the contemplative spirit of the town, it is an inconspicuous set of buildings with no signs or hostelry razzle-dazzle to spoil the scene. Built of brick in a style that evokes the institutional-dormitory look of the Harmonists' communal buildings, it offers rooms that are spare and simple, furnished with Shaker reproductions. No shag rugs on these clean wood floors; no velvet paintings on the walls; no rumbling ice machine outside your door. The Inn does have all the modern amenities, such as a pool, a health club, and tennis courts. But our favorite entertainment was opening the window of our room, gazing across the ripples in the pond out back, and listening to birds chirp.

The Inn's grand restaurant is called The Red Geranium, where the best things to eat are meat-and-potatoes square meals. We dug into a plate-size cut of prime rib, and a surf 'n' turf filet mignon and lobster tail combo, accompanied by custard-rich escalloped corn, then topped things off with the specialty dessert of the Inn—Shaker lemon pie—for which Inn manager Gary Gerard was kind enough to provide the recipe.

CROSS CREEK LIME PIE

GRAHAM CRACKER CRUST:

1½ cups graham cracker crumbs
⅓ cup sugar
¼ teaspoon cinnamon
8 tablespoons (1 stick) butter, melted

Preheat oven to 350 degrees.

Mix together graham cracker crumbs, sugar, and cinnamon. Stir in melted butter until well-blended. Empty mixture into 8- or 9-inch pie plate and pat (by hand) so mixture evenly covers the bottom and sides of the pan. Bake 8 minutes, until crust is firm. Remove from oven and allow to come to room temperature before filling.

FILLING:

1 15-ounce can sweetened condensed milk
5 egg yolks, beaten
zest of 2 limes
½ cup lime juice
2 tablespoons (6 teaspoons) 151 proof rum
4–6 drops green food coloring (optional)
1 cup whipping cream
2 tablespoons confectioners' sugar

Beat condensed milk and egg yolks together until smooth. Stir in zest, lime juice, and 2 teaspoons of the rum. If a green pie is desired, stir in food coloring. Pour into prepared graham cracker crust. Freeze 2–4 hours, until pie is firm.

Whip cream with confectioners' sugar and remaining 4 teaspoons of rum. Spread over firm, chilled pie.

Makes 8 servings.

The Yearling, Route 325, Cross Creek, Fla.; (904) 466-3033.

Cross Creek Lime Pie

CROSS CREEK, Fla.—Most of us who visit Florida see only the coasts. But there is another Florida, less modern, without crowds of tourists, secluded and peaceful. Marjorie Kinnan Rawlings, author of *The Yearling,* described it as a place that "belongs to the wind and the rain, to the sun and the seasons, to the cosmic secrecy of seed, and beyond all, to time."

Miss Rawlings was writing about Cross Creek, a village near Gainesville where a slow pace prevails. Here one is reminded that Florida is very much part of the deep South, with a heritage of simple country living.

Marjorie Rawlings's home stands south of the bridge that travels over Cross Creek. Restored as a historical site, the house is modest, designed to be practical in this steamy climate, its kitchen slightly removed from the rest of the structure so that heat from cooking stays out. The simple kitchen is where Miss Rawlings and her visiting neighbors prepared many of the recipes that appear in *Cross Creek Cookery,* a deliciously anecdotal book that not only gives recipes, but also provides a textured account of everyday life in the sleepy community she immortalized.

Our favorite way to savor the charms of inland Florida is to eat a meal at The Yearling, an inn and restaurant adjacent to the Rawlings home.

The Yearling is a place where many native Floridians like to vacation. There is a handful of cabins for overnight guests, a lake well-stocked with speckled perch and bass, and woods for hunting. The dining room at the inn is a gracious place, a bit fancier than one might expect in these down-home surroundings, but true in every way to the heritage of Cross Creek cooking.

Here you can taste the "cooter" that Marjorie Rawlings liked so much—delicate chunks of native soft-shell turtle dipped in flour and pan-fried. The menu also lists local favorites such as frog legs, catfish, gator tail, quail, and bass, all accompanied by fluffy-centered, golden-crusted hush puppies.

Many of the ingredients used to make Cross Creek dinner entrées are pretty hard to find in supermarkets outside Florida, so the recipe we'd like to share from The Yearling is one for dessert. This, too, is a dish that is uniquely Floridian—actually more typical of the southern Keys than of the inland north. Few people dine at The Yearling without topping off the meal with a slice of lime pie.

In the Florida Keys, of course, it is known as *Key* lime pie, and (if you are lucky) it is made with genuine Key limes—tiny little fruits with a distinct flavor all their own, tangier than ordinary limes, almost effervescent in their zest.

If you can get real Key limes and Key lime juice, by all means use them in our adaptation of The Yearling recipe. If not, don't worry. Made with ordinary limes—as it is done in Cross Creek—this pie is delish. Its graham crust is thick and buttery—almost like candy.

Chocolate Peanut Butter Pie

MARION, Ind.—"They are so giant that they look like a spaceship has just landed on your plate." So began a breathless letter we got from reader Jill Maidenberg of Madison, Wisconsin. Jill was describing that beloved Midwestern specialty, the tenderloin sandwich. Her letter included not only an elaborate account of the perfect 'loin ("ordered with everything, including pickles"), but detailed illustrations of how to eat one. (They are so large you cannot pick them up in two hands like an ordinary sandwich, so she suggested cutting the breaded pork cutlet in half or folding it over itself inside the bun, then eating the sandwich as a double-decker.)

Jill's letter concluded with a recommendation—the Nobby Grill in Marion, Indiana. The Nobby, she exclaimed, makes "undoubtedly the best tenderloin in Indiana. Being a former Hoosier, I ought to know. They also serve a mean slab of homemade cream pie. Try the butterscotch or banana cream!"

We were on our way. The Nobby was listed in the local phone book on 4th Street, just east of the town square. And there it was on the menu, the HOUSE SPECIALTY: "Our Giant Tenderloin—the all-time favorite of the Nobby crowd." We ordered one, and sure enough, a spaceship was soon launched our way from the back of the little luncheonette. The breaded and deep fried pork cutlet was so large it covered both halves of an opened burger bun. It was a real, hand-breaded cutlet, slim but moist and succulent inside its crusty golden skin. We ate it like a couple of rubes—with knife and fork—then set our sights on those pies that Jill had recommended.

The day's selection included coconut cream, banana cream, butterscotch, strawberry, and a chocolate peanut butter wonder listed by its brand-name inspiration, Reese's Pieces pie. Each type we sampled was a beaut, but it was the chocolate peanut butter combo that made us weak-kneed—its velvety chocolate filling swirled with veins of peanut butter, heaped with whipped cream, and dotted with chocolate chips.

We definitely recommend the Nobby to all adventurous eaters passing through north central Indiana. The giant tenderloin sandwich is an eating experience not to be missed, and virtually impos-

CHOCOLATE PEANUT BUTTER PIE

4 eggs

1 cup butter, softened

6 ounces semisweet chocolate, melted and cooled

2 cups confectioners' sugar

3/4 cup peanut butter (smooth, not chunky)

1 cup heavy cream

1 baked 10-inch pie shell

semisweet chocolate chips or shavings as garnish

Beat eggs with 3/4 cup of the butter, the melted chocolate, and the sugar for 5 full minutes, until smooth and thick.

In a separate bowl, beat peanut butter with remaining 1/4 cup of butter. While you are beating, add up to 1/3 cup of the cream, in order to make the peanut butter a spreadable consistency that will swirl readily into the chocolate mixture.

Spoon chocolate mixture into pie shell. Swirl peanut butter into chocolate mixture.

Beat remaining heavy cream until thick enough to spread across the top of the pie. Garnish cream with semisweet chocolate. Refrigerate until ready to serve.

Makes 8–10 servings.

The Nobby Grill, 213 E. 4th St., Marion, Ind.; (317) 664-1335.

sible to duplicate at home. And the chocolate peanut butter pie is the height of wanton dessert indulgence.

Chocolate Milk Pie

CARRABELLE, Fla.—Nestled among a grove of tall evergreens along Route 98 southwest of Sopchoppy and Tallahassee is a low-slung brick café named Julia Mae's Town Inn.

This is the place to taste what some locals refer to as "cracker cooking"—a lusty downhome cuisine with a Southern accent, based on groceries that are uniquely Floridian.

Oysters by the dozen, local fish, turtles, alligator tail, plus Dixie favorites from grits and hush puppies to banana pudding, are all part of the repertoire of the cracker cook. Whatever the ingredients, true cracker cooking is never fancy or expensive.

That is why Julia Mae's Town Inn is the perfect place to eat it. Rumble on in to the dusty gravel parking lot, saunter inside, and find yourself a booth. The seats are molded plastic; the walls—draped with a few shells, nets, etc.—are made of woodlike panels reminiscent of a well-kept mobile home. If there was any music playing, we couldn't hear it: We visited Julia Mae's in May, and the multiple air conditioners were already groaning full blast.

Along came a waitress, who set down a card announcing, "Hello, my name is Toni." Every table in the house was set with tartar sauce: gentle, creamy white, with just a tad of pickle smack. Coleslaw was served in a plastic-foam cup. The menu listed local specialties such as scamp, Florida lobsters, grouper burgers, even fried grouper throat (which Toni explained was the meat from behind the gills).

We feasted on shrimp "Franklin," each crescent wrapped in bacon with broiled tomato, then moved on to spicy deviled crabs served in an aluminum shell, accompanied by a formidable Greek salad loaded down with a mountain of feta cheese. Portions are country style—enormous!

The most delicious local specialty we sampled was fried mullet—rich and smoky-flavored, with a sharp crunch to its breading, accompanied by tubular hush puppies and French fries. All of Julia Mae's seafood is served with wedges of lime to bring out the fish's natural sweetness.

Julia Mae's pies are climactic, piled high with toasty-topped meringues, cut into jumbo wedges guaranteed to satisfy. The lemon meringue was sharp, tart, and jiggly. Our favorite was chocolate pie—creamy smooth and thoroughly chocoriffic. Julie Mae's

CHOCOLATE MILK PIE

6 ounces semisweet chocolate
4 tablespoons butter
1/2 cup sugar
2 cups milk
2 tablespoons cornstarch
2 tablespoons water
3 eggs, separated
2 teaspoons vanilla
dash of cream of tartar
1/4 cup sugar
1 9-inch pie crust, baked

In top of double boiler over simmering water, melt chocolate and butter together, stirring until smooth. Add sugar and milk. Continue stirring over simmering water until well-blended.

Dissolve cornstarch in 2 tablespoons water. Beat in egg yolks. Stir in vanilla. Gradually beat into milk mixture in top of double boiler. Cook and continuously stir over simmering water, until chocolate mixture is smooth and thick enough to hold the trail of a spoon. Remove and cool to tepid, stirring occasionally.

Pour chocolate into prepared pie shell. Chill in refrigerator until set (at least one hour.)

To make meringue, beat room-temperature egg whites with cream of tartar, slowly adding sugar as whites stiffen. Spread edge to edge across cooled pie and toast under broiler barely one minute, until top of meringue begins to brown. Watch constantly—meringue can burn in just a few seconds.

Makes 6–8 servings.

Julia Mae's Town Inn, Highway 98, Carrabelle, Fla.; (904) 697-3791.

original recipe is based on chocolate milk. This variation mixes whole milk and semisweet chocolate. (We recommend using chocolate chips.)

Egg Custard Pie

FORT WORTH, Texas—The exact right time to each lunch at the Paris Coffee Shop is 11 A.M. That will be well after the breakfast crowd has gone, and a bit before the noontime bunch arrives, so you'll have a choice of tables. But the real reason to come mid-morning is the pies: coconut, chocolate, banana meringue, cherry, apple, and pecan; lemon on Friday; egg custard every day. By 11 A.M., the day's selection is ready to serve.

If you are lucky, as we have been each time we've eaten lunch in this businesslike downtown café, the pies will be cooled to proper eating temperature at the precise time you are mopping the last of the chicken-fried steak gravy from your plate.

Slices will arrive at the table still slightly warm, the custard set but jiggling precariously, a bit of steam still escaping from underneath the top crust of the apple pie.

Eating pie in the Paris Coffee Shop—even if you dine here at 2 P.M. and the morning's selection has reached room temperature—is one of America's distinctive culinary experiences. Pie and coffee in a home-cooking café, after all, is as American as . . well, as apple pie.

Indeed, someday we would like to draw a pie map of this country, a map whose topography would ignore such trivia as mountains, rivers, and state lines in order to pinpoint the important pie lodes coast to coast. We would mark Duarte's Cafe in Pescadero, California, and Helen's in Machias, Maine; the vast sour cream-raisin treasure trove in Wisconsin, Minnesota, and Iowa; the berry belt across northern Indiana; the twin apple pie peaks of Vermont and Virginia; and the Key lime bonanza of south Florida.

Fort Worth is at the western end of the richest of all of America's custard pie reserves—a broad swatch of cafés with its easternmost border on the streets of Memphis, Tennessee (at Buntyn Cafe in particular), and its fullest expression in truck stops, town cafés, and roadside eateries throughout Arkansas and Oklahoma. Travel along the highways and into the small towns of this part of the Southwest, and it won't be easy to find a bad piece of custard pie. With few exceptions, even the humblest eat shops hand-crimp their crusts, and whip up their custards every day.

EGG CUSTARD PIE

1½ cups milk
1 tablespoon butter
4 eggs
¾ cup sugar
2½ teaspoons vanilla extract
1 9-inch pie crust (unbaked)

Preheat oven to 450 degrees.
Scald milk and butter.
Beat together eggs, sugar, and vanilla.
Stirring vigorously, gradually add milk and butter to beaten egg mixture. Continue beating until foam forms on top. Pour into prepared crust.
Bake 5 minutes. Reduce heat to 375 degrees. Cook 20 minutes more, or until firm.
Cool and serve.

Paris Coffee Shop, 704 W. Magnolia, Fort Worth, Texas; (817) 335-2041.

Few of the pies you find in this territory are elaborate or unusual. It is a region of the country where classics prevail. That is why we asked Mike Smith, owner of the Paris Coffee Shop, for the simplest of all custard pie recipes, an unimprovable combination of elementary ingredients.

Before we get to the recipe, however, we have to tell you that it isn't only custard pies that have endeared the Paris Coffee Shop to the people of Fort Worth since Vic Paris opened it in 1926. Meals that precede the pies are classics, too.

Here is true café cooking unadulterated by food trends and fancy notions of gourmet cuisine. Every Monday, you can come to the Paris for turkey and cornbread dressing with giblet gravy. On Tuesday, they make meat loaf; Wednesday, beef brisket; Thursday, chicken and dumplings; Friday, fried chicken. Any day you can come to the Paris for a serious chicken-fried steak smothered in gravy, accompanied by a mountain of mashed potatoes. Another meal we like is "the Arkansas traveler": a slab of cornbread topped with hot roast beef, accompanied by mashed potatoes, pinto beans, and biscuits for mopping up the gravy. Breakfast features yeast-rise biscuits and bacon cream gravy, bone-in country ham, and hot sweet rolls.

We don't recommend the Paris Coffee Shop to everyone—only to people who really like to eat.

MAPLE SYRUP A PP LE PIE

CRUST (FOR TWO-CRUST PIE):

2¼ cups flour

½ teaspoon salt

¾ cup lard or solid vegetable shortening

6 to 7 tablespoons ice-cold water

Mix flour and salt. Cut in shortening until crumbly. Sprinkle in water, I tablespoon at a time, stirring lightly or ly until dough holds together. Cut dough i n ha lf. Roll one half out to ⅛-inch thick o n a l ightly floured surface. Place into lightly floured 9-inch pie pan. Preheat oven t o 40 0 degrees, and proceed as follows .

FILLING:

8 cups cored, p eeled, thinly sliced apples

⅓ cup sugar

4 tablespoons butte r, melted

¼ cup maple syrup

milk

Mix apples wit h sugar. Place in bottom crust.

Mix butter wi th syrup. Pour over apples. Roll out remaini ng dough and lay over filling. Cut stea m vents in top. Trim top to fit bottom, leavir g enough dough to crimp top and bottom s ecurely together. Brush top with milk. B ake 30–40 minutes, until golden brow n.

Cool on pie rack. Serve slightly warm with sharp che ddar cheese or vanilla ice cream.

Maple Syrup Apple Pie

WEST HARTFORD, Conn.—Have you ever eaten fifteen different kinds of apple pie in one sitting? We did; and let us tell you, it was hard work! Delicious work, but to be perfectly honest, we would have been happy eating only ten pies, or maybe a dozen. But no, our task was to taste every one and, along with West Hartford restaurateur Ann Howard, select the best.

The occasion for this exercise in applemania was Noah Webster's birthday party on September 27, 1986. Mr. Webster, as you may know, wrote the first American dictionary. To honor him each year, the Noah Webster Foundation and Historical Society has a party at the home where he was born in 1758.

It is a cranberry-red clapboard farmhouse built around a central chimney. Furnished with authentic eighteenth-century antiques, it also includes a working loom for weaving, a full array of kitchen implements, and interpreter/guides in colonial dress. Noah's house feels like a home where someone lives—not just an impersonal museum. If you visit, you will likely see the kitchen fireplace at work, turning out Yankee fare such as Indian pudding, hoe cakes or "matrimony knots."

For Noah's birthday party the curators have an open house—an all-day event featuring crafts demonstrations and (of course) a spelling bee. Because apple pie was Noah Webster's favorite food, the festivities include an apple pie bake-off.

The rules for pies were simple: The crust had to be homemade, and the apples had to be fresh. Lucky for us, late September is the height of apple season, and so the range of apple flavors alone gave the entries a wondrous spectrum between tart and sweet.

Beyond the apples, the variety of pies was eye-opening. Of the fifteen, no two were even vaguely similar. Some came in health-food crusts made with whole wheat flour. There were lattice tops and crumb tops, flaky lard crusts and butter cookie crusts. There were apple pies with raisins, with cranberries, with rhubarb; there was even one that had a thick ribbon of cheddar cheese baked among the apples. Some fillings were mushy applesauce; others were nearly as crisp as an apple off the tree. Most had plenty of cinnamon and/or nutmeg; but one tart "English style" pie (to be served under a mantle of heavy cream) had barely any spice at all.

After much tasting and retasting, we chose a pure classic as our winner: Lill Quinn Costello's elegant-crusted pie with a filling that was nothing more than eight thinly sliced apples sprinkled with a cup of sugar and a half teaspoon of cinnamon.

We also tucked a runner-up's recipe into our pocket, saving it

DEEP-DISH APPLE PIE

enough dough for 2-crust pie
10 cups peeled, cored and sliced (½-inch-
    thick slices) apples (we like Granny
    Smiths best)
¼ cup lemon juice
½ cup white sugar
⅔ cup dark brown sugar
½ teaspoon cinnamon
½ teaspoon nutmeg
¼ teaspoon salt
3 tablespoons flour
4 tablespoons butter
2 tablespoons cream (or milk)

Preheat oven to 400 degrees.
Roll dough out on floured board, slightly thicker than ⅛ inch.
In large bowl, toss apples with lemon juice.
Mix sugars, cinnamon, nutmeg, salt, and flour. Stir thoroughly into apples.
Pack apples into 4 ovenproof 2- to 3-cup bowls. Dot with butter, then drape with dough. Pinch and crimp rim firmly around edge. Cut 3 to 4 vents in dough. Brush with cream. Place in oven, with a rimmed cookie sheet on the shelf below to catch any dripping juices. Bake 15 minutes. Reduce heat to 350 degrees. Bake 30 to 35 minutes more, until crust is a rich, golden brown. (Apples will "settle" below crust as pies bake. This is a good place to add ice cream or cheddar cheese, through a break in the crust, just before serving.)
Serve warm.
Makes 4 pies, 8 portions.

Dory Cove, Logan Road, Lincoln City, Ore.; (503) 994-5180.

for the spring maple sugar season. Karen Mitchell's maple syrup apple pie has a fine, subtle sweetness, its minimal sugar augmented by the woodsy smack of maple syrup. If you live anywhere near maple trees, we suggest you visit a sugar house and buy some grade B or grade C syrup, rather than fancy grade A. Any pure maple syrup works fine in this recipe, but the cheaper grades are more intensely mapley, all the better to harmonize with apples.

Deep-Dish Apple Pie

LINCOLN CITY, Ore.—Dory Cove Restaurant is known to its friends as Road's End Dory Cove because it is at the end of Logan Road. But the overly descriptive name suggests more than that mere geographical fact. Dory Cove *feels* like the end of the road—just the kind of home-cooking café a weary driver might hope to find in the wetlands west of Oregon's seacoast highway.

It is an American classic, this little wood-shingle bunker with its fishnet decor, a really fun place to eat. Lincoln City locals come for baskets of fish and chips or giant-size hamburgers, followed by splendorous wedges of pie. Travelers from all regions of the country have sung hosannas to us about Dory Cove's broiled salmon steaks and its Oregon-style extra-thick clam chowder.

It is not the kind of restaurant that a fastidious gourmet will appreciate. The cuisine and ambience are strictly for the roadfood connoisseur. Waitresses are friendly, fast, and gabby. Beverages are served in large Mason jars with handles.

Hamburgers are probably the most popular item on the menu. They are juicy, sloppy, satisfying hunks of beef, the kind you cannot get at a fast-food window. The head of the list is the mammoth Road's End Burger—a half-pounder topped with cheddar cheese and Canadian bacon on an onion bun. For meat-eaters who want to use utensils, the menu also lists steaks.

Seafood baskets are what we like to eat when we come to Dory Cove. This kitchen knows how to properly fry shellfish, so there is plenty of crunch and chew to the halo of golden batter that surrounds each oceanic nugget (shrimp, oysters, clam strips, or scallops), but not so much that whatever is inside gets lost. You taste the seafood, and its marine smack is even accentuated by the heft of the crisp fried jacket all around it. Baskets are accompanied by another oily-good thing: garlic-Parmesan French bread.

Dory Cove pies, like everything else on the menu, are hearty fellas. Sever a bite-size portion of cream pie from your wedge, and you will feel its gravity weighing on your fork; sour cream raisin is especially substantial—and tasty. Even chiffon pies are thick, sweet, and goopy. Last time we drove up the Oregon coast, we were faced with a choice of pineapple cream, banana cream, chocolate peanut butter cream, nectarine chiffon, lemon meringue, lime, sour cream raisin, walnut, and deep-dish apple pie served steaming hot.

There is something gluttonously satisfying about getting a whole deep-dish pie all for one's self . . . and something quite cozy about a deep-dish pie for two, as in our Dory Cove-inspired recipe. These measurements make enough pie for eight people, however you divide it: into four 2- or 3-cup ovenproof bowls, or into eight individual servings. If you make it in eighths, cut the baking time by 10 to 15 minutes. If you make it all in one big 2½-quart casserole, add 10 to 15 minutes.

Mock Apple Pie

Have you ever tasted mock apple pie? It is entirely possible that you may have eaten it without even knowing. Made properly, the bogus version—consisting of little more than crackers, sugar, and spice—does a remarkable impersonation of the real thing.

It is a phenomenon bordering on miraculous the way a few common kitchen spices can come so close to the flavor we all recognize as apples, and the way the crackers swell and soften and attain the texture of well-baked Granny Smiths.

Why bother? There are three good answers to that question. First, crackers are considerably cheaper than apples. Second, there are times of the year when good baking apples can be hard to find in some regions of the country. Third, it's a heap of sneaky fun. Fool your friends and family with this amazing trick; and even if you don't actually fool them, amaze them with how you have turned kitchen miscellany into something really good to eat.

We always assumed that mock apple pie was a modern invention dating back to the convenience-crazed 1950s. That was an era when many food manufacturers encouraged housewives to take up jiffy, no-fuss, shortcut cookery that involved using crackers, cereals, potato chips, and soda pop as substitutes for fancier or more sophisticated ingredients. For example, our files contain recipes for fried chicken "breaded" with corn flakes; roast duck glazed with ginger ale (tastes great!); cookies made with chow mein noodles that are supposed to resemble coconut; and—are you ready for this one?—meringue laced with crushed potato chips.

Many people know about mock apple pie because of the Ritz

MOCK APPLE PIE

Dough for one 8-inch, double-crust pie
5 cups unsalted soda crackers, broken into
  bite-size pieces
1¼ cups warm water
1 tablespoon lemon juice
1 tablespoon grated lemon zest
1 cup sugar
1 teaspoon cinnamon
½ teaspoon nutmeg
¼ teaspoon salt
2 tablespoons butter
1 tablespoon cream

Preheat oven to 425 degrees.

Fit bottom crust into 8-inch pie pan.

Soak crackers 2–3 minutes in warm water until soft. Sprinkle with lemon juice and zest. Combine sugar, cinnamon, nutmeg, and salt; mix with crackers. Place mixture in pie shell. Dot with pinches of butter.

Moisten edge of bottom crust. Drape with top crust, crimping firmly all around to seal. Trim edge. Cut slits in top or poke with fork. Brush with cream. Bake 30–35 minutes, or until top is golden brown.

Old West Cookbook is available for $14.98 plus $2 postage from Bob Evans Publications, Perkins, Okla. 74059.

cracker box, where the recipe has often appeared. No doubt about it, Ritz crackers make a terrific mock apple pie; but the fact is that the idea goes way, way back—to long before the 1950s, before Ritz and Nabisco.

Food historians believe that mock apple pie was created by pioneers, probably some time in the middle decades of the nineteenth century. They made it from ingredients that stored and traveled easily. Apples weren't always readily available, but sugar and spice and crackers were staples of any chuck wagon.

We've been thinking about frontier cookery quite a bit recently, ever since we got hold of a copy of Barbara Blackburn's *Old West Cookbook*—a big spiral-bound volume with recipes that range from cowboy coffee ("dump the grounds right into the water") to jugged hare to carrot cake made with cattail pollen. Barbara, who lives in Williamsville, New York, is the recipe editor for Western Publications, which publishes *Old West*, *True West*, and *Frontier Times*. She traces her recipe for mock apple pie, from which ours is adapted, to a one-hundred-year-old book called *Reminiscences of a Soldier's Wife*.

Millionaire's Pie

INDIANAPOLIS, Ind.—How does Laughner's do it? How is it possible to make so much food look so darn good?

Partly, it's the lighting: Overhead lamps shine down on gleaming muffin tins overflowing with swirly buns and rolls; focused lights for close-up carving make the great round of beef glisten, and expose the juice-heavy texture of each pink flap as it is severed from the roast; Jell-O salads seem to glow like oversized gelatinous gems—emeralds, rubies, and sapphires that have magically ingested nuts, carrot or cabbage shreds, raisins, sliced olives, or sweetened coconut.

Then there is the wait. That really gets the gastric juices flowing. Every Sunday and many weekday meals, too, chances are you will spend time in line before you even get to the food. But the proprietors of this place are clever folks. Instead of leading you along some boring corridor, their line doubles back along itself, snaking you right past the food waiting to be chosen. That, friends, is a killer: watching people way ahead of you in line, yet close enough so you could snatch a buttered new potato off their tray, receive plates heaped with turkey and dressing or baked ham and sweet potatoes.

We are nuts about cafeterias. We are certain that food-service in heaven is cafeteria-style. And we wouldn't be a bit disappointed to find that the Laughner family had the concession for all meals served in that great cafeteria in the sky. These people know how to do it right.

They ought to by now, since they've been in the food business for a century, beginning with J.W. Laughner's Indianapolis confectionary store in 1888. In the early 1900s, J.W. decided to open an efficient kind of eatery at which customers would select their own food from a steam table, carry their trays, and find their own place—either at a marble-topped table or in individual school chairs with attached side-arm tables. The place was called Laughner's Dairy Lunch and was one of the first cafeteria-style restaurants in America.

Business has been good these last hundred years. The Laughner family now reigns over nine cafeterias in central Indiana, most of them alongside interstate highway exits on the outskirts of Indianapolis. As cafeterias go, they are the height of elegance: fireplaces, fine draperies, thick carpets, stained glass windows, Colonial wallpaper and oil paintings, comfortable upholstered chairs. Although it isn't really necessary, many customers dress for dinner at Laughner's: It's that swell.

As for the food, it is a vast roster of Americana from Hoosier fried chicken and warm cinnamon buns to a heartland repertoire of fruit pies, cream pies, and custard pies.

We always take two desserts at Laughner's, because it would be wrong to eat here and not have sugar-cream pie, an Indiana specialty, and not also have millionaire's pie, for which only Laughner's cooks have the recipe. Until now, that is: In response to our request, Laughner's agreed to share their recipe for Millionaire's Pie with "Taste of America" readers. If you are looking for an ultra-rich dessert, there's none more ultra than this.

MILLIONAIRE'S PIE

1 partially baked 10-inch pie shell, in its pan
1 cup coconut flakes
1 cup semisweet chocolate chips
1 cup chopped pecans
1/2 cup brown sugar
3/4 cup white sugar
pinch of salt
1 1/2 tablespoons margarine, melted
1/2 cup light corn syrup
1/4 teaspoon vanilla
4 eggs, beaten

Preheat oven to 325 degrees.
Toss together the coconut flakes, chocolate chips, and chopped pecans. Place in pie shell.
Mix sugars, salt, and melted margarine. Beat in corn syrup and vanilla. Gently fold eggs into sugar mixture. Pour evenly over ingredients in prepared pie shell. Bake 55–65 minutes, or until deep golden brown on top and nearly set in center. Cool at room temperature.

Laughner's, Washington St. E. at I-465; (317) 356-3388. (For other locations, call 783-2907.)

Doris's White Christmas Pie

INDEPENDENCE, Kan.—There really was a Little House on the Prairie—home of author Laura Ingalls Wilder in 1869 and 1870. Her pioneer reminiscences, the basis of nine children's books and a long-running television series, were set on the high prairie, south of Walnut Creek, silhouetted by a dramatic horizon of Montgomery County bluffs.

Head south on Highway 75 toward Oklahoma, and you will find a log cabin standing on the site where Laura lived. The cabin was constructed in 1977 by local volunteers, using the descriptions in her books as a guide. Along with it is the Sunnyside School, built in 1872 and used right up until 1947, and the turn-of-the-century Wayside, Kansas, post office.

Awhile after Ma and Pa Ingalls and their children moved on, Lillian Jones Horton, age three, came to the Wayside area in a covered wagon with her parents. Mrs. Horton was the mother of Wilma Kurtis, who today maintains the Little House site as a small museum.

Mrs. Kurtis is also the author, with Anita Gold, of *Prairie Recipes and Kitchen Antiques,* an evocative collection of country cooking interspersed with photographs of old-fashioned farm tools and Ingalls family memorabilia. Here are descriptions of seed corn trees for drying ears of corn, pie crimpers, biscuit tins, herb mills, and pans for spider corn cake. One of the pictures is of Pa's famous fiddle. "Sometimes, if you close your eyes and listen hard," according to the caption, "you can still hear his fiddlin' on the Wayside prairie."

Along with the pictures of antiques are recipes equally reminiscent of country ways: home-churned butter, cracklin' cornbread, beet relish, and persimmon cookies. The recipes—many of them hand-me-downs from pioneer days—were all collected from local families. There are even a couple of home remedies, including Grandma Zenor's mustard poultice, which is good for whatever might ail you.

Along with the old-time recipes, Mrs. Kurtis and Mrs. Gold's book contains a bounty of practical home cooking, classics that have stood the test of time: spoon bread and biscuits, fricasseed chicken, and mulligan stew. We especially enjoyed reading the chapter on canning and preserving, with its recipes for Mary Jane's End-of-the-Garden Relish, Mrs. Floyd's Plum Conserve and Mom's Cranberry Jelly. This is a book with real personality: Almost all the recipes have someone's name attached. So even if you don't intend to cook from it, browsing through it offers a vivid taste of prairie life. Those people knew—and still know—how to eat.

We were clued in to the Little House on the Prairie site and its cookbook by one of the best eaters we know, ace television anchorman Bill Kurtis. Bill is Wilma's son, and he grew up in the vicinity of the Little House. "One festivity I would like to have attended," he writes in a prologue to the book, "was one of the traditional last-day-of-school dinners. That sounds like good food unlimited."

The pie chapter includes an old family recipe contributed by Mrs. Kurtis's sister Doris, suitable for special-occasion dinners. "A delicious dessert," Mrs. Kurtis writes. "One might call it elegant."

Hot Milk Sponge Cake

ST. LOUIS, Mo.—We panic when we've got only two days in St. Louis and about a hundred different restaurants to sample. Few cities in America offer such a palate-boggling variety of good eats, including out-of-this-world Italian specialties, super soul food, heartland square meals, and cutting-edge new American cuisine.

Name your pleasure, and you will likely find it, but if you want to zero in on the true culinary spirit of St. Louis, we suggest a sampler of restaurants that cater to the Gateway City's amazing sweet tooth.

How sweet it is! If the truth be told, it is candy and dessert we eat first whenever we breeze into town. We go to Bissinger's confectionery for king-size hand-dipped chocolate strawberries or spun molasses puffs; to Ted Drewes on Chippewa for old-fashioned custard cones and "concrete" milk shakes; to the Crown Candy Kitchen (since 1913) for fresh banana malteds.

Even the funky soul food storefronts (where, in other cities, dessert is at best perfunctory) offer an alluring array of sweet finales to their spicy meals: definitive single-serving pecan pie at C & K Bar-B-Q, or sweet potato pie and eight varieties of triple layer cake at Mister Austin's Bar-B-Q.

The undisputed queen of sweet things in St. Louis is Miss Hulling, whose restaurants, cafeterias, and creameries are built upon a bakery tradition that goes back to 1930. That was when Florence Louise Hulling opened a small cafeteria downtown to serve business people. Her good food and good value were an immediate success, luring as many as four thousand customers a day, lined up around the block.

There are now table-service restaurants and bakery branches around town, but it's the original cafeteria on Locust Street we like best. Here are coconut ambrosia pies, glazed fruit pies, cream

HOT MILK SPONGE CAKE

1 cup milk
1 tablespoon butter
1 teaspoon vanilla
4 eggs
2 cups sugar
¼ teaspoon salt
2 cups sifted cake flour
2 teaspoons baking powder

Generously butter three 8-inch cake pans. Line bottoms with waxed paper, then generously butter top of paper. Flour pan. Preheat oven to 325 degrees.

Bring milk and butter to boil. Remove from heat and cool slightly. Stir in vanilla.

Beat eggs with sugar and salt until thick and lemon-colored.

Sift flour with baking powder and fold gently into egg mixture. Gently combine with milk and butter until smooth. Pour into prepared cake pans. Bake 20–25 minutes, or until cake tester comes out clean.

Invert pans onto wire racks, remove cakes, and allow cakes to cool before filling or frosting them.

Miss Hulling's, 1103 Locust, St. Louis, Mo.; (314) 436-0840.

pies, meringue pies, puddings and custards and frappes, cakes baked in blocks and circles, including five-layer chocolate split cake and swirling mocha angel food with strawberries on top: Get the picture? Do you understand why we panic when we come to town? There is no way two normal human appetites can even make a dent in what's available. But we sure try.

Aside from the lure of its food, Miss Hulling's—now run by her son, Steven Apted—has charms that make it a happy place to be. Decorated in cotton-candy shades of pink, with a wall mural of café society and reassuring portraits of Miss Hulling and her family near the entryway, it is a nostalgic reminder of old St. Louis, the city you might remember if you saw the movie *Meet Me in St. Louis*.

Many of Miss Hulling's bakery goods are too complex to make at home. But one of the simplest specialties, suitable for fancying-up any way you please, is this hot milk sponge cake. Sandwich the layers around whipped cream and fruit, or fill them with custard and top the cake with a chocolate glaze to make it into Boston cream pie. Or soak it with booze and make your own babas au rhum!

Whipping Cream Pound Cake

TUPELO, Miss.—January 8 is Elvis Presley's birthday. Although it has been nearly a decade since the death of Tupelo, Mississippi's, native son, Elvis continues to be a provocative symbol. He is more popular than ever, with legions of fans who still adore him.

Year around, pilgrims of the Elvis World come to Memphis, Tennessee, to tour Graceland, his mansion on a hill. Then they take an hour's drive southeast along Highway 78 to Tupelo, to visit the house where he was born. It is a tiny wood-frame shack on what used to be the wrong side of town. Not an auspicious beginning; but the fair-haired boy born here on that "cold and frosty morn'" to Gladys and Vernon Presley grew up to become—in the words of the Smithsonian Institution—"the single most important event in the history of American music."

Today, Elvis is part of our culture, known not only for his musical gifts, but for his flamboyant personality—his pink Cadillacs, his glittering stage attire, his taste for gigantic diamond rings, and not least, his Homeric appetite.

Elvis Presley loved to eat. All his life, from the time he was a skinny twenty-year-old "Hillbilly Cat" playing rock and roll in high school gyms throughout the South to the final years when his metabolism finally caught up and he began gaining weight, he relished country-style food.

4E 77
ELVIS ARON PRESLEY

Elvis Presley was born in Tupelo, Mississippi
on January 8, 1935, the son of Vernon and
Gladys Presley. He moved to Memphis 1948.
Soon after signing a contract with RCA Records
in 1954 he achieved tremendous success. His
musical and acting career in many movies,
television, and concerts made him
most successful and outstanding
the world. He died on August 16,
here at his Memphis home.

WHIPPING CREAM POUND CAKE

3 cups sugar
½ pound butter, softened
7 eggs, room temperature
3 cups cake flour, sifted twice (do not use "self-rising" flour)
1 cup whipping cream (not whipped)
2 teaspoons vanilla extract

Butter and flour a 10-inch tube pan.
Thoroughly cream together sugar and butter.
Add eggs one at a time, beating extremely well after each addition. Mix in half the flour, then the whipping cream, then the other half of the flour. Beat five full minutes. Add vanilla.
Pour batter into prepared pan. Set in cold oven and turn heat to 350 degrees. Bake 60–70 minutes, until a sharp knife inserted in cake comes out clean.
Cool in pan 5 minutes. Remove from pan and cool thoroughly. Wrapped well, this cake keeps several days.

Elvis Presley Birthplace, 306 Elvis Presley Drive, Tupelo, Miss.; (601) 841-1245.

His taste was never fancy or exotic. Elvis hated sauced-up rich man's cooking, and avoided highfalutin restaurants whenever possible. He liked pork chops and meat loaf and well-done cheeseburgers, biscuits and cornbread, vanilla ice cream, red Jell-O, and pound cake.

While researching our book, *Elvis World,* we had the opportunity to sample many Presley family recipes for things he liked to eat. Todd Morgan, Graceland's manager of communications, introduced us to a Tupelo friend of Elvis's who still stops by the mansion to deliver Christmas presents to the staff. This friend, who knew Elvis from the time he was two years old, is a lady who really knows how to cook. Among the presents she brings are pound cakes. She told us Elvis adored these cakes; so each Christmas, and for his birthday, she would bake some and bring them to him at Graceland. Todd is now the lucky inheritor of this legacy, and gets two large cakes every year.

We all went out to "talk Elvis" at Gridley's (our favorite place for barbecue), but instead of having Mrs. Gridley's lemon pie for dessert, we returned to the Graceland offices and dug into one of the pound cakes from Tupelo. What a classic! Moist and dense and buttery, simple and totally satisfying, it is a cake that can be improved only by a scoop of ice cream set atop each slice.

The cake-maker, who prefers to remain anonymous lest she be deluged by Tupelonians requesting her cakes for birthdays and special occasions, shared her recipe with us. She said it was her mother's, and her grandmother's before that. As far as we're concerned, it makes the ultimate pound cake—all the more fun to eat when you know it was Elvis Presley's favorite.

Strawberry Shortcake

ESSEX, Conn.—New England has a love/hate relationship with dessert. Who but a Yankee would name a happy fruit cobbler a "grunt" or a "slump"? In what other part of the country would donuts (raised, unsweetened) and maple syrup (for dunking) be accompanied by sour dill pickles?

Apple pan dowdy and vinegar pie, hermit bars, duffs, and "dumfunnie" donuts: the repertoire of traditional New England sweets is long and eccentric. No region in the country eats more ice cream (23.1 quarts per person per year!); and New Englanders love pudding so much that they regularly make it not only with tapioca and rice, but with Grape-Nuts and cornmeal.

Despite its affinity for sweets, New England cookery looks down its nose at white sugar, an attitude that has less to do with Pritikin than with Puritan. To sweeten baked beans, the diehard Down East chef uses molasses. For cakes and pies, maple sugar is preferred. Such dark-colored sweeteners, we reckon, are more serious-looking than glistening granulated sugar, and therefore allowably dowdy in a no-nonsense kitchen.

A lot of Yankee cooking may be homely, but there is no denying the winsome charms of strawberry shortcake. Shortcake is an essential summer food throughout the region, especially when residents gather at outdoor parties, to listen to the evening music of a town square band concert. On Independence Day, when the rest of the country is chowing down on hot dogs, Yankee chefs serve a traditional poached salmon supper to celebrate an early midsummer harvest of new potatoes, baby green peas, and the running of the salmon on the inland rivers. This jamboree is always followed by strawberry shortcake.

But this is not shortcake like what the rest of the country puts under its berries. New England chefs, you see, have declared all the other versions too sweet. Real strawberry shortcake, they will tell you, is served on a biscuit. Not cake, but a plain baking powder biscuit, without a grain of sugar in it. Furthermore, the strawberries must be sliced, not mashed. The biscuit may be buttered (if it is piping hot from the oven) or spread with heavy cream, but there is no room between it and the sliced berries for ice cream. A dollop of whipped cream (or very heavy farm cream) topping is optional.

One of the most appropriate places we know to enjoy New England strawberry shortcake is the Griswold Inn in Essex, Connecticut. The Griz, as it is known to its friends, is a quintessential country inn, over two centuries old, with a dining room constructed out of an old covered bridge and guest rooms that list gently with age.

STRAWBERRY SHORTCAKE

3 pints strawberries, cleaned and sliced
2 cups cake flour
¾ teaspoon salt
5 teaspoons baking powder
½ teaspoon cream of tartar
¾ cup (1½ sticks) cold butter
1 egg, beaten
¼ cup milk
1 cup heavy cream
1 cup heavy cream, whipped

Mix strawberries with 2–3 tablespoons honey, if desired; refrigerate.

Preheat oven to 400 degrees.

Sift together flour, salt, baking powder, and cream of tartar. Cut in butter until mixture is crumbly. Beat egg and milk together and mix into flour mixture, only until ingredients hold together.

With floured hands, put dough onto well-floured board, and knead gently a few times. Handle dough as little as possible. Pat out to ½-inch thick. Cut with floured 2- to 2½-inch cookie cutter (makes 10–12). Place on ungreased cookie sheet. Bake 12–15 minutes, or until barely browned.

Place half the biscuits at the bottoms of wide, individual bowls. Drizzle with heavy cream, add strawberries, then top with another biscuit. Add another 3–4 tablespoons strawberries and top with whipped cream.

Serves 5–6.

The Griswold Inn, Main Street, Essex, Conn.; (203) 767-0991.

The town of Essex, on the Connecticut River just north of Long Island Sound, is a favorite port-of-call for sailors; a sign inside the Griz advises that because the inn caters to yachtsmen it does not require jackets and ties. It's a casual but classy kind of place.

The best things on the menu are nautical, too: local bluefish, Block Island swordfish, and Nantucket Bay scallops. For dessert— in addition to prune-flavored ice cream (an old Connecticut favorite)—there's the real thing, strawberry shortcake on a biscuit.

The Griz biscuit recipe, given to us by innkeeper William Winterer, is made with a sprinkling of powdered sugar. Lest our shortcake be deemed too frivolous by traditionalists, we've cut sugar out altogether. If the berries are ripe, they'll be sweet enough. If you want them sweeter, soak them in a few ounces of honey while the biscuits are prepared. And if you insist on a really sweet dessert, add a few tablespoons of sugar to the cream as it's whipped.

Rice Pudding

CHICAGO—In a world overrun with mousses, pudding is getting hard to find. Mousse is everywhere on menus: mousse du jour, mousse pie, mousse cakes and tarts and even ice creams. Ever so much classier than its poor relation, pudding, mousse is always ultrarich, sometimes described by swooning food writers as "sinfully" rich, even decadent.

Pudding, on the other hand, is an old friend. Nothing sinful about it; nothing highfalutin or wealthy. It is childish food, even silly, especially if it's chocolate with a splash of milk on top; or if it is made with bananas and vanilla wafers and goes by the nursery name of 'naner pudding.

Serious pudding people—ourselves foursquare among the fanatics—are especially persnickety about rice pudding. We don't like it if the grains of rice are still raw and chewy; nor is it any good if the rice is so overcooked that it bloats and loses its texture.

Then, there is the raisin issue. We have nothing against them; in fact, we rather like a few raisins in a rice pudding. But not hordes of them. An overpopulation of raisins can turn rice pudding into something sweet and fruity, rather than the bland, unblemished pap it is supposed to be.

As for flavoring, a tad of vanilla is all that's called for. Oh, maybe a sprinkle—just a puff—of nutmeg might be all right, but heaven help the chef who gets delusions of rice pudding grandeur and tries to add chocolate or booze.

The major decision to be made about rice pudding is whether it should be baked or made atop the stove. Most recipes call for baking; for years, we have made a pudding that starts on the stove, then gets finished in the oven. One of the greatest rice puddings in America, for which we have secured the recipe, is strictly a stovetop affair.

The extraordinary stuff is a specialty of Cricket's Restaurant in Chicago's Tremont Hotel. As puddings go, it's the swankiest of all, the most luxurious dessert any pudding-o-phile could hope to eat.

Cricket's itself is a pretty fancy place, a clubby establishment frequented by local epicures and visiting high rollers. What is great about the exalted pudding is that although it's rich, there is nothing tarted-up or mousselike about it. It is balmy, gentle, and kind; its magic is that the custard is etherealized by an infusion of whipped cream. If you are a rice pudding lover, we implore you to try this deluxe version and see if you don't melt as we do every time we eat pudding in Chicago.

RICE PUDDING

1½ cups milk
3½ cups cream
½ cup uncooked rice (do not use "converted rice")
½ cup sugar
pinch salt
1 teaspoon vanilla extract
2 egg yolks at room temperature, beaten

Combine milk, 2½ cups of the cream, rice, sugar, and salt in a heavy, non-aluminum saucepan. Gently simmer, uncovered, stirring frequently, for 50 minutes as mixture thickens and liquid is absorbed into rice.

Remove from heat. Stir in vanilla. Whisk in egg yolks very vigorously (don't let them sit unattended in the warm pudding for even a second). Let cool to room temperature.

When pudding is cool, beat remaining cup of cream until stiff. Fold into cooled rice pudding. Pudding may be served immediately or chilled. It can be served cold, but we like to warm up servings for 20–30 seconds in the microwave.

Serves 6–8.

Cricket's, 100 E. Chestnut St., Chicago, Ill.; (312) 280-2100.

Turtle Candy Sundae

AURORA, Ill.—Remember glass bottles of milk that you returned to the dairy to be refilled? Remember old-fashioned super-heavy top cream (36 percent butterfat) that tasted rich as sweetened butter? Remember soda fountain specialties such as a tin roof, a rocky road, and a triple-dip banana royal?

Oberweis Dairy is one of the few places we know where you can still enjoy such bygone Americana. It is an independent dairy that collects most of its raw milk from small local farms every day. The milk is processed in the back room and sold in the front. And some of it gets taken by the Oberweis milkmen (remember milkmen?) who have their regular routes through north-central Illinois.

Many Oberweis customers don't wait for the milkman. They carry back their own empties, rattling in the metal racks supplied by the dairy. That way they can stop for an ice cream sundae on their way home.

From its beginning in 1927 until 1951, Oberweis was strictly in the milk business. But thirty-five years ago, at the urging of John Oberweis's mother, who, John confided, "is kind of an ice cream nut," they added a soda fountain.

It is still nothing but a soda fountain, selling no cooked food at all: just sundaes, shakes, sodas, malts, and ice cream cones. There isn't even a counter to sit at, merely a handful of tables with a view through a glass wall to a room in back where milk is bottled (in the morning) and ice cream packaged (in the afternoon). Find a seat,

TURTLE CANDY SUNDAE

CARAMEL SAUCE:
30 Kraft caramels
¼ cup milk

Melt caramels and milk in the top of a double boiler, stirring occasionally. Serve warm.

FUDGE SAUCE:
4 ounces unsweetened chocolate
3 tablespoons butter
½ cup cream
½ cup granulated sugar
½ cup dark brown sugar, firmly packed
1 teaspoon vanilla extract

Over hot but not boiling water, melt chocolate and butter in top of double boiler. Stir in cream, then gradually add both sugars, stirring constantly. Cook, continuing to stir, until fudge is smooth and all the butter is incorporated. Turn off heat, stir in vanilla extract, and keep warm until ready to serve.

ROASTED PECANS:
1 cup pecan halves

Spread out pecan halves in a baking dish and bake at 300 degrees, tossing frequently. Cook until crisp, 15–20 minutes, but do not scorch or nuts will become bitter.

ASSEMBLING THE TURTLE CANDY SUNDAE:
The foundation is two scoops of vanilla ice cream. Top them with hot fudge, then warm caramel sauce, then nuts. Garnish with whipped cream and a cherry.

Oberweis Dairy, 945 N. Lake St., Aurora, Ill.; (312) 897-0512.

Oberweis Dairy

FOUNTAIN MENU

FOUNTAIN HOURS
DAILY — 9:00 a.m. till 10:00 p.m.
SUNDAYS and HOLIDAYS — 10:00 a.m. till 1:00 p.m.

look over the menu, then tell the waitress at the front counter what you want.

The selection is classic: single-, double-, or triple-dip ice cream sundaes, topped with chocolate, pineapple, marshmallow, caramel sauce, or strawberries. You can get an orange float or a black cow, a "cheery cherry" milk shake, a banana malt, or a "lusty lemon" super soda. Then there is a list of "special sundaes," for serious pigging out. Rocky road—chocolate marshmallow ice cream topped with marshmallow topping and Spanish peanuts. Banana royal—vanilla, chocolate, and strawberry ice cream heaped with fudge and bananas, plus strawberries and pineapple.

All the sundaes come crowned with a billowy cloud of Oberweis's glossy smooth whipped cream and a single maraschino cherry. Ah, what nostalgic bliss!

One of the greatest things to eat at Oberweis Dairy is plain vanilla ice cream. It is simple, silky white, elegant, and refined—nothing like the grossly overrich designer ice creams that sell for twice the price.

"Only for the big spender!" warns the menu about the turtle candy sundae (although at $2.60 for the triple-dip version, we gladly splurge every time). "Turtle," of course, refers to turtle candies, in which caramel and pecans are bound in chocolate. As children we always craved turtles because they seemed like rich man's food, costing two or three times as much as ordinary candy bars. There is still something fine and fancy about the triple whammy ingredients on a turtle candy sundae, even though they are as goopy and gloppy as all get-out.

Strangely, turtle sundaes seem unknown in other regions of the country. Grater's in Cincinnati makes a mean one, as does the Crown Candy Kitchen in St. Louis; but east or west or south of those points, we've never seen a turtle sundae. (A subject for further investigation is the Midwest's passion for caramel-flavored things in general, such as its superior caramel corn and the fantastic caramel sauce served on apple pie at the Winnetka Grill in Winnetka, Illinois.)

Buy a decent quality ice cream, and make your own sauces. Don't short-cut toasting the nuts, either. Their crunch is essential. These measurements make enough caramel and hot fudge sauce for four to six sundaes.

Dusty Road Sundae

BUFFALO, N.Y.—What is the true nature of a dusty road?

Is it built upon coffee ice cream, or vanilla, or an equal mix of chocolate and vanilla?

Is molten marshmallow a suitable topping?

Should the sauce be cool chocolate or hot fudge?

Whipped cream or bare-topped?

Maraschino cherry?

Nuts?

The only culinary principle about which every good soda jerk agrees is that the essential ingredient—the soul of the dusty road sundae and the inspiration for its name—is malt powder. (We won't even get into the sticky regional issue of whether it is properly called a sundae or a frappe.)

Even the malt powder gives rise to its own disputes. Where does it go? Directly on the ice cream, to be blanketed with sauce? Or is it sprinkled atop the finished sundae like a fine film of calorific dust? What happens if chocolate malt powder is substituted for plain? Hidebound malt devotees accept no brand other than Horlick's.

We got to thinking about dusty roads—and rocky roads, and tin roofs, and egg creams, and peanut butter fudge banana splits—after a visit to one of the prettiest ice cream parlors on this earth: Parkside Candy of Buffalo.

Built in 1927, it is an old-fashioned candy factory specializing in saltwater taffy, all-day suckers, bon bons of every size and shape, and a spun molasses specialty known as sponge candy (or honeycombs).

Walk into this place and your nose fills with a liquorish cocoa butter aroma even before your eyes can focus on the stunning interior decor. In a grandiose oval room lined with classic columns and umbrellaed by a domed ceiling, candies are sold from a series of vending stations around the circumference. Soft background music and subtle indirect light create the reverential atmosphere of a fine art museum. In the center of the room, on a checked tile floor, are a group of wooden tables and chairs where customers peacefully contemplate the fine gastronomic artistry of their Creamsicle frappes, root beer floats, and maple nut sundaes.

You can even eat a meal. Breakfast on homemade muffins, stuffed croissants, French toast, or a Belgian waffle. At lunch, the sandwich list includes the unique sandwich known around here as "beef on weck"—thin-sliced roast beef au jus on a hard roll crusted with salt and caraway seeds.

Nice eats, but the really good part is what comes from the soda

DUSTY ROAD SUNDAE

2 scoops coffee ice cream
2 tablespoons Horlick's malted milk powder
¼ cup chocolate syrup (not hot fudge)
whipped cream to taste
maraschino cherry

Place ice cream in a tulip glass. Sprinkle malt powder evenly over ice cream. Gently drizzle on chocolate syrup. Top with whipped cream and a maraschino cherry.

Parkside Candy, 3208 Main St., Buffalo, N.Y.; (716) 833-7540.

fountain: floats, shakes, sodas, and coolers. The menu lists more than a dozen different sundaes, including "Mexican" (made with little peanuts) and out-of-this-world bittersweet chocolate. Frappes, which in this case are simply complex sundaes, come in twenty-four different varieties, from classic hot fudge and triple-tiered banana split to new-wave cookie crunch and cocoa-kill triple chocolate.

If the Parkside fountainmaster will pardon our impertinence, we must say that some of these frappes seem quite iconoclastic. Rocky Road, for instance, is made with heavenly hash ice cream, instead of ice cream with mini-marshmallows on top. The pecan turtle is served underneath an actual candy turtle. We love the Creamsicle frappe, made with vanilla ice cream and orange sherbet, but the candy mountain frappe, heaped with chocolate candies, is too, too much.

Parkside's Dusty Road is a break with tradition as we know it. They use vanilla and chocolate ice cream, top it with marshmallow, then whipped cream. Malt gets sprinkled on top. That is wrong! (OK, so it tastes swell; but it is *not* tradition.)

The classical way to do it, as detailed to us in a letter written by Dusty Road aficionado Gail S. Murphy of Wayland, Massachusetts, appears here. Gail hails it as "the greatest sundae of all."

Brazilian Snow

TAMPA, Fla.—Even contrary people who might not agree that Bern's Steak House serves the best steaks in America are bound to admit that this is one spectacular restaurant. And we aren't only referring to the splendor of the gilt-edged decor in the dining rooms.

Bern's menu, entitled "Art in Steaks," offers eighty-three different steaks—every cut you've ever heard of, butter basted and broiled over charcoal to one of eight degrees of doneness. The choices range from a one-inch-thick, 6-ounce filet mignon to a three-inch-thick, 4½-pound sirloin strip (to feed six).

If beef is your dish, Bern's has it the way you like it—prime grade, aged two months, trimmed and cut to order. The last time we ate at Bern's, we feasted on a well-aged two-inch-thick porterhouse, its broad crust glistening black, its inside fibers red and running mineral-rich juices. It was a taste of all-American luxury, a dizzyingly delicious celebration of concentrated red meat protein.

With the steak, you eat salad and vegetables that are grown on Bern Laxer's own organic farms and delivered to the restaurant

BRAZILIAN SNOW

I pint high-quality vanilla ice cream
4 ounces dark-roasted coffee beans (or 8
*   tablespoons fresh, finely ground coffee)*
whipped cream as garnish

Chill a large mixing bowl and ice cream dipper.

Allow the ice cream to soften to a consistency that allows you to run a dipper through it easily. But don't let it get soupy!

If using beans, grind them as fine as your coffee grinder will go. Reserve I tablespoon of this grind.

Empty the softened ice cream into the chilled mixing bowl. Sprinkle a thin layer of the ground coffee over the ice cream, then turn up the surface with a dipper. Sprinkle on more coffee, using the dipper once more. Continue, a tablespoon at a time, dipping quickly and efficiently as the coffee is blended in.

Divide into four serving dishes. Garnish with whipped cream. Sprinkle each with a dash of the reserved ground coffee. Serve immediately.

Bern's Steak House, 1208 S. Howard Ave., Tampa, Fla.; (813) 251-2421.

kitchen every morning. If you want a bottle of wine to accompany dinner, you choose from the largest collection ever assembled anywhere in the world—approximately five-hundred thousand bottles. The wine list, complete with stories behind the wines, maps, and prices, is an oenophile's dictionary over two-thousand pages long.

Teas ("tips and flowering tops only," the menu advises) are custom-blended. Coffee is made from a blend of fourteen different beans, each individually roasted to its optimum flavor, then freshly ground and brewed to order.

"We have four people working in our test kitchen," Bern told us, "doing nothing but testing recipes. We're working on a white cake now; we've gone through 261 attempts, and I think we finally have it just right." Desserts are extravagant, from curaçao-spiked "Blue Bern" to hot-fudge sundaes made with fresh macadamia nut ice cream.

Bern's homemade vanilla ice cream forms the basis of a relatively simple, but incomparably wonderful dessert known as Brazilian Snow. Suggested years ago by a customer, it is unique to Bern's Steak House, but with a distinct Tampa taste. That is because it depends on superior coffee; and there are few places that take their coffee as seriously as Tampa. When you walk the streets of Ybor City, Tampa's Spanish and Cuban enclave, you smell powerhouse coffee in coffee shop kitchens. One cup of this strong, dark brew in the morning, even served con leche (diluted with milk), will snap open the sleepiest eyelids.

There is nothing more to Brazilian Snow than coffee and ice cream. But to do it right, the way they do it at Bern's Steak House, you've got to use the best ice cream and the freshest ground coffee. Brazilian Snow cannot be made in advance and stored in a freezer. The beans should be ground, then mixed with the ice cream immediately before serving. Freshly ground coffee packs taste and aroma, and it also adds a weird and enjoyable gritty texture to ice cream.

For best results you need a home coffee grinder. If you don't have one, it is possible to have the beans ground in a coffee shop or at the supermarket . . . but remember that it is the heady perfume of freshly ground coffee that makes Brazilian Snow a startling bowl of dessert. As that intensity evaporates, so does the magic of the dish.

Princess Cup

NEW ORLEANS, La.—Canned fruit cocktail is sad-looking food. It's so pale and wan, with the exception of the maraschino cherry halves. Even the cherry scraps seldom have the festive red dye vivacity one sees in jars of high quality whole, stemmed maraschinos.

As for taste, we defy anyone to identify which fruit is which. There are square segments and round ones, and there are skinned ones, too (they, one assumes, are grapes). Some are vaguely orange, some yellow. They all taste of syrup; or if not syrup, they taste more like generic fruit than any one variety. Texture-wise, it's pretty much the same story. The grapes are more slippery than any of the other things; but each geometric shape shares a rubbery, water-logged consistency.

Sad, indeed; yet we cannot help liking fruit cocktail. By the standards of knee-jerk gourmets, who automatically condemn anything in a can, it is a crime against the almighty god of freshness. But we contend there are certain occasions when canned fruit cocktail is preferable to fresh fruit.

For example, when making fruited Jell-O for the weak and the ill, you don't want to shock their sensitive palates with large clods of strong-flavored fruit suspended in the pastel gelatin. You want the colorless, bland little shapes from the can.

Perhaps the most convincing *apologia* for fruit cocktail comes in the form of Princess Cup, the famous—or should we say notorious?—dessert of Galatoire's restaurant in New Orleans.

Galatoire's, as you may already know, is one of the definitive citadels of Creole cuisine. Its time-honored dining room is famous for French Quarter specialties such as shrimp *remoulade*, oysters *en brochette*, trout *meuniere* or *Marguery*, eggs *Sardou*, Creole gumbo, crisp bread, and strong coffee.

Other than the masterpieces turned out by the kitchen, nothing about Galatoire's is posh: Illumination is by means of bare bulbs overhead, the floor is plain tile, the waiters are gruff. Neither credit cards nor reservations are accepted.

"Princess Cup" is the name Galatoire's gives to its fruit cocktail dessert. (It is also possible to have a fancier dessert of crepes rolled around currant jelly.) Its ingredients are vanilla ice cream, fruit cocktail, and some sort of liqueur.

You can use gourmet ice cream if you wish (it isn't necessary); and the choice of liqueur is up to you: Cointreau is suggested by Rima and Richard Collin in their *New Orleans Cookbook;* Duncan Hines used to make his Princess Cup with port wine; we skip the

---

PRINCESS CUP

2 cups fruit cocktail in syrup

²/₃ cup Cointreau or port wine or liqueur of choice

1½ pints vanilla ice cream, at serving temperature

Pour off most of fruit cocktail syrup, leaving enough so fruit isn't dry (but neither do you want it soupy). Combine fruit cocktail with liqueur if desired (in which case, you will need to keep less of the canned syrup).

Place a bit of the fruit cocktail, with its juices, at the bottom of a parfait or sundae glass. Top with ice cream. Top ice cream with more fruit cocktail. Serve.

Makes 4 servings.

Galatoire's, 209 Bourbon St, New Orleans, La.; (504) 525-2021.

booze altogether and use a dash of extra syrup from the fruit cocktail. What *is* essential is that you use canned fruit. Fresh fruit would have too much texture, and be without the processed-sugar sweetness upon which Princess Cup is founded; fresh fruit would work against the dairyfat luxury of ice cream, and give this wanton dessert an unwelcome natural-food character.

The recipe sounds ridiculously simple—and it is. To assemble Princess Cup requires no skill whatsoever. And yet, this elementary combination of ingredients is magic.

GRAPEFRUIT ICE

3 cups grapefruit segments and juice
(fresh—about 5–6 large grapefruits, pink
or white; be sure to remove as much
seeds, pith, and skin as possible)
I cup sugar
2 tablespoons water

Combine I½ cups grapefruit with sugar and water in heavy saucepan. Bring to boil, stirring and cooking until it reaches the softball stage (239 degrees). Remove from heat.

Immediately add remaining grapefruit to cooked fruit. Stir well.

Purée until fine. Strain.

Process in ice cream machine. Store in freezer. Serve with delicate butter cookies, and/or topped with puréed kiwi fruit.

Yield: I½ pints.

London Chop House, I55 W. Congress, Detroit, Mich.; (3I3) 962-0277.

Grapefruit Ice

DETROIT—The London Chop House is the Cadillac of Detoit restaurants—the undisputed best. It is where Michigan high rollers eat, where Motor City deals are made, where Fords and Iacoccas have regular tables. For the rest of us normal people, it is a restaurant for celebrating special occasions, the only place to go if you are visiting and have time for one grand meal.

In some ways, it is very old-fashioned, a clubby sort of establishment reminiscent of the 1940s, located in a cellar down an inauspicious flight of stairs. The lighting is low; the tables (covered with paisley cloth) are spacious, many ringed with banquettes rather than chairs to allow a greater sense of privacy. Service is swift, seamless, and professional. Live music and a small dance floor provide entertainment; sketch artist Hy Vogel roams from table to table doing caricatures. (The walls are covered with Mr. Vogel's renderings of the rich and famous.) And if, during or after dinner, monsieur would like to buy a little gift or trinket for milady, a discreet counter near the door offers perfumes and cuddly stuffed animals for sale.

The food—some of it, anyway—is in keeping with the aura of classic luxury. Few restaurants anywhere in America offer better meat-and-potatoes meals: the primest of prime steaks, herbed lamb chops to make a lamb lover swoon, and flavorific potato skins like you've never known before. Of course, first-class seafood is imported from the East, West, and Gulf coasts. And for a unique taste of the Great Lakes, you can order perch—a pile of firm-fleshed buttery fillets that are listed on the menu by their proper (if somewhat uncouth) group terminology: "a mess of perch."

When we first ate at the Chop House about a dozen years ago, it was owned by a celebrated gourmet named Lester Gruber, who used to publish a pamphlet guide to the world's fine restaurants (and art museums) called "Itinerary of Taste." It was Mr. Gruber who fashioned the Chop House as a Midwest mecca for gastronomes. It was he, also, who hired young Chef Jimmy Schmidt to revitalize the kitchen. Under Jimmy's directorship the Chop House blossomed; the familiar fancy menu was still available, but it was supplemented with inventive, way-out dishes like oysters in champagne sauce, interesting pastas, and exotic-fruit sorbets.

When Mr. Gruber died, fans of the Chop House panicked at the thought of losing his sure touch. In fact, Max and Lanie Pincus were so worried that the Chop House might change if it fell into the wrong hands that they bought it. Jimmy Schmidt has moved on (to the Rattlesnake Club in Denver), but Tom Varee, the new chef, has everything under control. The Chop House is still the top of the line of Detroit restaurants—all the way from such delightfully unpretentious menu listings as "a heap of frog legs, roadhouse style" to the most ethereal frozen hazelnut soufflé.

When we asked for a recipe, the folks at the Chop House gave us one that is easy to make, yet ultra elegant. It does require an ice cream machine, but if you have one (hand-crank or electric), it's easy. They said they recommend serving grapefruit ice with a sauce of puréed and sweetened kiwi fruit; but we like it fine without any sauce—just a cool, tart bowl of refreshing slush.

Palacinke

CLEVELAND, Ohio—Our waitress, a motherly lady in a crisp uniform who is wearing the special open-toe and open-heel shoes that are the true sign of a genuine Hungarian waitress, insists we can each eat a large Wiener schnitzel. Who are we to disagree, especially when the price—even for a top-of-the-line large one—is so low?

This schnitzel is at least one foot in diameter. It eclipses its plate. A fragile crust adheres to a pounded-thin veal cutlet that is so delicate that it melts in your mouth like warm butter, its milky tenderness counterpointed by the crunch of the golden envelope around it. On the side are nockerli—squiggly little dumplings—in a cream gravy faintly pink with paprika. It's no problem polishing off this handsome cutlet.

What a grand meal it is! Beautiful, delicious—and cheap. The Balaton Restaurant, with its wood paneling and plain paper placemats, is a diamond in the rough that all hungry visitors to Cleveland ought to know about. The specialty of the house is Hungarian cooking. As in so many of the great urban restaurants of the melting-pot Midwest, the food is even tastier because the restaurant itself is so real.

PALACINKE

2 eggs, well beaten

2 egg yolks, beaten

1/3 cup water

1/2 cup skimmed milk

1 tablespoon rum

1 tablespoon Grand Marnier (or strained
    orange juice)

1/2 teaspoon vanilla extract

grated zest of 1 orangae

grated zest of 1 lemon

1 cup flour, sifted

1/2 teaspoon salt

1/2 teaspoon baking powder

Beat eggs and yolks until lemon colored. Add water, milk, rum, Grand Marnier (or orange juice), vanilla extract, and zests. Mix flour, salt, and baking powder, and gradually beat into liquid, beating well until smooth. Chill one hour.

When ready to make palacinke, beat mixture again. It should be the consistency of·heavy cream. (If necessary, thin with chilled milk or thicken with a sprinkle of sifted flour.)

Brush a 7-inch crepe pan or Teflon skillet with melted butter or vegetable oil. Over medium heat, pour scant 1/4 cup batter into the skillet, tilting the pan quickly so the bottom is covered evenly—you want palacinke to be very thin. Cook 2 minutes, until light brown. Flip; brown other side (about 1 minute).

Keep palacinke warm in low oven, separated by a sheet of wax paper, until ready to serve. To serve, roll each into a tube around marmalade or jam, or simply roll and sprinkle with powdered sugar.

Yield: 12–15 palacinke (dessert for 4–6).

Balaton Restaurant, 12523 Buckeye Road, Cleveland; (216) 921-9691.

It is nothing more than a friendly neighborhood café, favored by local workers who come for a three-dollar lunch of gulyas soup (beef and diced potatoes in paprika-zapped broth) and rye bread, followed by a slab of dobos torte or palacinke stuffed with apricots and poppy seeds.

Wiener schnitzel is the thing to get if you are coming to the Balaton but once. After that wide wonder has been sampled, we recommend the goulash, made with chunks of unbelievably tender pork. Then there is chicken paprikash—"served disjointed"—with nockerli in gravy. And stuffed cabbage—a glorious melange of beef, pork, and rice, wrapped inside a tender sheaf of steamed translucent leaves, accompanied by zesty sauerkraut.

Dessert is where Hungarian cooks really strut their stuff. Look, for example, at the Balaton dobos torte, a multi-tiered extravaganza known as "the queen of pastries"—eight layers of moist sponge cake separated by seven velvety ribbons of cream filling, haloed by a thin sheen of slick chocolate glaze. And there are strudels, and chestnut cakes, and mocha rolls, customarily accompanied by small gold-rimmed glasses (not china cups) of powerhouse espresso coffee.

The Balaton, like most Hungarian restaurants, also features palacinke for dessert. Palacinke are very thin pancakes—sweet crepes—that are rolled up around a filling of choice: apricot preserves, marmalade, poppy seed filling, or melted bittersweet chocolate. Or they can be served unfilled, simply rolled up and dusted with powdered sugar. Our own recipe is for crepes with a built-in rum and citrus flavor; therefore, minimal filling is needed.

Stuffed Pears

WESTPORT, Conn.—Homesickness is the down side of our profession. As much as we love traveling, we miss our dogs, the daily mail, and our own refrigerator.

The other thing we miss is local grocery shopping. Oh, it's wonderful to snoop through grocery stores away from home. But it can be frustrating: itinerants such as ourselves, with a pantry no bigger than a car's trunk, cannot stock up on "boudin noir" in a Louisiana butcher shop, or Tillamook cheddar in Oregon, or black bing cherries in northern Michigan. One of our favorite rituals upon returning home is going to a nearby farm market named Hay Day, where we buy a cart full of perishable vegetables, unwieldy pies, short-lived herbs, brown eggs, runny cheeses, and ready-to-eat ripe fruits—all the wonderful comestibles you need a home life to fully enjoy.

STUFFED PEARS

2 cups water
1 tablespoon lemon juice
1/2 cup sugar
4 firm, ripe pears
1/4 cup ground pecans
1 tablespoon sour cream
2 tablespoons brown sugar
1/2 teaspoon vanilla extract
1 teaspoon rum
1 cup cream, whipped stiff with 2
*   teaspoons rum*
1 cup chocolate sauce, warm

Simmer water, lemon juice, and sugar for 10 minutes in a saucepan. Peel pears and core from large end, leaving stems intact. Gently drop pears into hot syrup and simmer until tender. Turn pears while cooking if syrup doesn't cover them. Cool fruit in syrup.

Mix together pecans, sour cream, brown sugar, vanilla, and rum. Stuff about 1 tablespoon of filling into cored end each pear. Chill.

To serve, arrange pears on a bed of whipped cream and spoon a little hot chocolate over each. Serve remaining chocolate sauce on the side.

Hay Day, 1026 Post Road East, Westport, Conn.; (203) 227-9008.

For doting over varieties of foodstuffs, there is no place we know quite like Hay Day. Most of its fruit and vegetable inventory is seasonal—a changing array of produce that serves as an education in small-scale agriculture. During autumn apple season, for example, the varieties on display usually include Rhode Island Greenings, Winesaps, and Northern Spies, Roxbury Russets and Rome Beauties, all suitable for pies, sauce, and cider. There are eating varieties, too, from familiar Delicious to Mutsu and Spartan. One bountiful day during a recent summer plum season, they managed to offer nineteen different varieties of plum for sale.

What's great about the selection is that each wooden fruit bin is labeled not only with the name of the variety, but with a description of what it's like. Muskmelons are described as "very sweet, with a musky cantaloupe flavor and strong aroma." Galia melons have "a nectarlike flavor." Crenshaws are "mildly spicy." Santa Claus melons (yes, there really is such a variety) are "good with Italian proscuitto or smoked ham."

Even better than the descriptions are the samples. Hay Day always has samples set out to eat. If it's winter and you're wondering whether you want a Minneola tangelo or a Murcott Mandarin tangerine, it is likely there will be segments of each set out to taste. So you discover that the Murcotts, although seedy, have a deep orange flavor and aroma; while the tangelos in question are slightly tart, with fewer seeds.

One of the best areas in the store for snacking and tasting is the cheese counter. Here is the pick of the world's cheeses, from Wisconsin or New York cheddar and Maytag Iowa blue to real English Stilton and exotic French triple-cremes. Hard cheeses are set out near a crock of mustard for dipping; spreadables are smeared across a piece of Hay Day's own tender-crumb "peasant bread." And across from the fruits—to balance your grazing—is an assortment of salamis, smoked fish, and patés to nibble.

In recent years, Hay Day has expanded its repertoire beyond groceries to prepared food—pies, breads, ready-to-eat dinners, and desserts. These things are really good, and not just because they contain ingredients from Hay Day's own shelves. They are made with skill using extraordinarily well-thought-out recipes.

That being the case, we were pleased as punch when Hay Day put out its own cookbook last year (*The Hay Day Cookbook*, by Maggie Stearns and Sallie Y. Williams, published by Atheneum), loaded with ways to use their vast array of groceries—such as this recipe for stuffed pears nestled in whipped cream, topped with hot chocolate.

13

Sandwiches and One-Dish Meals

225

Souvlaki and Tzatziki

NORWALK, Conn.—Most restaurants are merely businesses. Some have personalities. You *like* them, not just because they serve good food, and not even because you happen to like the people who work there. It is the restaurant itself that wins your affection and loyalty.

That's the way we feel about the Silver Star. It is a huge establishment, a modern modular diner with a long counter, two dining rooms, booths, tables, chandeliers, busts of classical philosophers, and a pastry case filled with specimens of the baker's art that are so magnificently constructed they would make a baroque sculptor jealous.

It was not the diner's grandiosity that first won our hearts. It was the air conditioning. Many years ago, during a severe summer heat wave, we ate lunch and dinner at the Silver Star all week long. It was so cool; its upholstered booths were so comfortable; and its multipage menu, approximately one zillion items long, allowed us to order something new and different every meal. (And the prices were low enough so that we could afford our spree.)

We ate farmer's omelettes and fisherman's platters, Jewish blintzes, Italian spaghetti, French toast, Texas T-bones, New England chowder, and superb Greek specialties from feta-topped salad to spanikopita and baklava. We went around the world in a dozen meals, and always into the stratosphere for one of those celestial desserts. Since that sweltering week, the Silver Star has become a regular haunt for us: old reliable.

Although it is a democratic restaurant that welcomes every class of clientele, there is something distinctly luxurious about the Silver Star. The booths are extra-wide and tables are set far apart. You get the feeling when you settle in that no expense has been spared to make guests comfortable.

SOUVLAKI

5 pounds lean, boneless pork, cut into
    1-inch pieces
1 cup imported olive oil
juice of 2 lemons
¼ cup dry white wine
¾ tablespoons dry oregano
½ tablespoon black pepper
5 garlic cloves, crushed
6 to 8 large pita bread rounds
2 whole tomatoes, chopped
1 medium onion, chopped
½ cup shredded iceberg lettuce

    Place pork cubes in large bowl. Make
marinade of oil, lemon juice, wine, oregano,
pepper, and garlic. Pour over meat, toss,
cover, and refrigerate overnight.
    Thread meat on skewers and grill over
hot coals or 6 inches below broiler, brushing
with remaining marinade, turning
frequently until cubes are cooked through.
    Remove meat from skewers onto warm
pita bread rounds. Garnish with tomato,
onion, lettuce. Serve Tzatziki on side (recipe
follows).

TZATZIKI

4 cups plain low-fat yogurt
2 medium cucumbers, peeled, seeded, and
    diced
2 cloves garlic, finely minced
3 tablespoons fresh dill, finely chopped

    Combine all ingredients in glass or
earthenware bowl and chill several hours.
Serve as dip with souvlaki or on lettuce
leaves as salad dressing.
    Makes 6–8 servings.

Silver Star, 210 Connecticut Ave., Norwalk,
Conn.; (203) 852-0023.

And then there are the Savvidis brothers, and their large extended family, who own and operate it. These guys—Andreas and Alex and Tasos and their gal Friday, Nancy—invented hospitality. We cannot count the number of times we have swapped stories with other local eaters about the Savvidis's spontaneous generosity: the Christmas fruitcakes Alex gave away; the champagne Andreas uncorks for special birthday meals; and the way the brothers turn on their irresistible Hellenic charm when meeting friends and relatives of their regular customers. Even if they know you only as the folks who come in every Friday for lemon chicken and rice pudding, you quickly begin to feel you have a second family at the Silver Star.

The really good things to eat are the Greek specialties. Our favorite is Souvlaki, a garlic-perfumed grilled open-face pork sandwich, for which Nancy Gierwielaniec provided the diner's recipe. It tastes best if you grill the meat over an open fire and serve it on top of broad, thick (preferably homemade) pita bread rounds.

KENTUCKY HOT BROWN

ITALIAN MEAT SAUCE:

¼ cup olive oil

2 medium onions, finely chopped

2 cloves garlic, finely chopped

¼ pound lean ground beef

⅓ cup tomato paste

1 cup chicken stock

⅓ cup dry white wine

2 bay leaves

½ teaspoon oregano

salt and papper to taste

Heat olive oil over medium heat in large skillet. Sauté onions and garlic. When onions soften, add meat, stirring with a fork to keep it pebbly. When well-browned, stir in tomato paste. Cook 2 minutes. Add chicken stock, wine, bay leaves, and oregano. Stir and taste. Add salt and pepper to taste (you won't likely need salt if using canned chicken stock). Lower heat, cover, and simmer, stirring occasionally, 2 hours. Sauce should be quite thick. If not, uncover for final 15 minutes of cooking time. Remove bay leaves.

Kentucky Hot Brown

ROANOKE, Va.—We want to remain welcome visitors in the state of Kentucky, so we shall begin this ode to one of America's great sandwiches by making it clear that the Hot Brown is a product of Louisville.

It was originated by the Brown Hotel; and it was called a *hot* brown to distinguish it from the Kentucky hotel's other well-known sandwich, which was a *cold* brown. The cold one was a summertime special: open-face turkey, tomato, hard-boiled egg, and Thousand Island dressing on crustless rye. Its traditional companion was a wide glass of iced tea in which a scoop of lime or lemon sherbet was set to float.

The original hot brown was a cold-weather meal: turkey and crisp-cooked bacon on toast topped with creamy melted cheese sauce. The basic idea has since proliferated throughout the mid-South, where one finds hot brown sandwiches made with chicken or turkey, with bacon or ham, with cream sauce, cheese sauce, or pepper gravy, served on white bread, rye bread, dinner rolls, and jumbo biscuits.

One of the most interesting and elaborate variations on the theme was created at the Roanoke Hotel in Roanoke, Virginia, whose Regency Room has been known as a citadel of gourmet cooking since 1882. A great Tudor edifice across from the Roanoke & Western Railway tracks, the hotel with its broad front lawn is truly a grand-looking place, reminiscent of an era before high-rise towers of glass.

Its cuisine is the finest Old Dominion fancy food, including such Jeffersonian glories as a dessert of "crepes soufflé à la Shenandoah" filled with orange-tinged meringue and topped with rum sauce.

The Regency Room's Kentucky Hot Brown is like no other we've sampled. Unlike most quickie hot browns, it requires advanced planning to make the Italian sauce. The results are more substantial than any ordinary sandwich. This recipe, which we adapted from the Regency Room's pamphlet of "Most Requested Recipes," makes a hearty meal for six. All you need to round it out is a small green salad.

CHEESE SAUCE:
3 tablespoons butter
½ cup minced onion
3 tablespoons flour
2½ cups warm milk
I cup finely chopped Swiss cheese
I bay leaf
½ cup dry white wine
½ teaspoon white pepper

In a medium-size saucepan, sauté onion in butter until soft. Sprinkle in flour, stirring constantly. Cook over low heat 3–5 minutes, stirring until smooth. Slowly add warm milk. Continue stirring with a wooden spoon. As sauce thickens, stir in cheese. Add bay leaf and white wine. Add white pepper. Cook over low heat 20 minutes, stirring very frequently. Remove bay leaf.

TO ASSEMBLE SANDWICHES:
6 large, thick slices white bread, well
   toasted
Italian meat sauce (above recipe)
½ pound white meat turkey, sliced
18 strips bacon, cooked crisp
Cheese sauce (above recipe)
I beefsteak tomato, sliced

Preheat oven to 400 degrees. Place toast on ovenproof serving dish or dishes. Spread Italian sauce on toast. Layer with turkey and bacon. Top with cheese sauce. Garnish with tomato. Bake 10–15 minutes, until sauce is bubbly. Serve immediately.
   Serves 6.

Hotel Roanoke, 19 N. Jefferson St., Roanoke, Va.; (703) 343-6992.

RUNSKIS

RUNSKI BUN DOUGH:

2 cups flour

1 tablespoon sugar

1¼ teaspoons salt

2½ tablespoons non-fat dry milk

*4 tablespoons unsalted butter, at room
  temperature*

*1 package yeast, dissolved in 3 tablespoons
  110-degree water with 1 teaspoon of
  sugar*

*1 egg, lightly beaten with ¼ cup very cold
  water*

*Combine flour, sugar, salt, and dry milk.
Cut in butter. Add yeast mixture and egg-
water mixture and knead vigorously 3 to 4
minutes until silky, adding flour if necessary
to make dough workable. Cover and let rise
in warm place 1 to 2 hours, until double in
bulk.*

RUNSKI FILLING:

1 pound ground chuck

½ teaspoon salt

¼ teaspoon coarse ground black pepper

¼ teaspoon dry English-style mustard

⅛ teaspoon garlic powder

1 to 2 dashes hot pepper sauce

1 teaspoon Worcestershire sauce

*2 tablespoons dehydrated minced onions,
  soaked 10 minutes in ¼ cup warm water*

¼ cup dehydrated instant potato flakes

*½ of 1-pound can sauerkraut, drained but
  not rinsed*

Runskis

MOUNTAIN VIEW, Ark.—A dozen years on the road looking for good things to eat has yielded some fringe benefits: pen pals coast-to-coast with whom we regularly exchange recommendations about newly discovered restaurants. We don't meet most of the tipsters, but after a few letters we do get to know them.

We pegged correspondent Mike Warshauer as a serious sweet tooth when we noticed that his letters always focused on pies wherever he went. How high is the meringue? Is the crust hand-crimped? Do the cream pies taste of real cream and fresh eggs?

In one letter, Mike 'fessed up that he is a baker; he's also a "spelunker" (cave explorer)—an interest that attracted him to Arkansas, where he opened his own bakery in 1982. "People needed an alternative to pasty balloon white bread," he explained.

His Hearthstone Bakery, in the Old Commercial Hotel on the square in Mountain View, produces sixty varieties, from pillowy potato rolls to rough-grained, unchopped sprouted wheat.

Natch, the Hearthstone makes pies—some of those recipes inspired by the four-star pies Mike has eaten at *Roadfood* restaurants such as the Norske Nook in Osseo, Wisconsin, and the Family Pie Shop in DeValls Bluff, Arkansas. "Our products," Mike explained, "have always been a mix of healthy breads and 'decadent' sweets. As time went on, we definitely grew more decadent!"

It is thanks to Mike that we finally got an answer to a culinary riddle that had vexed us for years: the origin of "Runza"—a trade-marked name for a scrumptious pocket sandwich unique to the area around Lincoln, Nebraska. Mike said that Runzas are related to Polish "pierogi," and were brought to the prairie by Germans who had settled in the Ukraine, then moved to the United States. Runza Drive-Ins are all over eastern Nebraska—clean, uniform establishments selling the hefty meat-filled sandwiches just like a fast-food burger.

Hearthstone Runzas, called "runskis," are meals in a bun—the beef seasoned with a luscious tang, wrapped in a buttery sweet dough. In Mike's words, they are "filling, nourishing and tasty as all get-out, with a memorable junk-food aroma!"

Preheat oven to 350 degrees. Mix all
ingredients except potato flakes and
sauerkraut. Roast in shallow pan 30
minutes until meat is no longer pink. Break
up large pieces of meat. Drain off grease.

Mix in potato flakes and sauerkraut.
Cool to room temperature.

RUNSKIS:
dough recipe (above)
filling recipe (above)
1 egg beaten with 1 tablespoon cold water
9 1/2-ounce slices Colby or other mild, semi-
    hard cheese

Pat out risen dough on lightly floured
surface. Roll into square 1/4-inch thick,
about 18 by 18 inches. Cover and let rest 5
minutes. Cut out 9 squares, 6 inches per
side, using a ruler as a guide.

Lightly brush each square with egg and
water mixture. Place slice of cheese on
lower center of square, then 1/3 cup filling
over cheese. Fold corner-to-corner, forming
an envelope, pressing to seal. Place on
lightly greased and floured sheet pans.
Cover and let rise one hour.

Preheat oven to 375 degrees. Brush risen
runskis with egg wash and sprinkle with
sesame seeds if desired. Cut 2 or 3 slits in
top of each for steam to escape. Bake 25
minutes, or until golden-brown. Cool on
rack. Serve warm.

Makes 9 runskis.

Hearthstone Bakery, Commercial Hotel
on the Square, Mountain View, Ark.;
(501) 269-3297.

NEW HAVEN WHITE CLAM PIZZA

DOUGH:

I cup tepid water (100–110 degrees)
I package dry yeast
I teaspoon sugar
2½ to 2¾ cups all-purpose flour
2 teaspoons salt
cornmeal

Dissolve the yeast and sugar in ¼ cup of the warm water. In a separate bowl, add the remaining ¾ cup water to 2½ cups of flour; add salt. When the yeast begins to foam, add it to the flour mixture. Stir together vigorously and turn out onto a floured board. Let dough rest while you clean the bowl and rub the inside with olive oil.

Knead continuously for a full 15 minutes, adding flour if necessary to create a silky dough. Return to bowl, roll the dough around to coat it with oil, then cover bowl with two tight layers of plastic wrap, and let rise in a warm (but not hot) place (such as a gas oven with a pilot light, or an electric oven with the light on) until double in bulk, 2–3 hours.

New Haven White Clam Pizza

NEW HAVEN, Conn.—You can eat barbecued pizza in Memphis (at Coletta's), caviar pizza in Hollywood (at Spago), pizza soufflé in Chicago (at Edwardo's), double-decker pizza in Old Forge, Pennsylvania (at Ghigiarelli's), whole-wheat pizza topped with broccoli in Cambridge, Massachusetts (at Bel Canto), even pineapple pizza in New York (at the original Ray's on Prince Street).

We have tried them all and, like Will Rogers, never met a pizza pie we didn't like. But there is no doubt in our minds that the pinnacle of pizzas is a variation unique to New Haven—white clam pizza.

If we were given one last meal, anything on earth, white clam pizza would be it. We would ask to have it served just the way it's done at Pepe's Pizzeria Napoletana on Wooster Street in the Italian part of town—in a booth, without plates or silverware, on a battered metal tray. We are talking here about the best pizza in America.

No tomato sauce, no mozzarella cheese, no sausage or pepperoni or mushrooms; white clam pizza is simplicity itself: a round of thin dough, poised precisely between crunch and chew, frosted gold with olive oil, topped with littleneck clams, grated cheese, oregano, and a shower of garlic. The cheese and garlic have a bite, the clams a vibrant marine zest; and the crust's circumference is a sumptuous mottled ring of pliant bready pillowettes.

Preheat oven to 450 degrees. (If using pizza stone, preheat it in the oven.)

Punch down dough and flatten it on a lightly floured board. Divide it in half, returning one half to the bowl covered with plastic wrap. Pounding with the heel of your hand or using a rolling pin, carefully and methodically work each half into a pizza about 12 inches in diameter. Sprinkle a baker's peel or a cookie sheet well with cornmeal, and put the dough on it. Put on the topping.

TOPPING:

3 tablespoons olive oil
2–3 large garlic cloves, finely minced
I dozen littleneck clams (or a 6½ ounce
    can of minced clams, drained)
I teaspoon oregano
1½ tablespoons grated Parmesan cheese

Mince the garlic into the olive oil. Brush the oil and garlic on the pizza, leaving a half-inch rim untouched. Spread clams around the pie with a dash of their own juice. Sprinkle on oregano and cheese.

TO BAKE:

If using a baker's peel, transfer pie to preheated pizza stone in 450-degree oven. Or put cookie sheet with pizza on it onto the oven's middle shelf. Bake 15 minutes, or until crust is light brown. Remove, slice, and serve with beer or soda and plenty of napkins.

Yield: Two 11-inch pies, enough for dinner for two, or hors d'oeuvres for 4–6.

Pepe's Pizzeria Napoletana, 157 Wooster St., New Haven, Conn.; (203) 865-5762.

Here is pizza that is soulfully Mediterranean yet Yankee plain, that tastes elegant but eats raunchy, favored equally by Yalies and townies who mob Pepe's booths every night.

The special savor comes from freshly opened Rhode Island clams—tiny morsels whose juices mingle in perfect harmony with the olive oil and garlic. "They are sweeter and tastier than clams from anywhere else," said Ralph Rosselli, son-in-law of Frank Pepe, known hereabouts as "the Michelangelo of pizza."

In an attempt to replicate the recipe, we have fiddled with homemade pizza for years, using all manner of oven bricks and stones, cookie sheets, and bakers' peels; and we have come extremely close to Pepe's magic formula, which depends on a coal-fired, brick-floored oven that heats up to 800 degrees. The oven's high heat means the dough bakes fast, without drying; a porous brick floor allows the heat to penetrate and perfectly crisp the crust.

The way to get that effect at home is with a pizza stone (sold in any gourmet store). Heat the stone with the oven, prepare your pizza on a baker's peel sprinkled with cornmeal, then slide the pizza in. It may be a mess getting the pizza off the peel the first few times you try. But pizza-making skills improve fast with practice; by your third pie, you will want to twirl the dough overhead to stretch it out (although such show-off flourishes, considered very "New York," are never indulged in at Pepe's).

Hawaiian Pizza

NEW YORK—Designed long ago for pushcarts and pedestrians, Prince Street is a narrow, all-day traffic jam. Drivers cuss jaywalkers and honk at double-parked delivery trucks. On the block between Mott and Elizabeth streets, rickety tables spill out of a storefront eatery onto the sidewalk. People stroll past, sideswiping lunch with their portfolios or billowy shirttails. The air smells of basil and olives, sausage and peppers, yeasty crust and sizzling cheese.

Here at the heart of the commotion is Ray's Pizza—along with John's on Bleeker Street and Totonno's out in Coney Island, one of the few genuine old-fashioned pizza parlors in New York.

New York-style pizza—with its small proportion of toppings and its chewy thin crust—is a direct descendant of the "pizza Napoletana" made at America's first pizzeria, Lombardi's, around the corner from Ray's at 53½ Prince Street.

Lombardi's is now a full-blown Italian restaurant, but when it was opened by Gennaro Lombardi eighty-five years ago, it was a grocery store and bakery without tables and chairs. All the pizza was made "to go." For years, at Lombardi's and at similar bakery-pizzerias in the Italian neighborhoods in cities all along the Eastern seabord, pizzas were a sideline so that bakers could keep their bread ovens working even after the morning loaves were baked.

At Ray's, you can buy New York-style pizza by the slice, or thick-crusted "Sicilian" pizza; but the fun of the place is its nontraditional whole pies. Huge, wide-bodied, thin-crusted behemoths come topped with spinach, broccoli, or zucchini and ricotta cheese; or with eggplant; or with pesto sauce and black olives.

One of the weirdest and most wonderful of Ray's creations is the one known as the "white Hawaiian pie," made with ham, chunks of pineapple, ricotta, and mozzarella cheese. It is tropical and savory, mild compared to most tomato-sauced pizzas. We serve our version in the summer, as a meal or hors d'oeuvres.

While a pizza stone or screen does make a crisper crust, this pie is quite delicious when assembled and baked on a well-greased baking sheet.

HAWAIIAN PIZZA

1 package yeast
1 teaspoon sugar
1¼ cups warm water (110 degrees)
3 to 3½ cups all-purpose flour
1 teaspoon salt
vegetable oil
1 cup ricotta cheese
1 cup pineapple chunks, very well-drained
   (most of a 20-ounce jar)
¾ pound ham, cut into small pieces
8 ounces low-moisture mozzarella, grated

   Combine yeast and sugar with ¼ cup warm water. Combine remaining water with 3 cups flour and salt. When yeast is foamy, add it to flour and stir vigorously. Turn out on floured board and let dough rest while you clean and oil bowl.

   Knead dough 10 minutes, adding flour if necessary to create a smooth, silky mass. Return to bowl, roll around to coat with oil, cover with double layer of platic wrap, and let rise until double in bulk (about 2 hours).

   Preheat oven to 500 degrees.

   (If using a pizza stone and baker's peel, heat stone in oven. Dust baker's peel with a sprinkle of flour; stretch out pizza, lay it on the baker's peel, and assemble it on the peel, sliding it onto the pizza stone in the oven.

   (If using a cookie sheet, it should be about 10-by-20 inches. Preheat the oven, grease the sheet well with vegetable oil, but don't put it in the oven.)

*Punch down dough. Knead again for 3
minutes. Cover and let rest. Flour board
and flatten dough out on it. Pounding and
pressing with the heel of your hand, work
dough into a circle. When it is about ½-inch
thick, pick it up and use your fists
underneath to stretch it further. Proceed
slowly until pizza is the size of your baking
sheet. Lay it on the sheet and lightly spread
the top with vegetable oil.*

*Spread dough with pinches of ricotta,
then pineapple and ham, then mozzarella.*

*Bake 10–12 minutes, or until crust is light
brown. Serve still hot, directly from sheet,
using scissors to cut slices.*

Serves 3–4.

*Ray's Pizza, 27 Prince Street, New York,
N.Y.; (212) 966-1960.*

America's Best Hamburger

LOS ANGELES—Where is the best hamburger in America? Our
list of nominees includes:

Louis Lunch in New Haven, Connecticut, where it is said the
hamburger was invented nearly a century ago by a man named
Louis Lassen. Mr. Lassen ground up raw steak scraps, formed
them into patties, broiled them, and presented the result between
two pieces of toast. The legend says he served newfangled sandwiches to a bunch of rowdy sailors from Hamburg, Germany.

Whether or not it is the cradle of the hamburger, Louis Lunch is
an essential stop on the itinerary of anyone searching for the ultimate in grilled ground beef. Ken Lassen (Louis's grandson) still
grinds his own, and still employs the original ancient ovens. You
can get a cheeseburger, for which the toast is spread with Cheez
Whiz, or you can get a double burger (two patties' worth of meat
mushed into one).

Nominee number two in our quest for the best is *Conway's Red
Top* of Colorado Springs (p. 84), where the motto is "One's a Meal."
Each patty is six inches wide, served on a six-inch bun. It is a slim
burger, quite juicy, but not oozingly so. The meat and puffy bun are
a perfect balance of beefy smack and bread cushion. We also like
the French fries: thin and crisp, some with crusty shriveled tips.

If thick burgers are your pleasure, try *Hackney's* in Chicago. A
Hackney's hamburger is a half-pound loaf of meat, the breadstuff
around it mere decoration. The great rosy mound is coarse-tex-
tured and barely holds together when you slice it with a knife. On
the side of this Gargantua, get a brick of deep-fried onions. Crisp,
wispy, utterly uncouth and absolutely irresistible, they are fragile
around the edges, but the deeper you go into the brick, the naugh-
tier and oilier they get.

In Texas, the temple of sloppy hamburgers is the legendary *Kincaid's* of Fort Worth. Kincaid's is a grocery store, and there isn't a
seat in the house. That doesn't bother the thousand loyal fans who
flock to the back counter every day to order their big fat burgers
with the works, then find a place along the shelves of groceries to
eat lunch.

It must be acknowledged in our search for perfection that some
people do not believe that bigger is better. Connoisseurs condemn
fat patties as freakish, going beyond the limits of honest bur-
gerhood toward the epicureanism of Salisbury steak. To purists, a
burger is a burger only if it is a quarter-inch thin, gray throughout,
with enough oil from the grill glistening on its surface to dampen
and season the bun.

AMERICA'S BEST HAMBURGER

The flame should be high. The meat should be lean, but not too lean, lest the hamburger be dry. Twenty percent to 30 percent fat is just right. Form it into a patty by hand, handling it as little as possible. One inch thick is as tall as you can go without running into the serious problem of burnt crust and raw insides.

Cook the hamburger about 6 inches from the flame, on a rack that lets the grease drip away. Each side should be seared, then each cooked 2–5 minutes, depending on desired doneness. The grill should be oiled lightly before the burger is slapped on.

Never mix seasoning into the meat. Add it after the hamburger comes off the grill. For cheeseburgers, use the broiler or a toaster oven to melt the cheese onto the bun (toasted inside up), rather than the burger.

Cassell's, 3300 W. 6th St., Los Angeles, Calif.; (213) 480-8668.

For that perfect lunch-counter burger, we recommend the *Avalon Drug Company* of Houston, a forty-year-old pharmacy where the patties are slim, cooked on a griddle, and sandwiched inside lightly toasted buns. Or if you really want to get thin—we're talking no thicker than a dime—check out the *Cozy Inn* of Salina, Kansas, where the patties are fried with onions on a griddle and sold for 39 cents apiece. They resemble White Castles, but better. Cozy Inn has been serving them since 1922, when they sold for a nickel apiece. Customers buy them—and eat them—by the dozen.

And now—the envelope, please—our last-but-not-least nomination for the best hamburger in America: *Cassell's* of Los Angeles. Cassell's is a self-service burgerteria that makes the pinnacle of patties from lean chuck, ground into one-third- and two-thirds-pound sizes, broiled under an open flame, just long enough to char. When the blackened crust is broken, it splits to reveal pebbly pink meat, running rivulets of savory juice.

Cassell burgers are served on thick cardboard trays, which customers tote to a dazzling condiment bar that includes all the usual toppings plus potato salad, fruit salad, cottage cheese, homemade mayonnaise, and relish. After piling trays with goodies, hamburger eaters carry them out back to Cassell's patio, where they dig in under a warm California sun.

"The important thing," Cassell's owner Al Smith advised us, "is to broil—not fry—the meat. We cook it on a slant, so the grease runs off."

Ambrosia Burgers

BIG SUR, Calif.—High above the Pacific Ocean, on Big Sur's dramatic coastline, there stands a restaurant that transcends its food. Nepenthe is proof that the joy of eating is due only in small part to what is on a plate. The deepest effect of a meal comes from everything around that plate: the setting, your dinnermates, the mood of the evening.

Not that there is anything wrong with the food. On the contrary, it is easy to pick a winner from the cheerful, unpretentious menu of sandwiches, steaks, and salads. We love "Lolly's roast chicken dinner," with its sage dressing and cranberries. And the Nepenthe chefs salad, topped with a healthful sprinkle of seeds and sprouts and garden goodies, is a model of vegetarian assemblage. We could nibble from Nepenthe's fruit and bread and cheese board all night long. There is even a "slim-n-trim plate" for weight watchers, or a big juicy steak for serious carnivores. And the ambrosia bur-

AMBROSIA SAUCE

1 whole egg
1 extra egg yolk
1/4 teaspoon salt
1 1/2 teaspoons sharp Dijon-style mustard
1 1/4 cups olive oil
4 teaspoons lemon juice
1 tablespoon boiling water
3/4 cup tomato sauce
2 tablespoons red chili salsa

In an electric blender, mix egg, the extra yolk, salt, mustard, and 1/4 cup of the olive oil. With the blender on high speed, slowly drizzle in all remaining oil. When oil and eggs are blended, mix in lemon juice and boiling water.

Pour into bowl. Use a wire whisk to blend in tomato sauce and salsa. Refrigerate to store.

Yield: 2 1/2 cups.

Nepenthe, Route 1, Big Sur, Calif.;
(408) 667-2345.

ger—which we'll get to in a minute—is a model of hamburger excellence.

All good food. But it is the place that stirs one's soul. Named for the ancient drug that was supposed to induce forgetfulness, Nepenthe could be a vision pulled whole from some romantic poet's grandiose dream of glory. On an oak-shaded cliff 808 feet above sea level, built of redwood and adobe, with a vast windowed wall and stone terrace overlooking the Big Sur coastline, it is accessible by car—but only barely. One parks in a lot down below, then walks up to the majestic pavilion.

The air is clear up here. On one side are the dense, unspoiled pine and redwood forests; on the other is a raging Pacific surf. And in the middle, underneath the high-perched restaurant, is a jagged coastline of towering cliffs. There are seats outside—plain director's chairs—where customers sit enjoying drinks along with cheese and crackers or baskets of good French fries.

The dining room, lighted by candles, is a sweeping open space circling a huge fireplace. There are tables and choice window benches, set with random pillows and cushions for slow-paced dining, lounging, or listening to live music. Could there be any location in America that offers a more romantic sunset?

It would be impossible for any kitchen to try to compete with the setting; wisely, Nepenthe sticks to unfancy food—nothing that would divert one's attention from the spiritual trance inevitably induced by the view, accompanied perhaps by a bottle of California wine.

Although we have eaten up and down the menu, the meal to which we always return is the good old hamburger, known as an Ambrosia Burger because of its Ambrosia Sauce—an elementary mixture of mayo and salsa. The meat itself is ground chuck formed into a fat five-ounce patty, broiled and served on a French roll in a basket. It is accompanied by a kosher pickle and either coleslaw, green salad, or a crunchy bean salad made with garbanzos, sweet onions, and kidney beans.

Ambrosia Sauce is just fine when made with bottled mayonnaise. But if you really want to make it sparkle, start from scratch, as in our adaptation of the Nepenthe recipe. It's pretty goopy stuff, so be sure to serve Ambrosia Burgers with plenty of napkins.

Caesarburger

OKLAHOMA CITY—One of the best eaters we know is a fellow named Richard Story, who hails from Oklahoma City. Richard knows good food, from lick-your-fingers fried chicken to haute cuisine, so the last time we headed southwest to the Sooner State, we called him and asked where to eat. Richard and his brother Craig put their heads together and came up with a long list of OK eateries, including grand cafeterias, trendy trattorias, bars and barbecues, steakhouses and cheese grits grills.

We were in heaven. For a delirious few days, with a few breaks to visit the Cowboy Hall of Fame, we ate ourselves silly all across town, feasting on the foods of the American Southwest, from chicken fried steak and Tex-Mex fajitas to barbecued balony and burnt sugar chiffon cake.

One of the specialties of Oklahoma City that Craig Story had insisted we sample during our visit was hamburgers. Hamburgers, a specialty of Oklahoma City? That's right, because these are no ordinary hamburgers. Oklahomans, Craig explained, like their burgers dolled up, really weird. To prove his point, he directed us to two burger joints: Johnnie's and The Split T.

There are four Johnnie's outlets around the city. They are modern, molded-chair, Formica-counter-type places—nothing special to look at. But you can smell the difference as soon as you enter. What you smell is onions.

Johnnie's pièce de résistance is an onion burger, made like this: The griddle man grabs a ball of raw ground beef and a fistful of sliced red onions, then uses a skillet to mash them down together on the hot griddle. He presses hard as the burger cooks, flipping onion and meat patty at the same time, so that by the time it's done, the hamburger is permeated with the taste and smell of the sliced onions that are stuck to it. The whole luscious mess is then inserted into a bun along with a sheaf of pickle chips. It's great, especially with a spill of hot jalapeño peppers added for extra pep (twenty cents extra).

Of course, Johnnie's offers variations on the onion burger: double patties, chiliburgers, lettuce and tomato garnishes. For crisp munchies to accompany the sandwich, you can get French fries (fresh cut) or onion rings or, best of all, bite-size morsels of golden fried okra.

While an onion burger isn't what you'd call exotic, Oklahoma City's other favorite burger, specialty of The Split T Bar, is genuinely odd. The Split T is the home of the Caesarburger.

You needn't be a detective to figure out what a Caesarburger is:

CAESARBURGERS

4 hamburgers, charcoal broiled to taste
4 buns or large pita breads

CAESAR CONDIMENT:
½ cup mayonnaise
¼ cup grated Parmesan cheese
1 raw egg yolk
2 tablespoons olive oil
½ teaspoon coarsely ground black pepper
1 clove raw garlic, finely minced
1 anchovy fillet (optional)
2 to 3 leaves romaine lettuce, torn into small shreds

Combine all ingredients. Heap atop hamburgers in buns. Makes 4 Caesarburgers.

The Split T Bar, 57th & N. Western, Oklahoma City, Okla.; (405) 842-0331.

a combination of a hamburger and Caesar salad. When we first heard about it from Craig, we wondered how the two could possibly fit together and not be an impossible-to-eat, total mess.

The answer is: They cannot. A Caesarburger is a handful of edible chaos, which is why The Split T serves them wrapped inside an envelope of paper that cups all the ingredients until you are approximately halfway through the sandwich. By that time, so much of the Caesar dressing has oozed out, along with juices from the patty and shreds of lettuce, that the paper wrapper is disintegrating and the plate below (or your lap, if you choose to eat in the car) becomes the receptacle for the spillage.

It is a sloppy sandwich, all right, but what a winning combination of flavors! The hamburger is thick enough to ooze natural gravy from inside its charred crust. The salad is a wild combination of garlic, pepper, and sharp cheese. In fact, the topping is considerably thicker than the kind of salad you'd serve in a bowl, actually closer to sauce than salad.

We suggest serving Caesarburgers on a plate, with a knife and fork, or stuffed inside pita pockets. They won't be as much fun as the messy way of doing things at The Split T, but the civilized method in our recipe will definitely save on dry-cleaning bills!

Piggie Pocket Burgers

WEST COLUMBIA, S.C.—Since the 1930s when Joe Bessinger opened a café in Holly Hill, South Carolina, the Bessinger family name has meant great barbecue. Joe's sons Maurice and Melvin kept the tradition by opening a series of Piggie Park barbecue restaurants in the early 1950s. Maurice's Piggie Park in West Columbia has become one of the biggest curb-service drive-ins in the country.

Dining at Maurice Bessinger's is a rousing experience. It is the kind of uniquely American meal to which we would eagerly take visitors from another country if we wanted to show them the spunk, character, and quality of American gastronomy. Pardon our emotionalism, but Piggie Park inspires patriotic thoughts, and not only because the food is so darn good. The largest American flag in South Carolina waves above its parking lot.

It is possible to eat at tables inside, but most customers prefer dining in their cars, parked in Piggie Park's tin-covered car slots with illuminated menus and individual intercoms. The menu guarantees three-minute serivce—by carhops in crisp red, white, and blue uniforms.

PIGGIE POCKET BURGERS

2 pounds lean ground beef
8 ounces shredded American or cheddar
  cheese
1/2 cup chopped onion
1/2 cup barbecue sauce
1/4 cup melted margarine
salt and pepper to taste

Between sheets of waxed paper, roll out 8 equal-size 1/4-inch thick patties of ground beef.

Mix cheese, onion, and sauce. Spread this mixture onto four of the thin patties, leaving a 1/2-inch border around the edge. Take the remaining four patties and use them to cover the ones topped with cheese and sauce. Crimp the edges to seal thoroughly.

Use a spatula to gently place the burgers on a broiling pan. Broil 6–8 inches from flame until top is done as desired. Carefully flip and broil the other side.

Season to taste. Serve in large buns or pita pocket breads, with extra barbecue sauce as condiment.

Makes 4 big burgers.

Maurice's Piggie Park, 1601 Charleston Highway, West Columbia, S.C.; (803) 796-0220; for mail order sauce, write to Box 6847, West Columbia, S.C. 29171; or call (803) 791-5887.

Roll the windows down, because the tantalizing smells of burning wood and sizzling hams make the lot an aromatic feast. Piggie Park chefs cook their pork the old-fashioned way. Round the clock, every day, hogs are roasted over hickory coals (note the woodpile by the sooty chimney). Although the menu is vast, including foot-long hot dogs, chicken baskets, and beefalo burgers, pork is the star.

Some like it in a sandwich: Big Joe Q Pork or Little Joe Q Pork ("with skin $.20 extra"). The smoky-flavored meat is finely chopped and accented with a dash of sauce. The sauce is a shock if you have never had the pleasure of pig-pickin' (eating barbecue) in or around Columbia. Unlike the tomato-red stuff common everywhere else in the Q-belt, central South Carolinians like a golden mustard-based glaze. Bessinger's version—known as the "million-dollar heirloom recipe"—is apple-cider sweet, zesty but not burning hot.

Our recommendation is a Q Rib or Q Pork Plate. The ribs are big messy bats, their lode of meat permeated with smoke. Pork is cut into big chunks—"inside" pieces that are pale white and tender; and "outside" strips, encrusted with roasted-on sauce. Be sure to get some skin on the side. It is dark mottled brown, fried to a crisp.

If you are not going to be visiting Columbia in the near future, you can get a taste of its unique barbecue sauce by mail. Simply order some from Maurice. We recommend it for mopping on any barbecued meat, for mixing into meat loaves, for adding to any Crockpot-cooked meal. It is sold three ways: regular, hot, and hickory-flavored.

If you do get some, try it in this recipe Maurice Bessinger sends with his sauce. Of course, you can use any ordinary barbecue sauce in the recipe; but Maurice's tart mustard potion is what gives these surprise-inside patties their kick.

Cheese-Br-Ger

COLUMBUS, Ind.—Zaharako's is a working soda fountain where they still know how to concoct a green river, a black cow, and a double chocolate malt.

It opened as a confectionery in 1900. Five years later, the Zaharako brothers brought back a couple of soda fountains from the St. Louis World Exposition. The fountains were ornate fixtures, set into a backbar of solid mahogany, Italian marble, and onyx pillars. The Zaharakos installed a counter of Mexican and

CHEESE-BR-GER

MEAT SAUCE:

1 clove garlic, minced

2 tablespoons vegetable oil

½ cup chopped onion

1 pound ground beef

2 tablespoons brown sugar

2 teaspoons salt

½ teaspoon black pepper

1 teaspoon Worcestershire sauce

5–10 drops Tabasco sauce, to taste

¼ cup ketchup

½–1 cup tomato juice

Sauté garlic in oil over medium heat in large skillet. As garlic begins to brown, add onion and sauté until soft. Stir in beef with fork; continue stirring constantly to keep it loose as it browns.

When meat is brown, drain off excess oil, then add remaining ingredients, using enough tomato juice to create a sloppy but not soupy mixture. Simmer, stirring occasionally, 10 minutes.

Yield: Sauce for 4 cheese-br-gers.

CHEESE-BR-GER:

2 slices white bread

1 slice American cheese

1–2 tablespoons butter or margarine

Spread meat sauce across a slice of bread. Top with slice of cheese, then another slice of bread.

In skillet over medium-low heat, melt butter or margarine. Grill sandwich on both sides until golden brown.

Zaharako's, 329 Washington St., Columbus, Ind.; (812) 379-9329.

Italian marble, and a Tiffany lamp on an onyx stand. Today, everything looks as it did back then, but haloed with a fine patina of age. It is a dazzling experience to walk into Zaharako's for the first time and confront the gleaming silver and polished wood in the front room, or to continue beyond the fountain, through the trellised wood divider, toward the tables in the back room, surrounded by walls covered entirely with mirrors.

At the back of the back room is the most spectacular of Zaharako's antiques: a full concert German pipe organ, purchased in 1905. It features 185 pipes and complete orchestration: trumpets, bass drum, snare drum, cymbals, flutes, and a triangle. The organ is played like a player piano, with punched paper rolls, each five to ten mintues long. It still works perfectly, providing gay-nineties background music for sipping sundaes and eating sandwiches.

The menu at Zaharako's is limited to soda fountain specialties and sandwiches. The only cooking utensil in evidence, other than the mixological instruments, is a small grill. It is used for making grilled cheese sandwiches and a unique item listed on the board above the serving area as a Cheese-Br-Ger.

If you guess a Cheese-Br-Ger is like a cheeseburger, you'd be close to correct. But there is a difference. A Cheese-Br-Ger is made with meat sauce instead of a meat patty, and it gets grilled inside two slices of white bread instead of a bun. The secret of its goodness is the spice in the sauce—a Greek-accented combination of sweet and hot reminiscent of Cincinnati five-way chili.

How to Cook a Hot Dog

TONAWANDA, N.Y.—We are about to get ourselves into hot water by suggesting how people ought to cook a wiener, since most connoisseurs of the all-American tube steak have their own favorite way of doing it. Wieners, and wiener cookery, are a subject that stirs regional pride and nostalgic passion to a degree equaled only by chili, barbecue, fried chicken, and apple pie.

Most of us are loyal to the hot dogs we grew up eating: ballpark franks in Fenway Park, kosher dogs on the Lower East Side of Manhattan, Chicago red-hots smothered with a gardenful of condiments, white hot wieners of upstate New York, Chris's garlic links in Oakland (California), Washington, D.C., half-smokes, Sheboygan (Wisconsin) brats, split wieners of the Connecticut shoreline, Coney Islands of Cleveland, chili dogs of Detroit, or itty-bitty "New York System" piglets of Rhode Island. You could travel coast to coast eating nothing but hot dogs, and never have the exact same meal twice. (A gustatory trip we recommend only in theory!)

Probably the most popular way of cooking hot dogs is to steep them in hot water. The point of this easy technique is to merely heat the meat inside the casing (since it is already cooked when you buy it). Steeping a hot dog keeps it pink and plump. It is also a convenient method, since most people don't mind letting the dogs wallow in hot water until everything else (buns, French fries, milk shakes, etc.) is ready.

Serious steepers, however, insist that the only proper way to do it is to get everything else ready first, then set the pot of water to boil. When it is boiling furiously, drop in the hot dogs, *turn off the heat underneath the pot,* cover the pot, and let the dogs steep for 6–8 minutes. Remove them, pat them dry, and place them in their buns.

While steeping is easy, we recommend it only if you have hot dogs that are delicious to begin with. Water contributes nothing to their taste, so the results with less than a four-star frank can be drab.

For adding a bit of zest to a hot dog, take a lesson from Ted's Jumbo Red Hots restaurant in Tonawanda, New York. Tonawanda is part of greater Buffalo, where people are crazy for hot dogs; and Ted's is where those in the know go for the best in town. What they do at Ted's is to grill them over charcoal. As they grill, the chef whacks them with a spatula and pokes them with a fork, mashes them hard against the grates of the grill, and generally uglifies them, so that the finished tube steak is scarred, charred, and crusty.

It's a wonderful technique because it forces the hot dog to absorb the flavor of the fire. Of course, you do lose the natural ooze of the dog by cutting into it. Instead of a fat-packed tube loaded with juice, you get a crusty, withered log. For those of us who like the fiery crunch of grilled food, it is a worthwhile trade-off.

The other thing that makes Ted's Jumbo Red Hots especially delicious is the homemade hot sauce applied by an employee known as "the dresser" stationed at the "dressing station" behind the counter. It is laced with relish and has a spicy tingle that sets a tongue on fire. Great stuff, although being traditionalists, we prefer bright yellow mustard.

Regardless of how hot dogs are cooked, the most important issue that a hot dog chef must face is this: pork or all-beef? The difference in flavor between a porcine hot dog and a beef hot dog is enormous; so is the difference in price (beef is higher). Having studied the problem, we have concluded that the best pork hot dogs ought to be steeped, because steeping maintains the moist piggyness that gives them their character.

When it comes to all-beef dogs, on the other hand, we insist on grilling. The flavor of the fire brings out a certain beef-and-garlic snap that never comes alive when they are steeped. Grilling is almost as easy as steeping. You can do it outdoors on a barbecue grill, or under any kitchen broiler (gas or electric).

Here's how: Slash the hot dogs before you put them over the flame (or indoors, 6–8 inches below the broiler). Cut into them a quarter to a half-inch, with either random incisions or a spiral cut going end to end. Or if you really want to get fancy, cut a trough along the length of the hot dog, grill it, and when it's almost done, lay in some cheese and continue broiling until the cheese begins to melt. Watch closely when you grill hot dogs. You want them browned and charred, maybe even blackened along the edge; but don't let them turn to cinders!

Ted's Jumbo Red Hots, 2312 Sheridan Dr., Tonawanda, N.Y.; (716) 836-8986.

Hoppelpoppel

AMANA, Iowa—The man in the lederhosen strolls through the dining rooms playing his accordion and singing, as tables full of happy families dig into pork chops and sauerbraten, Amana ham, and T-bone steaks.

Mealtime at the Ronneburg Inn wasn't always so cheerful. Back in the 1920s, men and women were required to eat at separate tables. Allotted fifteen minutes to scarf down the grub, they had no time for conversation. Music was forbidden.

The Ronneburg was the mess hall for a long-running experiment in communal living begun by Lutheran separatists in the 1850s. Nineteenth-century America was rife with such utopias. This one arrived in the new world from Germany in 1842, calling itself the Ebeneezer Society when members settled outside of Buffalo, New York. They soon needed more space for farming, so they came to Iowa, establishing a cluster of small towns known as the Amana Colonies. All land, livestock, and homes were held in common by the group.

The goal of this "Community of True Inspiration" was to be completely self-sufficient, so they developed every kind of skill they needed. They farmed, they crafted furniture, they smoked their own meat, baked their own bread, pressed their own grapes for wine.

HOPPELPOPPEL

*3 pounds small potatoes, washed but
    unpeeled
1 pound thick-sliced bacon, cut into 2-inch
    lengths
1½ cups onion, finely chopped
12 eggs
3 tablespoons milk
6 tablespoons finely chopped parsely
1 teaspoon salt
¼ teaspoon pepper*

*Boil potatoes until they can be pierced
with a fork, 20–30 minutes; do not cook
until soft. Drain (peel if desired). Cut into ¼-
inch slices and set aside.*

*Cook bacon in large nonstick skillet over
moderate heat until brown and crisp.
Remove with slotted spoon and drain on
paper towels. Pour off grease and return ⅓
cup of grease to skillet.*

*Fry onions in bacon grease, stirring
frequently until onions are transparent but
not brown, about 5 minutes. Add potatoes
and more grease if necessary. Cook 10–12
minutes, stirring occasionally, until potatoes
are light brown.*

*In a bowl, beat eggs, milk, parsley, salt,
and pepper.*

*Reduce heat under skillet to low. Add
bacon to potatoes. Pour in egg mixture and
stir once or twice as eggs begin to cook.
Cover and cook without stirring 6–8
minutes, until eggs are set but still moist.*

*Serve directly from skillet. Makes 6
servings.*

*The Ronneburg, Amana, Iowa;
(319) 622-3641.*

The cloistered life lasted until 1932 when private ownership was restored to the community. After the "change," Elsie Oehler's grandparents and parents bought the place they had been assigned to live in: two connected brick buildings that included the village kitchen. Elsie's grandmother had been a "kitchen boss" in commune days, and it was with her inspiration and her mother's help that Elsie and her husband, Don, began the Ronneburg Restaurant.

Named after the medieval fortress that sheltered the original separatists from persecution in the 1700s, the Ronneburg still serves meals in the original dining room, and prepares them in the kitchen Elsie's grandmother once bossed. But the spirit of the dinner hour has changed completely.

The Amana Colonies are now a popular tourist attraction. And the Ronneburg is the best of several eateries where visitors can sample a culinary heritage that expresses heartland meat-and-potatoes taste with a strong German accent.

It is immigrant farm food, the emphasis on Iowa pork: zesty homemade sausage; pork chops (three per order) with gravy and sauerkraut; cured ham, fried or baked; and a fantastic appetizer of pickled ham and onions. On the side at dinner comes bowls full of hashed brown potatoes, butter-sopped sweet corn, potato dumplings, crumble-topped spaetzle, cottage cheese, chicken giblet dressing, white bread, dark bread, etc. One Sunday afternoon we stopped mid-meal and counted twelve different bowls of food on our table.

It is possible to accompany the food with French or German wine; or you can get Amana wines produced by the winery one block away: blackberry or cranberry, even wine made from local rhubarb.

We left Amana with a copy of Elsie Oehler's *Ronneburg Recipe Album*, illustrated with pictures of life in the communal colonies. It is a pamphlet of real farm cooking such as fresh dandelion salad and dill weed bread, plus Ronneburg favorites such as crusty fried potatoes and old-fashioned rhubarb pie.

Among Mrs. Oehler's favorite recipes is hoppelpoppel, which she recommends for breakfast, Sunday night supper, or late night snacks. On Christmas morning, the Oehlers serve it along with stollen and hot coffee. How Hoppelpoppel got its name, she doesn't say.

1920s Milk Toast

ANN ARBOR, Mich.—Drake's Sandwich Shop is a place of many culinary virtues.

First, and most obvious when you walk in the door, is all the candy it sells. The shelves are lined with jars full of licorice whips, jelly beans, caramels and kisses, nougats, lozenges, and lollipops: a confectionery dream. Buy them boxed, or weigh out bagsful according to your own taste.

Next thing to know about is Drake's pecan roll, Ann Arbor's favorite midmorning (or midafternoon, or late-night) snack. It is a sticky swirling bun that connoisseurs ask for "twice cooked," which means it gets buttered and toasted on a grill.

Now look at the cake tray on the soda fountain counter. Every other day, Drake's sets a new kind of cake upon a pedestal. They are double-layer cakes, moist and fragile, lathered with appropriate frosting. Spice cake is our favorite, followed closely by banana, peanut butter, then double chocolate.

Before getting on to any more of the good food at Drake's, let us step back and consider the place itself. Sixty-plus years in business hasn't changed it a bit. The 1920s marble soda fountain still has all the proper malt dispensers, milk shake mixers, syrup taps, and soda squirters. Booths in back are high-backed wood aged to a lustrous dark patina.

Upstairs, Drake's has a newfangled annex with a different kind of nostalgic appeal. Here is the "Martian Room," decorated during that midcentury era when Formica and boomerangs were the height of fashion.

Another thing we like about Drake's is the way you order your food. Study the menu, write your own ticket on a small pad provided, then hand it to the people behind the counter.

It is what's on the menu we like best of all—a journey back to days of sweet shop innocence. Of course there is an array of soda fountain specialties: malts, shakes, sundaes, and banana splits. And because Ann Arbor is a college town, the dagwood sandwiches have collegiate names: the "Cornell" (tuna and tomatoes), the "Northwestern" (ham and Swiss), and the home town favorite, "Michigan" (chicken and tomatoes).

Many Drake's aficionados contend that the best things to eat, other than the pecan rolls and cakes, are the dainty ones: cucumber sandwiches on buttered white bread, accompanied by freshly squeezed limeade. Or cream cheese and jelly. Or ordinary grilled cheese.

Or—we have saved the best for last—milk toast. Milk toast, that

---

1920s MILK TOAST

2 thick slices toast
1 cup milk (or cream, or half-and-half)
2 tablespoons butter
salt to taste

Tear or cut toast into bite-size pieces and place in shallow bowl.

Warm milk. Pour over toast. Immediately dot with butter. Sprinkle with salt. Serve immediately.

Makes 1 serving.

Drake's Sandwich Shop, 709 N. University, Ann Arbor, Mich.; (313) 688-8853.

great antique dish of nursery comfort food, is nowhere more at home than in this venerable 1920s eatery. In fact, we cannot think of another restaurant, anywhere other than a few grand hotels in the East, that even offers milk toast any more. It's so passé, so prim. But for a quiet breakfast, or a midnight snack after a long, hard day, no meal on earth is as kind and tender.

Few dishes are easier to prepare, either. The ingredients, after all, are little more than milk and toast. But there are some subtleties and variations you might want to know about.

The first rule of making good milk toast is to have the bread properly toasted. It ought to be white bread—high quality white bread, preferably homemade and definitely sliced thick. Toast it only until light brown, so the outside is crisp, but the interior still has some "give."

Toast should be torn or cut into bite-size pieces before you put it into the bowl. This is most important, as it eliminates the need for sawing and cutting while eating: it is crucial that the actual eating of the toast be baby-food easy.

The milk (or cream, if you want it extraluxurious) must never be boiled. Heat it to near scalding, enough to quickly melt the butter.

Finally, although traditional milk toast is simple and savory, consider other versions: Sprinkle it with a tablespoon or two of cinnamon-sugar instead of salt; or spread a layer of honey or peanut butter on the toast before you cut it. Or—if you really want to go wild—make it a bowl of hot chocolate milk toast, and garnish it with fresh raspberries.

14
Cookies and Snacks

Buttermilk Shake

YOUNTVILLE, Calif.—One of the sad things about growing up is that adult life contains no milk shakes.

Too many calories, too sweet, too juvenile, too filling: Logical arguments against shakes abound. But none deals with the main reason milk shakes were a vital part of most people's teen cuisine. Milk shakes are fun! They are the only proper companion for a meal of cheeseburgers and French fries. They are the unofficial drink of American childhood.

Think about it: When was the last time you saw milk shakes on the menu of a serious restaurant? Can you imagine asking a waiter for the kitchen's suggestion of a beverage to accompany your surf 'n' turf, and having him respond, "Yes, monsieur, tonight the chef recommends a double chocolate milk shake, extra thick, with a soupçon of malt powder."

Milk shakes are the pride of the soda fountain. For maximum enjoyment, that is where they ought to be enjoyed: on a leatherette booth or stool at a Formica table or counter, presented in a tall silver beaker that holds enough to fill a glass two or three times. They should be served with background music from a jukebox, accompanied by the whirr of more milk shakes being blended, by the sizzle of burgers on a grill, and by the perfume of honeytone shoestrings or curly-Q potatoes emerging from bubbling oil in the Friolator.

There *are* places like that; the problem is that most of them are strictly for kids. Where do oldsters like us go if we want a milk shake served in adult surroundings?

Answer: to Yountville, California, and a restaurant called The Diner. The Diner has a counter and stools, and booths, and its menu lists some tasty hamburgers along with the milk shakes, cherry Cokes (made from syrup and seltzer, not poured from cans), hot fudge sundaes, and banana boats. But it is no relic from the mists of soda fountain history.

Begun in the late 1970s by Cassandra Mitchell and her friends, The Diner is a converted bus depot conceived as an ode to real American food. Cassandra doesn't serve only good hamburgers and classic ice cream specialties. She also bakes whole grain breads every day. She cooks her fudge sauce from scratch. To accompany breakfasts ("served all day") she makes her own luscious sausage patties, using ground seasonings from her backyard herb garden.

Each night, The Diner offers a special menu titled "El Diner," featuring Cal-Mex cooking such as chicken and cream enchiladas and tacos stuffed with the most wonderful freshly made guacamole.

Cassandra's soda fountain offers a full roster of all the usual splits, shakes, and sodas, plus a specialty we've seen only in the San Francisco area: buttermilk shakes.

There is nothing complicated about the basic formula; it's hardly more than buttermilk and ice cream. (Of course, the possible variations, using different flavored syrups, liqueurs, and fancy ice creams, are spectacular.)

But before we get to the recipe, a few basic points should be made about soda fountain mixology. Any blender is fine for making milk shakes, although the kinds with the wand and small, rectangular blades work best. Blenders with large knifelike blades tend to pulverize the ice cream quickly, yielding a too-thin shake. Other than length of blending, the primary determinant of a shake's thickness is the ratio of ice cream to milk (or buttermilk). A good starting formula for a shake that is fairly thick but can still be sucked up through a straw is four scoops of ice cream to a cup of milk.

As for flavoring, the shake-maker's best friend is pure vanilla extract. (You should use a dash even in a chocolate shake.)

When using buttermilk, go easy on the other flavorings so as not to overwhelm its tang. The best buttermilk shakes, we think, are plain vanilla with a dash of lemon—producing a beverage that Cassandra Mitchell described as "like liquid cheesecake"!

BUTTERMILK SHAKE

4 scoops high-quality vanilla ice cream
I cup buttermilk
½ teaspoon vanilla extract
I tiny drop of lemon extract
I teaspoon lemon rind (optional)

Mix all ingredients in blender just long enough to blend. Yield: about 2 cups.

The Diner, 6476 Washington St., Yountville, Calif.; (707) 944-2626.

Fuzzy Navel Milkshake

YELLOW SPRINGS, Ohio—If you are traveling along Interstate 70 through Ohio (a route we recommend to anyone who enjoys eating), we've got a tasty little detour for you, just east of Dayton. Get on Highway 68 heading toward Zenia, home of the Apple Tree Inn; but before you get to your big meal at the Inn, look on the left for a life-size statue of a cow perched high atop a sign overlooking the road.

The cow is brown and white, a symbol of Young's Jersey Dairy, a roadside stand and store that has long been a favorite haunt of students from nearby Antioch College. Young's is a working farm, with barns full of cows nearby. It is a bakery, too, with fresh breads available every day. It is a soda fountain, an ice cream store, and a sandwich shop. Best of all, it is open twenty-four hours a day, seven days a week.

Pull into the parking lot, and a choice of activities awaits. You

FUZZY NAVEL MILKSHAKE

4 scoops high-quality vanilla ice cream
1 cup cut-up peaches (peeled and pitted)
1 cup cold orange juice
2 strawberries as garnish

Combine ice cream, peaches, and orange juice in drink mixer. Blend only until mixed, but don't worry about an occasional lump of unblended peach. Pour into tall glasses and garnish with strawberries. Serve with long-handled spoons. Makes two tall drinks.

Young's Jersey Dairy, 6880 Springfield-Xenia Road, Yellow Springs, Ohio;
(513) 325-0629.

can walk to the goat pen nearby, buy a handful of feed for a dime from the dispensing machine, and give the cloven-footed Nubians a snack. (If you don't buy any feed, they seem nearly as happy nibbling on a passing sleeve or pants cuff.)

Beyond the goat pen is a model cow barn, filled with pulchritudinous dairy animals, occasional calves, and even a couple of hefty bulls (whom visitors are advised to circumnavigate by at least five feet).

On the other side of the parking lot is Young's Farm Store, a large, sunny room with tables and chairs at one end for eating sit-down meals.

The menu is not particularly thrilling to read: eggs, pancakes, biscuits, and gravy for breakfast; soup, sandwiches, and chili for lunch. But if the kitchen's repertoire is not original, its food sure is good. All the breadstuffs are homemade—white or whole wheat toast, biscuits, or "English muffin bread." French toast is made from a loaf of sourdough. You can get bacon, egg, and cheese inside a Young's-made croissant. The double cheeseburger on a homemade bun, with bacon, lettuce, and tomato, French fries on the side, is a meal we'd be happy to eat nearly any day.

Of course the really good thing about eating at Young's is getting something from the dairy bar, whether it's a simple glass of pure "Jersey milk" or an ultra-thick, eat-it-with-a-spoon "cow shake." Even more luxurious than the cow shake is a "bull shake," which comes with a whole, unblended scoop of ice cream (pick your flavor) floating on top. For real fanatics, Young's offers a monumental "King Kong sundae," which is a trough loaded with enough ice cream and syrup to feed a family.

The array of soda fountain specialties includes familiar classics as well as a seasonally changing roster of fresh-fruit shortcakes and sundaes. Most of the business in sodas, shakes, sundaes, frappés, cups, and cones is transacted at a long counter at the back of the store, from which customers tote their ice cream concoctions out to eat in the car or at one of the picnic tables near the goat pen.

The last time we stepped up to the counter, it was a hot day late in the spring, and hand-written signs announced strawberry shortcake and fuzzy navels as the day's treats. The shortcake was swell: a biscuit (homemade, of course) topped with fresh sliced strawberries, vanilla ice cream, and gobs of thick whipped cream. The fuzzy navel was something different! It was made with Young's own peaches and cream ice cream, blended with orange juice, served with a strawberry on top.

The fuzzy navel was such a memorable way to beat the heat that when we returned from our trip, we got out our milk-shake maker, determined to devise a recipe we could share with readers who, like us, don't have ready access to Young's peaches-and-cream ice cream. If you've got fresh, ripe, sweet peaches, it's a snap to make. If they aren't quite sweet, you may want to sprinkle them with sugar. Even defrosted frozen peaches do the job in an emergency. We recommend making fuzzy navels on a hot afternoon when you need a tall, cool glass of sheer luxury.

MOLASSES KRINGLES

¾ cup rendered chicken fat and solid
   vegetable shortening (the ideal mixture is
   about half-and-half)
1 cup packed light brown sugar
1 egg, beaten
¼ cup molasses
2¼ cups sifted flour
¼ teaspoon salt
2 teaspoons baking soda
½ teaspoon ground cloves
1 teaspoon cinnamon
1 teaspoon ginger
granulated sugar

Cream shortening and sugar. Beat in egg, then molasses. Sift together flour, salt, baking soda, cloves, cinnamon, and ginger. Beat into cream mixture. Cover and chill 1 hour. (Dough may be frozen at this point.)

Preheat oven to 350 degrees. Form dough into walnut-sized balls; roll each ball in granulated sugar. Place 2 inches apart on ungreased cookie sheets. Bake 10–12 minutes. Let cool slightly on sheets before removing. Cookies will puff up in oven, then "krinkle" and flatten as they cook. They will be soft when done, but firm up as they cool.

Makes 4 dozen molasses kringles.

O & H Danish Bakery, 1841 Douglas Ave., Racine, Wis.; (414) 637-8895.

Molasses Kringles

RACINE, Wis.—People in southern Wisconsin have a nickname for the city of Racine: Kringleville. If you know your pastries, the name will clue you in to the fact that there are a lot of Danish people in Racine—because in Denmark, "kringle" is the term for cookies and tea cakes made with butter.

In Racine, however, it means only one kind of pastry. When you say kringle hereabouts, you are referring to a broad cake wider than a dinner plate. It is less than an inch high, a lightweight sheaf of several dozen near-microscopic layers of dough and butter—like an enormous croissant but flakier—glazed with brown sugar and cinnamon, then filled with pecan, apple, date, prune, or cheese, and finally iced with a clear sugar frosting. One kringle serves about a dozen people.

The kringle is Racine's alone; it is the food that makes the city proud. Let New Orleans keep it beignets and New York its bagels; when it is breakfast time (or tea time, or dessert time, or midnight snack time), Raciners reach for kringles. They are usually served warm—either straight from the baker's oven, or heated from a home freezer (where they keep well); and despite the vast amounts of butter in the dough, true patriotic residents of Wisconsin—"America's Dairyland"—top each slice with an extra pat or two of butter.

At least a half-dozen Racine bakeries specialize in kringles. Our favorite is O & H Danish Bakery on Douglas Avenue, which has been a family business for more than half a century. O & H makes two hundred to three hundred kringles per day, some of them shipped (via Federal Express) to Wisconsin expatriates now living in kringle-deprived regions of the country.

If you want to sample an authentic Racine kringle, call O & H and have them send you a few. The truth is, they're difficult to make at home. Once the dough has been mixed and kneaded, it must be folded three dozen times over butter, then it has to rest in the refrigerator three days before it gets shaped, filled, and glazed.

So instead of telling you how to make a true Racine kringle at home, we have a dilly of a recipe for molasses "kringles" that are easy to make . ... and even easier to eat. They're cookies, not fancy pastries, from a different branch of kringledom than the Wisconsin pastry, but they are eminently practical for the home cook. You can double this recipe to make a big batch of dough, freeze it, then defrost as much as you need when the cookie urge strikes.

The recipe comes to us courtesy of Mrs. Max Gibbs of St. Petersburg, Florida, who was intrigued by our mention in our column of the use of chicken fat as an ingredient in cookies. Mrs. Gibbs turns out to be an expert on the subject. "I find that substituting half chicken fat for the shortening in any cookie recipe makes a tastier cookie," she advised. "It 'shortens' more dry ingredients per ounce than any other shortening."

You don't need to use chicken fat in her recipe, but try it if you can. It is the secret ingredient that makes these kringles meltingly lush.

KRINGLE

1 cup butter, slightly softened
3¼ to 3¾ cups sifted flour
1 package dry yeast
¼ cup sugar (4 tablespoons)
¼ cup tepid (110 degrees) water
1 egg, beaten
¾ cup milk
1 teaspoon salt
1 teaspoon ground cardamom
2 cups sifted confectioners' sugar
2 tablespoons cream
1 cup golden raisins
1 beaten egg
¼ cup sugar
½ cup slivered almonds

   Cream ¾ cup of the butter with ¼ cup of the flour. Roll the mixture between two sheets of wax paper to a 10-by-4-inch rectangle. Chill thoroughly (about 45

Kringle, Part 2

Kringle is one popular pastry! After complaining that kringle was too hard to make at home, we were deluged with letters from kringle aficionados coast to coast. Many of them had grown up in Racine, Wisconsin (known as Kringleville because of all the bakeries specializing in kringle), and wrote us to share their fond memories of the multi-sheaved pastry oval filled with cinnamon or fruit filling.

Readers sent us dozens of different recipes for genuine kringle: yeast-leavened kringle, "kriss kringle" dough for making cream puffs, quick kringle made with sour cream. One generous person from New Jersey actually sent us her own homemade butterscotch kringle—wrapped tightly in foil and enclosed inside a Gucci gift box!

Our kringle bonanza also included a letter and brochure from Daniel Kohel, owner and baker at Kringles Fine Bake Shoppe in Fort Collins, Colorado, where the specialty is—you guessed it— Racine-style kringle. Mr. Kohel worked at a bakery in Racine for eighteen years before moving west. Mr. Kohel regularly bakes nine kinds—filled with pecan, almond, raspberry, apricot, cherry, apple, blueberry, cherry-cheese, and chocolate chip. As is traditional at the Racine bakeries, he specializes in mail-order sales, *minutes) while preparing dough. Let remaining ¼ cup butter continue to soften at room temperature.*

Mix yeast and 1 tablespoon of the sugar in warm water. Combine egg, milk, remaining sugar (3 tablespoons), and salt. When yeast begins to foam, add it to mixture and mix well. Stir in 3 to 3½ cups flour to form a soft, raggedy dough. Using a floured rolling pin, roll out to 12-inch square on well-floured board.

Place chilled butter rectangle in center of dough. Overlap long sides of dough over butter rectangle. Turn dough one-quarter way around. Roll to 12-inch square. Repeat folding and rolling twice, flouring board and pin as necessary. Wrap in wax paper. Chill 30 minutes.

As dough chills, add cardamom to ¼ cup of softened butter. Beat in confectioners' sugar, then cream. Mix in raisins.

Roll chilled dough to 24-by-12-inch rectangle. Cut lengthwise in two strips. Spread each with half of the raisin filling. Roll up like jelly roll to form a 24-inch tube. Moisten edges and seal. Stretch to 30-inch length without breaking. Place each roll seam-down on greased baking sheet, shaping into a horseshoe. Flatten to ½ inch with rolling pin. Brush rolls with beaten egg. Sprinkle with ¼ cup sugar and almonds. Cover with wax paper and damp cloth. Let rise until almost double, about 45 minutes.

Preheat oven to 375 degrees.

Remove cloth and wax paper from kringles. Bake 30 minutes, until golden brown.

Serve warm with curls of butter as garnish.

Yield: 2 kringles. Each will serve 6–8. (Kringle may be well-wrapped and frozen.)

serving kringle-starved customers around the country. (Write to Kringles Fine Bake Shoppe, 4020 South College No. 4, Fort Collins, Colo. 80525; or call 303-223-2253).

For the authentic kringle recipe that follows, we have Louise Elsen to thank. Mrs. Elsen lives in Denver but her parents came from Racine, and she wrote to tell us that she enjoyed many a kringle as a child. It is a complicated recipe, but believe us: There are few snacks as scrumptious as freshly made kringle, still warm from the oven, served with a pot of hot coffee.

Cardamom Shortbread

PORTLAND, Ore.—For those of us whose beat is American food, it is impossible to eat around Portland without being reminded of James Beard and the Northwest heritage on which he cut his teeth. This is where Beard grew up and developed a taste for razor clams, Dungeness crab, wild Oregon berries, and black bottom pie.

The last time we visited Portland, we were lured by its bibliopolic rather than culinary charms. We came to wallow in the wonders of a book store called Powell's—the largest used book store in the West, its million-plus volumes occupying a full city block.

Having browsed through old books (old cookbooks in particular) all morning, we were ravenous by lunchtime. But rather than go to an old favorite place to eat, we found a new one: the Bread and Ink Cafe. One meal, and we were hooked. This is a restaurant James Beard would have loved.

It is a casual kind of urban eatery, its bright store-front window ledge strewn with newspapers and magazines to read while you dine. White tablecloths are covered with butcher paper.

There is no easy way to summarize its food. On one hand, the hamburger is first-rate: a hefty patty grilled to crusty succulence, on a fresh onion bun, accompanied by ramekins of *homemade* mustard, catsup, and mayonnaise. It is available with cheddar or Gruyère cheese, or accompanied by guacamole. The guacamole is not to be missed, with or without the burger. It is piercingly spiced, vibrant green, sold as a little dinner or big appetizer with a complex tomato salsa.

Most meals are fancier than burgers. You can begin dinner with hors d'oeuvres such as garlic and onion soup, garnished with Parmesan croutons, or a silky sweet red pepper soup. Or there is a zesty chaw of a dish called pan bagna, a length of bread dolled up with anchovies, tomatoes, olive oil, and herbs. Even the regular

CARDAMOM SHORTBREAD

1 cup butter, softened
1/2 cup confectioners' sugar
1/2 teaspoon vanilla extract
2 cups flour
1/4 teaspoon salt
1 teaspoon ground cardamom

Preheat oven to 325 degrees. Lightly grease a cookie sheet.

Beat butter until smooth, adding sugar and vanilla.

Mix together flour, salt, and cardamom. Beat into butter mixture.

Pat dough onto greased cookie sheet, using a lightly floured rolling pin to roll it to 1/2-inch thick, about 12-by-7 inches.

Bake 25–28 minutes, or until the edges barely begin to brown. Remove from oven and while still hot, cut into 14 fingers about 1-by-6 inches.

Makes 14 cookies.

Bread and Ink Cafe, 3610 S.E. Hawthorne Blvd., Portland, Ore.; (503) 239-4756.

bread set on the table is terrific—chewy and yeasty, with a brittle crust.

Grilled loin lamb chops are marinated in juniper berries, olive oil, and rosemary. Chicken is dipped in ground walnuts and Parmesan cheese and fried in butter. The menu might offer Vietnamese spring rolls as an appetizer and Italian cassata (liqueur-sopped cake and cream) for dessert.

One of the really great items at Bread and Ink is cheese blintzes—served at lunch, dinner, and on Sunday, when the restaurant features a "Yiddish brunch," including chopped liver and scrambled eggs with lox and onions. The blintzes come as a threesome—tender crepe pillows filled with ricotta cheese, accompanied by sour cream and raspberry jam.

Although the pie, cake, and pastry list is impressive, one of the things we like about Bread and Ink is that you can buy cookies by the piece. For a farewell meal in Portland, before heading north to Seattle, we finished things off with a plate of chocolate chip cookies, cardamom shortbread, good coffee, and a glass of sweet dessert wine. It was the shortbread that left the most lasting impression: a pale, aromatic finger of buttery luxury that makes a great light dessert or tea time snack. As soon as we got home, we whipped up this recipe to replicate it.

Glazed Devil's Food Donuts

WESTPORT, Conn.—We eat donuts a couple dozen times a year, at the most. One or two of those times are in response to a strange craving for cheap awful ones. You know which: the mass-produced donuts they sell in franchised stores, or even worse, the prepackaged ones on supermarket shelves. Don't ask us to explain or justify it, but somehow these hideous things appease a yearning that good pastry cannot sate.

If, on the other hand, the itch is for excellent donuts, there is only one that will satisfy: the kind they make at a little café called Coffee An' in Westport, Connecticut.

The time to eat at Coffee An' is between seven and nine in the morning. It will be crowded; that's part of the fun. Observe the regulars at the twin counters on either side of the store, and at the seats along the front window. They've got their dunking-sipping-reading-the-paper routine down pat. Few of them eat just one donut; personally, we find it hard to limit ourselves to two. It is hard not to pig out when each variety—chocolate, cinnamon, plain, and glazed—is a paragon.

GLAZED DEVIL'S FOOD DONUTS

1½ cups Duncan Hines Devil's Food Cake Mix
1½ cups Bisquick
1 egg
⅓ cup ice water
oil or shortening for deep frying

GLAZE:
1½ cups powdered sugar
3 tablespoons honey
1½ tablespoons water

Beat together cake mix, Bisquick, egg, and ice water until dough clumps together. Turn out onto board and knead 5 or 6 times, until dough is about the consistency of Play-Doh.

Lightly flour board and roll out dough ½-inch thick. Let rest 8 minutes. Using a 2½-inch donut cutter, cut out donuts. Pull and stretch each one to make slightly wider and flatter. Let rest under plastic wrap 5 minutes.

Heat at least 1½ inches of oil in deep cast-iron pan or deep fryer to 360 degrees. Fry donuts, a few at a time, 2 minutes per side. Drain on paper towels.

Make glaze by combining powdered sugar, honey, and water in saucepan. Bring to boil. Simmer 1 minute, or until honey and sugar dissolve. Remove from heat.

Dip warm donuts into glaze until almost completely coated. Set aside a few moments until glaze sets.

Makes 8–10 donuts.

Coffee An', 343 N. Main St., Westport, Conn.; (203) 227-3808.

The kind we like most are the chocolate ones. First let us tell you that we are not chocoholics; so we don't automatically like them just because they're fudgy. Indeed, what's amazing about them is more texture than flavor. They have a heft and chaw, like rounds of cocoa pound cake gilded with a thin sugar glaze.

The genius responsible is Derek Coutouras, whom you will see in the back room every morning working at the fry kettles, hanging freshly cooked donuts on dowels to cool, drizzling on the glaze, and sprinkling sugar. Derek arrives at Coffee An' every morning at four o'clock.

For our waistlines' sakes we try to stay away from Coffee An'. But now that will not be so easy. The reason? We just read *The Donut Book* by Sally Levitt Steinberg. Never has a single foodstuff been so royally honored.

The Donut Book tells all: donut folklore, dunking etiquette, and more history than you ever thought existed about so plebian a piece of pastry. The author ought to know. Her grandfather was the Donut King—Adolph Levitt, the man who invented the donut machine in 1920.

There were donuts before Mr. Levitt's machine. Sally's book traces them back to the Celts. She also finds literary references to donuts in the works of Hemingway and Gertrude Stein. She explains the donut as a patriotic symbol. She psychoanalyzes it. She offers its taxonomy: "A Long John is an oblong, yeast-fried donut. A Hole-in-One is a donut with ice cream and fudge. Donut holes . . . are called Munchkins, Smidgets, PopEms." She finds outrageous donut lore regarding—can you believe this?—"Dr. Crum's Donut Reducing Diet" of 1941. Best of all, she fills her book with wonderful, silly, nostalgic pictures of donuts as they have rolled through decades of American popular culture.

There is no book quite like *The Donut Book* (its cover has a hole in it!). If you have an interest in donuts or in the eccentric side of American life, you'll love it. And if you like to eat donuts, try this recipe we cooked up, based on the best donuts in the world, as served at Coffee An'.

Caramel Apples

CHICAGO—Please, if you visit the Ideal Candy Store in Chicago, go to the bathroom while you are there. The facilities are way at the back of the building, and to reach them you've got to go behind the soda fountain through the room where the candy is made.

"Is this an antique collection?" we asked when we saw the great

CARAMEL APPLES

12 ounces salted skinless peanuts
2 pounds caramels
6 to 8 large, crisp eating apples
6 to 8 sturdy wooden sticks

Chop peanuts coarsely and place into deep bowl. Melt caramels in top of deep double boiler over simmering water, stirring until smooth (this can take a full 30 minutes).

Wash apples and dry well. Insert stick into stem, dip apples in warm caramel mixture until thoroughly coated. Let excess drip off, but slowly twirl the apple, trying to get as much caramel as possible to stick. Dip just-coated apple halfway into bowl of nuts, pressing with your hands if you have difficulty getting the nuts to stick to the caramel. Set on wax paper.

These may be refrigerated, but they must be served at room temperature, or the caramel will be too hard to eat.

Ideal Candies, 3311 N. Clark, Chicago, Ill.; (312) 327-2880.

circular equipment used for spinning out the candy. The machines look very old, but what made us think of them as museum pieces was the fact that they were spotless, so clean that you couldn't imagine they recently had been used for the messy business of confectionary work.

But they are used regularly, and one-half of the Ideal Candy Store bears testimony to their productivity. Mahogany and glass cases are filled with hand-dipped chocolates of every variety. When you buy a box of candy at Ideal, you aren't getting some old stale things that have been shipped from a faraway factory, then stored on a shelf for weeks. You are getting fresh, homemade candy.

Our favorite among the dozens of choices isn't any of the chocolates. It is Ideal's peanut brittle. The first astounding thing you notice about it is the size of the nuts. They are plump, tawny beauties, many of them only partially covered by the sheet of clear, hard sugar candy. When you bite into a chunk, you realize that they are fresh peanuts, with a wicked crunch; but it's a different crunch than that of the brittle amber plaque in which they are suspended.

To tell the truth, it is not the candy that draws us to Ideal. It is the soda fountain, with its marble counter and red-topped stools, its antique wooden booths, and its nostalgic menu of frappés, flips, and double dips. Malts and milk shakes, made from scratch, are available in three different thicknesses, from normal to a super-thick size that barely makes it up a straw. They are served in a tall silver beaker, from which you retrieve two or three glassfuls.

Or you can plow into superb hot fudge and hot butterscotch sundaes, banana boats, phosphates, egg creams, and black cows.

If it is autumn, it is possible to feast on a caramel apple. To the rest of the country, caramel apples may not seem like a soda fountain specialty, but in Chicago, they are. At least at Ideal and at the South Side's premier ice cream parlor, Gertie's (since 1901). Both specialize in hand-dipped caramel apples between September and December.

Ideal's apples, nearly too unwieldy to eat anywhere other than at a table or counter, are sheathed in from-scratch caramel sauce. A dip in chopped nuts is optional. Few snacks are as evocative of autumn, or as easy to make.

Of course, they can seem difficult—if you choose to make your own caramels. Actually, it isn't hard to do so, just exacting. In a heavy saucepan over low to moderate heat, stir together the following: 1½ cups sugar, 1½ cups dark corn syrup, 12 tablespoons butter, and ¾ cup evaporated milk. Stir continuously until a candy thermometer reads 242 degrees. Remove from heat and slowly stir in another ¾ cup evaporated milk. Return to heat, bring to 244 degrees, and immediately pour the mixture into a wide, well-buttered sheet-cake pan. Cool to room temperature, invert pan onto cutting board, and use a serrated knife and a quick sawing motion to cut caramel squares. (Yield: about 2 pounds of caramels.)

Wrap caramels individually in waxed paper and serve as candy, or remelt them to use in the following recipe, our own favorite formula for extra-gooey caramel apples. Some recipes suggest thinning the caramel coating so the apple is easier to eat, but we like the caramels straight—a chewy mess, blanketed with nuts, virtually impossible to manage without knife and fork and many napkins.

Caramel Corn

TOPEKA, Ind.—Our friend Lary (one *r*) Bloom has it all figured out. "If life were reduced to its bare necessities," he told us, "it would be a pot of coffee, whole-wheat bagels, and a day's supply of popcorn." We like Lary's idea of "a day's supply" of popcorn, the implication being that there ought to be no days without it. Every day after lunch, he buys a bag to take back to the office; on weekends, he pops his own.

At our house, it would be unthinkable to sit down for a night of television without a bowl hot off the stove. When we are on the road, the motel-room necessities of life always include club soda, M&M's, and a large bag of popcorn.

The devotion people have to their daily corn cuts across all gastronomic boundaries. Popcorn is beloved by gluttons and health-food nuts, oinkers and epicures. Dieters are free to gobble air-popped, unsalted, unbuttered corn by the gallon. Plain popcorn is low in calories and good for you!

Most people cannot think of popcorn without giving it a bath of melted butter. (Remember going to the movies and paying the popcorn lady five cents extra for a double squirt?) On the other hand, we know one gourmet cornhound who swears that melted margarine (the high-priced spread) gives a much better taste than butter. This man is so fanatical about the subject that he found a popcorn farmer who ships him kernels monthly, because no store-bought brands are fresh enough.

If you are really serious about popcorn, we recommend a visit to Elkhart and LaGrange Counties in northern Indiana, an area known as "Heritage Country." It is farmland, with a large population of dairy cows and work horses, and one of the greatest con-

CARAMEL CORN

8 tablespoons butter
I cup brown sugar
⅓ cup light corn syrup
¼ teaspoon salt
I teaspoon cider vinegar
⅛ teaspoon baking soda
½ teaspoon vanilla
3 quarts popped corn, lightly salted

Preheat oven to 250 degrees.

In a heavy-bottomed saucepan, melt butter, then add sugar, corn syrup, and salt. Cook over medium heat, stirring frequently for 5–10 minutes after it begins to simmer. When it reaches 260 degrees on a candy thermometer, remove from heat and immediately stir in vinegar, baking soda, and vanilla.

Spread popped corn out on lightly greased baking pan so it is crowded, but not more than 2 inches thick. Pour hot syrup over corn and stir until corn is evenly coated, trying not to break up kernels.

Bake one hour in 250-degree oven with the door ajar, stirring every 10 minutes to keep corn from sticking together. Makes caramel corn for 4.

Yoder's Popcorn Shop, County Road 200S, Topeka, Ind.; (219) 768-4051. For mail-order popcorn information, write to Yoder Popcorn Co., RR I, Box 126, Topeka, Ind. 46571.

centrations of antique stores and flea markets in America.

Drive carefully when you travel the narrow farm roads, because you share them with Amish people steering horse-and-buggies. Stop in any of the shops or cafés, and you find yourself elbow to elbow with the bearded men and bonneted women of the Mennonite sect. There is some good eating to be done here.

Head south out of the town of Middlebury toward Honeyville, and you are suddenly deep in farm country. In summer, the fields are thick with rows of corn. And just off County Road 200S, you will see a sign for the Yoder Popcorn Shop.

It is hardly a store, at least not like a store one would find in a town. It is a small room in the back of a popcorn farm—down the gravel driveway, past black Amish garments flapping on a clothesline, toward the corncribs and barn.

A hot-corny aroma perfumes the room. Before you have a chance to look around the pint-size office, the girl behind the counter looks up from her ledger book (her records are kept in longhand) and offers a small bag of freshly popped corn. Now, browse among the inventory of popcorn-related items: poppers, oils, and special salts, plus peanut brittle and locally put-up pumpkin butter.

For the connoisseur, Yoder's sells several varieties of popping corn. Of course there are white or yellow kernels, but have you ever seen *black* popcorn? Here it is, called "black jewel," a strange genetic mutation that doesn't really taste different, but sure looks odd. The cream of the popcorn crop is what Yoder labels "T.T." corn, meaning "tiny tender" kernels from the tip of the ear. These little pearls pop into an elegant, featherweight snack too fragile for gobs of butter.

Popping good corn is a simple but subtle technique best learned by trial and error. As it is the moisture inside the unpopped kernel that causes it to explode when heated, freshness is essential. Once you've got your corn popping perfected, you might want to gild the kernels with candy caramel. The recipe takes time and constant attention, stirring the candied corn in the oven so it doesn't harden into a solid mass, but the results are a sweet tooth's paradise.

Special Menus

Regional Meals

Breakfast in the Mid-South
- Ham and Red-Eye Gravy (Roanoke, Virginia; pp. 13–14)
- Sweet Potato Biscuits (Atlanta, Georgia; pp. 48–49)
- Candied Apples (Sevierville, Tennessee; pp. 147–48)

Downeast Breakfast
- Quahog Hash (Old Saybrook, Connecticut; pp. 6–7)
- Walnut Pineapple Corn Bread (Usquepaugh, Rhode Island; pp. 53–54) *or*
- Old Fashioned Egg Muffins (Gray, Maine; pp. 63–64)

A Hoosier Breakfast Combination
- Buckwheat Cakes (Winchester, Indiana; pp. 1–2)
- Apple Butter (Middlebury, Indiana; pp. 184–85)

Texarkansas Wake-Up Duo
- Migas (Austin, Texas; pp. 2–3)
- Quivering Jalapeño Corn Bread (Harrison, Arkansas; p. 55)

Polite Lunch, Southern Style
- Peabody Vanilla Muffins (Memphis, Tennessee, pp. 60–61)
- Crab Baked in a Ramekin (Carrboro, North Carolina, pp. 114–15)
- Belle Meade Buffet Squash (Nashville, Tennessee; pp. 151–52)
- Princess Cup (New Orleans, Louisiana; pp. 219–20)

White Glove Midwestern Ladies' Lunch
- Apple Muffins (Madison, Wisconsin; pp. 59–60)
- Herbed Buttermilk Dressing and Molded Tomato Salad (Winnetka, Illinois; pp. 77–78)
- Golden Noodle Bake (Indianapolis, Indiana; pp. 142–43)
- Tea Room Spinach Delight (Gallatin, Missouri; pp. 163–65)
- Hot Milk Sponge Cake (St. Louis, Missouri; pp. 207–8)

Hale, Hearty Pacific Northwest Lunch (or Dinner)	► Slumgullion (Newport, Oregon; pp. 31–32)
	► Basil and Cheese Hot Breadsticks (Gearhart, Oregon; pp. 52–53)
	► Dungeness Crab Cakes (Portland, Oregon; pp. 117–18)
	► Dee's Tartar Sauce (Westport, Washington, pp. 181–82)
	► Deep Dish Apple Pie (Lincoln City, Oregon; pp. 201–2)
A Manly Middle-of-America Meal	► This Is It Meat Loaf (Houston, Texas; pp. 86–88)
	► Chickasha Hot Sauce (Chickasha, Oklahoma; pp. 179–80)
	► Mashed Potatoes à la Riverside (Stockport, Ohio; pp. 169–70)
	► San Antonio Squash (Austin, Texas; pp. 152–53)
	► Egg Custard Pie (Fort Worth, Texas; pp 198–99)
A Big Meal for the Hottest Day of Summer	► Scandanavian Fruit Soup (Bridgeport, Connecticut; pp. 41–42)
	► Beaten Biscuits (Richmond, Virginia; p. 50)
	► Carrot Salad (Lakewood, Ohio; pp. 75–77)
	► Barbecued Salmon (Eureka, California; pp. 109–10)
	► Country Simple Yellow Squash (Plant City, Florida; pp. 150–51)
	► Fuzzy Navel Milkshakes (Yellow Springs, Ohip; pp. 249–51)
	► Lemon Chess Pie (Harrodsburg, Kentucky; pp. 191–92)
Full Dress Dinner	► Oyster Stew (Portland, Oregon; pp. 122–23)
	► Silver Spoon Wings (Georgetown, Connecticut; pp. 23–24)
	► Indonesian Lamb Roast (San Francisco, California; pp. 97–98)
	► Peanut Satay Sauce (Danbury, Connecticut; pp. 183–84)
	► Tipsy Sweet Potato Pudding (Lynchburg, Tennessee; pp. 166–167)
	► Millionaire's Pie (Indianapolis, Indiana; pp. 203–4) and/or
	► Brazillian Snow (Tampa, Florida; pp. 217–18)
A Big All-Ethnic Smorgasbord	► Knish (Forest Hills, New York; pp. 20–21)
	► Tripe à la Frank (New York, New York; pp. 22–23)
	► Orange Salad (Hartford, Connecticut; p. 71)
	► Creole Daube (New Orleans, Louisiana; pp. 91–92)
	► Zwiebelkuchen (Mequon, Wisconsin; pp. 172–73)
	► Palacinke (Cleveland, Ohio; pp. 221–22)

A Street Food Party

▸ Cheese-Br-Gers (Columbus, Indiana; pp. 240–41)
▸ Hawaiian Pizza (New York, New York; pp. 234–35)
▸ Hot Dogs (Tonawanda, New York; pp. 241–42)
▸ Sweet Onion Mustard (Clifton, New Jersey; pp. 175–76)
▸ Caramel Corn (Shipshewana, Indiana; pp. 257–58)
▸ Buttermilk Shake (Yountville, California; pp. 248–49)

**Sloppy Supper for
Children and Grownups**

▸ French Fried Eggplant (Dayton, Kentucky; pp. 168-69)
▸ Throwed Rolls (Sikeston, Missouri; pp. 47–48)
▸ Ham-Stuffed Apples (Dahlonega, Georgia; pp. 98–100)
▸ Turtle Candy Sundae (Aurora, Illinois; pp. 213–15)

Respectable Sunday Family Dinner

▸ Cinnamon Apple Jellied Salad (Pittsburgh, Pennsylvania; pp. 68–69)
▸ Strongbow Turkey Tetrazzini (Valparaiso, Indiana; pp. 134–35)
▸ Tea Room Spinach Delight (Gallatin, Missouri, pp. 163–65)
▸ Chocolate Milk Pie (Carrabelle, Florida; pp. 197–98)

**Downeast Supper
When It's Cold Outside**

▸ Blueberry Gingerbread (Machias, Maine; pp. 51–52)
▸ Salt Pork and Milk Gravy (Barre, Vermont; pp. 102–3)
▸ Maple Syrup Apple Pie (West Hartford, Connecticut; pp. 200–1)

*Mixed but Matched Meals—
Recipes from all around the country*

Farmlands Dinner

▸ Heart of Artichoke Soup (Pescadero, California; pp. 33–34)
▸ Brisket Roast (San Diego, California; pp. 90–91)
▸ Country Simple Yellow Squash (Plant City, Florida; pp. 150–51)
▸ Derby Dressing (Derby, Iowa; pp. 154–55)
▸ Shaker Lemon Pie (New Harmony, Indiana; pp. 193–94)

Mom-like Home Cooking

▸ Triple Layer Spoon Bread (War Eagle, Arkansas; pp. 58–59) *or*
▸ Throwed Rolls (Sikeston, Missouri; pp. 47–48)
▸ Granny's Beef Stew (Colorado Springs, Colorado; pp. 84–85)
▸ Rice and Gravy (Tallassee, Alabama; pp. 162–63)
▸ Peanut Butter Pie (Dallas, Texas; pp. 192–93)

Hoity-Toity Lunch
from Swanky Restaurants

▶ Roasted Garlic (Yountville, California; pp. 18–19)
▶ Tortilla Soup (Bel Air, California; pp. 39–40)
▶ Prawn Sauté Chardonnay (San Francisco, California, pp. 110–12)
▶ Onions and Potatoes (Beverly Hills, California; pp. 148–49)
▶ Grapefruit Ice (Detroit, Michigan; pp. 220–21)

A Blue Plate Special Diner Meal

▶ Diner Split Pea Soup (Remsen, New York; p. 38)
▶ Max's White Meat Loaf (San Francisco, California; pp. 88–89)
▶ Haystack Potatoes (Walnut, Iowa; pp. 170–72)
▶ Copper Pennies (Pensacola, Florida; pp. 161–62)
▶ Chocolate Peanut Butter Pie (Marion, Indiana; pp. 196–97)

The Nicest Nursery Supper

▶ Cream of Mushroom Soup (Reading, Pennsylvania; pp. 34–35)
▶ Ippy's Staff of Life Bread (Redding, Connecticut; pp. 62–63)
▶ Austrian Ravioli (Oklahoma City, Oklahoma; pp. 144–45)
▶ Spoon Bread (Berea, Kentucky; pp. 57–58)
▶ Rice Pudding (Chicago, Illinois; pp. 212–13)

Recipe Index

Restaurant Index by State